Other books by Ruth Ellen Gruber:

Jewish Heritage Travel: A Guide to East-Central Europe

Upon the Doorposts of Thy House: Jewish Life in East-Central Europe, Yesterday and Today

Virtually Jewish

The road made of fake tombstones that was used as part of the *Schindler's List*
set in Kraków and was later included as part of the *Schindler's List* tour, 1994.
(Photo by Ruth Ellen Gruber.)

Virtually Jewish

Reinventing Jewish Culture in Europe

Ruth Ellen Gruber

UNIVERSITY OF CALIFORNIA PRESS

Berkeley / Los Angeles / London

Permission has been granted to reprint the following material:

"Berlin 1990"; words by Michael Alpert, music by Michael Alpert and Alan Bern; published by JA/NEIN Musikverlag GmbH & Pinorrekk Musikverlag (GEMA), © 1993; played by Brave Old World on the album *Beyond the Pale* on Pinorrekk Records.

Czesław Miłosz, "Campo dei Fiori"; used by permission of the poet.

Jerome Rothenberg, "The Wedding," in *Poland/1931;* used by permission of the poet.

University of California Press
Berkeley and Los Angeles, California

University of California Press, Ltd.
London, England

Library of Congress Cataloging-in-Publication Data

Gruber, Ruth Ellen, 1949–
    Virtually Jewish : reinventing Jewish culture in Europe /
Ruth Ellen Gruber.
        p.   cm.
    Includes bibliographical references (p.) and index.
    ISBN 0-520-21363-7 (cloth : alk. paper)
        1. Jews—Europe—History—20th century.   2. Judaism—
Europe—History—20th century.   3. Jews—Europe—Identity.
4. Jews—Europe—Intellectual life.   5. Holocaust survivors—
Europe—Intellectual life.   6. Civilization, Modern—Jewish
influences.   7. Europe—Ethnic relations.   I. Title.

DS135.E83 G69   2002
940'.04924—dc21   2001027818

Manufactured in the United States of America

10   09   08   07   06   05   04   03   02

10   9   8   7   6   5   4   3   2   1

The paper used in this publication meets the minimum requirements of ANSI/NISO Z39.48-1992 (R 1997) (*Permanence of Paper*). ⊗

To my family,
and to the memory of three dear people
who continue to inspire me:
Fr. Mitchell Dahood, S.J.
Jonathan R. Lax
Geoffrey Wigoder

Contents

Illustrations

Acknowledgments

This book is the fruit of research carried out over a number of years and reflects a rapidly, and continuously, changing situation as it was in the late 1990s.

It is a pleasant duty to express my thanks to the many friends, colleagues, artists, performers, and others involved in the phenomenon I describe who offered me invaluable assistance and support. Many are mentioned in the text and notes. Were I to cite everyone, the list would fill many pages. But several people have been especially important. Francesco Spagnolo has been a constant sounding board, critic, and source of inspiration ever since we met. My brother, Samuel D. Gruber, as always, was generous with his comments, criticism, and valuable insights. András Kovács introduced me to the work of Hugo Bettauer and pointed me in many other right directions. Diana Pinto's pioneering work inspired and challenged me, and Michael T. Kaufman gave me invaluable advice when I needed it sorely. Among performers, I particularly would like to thank the members of Brave Old World—Stuart Brotman, Michael Alpert, Alan Bern, and Kurt Bjorling—for the many hours we spent together in various countries, as well as for their insights, and also Bob Cohen and Moni Ovadia.

Conversations and correspondence with many people, some of whom read parts of the manuscript in progress and some of whom took time to talk things through, helped me tremendously. Others simply gave me moral support (or a bed to sleep in). Among them I would like to mention in particular Barbara Walsh Angelillo, Lucyna Gebert and Rudi Assuntino, Sylvia Poggioli and Piero Benetazzo, Lena Bergman, Y. Michal Bodemann, Giacomo Bonaccorsi, Franco Bonilauri, Enrico Fink, Judit Frigyesi, Kostek Gebert, Henryk Halkowski, all the Harasztis, Marilyn Henry, Rebecca Kaufman, Barbara Kirshenblatt-Gimblett, Stanisław and Monika Krajewski, Carol Herselle Krinsky, Jack Kugelmass, Heiko Lehmann, Tony Lerman, Gilbert Levine, Frank London, John and Judith Macgregor, Janusz Makuch, Monika Miklis, Steve and Eve Miller, Laura and Olek Mincer, Sonia and Albert Misak, Sabine Offe, the Onyszkiewicz family, Wojtek and Małgosia Ornat, Arno Pařík, Leo Pavlát, Harriet Poland, András Román, Joel Rubin, Joachim Russek, Richard Chaim Schneider, Michael Schudrich, Willy Schwarz, Joachim Seinfeld, Edward Serotta, Krzysztof Śliwiński, Mark Slobin, Lena Stanley-Clamp, Michael Steinlauf, and Levente Thury. My parents, Jacob W. Gruber and Shirley Moskowitz Gruber, were especially important, as were my brother Frank Gruber and my sisters-in-law Janet Levin and Judith Meighan. *Tschiers,* too, to Johanna Householder and Carmen Householder Pedari, who were wonderful traveling companions.

I would like to express my appreciation to a number of organizations and institutions that enabled me to travel, carry out research for this book, or gain firsthand experience in the "virtual Jewish" phenomenon: first and foremost, the American Jewish Committee (AJC), which in 1996 commissioned and published my research paper, *Filling the Jewish Space in Europe,* from which this book has grown. I am particularly grateful to the AJC's director of research, David Singer, and director of international affairs, Rabbi Andrew Baker.

Thanks also to the U.S. Commission for the Preservation of America's Heritage Abroad, for which I carried out a survey of Jewish monuments in Slovenia in collaboration with the Slovenian Ministry of Culture. I presented this survey at a conference in Maribor, Slovenia, on medieval Jewish communities in central Europe and their cultural heritage, sponsored by the University of Maribor, in October 1997. I am grateful to the Bertelsmann Stiftung for having invited me to its German-Jewish Dialogue near Bonn in October 1997 and to the European Council of Jewish Communities and Institute for Jewish Policy Research for asking me to speak about non-Jewish interest in Jewish culture at the meeting "Strengthening Jewish Life in Europe" held in Strasbourg in June 1997. I also thank the organizers of the Mittelfest festival in Cividale del Friuli, Italy; the Festival of Jewish Culture in Kraków, Poland; Jewish Culture Days in Berlin; the Jewish Culture Festival in Venice; Shalom Trieste; and the International Klezmer Festival in Ancona, Italy (which invited me to speak on the klezmer revival) for their aid and hospitality. Likewise, thanks to Bernhard Purin and the Jüdisches Museum Franken for hosting me in Fürth. Thanks, too, to the organizers of the International Conference on European Jewish Heritage held in Paris in January 1999, to Ladislau Gyémánt and the Moshe Carmilly Institute for Hebrew and Jewish History in Cluj-Napoca, Romania, to the philosophy department of Milan University, and to the American Jewish Joint Distribution Committee and the Ronald S. Lauder Foundation.

I was able to publish articles or reports related to this book's subject for the Jewish Telegraphic Agency, the *Jewish Chronicle,* the *New Leader,* CBC Radio, and the *International Herald Tribune.* Some material herein also is drawn from earlier articles of mine in the *New York Times* and elsewhere. An article based on research for this book appears as a chapter in the yearbook of the Jewish Studies Program of Central European University, Budapest.

I was able to carry out my research thanks to grants from the Lucius N. Littauer Foundation and the Memorial Foundation for Jewish Culture, as well as from Marcia Kurtz. Many thanks for their assistance. I also want to thank my lifelong friend Donald Rasmussen for his support and encouragement.

Finally, I would like to thank my editor, Stanley Holwitz, as well as Laura Pasquale, Suzanne Knott, and Sheila Berg at the University of California Press for their care, support, and interest in this project. The anonymous readers for the press gave me invaluable critique. I want to add a particular note of appreciation to Doug Abrams Arava and to Marc Klein, who made the *shidduch.*

Henryk Halkowski, of the 200-member local Jewish community, stands at a souvenir stall selling carved wooden figures of Jews, T-shirts, and other keepsakes in Kraków's former Jewish quarter, Kazimierz, 1997. (Photo by Ruth Ellen Gruber.)

PART ONE

Afterlife

Berlin boasts its own klezmer bands, and Jewish thought/Jewish
art/Jewish spirit is everywhere on the shelves and on the airwaves.
In 1993, Germany is one of a very few countries where you can
make a living playing Jewish music. But for whom? A bord on a
yid? . . . A beard without a Jew behind it?

Liner notes for *Beyond the Pale*,
a compact disc recorded by the American
klezmer group Brave Old World

I

Cities without Jews

In the early 1920s, the Viennese journalist Hugo Bettauer wrote a novel that at the time must have seemed little more than a satirical excursion into a science fiction–style parallel universe. Titled *Die Stadt ohne Juden* (The City without Jews), Bettauer's brief tale describes what happens to Vienna, and to Austria as a whole, when parliament passes a law expelling all Jews from the country. The expulsion order clears Austria of its Jews in six months and includes elaborate "who is a Jew" classifications that uncannily foreshadow the Nuremberg laws decreed by the Nazi Third Reich.

Jews, of course, have been expelled from European cities and countries countless times during their more than two-thousand-year history on the continent. But Bettauer does not dwell on the hardships of the Jews forced, once again, to leave their homes. Instead, with irony and acid wit, he focuses on the predicament of the Austrian Christians left behind in their racially pure paradise. Without the Jews, Viennese culture dries up, newspapers become a yawn, coffeehouses empty out, and intellectual life comes to a juddering standstill. Political debate evaporates, and economic indicators plummet. Restaurants go downhill, vacation resorts are deserted, and men and women alike forsake elegant fashions for rough wool and sensible flannel. In short, the city—indeed, the entire country—becomes a drab, bleak, boring wasteland.

"Vienna's going to the dogs without the Jews!" one character exclaims. " . . . Vienna's going to the dogs, I say; and when I, a veteran anti-Semite, say that, it's true, I tell you!"[1]

In the end, the expulsion order is rescinded, and the novel concludes with the young man believed to be the first Jew to return to Vienna being greeted by a massive cheering crowd at City Hall, Vienna's famous Rathaus: "As the trumpets blared, the Mayor of Vienna, Herr Karl Maria Laberl, stepped out on the balcony, stretched out his arms in a gesture of benediction, and pronounced an impassioned speech that began with the words: 'My beloved Jew!'"[2]

Bettauer's book was an immediate sensation, selling a quarter of a million copies in less than a year according to Salomea Neumark Brainin, whose English translation of the novel appeared in 1926.[3] It was made into a film and inspired the Berlin-based author Artur Landsberger to write his own novel, *Berlin ohne Juden* (Berlin without Jews), in 1925. Bettauer himself, however, had little time to enjoy his fame. In March 1925 he was murdered by a proto-Nazi who was determined to save German culture from "degeneration." Bettauer received, as Brainin put it, "a fatal bullet as royalty for his novel."[4]

The Nazis came to power in Germany about a decade after *Die Stadt ohne Juden* was published and unleashed the Holocaust only a few years after that. (Artur Landsberger committed suicide when Hitler became chancellor in 1933.) Nazi Germany annexed Austria in 1938, the first step in its conquest of Europe; Hitler was welcomed by cheering crowds when he entered Vienna. By 1945 not only had almost all Austrian Jews fled the country or been deported to their deaths, but of the estimated 9 million Jews who had lived in Europe before World War II, 6 million had been murdered. Thousands of synagogues, too, had been demolished and Jewish cemeteries destroyed, not to mention Jewish homes, schools, and businesses. Torah scrolls, prayer books, ritual objects, and even the humdrum, everyday possessions of Jews had been smashed, stolen, or consigned to the flames. Bettauer's fantasy of a city—a country—without Jews had essentially become reality, not just in Austria, but in all of east central Europe and in much of the rest of the continent as well.

Today few Jews still live in the countries where the Holocaust took place. But the continuing physical absence of Jews in much of Europe is not the only way in which Bettauer's book has proved prophetic. More than half a century after the Holocaust, an apparent longing for lost Jews—or for what Jews are seen to represent—is also evident. In a trend that developed with powerful momentum in the 1980s and accrued particular force after the fall of communism in 1989–90, Europeans, like the fictional mayor of Vienna, Herr Karl Maria Laberl, have stretched open their arms to embrace a Jewish component back into the social, political, historical, and cultural mainstream.

The irony is inescapable. For decades after World War II, memory of Jewish history and heritage was often marginalized, repressed, or forgotten, not only in countries where the flames of the Holocaust had burned most fiercely, but also in countries less directly touched by the effects of the Shoah. Jews, their culture, and their history were often viewed as something distinctly apart, off-limits; even the Holocaust was regarded as an internal "Jewish thing," detached from the general flow of national history and national memory. In eastern Europe communist ideology made the extermination of the Jews and the world that was destroyed with them a footnote to the overall suffering in World War II. In Germany the psychic trauma left by the Nazis made people close their minds to the issue. In many countries Jews themselves kept low profiles.

By the late 1990s, though, the "Jewish phenomenon"—anything to do with Judaism, Jews, the Holocaust, and Israel—was increasingly recognized as part of the broad national experience, both on the personal level and as part of official policy. (Already in 1987, for example, the Parliamentary Assembly of the Council of Europe passed a resolution recognizing "the very considerable and distinctive contribution that Jews and the tradition of Judaism have made to the historical development of Europe in the cultural and other fields."[5] And in January 2000 political and government leaders from forty-six countries, mainly European, gathered in Stockholm for a first-of-its-kind international forum on the Holocaust, where in effect they officially acknowledged the Holocaust as part of their countries' national histories and embedded this recognition within the parameters of public national discourse.)

As part of this trend, Jewish culture—or what passes for Jewish culture, or what is perceived or defined as Jewish culture—has become a visible and sometimes highly visible component of the popular public domain in countries where Jews themselves now are practically invisible. From Milan to Munich, from Kraków to Cluj and well beyond, Jewish exhibitions, festivals, and workshops of all types abound, as do conferences and academic study programs on all aspects of Jewish history, culture, and tradition. Readings, lectures, seminars, talk shows, and films spotlight Jewish issues; and articles and programs on Jewish subjects are given frequent and prominent space in the print media and on prime-time television. Private volunteers and civic organizations clean up abandoned Jewish cemeteries and place plaques on empty synagogues. And new Jewish museums are being opened—often in towns where no Jews have lived for decades, often with government support, and often in synagogues newly restored after lying forgotten since the end of World War II.

Jews and Things Jewish, meanwhile, are popular attractions, even a category of commercial merchandise. *Fiddler on the Roof,* with German or Polish or Austrian actors pinning on beards and sidecurls, is a favorite on local stages, as are many other plays and performances on a variety of Jewish themes. Yiddish song, klezmer (traditional eastern European Jewish instrumental music), and other Jewish music—performed by Jewish and non-Jewish groups alike—draw enthusiastic (and overwhelmingly non-Jewish) audiences to concert halls, churches, clubs, and outdoor arenas. Hundreds—even thousands—of new books on Jewish topics are published in local languages, and new Jewish bookstores attract a wide clientele in such cities as Munich, Vienna, Berlin, Kraków, and Rome.

Old Jewish quarters are under development as tourist attractions, where "Jewish-style" restaurants with "Jewish-sounding" names write their signs in Hebrew or Hebrew-style letters, use Jewish motifs in their decor, and name their dishes—sometimes even dishes made from pork or a nonkosher mix of meat and dairy products—after rabbis and Old Testament prophets. In April 1997, for example, the Golem restaurant in the old Jewish quarter of Prague featured "Rabbi Löw Beefsteaks," made with ketchup, cheese, ham, and mushrooms, "Merchant Samuel Pork," and a "Rabbi's Pocket" filled with smoked meat and garnished with cheese. Kiosks, shops, and market stalls overflow with new Jewish kitsch; souvenir T-shirts and postcards sport imagery ranging from candlesticks and tombstones to caricatures of Franz Kafka. There are painted wooden carvings of hook-nosed, bearded Jews for sale in Poland and Golem statuettes and sidelocked Jewish puppets for sale in Prague. In the ancient ghetto of Venice, shop windows sparkle with brightly colored miniature Jews of hand-blown Murano glass. In Kraków a Ukrainian band at one "Jewish-style" café dresses up in Hasidic attire and plays Yiddish tunes for patrons sipping chicken soup and kosher vodka, while local travel agencies take visitors on "Schindler's List" and other Jewish tours, and a "Jewish" gallery has been known to display, among other things, antique Jewish clothing—including men's ritually fringed undergarments.

Many aspects of this phenomenon—from concerts to kitsch—are commonplace in the United States and Canada, particularly in cities where there are sizable Jewish populations. This is also the case in some cities in Great Britain and France, the countries that have the largest Jewish populations in Europe outside the former Soviet Union (600,000 in France and 300,000 in Britain) and where, as in North America, Jews are and have been a visible part of the postwar social and cultural landscape and also create their own important internal markets. (This discussion does not deal with Israel, where, of course, the Jewish internal market *is* the mainstream.) Particularly in America, the size, visibility, and sense of security of the Jewish population, not to mention the long-standing general ethnic and immigrant mix, enable a casual mainstream penetration or exchange of specifically Jewish habits, traits, customs, and characteristics. They also allow for a play on stereotypes, epitomized, perhaps, by the famous ad campaign that used photographs of African Americans, American Indians, WASPs, and other representative "goyish" types to make the point that "you don't have to be Jewish" to enjoy Levy's rye bread.

In most European countries today, however, particularly in those where most of the Jews killed in the Holocaust were concentrated, it is not at all "normal" to be Jewish. This is the result of the Holocaust and the other legacies of a long and troubled history. But it also holds true in simple numerical terms. Despite a dramatic, if still uncertain, revival of Jewish communal life in former communist states since the waning and fall of communism and despite energetic new efforts to promote a pan-European Jewish identity,[6] the Jewish population in most European countries is very small—and dwindling. The most pessimistic observers even predict that, as a result of demographic decline, intermarriage, emigration, and indifference, Jews may practically disappear from the continent within a few decades.[7] There are twice as many Jews in Los Angeles as in all of Britain, and single city blocks in New York are likely to be home to more Jews than are entire European capitals. Hungary has an estimated 100,000 Jews, the biggest Jewish population in a postcommunist state outside the former Soviet Union, but only a fraction have regular contact with organized Jewry. Only about 10,000 Jews live in Austria, out of 7 million people. There are 3,500 to 6,000 Jews out of a total population of 12 million in the Czech Republic, 10,000 to 20,000 Jews out of 38 million in Poland. Of the 60 million people in Italy, only 30,000 to 35,000 are Jews.[8] Only Germany, ironically, has seen a visible surge in Jewish population in recent years: their number has more than doubled, thanks to the arrival in the 1990s of tens of thousands of immigrants from the former Soviet Union. Even with this immigration, however, Germany's Jewish population remains minuscule—as of 1999, 80,000 Jews out of a population of 80 million.

Nonetheless, it is in countries such as these, where Jews make up only a tiny fraction of the general populace and where few members of the public may actually ever meet a living Jew, that the non-Jewish embrace of the Jewish phenomenon becomes a bear hug. Jews in these countries are of course among the participants, sponsors, and targeted public, and foreign and local Jews often play key roles in popularizing Jewish culture and bringing Jewish music, art, dance, literature, scholarship, and religious traditions to a broader public. But, for the most part, the outpouring and interest dwarf local Jewish populations and capacity. Organizers, audiences, performers, participants, and consumers are, to a great extent, Gentiles; the result is a form of Jewish culture, or at least Judaica, minus the Jews.

The motives behind this activity and interest are as varied as the manifestations themselves. Often, they are not fully clear, and the end results are not yet known. It is easy to dismiss much of the phenomenon as opportunistic "Shoah business" or a debased form of folklore, and some of it obviously *is* exploitative kitsch. Fashion, commercialism, and what can be described as post-Holocaust necrophilia also certainly play a role.

But the phenomenon is much more complex than passing fads, picking at sores, political correctness, or cynical exploitation. For one thing, it has expanded and diversified since the early 1980s, assuming new and changing forms as it has evolved. Aspects of it have become well entrenched in the most diverse of European societies. What started out in many cases as the private explorations of a limited number of intellectuals has often become institutional and also now the province of a much wider, more casual, popular awareness. In some countries aspects of the phenomenon that even a few years ago seemed startling (such as the klezmer craze or Jewish theme tourism) have simply become part of the norm. Generational changes also have had and continue to have an effect; "serious" motivations have given way in many instances to pop expression and simple cultural curiosity, and vice versa. For many, particularly younger, people, "Things Jewish" may merely be fun, even an ethnic flavor of the month in societies where "world music" and "multiculturalism" are chic political and cultural contemporary catchwords. For others, casual pop encounters have led to a much deeper academic, artistic, humanitarian, or other involvement.

Thoughtful reevaluations of history, culture, and identity are at play, as are sincere attempts to make up for the past. But Holocaust commemoration per se is only part of the equation. In many ways (at least in its initial stages) the phenomenon has reflected a "third generation" syndrome: the desire to discover and seize hold of knowledge withheld, denied, or ignored by older generations, be they parents, grandparents, or ruling elites. Memory—memory of Jews—is employed as a vehicle for self-discovery and self-exploration. The recovery of Jewish history and culture as well as Holocaust memory is used, consciously or not, as a means of rethinking and redefining personal identity and national histories. This process may entail what some Germans label "memory work," a meticulous, sometimes ritualized approach to bringing to light that which the wartime generation sought to bury. Or it may be what eastern Europeans dubbed "filling in the blank spaces" created by communist ideology. It may be an intellectual or emotional attraction to Jews and to their lost world as metaphorical symbols—symbols of survival, of self-irony, and of identity maintained in exile; symbols of the Holocaust; symbols of what was suppressed under communism; symbols of democratic ideals; even simply symbols of the "good old days." Or it may be a much less complicated attraction to local legend and lore.

Clearly, various degrees of philo-Semitism—an idealization of Jews, sometimes linked to guilt or uneasiness about the Holocaust, sometimes linked to a fascination with what is perceived as an almost familiar exotica—play a role. Nostalgia, too, is involved, though it is likely to be expressed as a pseudonostalgia for stereotypes—be it the stage-set shtetl world of *Fiddler on the Roof* or a romanticized vision of the coffeehouse Jewish intellectual—rather than nostalgia for the highly nuanced and often highly contentious Jewish world that actually once existed or, for that matter, nostalgia for the complex, problematic, and far too often ugly relations between Jews and non-Jewish society.

The conflicting motivations can lead to a troubling ambivalence. The history and memory that are resurrected and tenderly restored to place are often distorted to suit specific local and personal needs. Sincere attempts to study or reintegrate what has been lost, destroyed, or forgotten coexist with superficiality, slogans, lip service, and show. State-, city-, or church-sponsored promotion of Jewish culture or celebrations of Jewish heritage—whether by the opening of a Jewish museum, the restoration of a synagogue, or the organizing of a Jewish cultural festival—can serve as institutional forms of cultural apology, consciously articulated mea culpas aimed at acknowledging, however tardily (and with however much self-serving political calculation), a part of history once deemed lost, if not indeed irrelevant. In addition, some governments, including several communist regimes in the 1980s, have not hesitated to play the Jewish card to win sympathy or support from Western nations and from what some perceive as an internationally powerful Jewish lobby or, more simply, to look good in the eyes of the world. Jews, too, are often viewed as symbols of all persecuted peoples: honoring lost Jews and their annihilated world can become a means of demonstrating democratic principles and multicultural ideals, regardless of how other contemporary minorities are treated, be they Turks, Roma, North Africans, or whatever.[9]

"Feeling," too, bears an influence on the reconstruction of what is perceived as fact. Nostalgia, stereotypes, and commemoration can become shorthand tools in the creation of what often, to rework a concept expressed by Umberto Eco in a 1975 essay on aspects of popular culture in America, become "absolute fake" environments, "where the boundaries of game and illusion are blurred" and where "absolute unreality is offered as a real presence."[10] Indeed, many who so tightly embrace Jewish memory and Jewish culture, who profess themselves interested in "bringing back to life" what was destroyed in the Holocaust, have manifested little apparent interest in the local living Jewish present.

The Paris-based historian Diana Pinto uses the term "Jewish space" to describe the place occupied by the Jewish phenomenon within mainstream European society today.[11] Jewish space, she has written, entails not so much the physical presence of Jews but the ways in which European countries now integrate Jewish history and memory, and the Holocaust, into an understanding of their national history, regardless of the current size, visibility, or activity of the local Jewish population.[12] "There is a Jewish space in Europe that will exist even in the absence of Jews," Pinto said at a 1995 conference in Prague on planning for the future of European Jewry. "The 'Jewish thing' is becoming universal."

In the early 1990s the sociologist Y. Michal Bodemann described the specific manifestation of this phenomenon in Germany as the emergence of a "Judaizing terrain" made up of "converts to Judaism, of members of joint Jewish-German or Israeli-German associations, and of many 'professional almost-Jews' outside or even inside the apparatuses of the Jewish organizations and [Jewish communities]." Jewish culture, he wrote, "is being manufactured, Jewish history reconstructed, by these Judaizing milieux—by German experts of Jewish culture and religion [who] enact Jewish culture from within German biographies and from within German history; this has an important bearing on the type of Jewish culture that is actually being produced: a culture that is not lived, that draws heavily from the museum, and that is still no less genuine for that." [13]

I think of this "universalization" of the Jewish phenomenon and its integration into mainstream European consciousness, this emergence of a "Judaizing terrain" and "Judaizing milieux" in all their widely varied, conscious and unconscious, manifestations, as a "filling" of the Jewish space.[14] This is a process that in turn encompasses the creation of a "virtual Jewishness," a "virtual Jewish world," peopled by "virtual Jews" who perform—or, as Bodemann put it, enact—Jewish culture from an outsider perspective, alongside or often in the absence of local Jewish populations. In doing so, they may take over cultural and other activities that would ordinarily be carried out by Jews. In other cases, they create their own realities that perpetuate an image of Jewish presence. Some go so far as to wear Stars of David around their necks, assume Jewish-sounding names, attend synagogue, send their children to Jewish schools, and follow kosher dietary laws, in addition to championing Jewish causes. Sometimes non-Jews consciously underscore the irony of their outsider status: local non-Jewish klezmer groups in Austria and the Netherlands punningly call themselves by the Yiddish name Gojim (Gentiles). Another, in Bremen, Germany, takes the pun a step further, calling itself the Klezgoyim.

Like any broad notion, the idea of a virtual Jewish world embraces several realms. There is a public political dimension and a dimension that is strictly personal. There is a physical dimension, exemplified by activities such as the restoration of synagogues, the documentation of Jewish monuments, and the redevelopment of old Jewish quarters. Another dimension is that of performance, which by definition embodies the use of virtualities: the created worlds presented onstage and in film or in museum displays, for example. Shifting definitions of "Jewish culture" and the manufacture, merchandising, and display of what can be called "Jewish cultural products"—books, music, art, souvenirs, and the like—constitute still other dimensions, as does the iconizing of the concept "Jew" or "Jewish identity" as a model, metaphor, symbol, or tool.

What is the scope of the "virtual Jewish" phenomenon? It is hard to quantify, but a few examples may help.

· In 1992 in Berlin—home to about nine thousand Jews at the time—an exhibition described as "the world's largest and most expensive ever" was mounted at the Martin Gropius Bau museum.[15] Sponsored by the city and costing more than $6 million to mount, the exhibition spilled far outside the walls of the museum to include a wealth of related performances, conferences, poetry readings, film series, specialized exhibits, and concerts—even a double compact disc (CD). Some 350,000 people saw the exhibition, called "Jüdische Lebenswelten" (Patterns of Jewish Life), and 115,000 attended the related events. Some sixty thousand copies of the catalog, which was nearly 800 pages long and included more than 740 illustrations, were sold.[16]

· The European Association of Jewish Studies (EAJS), founded in 1981 as an international voluntary association, began organizing annual international Jewish studies conferences in the early 1990s. In 1995 it established a permanent secretariat. Its first *Directory of Jewish Studies in Europe,* published in 1998, listed nearly three hundred institutions and university departments in twenty-two European countries (outside the former Soviet Union) where Jewish studies courses or classes were taught. It also listed nearly one thousand Europe-based scholars who taught (or in some cases carried out research in) various areas of Jewish studies.[17] Similarly, scholars, archivists, museum directors, and researchers from more than forty institutions all over Germany attended the 1997 annual meeting in Cologne of Germany's Association of Jewish Collections, and in Prague in March 2000 some forty representatives of Jewish museums in a dozen countries attended the annual meeting of the Association of European Jewish Museums.

· In Italy a January 1998 special program on state-run television featuring a cabaret act combining Yiddish music, Jewish jokes, and a discussion of Jewish traditions drew an audience share of one million viewers. On the day of the broadcast, the staid Milan daily *Corriere della Sera* splashed its entertainment section with the headline "Songs, Theater, and TV: It's Yiddish-mania" and ran a glossary of Hebrew and Yiddish terms with the article.

· In Kraków, Poland, a city with a Jewish population of about two hundred souls, the Center for Jewish Culture, operated and staffed by non-Jews, opened in November 1993. By August 1996 it had already programmed more than 625 events, including lectures, concerts, exhibits, and seminars. In 1995–96 alone, more than five hundred "serious titles" on Jewish history, literature, and culture were published in Poland, and Poland claimed the "world record" for the translation of works from Yiddish: more Yiddish books were translated in Poland than in the United States or Israel.[18]

- According to Rachel Salamander, founder of the Literaturhandlung Jewish bookstores in Munich, Berlin, and Vienna, as of 1997 about 1,200 new titles on Jewish topics or by Jewish authors were being published in German each year. Salamander, the daughter of Jewish displaced persons who settled in Germany after World War II, founded the first Literaturhandlung in Munich in 1982. It both responded to and helped catalyze interest in Jewish subjects among society at large. In its first fifteen years of operation, it expanded its inventory to include some 7,000 titles grouped in some forty subjects. Literaturhandlung also hosts readings, lectures, and other public events and annually publishes a successful mail order catalog. A similar catalog, divided into fifty categories, was published in 1997 by Rome's Menorah Jewish book shop and also posted on an Internet web site. Menorah initially made an effort to stock Italian university dissertations on Jewish themes on its shelves, but by the late 1990s, according to its owners, it had to abandon the practice because of the volume.

It is important to note that all these activities (and more) exist side by side with widespread ignorance and apathy and sometimes overt anti-Semitism and Holocaust denial. Numerous surveys and public opinion polls in various countries, east and west, have demonstrated this, and also that young people, in particular, are often quite ignorant of recent history or of anything to do with Judaism.[19] A series of studies carried out by the American Jewish Committee in 1998 and 1999 demonstrated that nearly a decade after the fall of communism, little was taught in state-run high schools in former communist countries about the Jewish phenomenon, and what was taught sometimes included anti-Semitic distortions.[20]

Ignorance combined with the visibility of Jews and Jewish concerns in the media, on theater stages, in bookstores, and the like, also produce mistaken impressions about the status of Jews in Europe today. "Considering the number of publications [and] exhibits and the large focus on Jewish topics in the media," the German journalist Katharina Ochse told a 1993 conference on emerging Jewish culture in Germany since 1989, "one could get the impression that the country had a few hundred thousand Jews and a blossoming German Jewish culture."[21] According to surveys cited but not identified by the Polish author Agata

Tuszyńska, "[One] in 4 Poles is convinced that from 350,000 to 3.5 million Jews are living in Poland. One in 10 believes that there are significantly more, perhaps 4 million, perhaps as many as 7 million."[22] Various surveys carried out in the 1980s and 1990s in Italy showed that Italians consistently overestimated the number of Jews in the country by hundreds of thousands or even millions.[23] Indeed, in summer 1998 a senior staff member at a local history museum in the northeastern Italian town of Gorizia, on the border with Slovenia, told me that she guessed there must be about 500,000 Jews in Italy—some fifteen times the actual number. ("I know there are only a small number of Jews in Italy," she told me, "and 500,000 seems small in a country with 60 million people.")

This woman may have gotten the impression that there were so many Jews from the attention paid to the Jewish phenomenon in Gorizia alone, not to mention in the national media. The town has a Jewish history stretching back to the Middle Ages. Though the Jewish community never amounted to more than three hundred fifty people, Jews played an important role in local development, and the community produced several prominent figures, including Carlo Michelstaedter, an early-twentieth-century poet and philosopher. Today Gorizia has only a handful of Jewish residents, but its large eighteenth-century synagogue is the epicenter of activity organized by a local club called the Association of Friends of Israel, which had about sixty members in 1998. It sponsored public meetings, exhibits, lectures, seminars, publications, guided tours to the onetime Gorizia ghetto, and other initiatives "aimed at the recovery of the history of Gorizian Jews and the diffusion of information about the state of Israel." The synagogue, abandoned after World War II, was fully restored by municipal and regional authorities and reconsecrated in 1984 at a gala ceremony led by the mayor, a man who later became president of a local institute for middle European Jewish studies. Throughout the 1990s the Association of Friends of Israel maintained its offices in the synagogue building and also managed the museum installed in a ground floor hall beneath the sanctuary. Until 1998 this museum comprised little more than an amateur display of ritual objects and historic memorabilia, but in 1998 the municipality sponsored a total overhaul that added didactic text panels on Jewish history and traditions, installations, multimedia presentations, and a special room dedicated to Michelstaedter. (The young architect who designed the new exhibition installation had little knowledge of Judaism, however: the minyan, or quorum for a Jewish service, she informed me, was fifteen, not ten, men.) This upgrade formed part of an overall municipal development plan for historical tourism in Gorizia, and it placed the Jewish museum and synagogue squarely within the official framework of the town's cultural sites. Antonella Gallarotti, president of the Association of Friends of Israel, a plump, smiling woman who wears a gold cross around her neck, oversaw the changes made in the museum presentation and exhibits. "The Jewish community gave a lot to Gorizia, to its cultural, social, and political fabric; to the life of the city on all levels," she told me. "And this has disappeared. Few survived to come back. So it seemed right to us to memorialize them, at least to keep their history alive for future generations to know what the Jewish community gave Gorizia and how unjust was their fate." As of September 1997, according to information Gallarotti provided me, twenty-four exhibitions had been mounted at the synagogue and four books and ten pamphlets had been published. Lectures, book presentations, and panel discussions were "too numerous to cite" individually.

A Question of Timing

In one form or another and to one degree or another, the reintegration of a Jewish component is a pan-European phenomenon, part of an unprecedented and widespread confrontation with history in which the past "has again become [a] battlefield of interpretation."[24] It can be seen in countries whose people were the perpetrators as well as the victims and bystanders of World War II and the Holocaust, in countries on both sides of Europe's north-south axis, in countries that straddle the onetime Iron Curtain that divided the Soviet bloc from Western democracy, and in countries where anti-Semitism is still alive, openly voiced, and sometimes, quite literally, kicking. Symptoms of the phenomenon—that is, the concrete ways in which it is manifested—are much the same across the continent, regardless of differing motivations and differing political history. Still, geography, postwar politics, and historical legacy obviously have had an inescapable impact, both on the attitudes of individuals and on public policy. The history and societal role of Jews, the impact of the Holocaust, and the course of postwar development were different in Poland from what they were in Italy, different in the Czech Republic from what they were in Austria, different in the postwar eastern and western parts of today's united Germany.[25]

"Blank spaces" regarding Jewish heritage and history, as well as regarding the Holocaust, were the result of much more than World War II annihilation. They were created and bolstered after the war by willful public amnesia, deliberate political agendas, or apathetic neglect—or a combination of all three. Indeed, the postwar years were a time both to rebuild and to forget. Across the war-ravaged continent, where entire cities had been reduced to rubble and where millions of people, not just Jews, had been made homeless, Jews and non-Jews alike scrambled to put the war, its horrors, and its effects behind them. Few Jewish survivors wanted to remain in the parts of Europe that had become a vast Jewish graveyard. Those who did remain tended to keep a low profile as they regrouped and recovered, or sought anonymity in total assimilation. Many, if not most, Jews remaining in communist-dominated countries chose (or were compelled) to conceal or deny their Jewish identity. Some wanted simply to slam the door on the tragic past. Some wanted to build a "safer" neutral identity for their children in countries where religion in general was repressed, Jewish topics were officially taboo, and grassroots as well as official anti-Semitism often lingered. Some, at least initially, embraced communism with enthusiasm, attracted by its internationalist promise of ethnic equality.[26]

Among non-Jews, the memory of prewar Jewish presence and history, along with the shameful or guilty memory of anti-Semitic persecution and of the Holocaust itself, was often repressed and even effaced. Among society at large, there was little desire to explore the meaning and specific horrors of the Final Solution or to make the painful effort of self-examination that that process would entail. On the one hand, the wound was too raw and too potentially disturbing; on the other, the fate of the Jews seemed incidental when compared in immediate terms to the fate of entire countries or to that of individual families and friends. In the view of many, the Holocaust had concerned "others," not themselves, and those "others" were now gone. People, too, were simply numb.

It took changing conditions and several postwar catalysts to enable the development of the non-Jewish embrace of the Jewish phenomenon. One of these was distance, first marked most vividly by the coming-of-age of the student generation of the 1960s and then marked by degrees as living memory became history. A generational attempt to confront both the wartime legacy and its prewar antecedents formed part of a broader general revival of interest in lost traditions and veiled history that also, for example, produced folk music, genealogy, and "alternative" lifestyle movements as well as Vietnam-era antiestablishment protests and political groupings.

In West Germany this coming-of-age led to a painful—often brutal —confrontation with family and national skeletons that was exemplified by the radical "'68 generation" directly asking the question "What did you do in the war, Daddy?"[27] Interest in Jews per se resulted in part from this fixation: The question What did you do in the war? became Whom did you do it to? and what did you destroy? This confrontation and how to deal with it, a sometimes clumsy balancing act of guilt, memory, atonement, and denial, has yet to be resolved. In West Germany it developed into a manifold, if far from flawless, process known as *Vergangenheitsverarbeitung*, "working through the past" (or *Vergangenheitsbewältigung*, "coming to terms with [or mastering] the past"), a process of making moral, material, and psychological amends for the Nazis, on both the institutional and individual levels, that encompasses everything from official commemorations and acts of reparation on the part of the state to the activities of religious and other groups that try to foster German-Jewish dialogue to a personal fascination with Jewish culture and traditions.

Another catalyst was the opening of the Christian world—particularly the Vatican—to Jews and Judaism, which also was initiated in the 1960s and gained momentum as the postwar student generations came of age. The landmark *Nostra Aetate* declaration issued in 1965 by the Second Vatican Council repudiated the notion that the "perfidious" Jews were collectively responsible for the death of Jesus. Its call for "mutual respect and understanding" between Catholics and Jews formally initiated an interfaith interaction that has by now become so routine that in some countries it is often taken for granted. Pope John Paul II, who saw the effects of the Holocaust and of communist anti-Semitism firsthand in his native Poland, made improving relations with the Jewish world one of the cornerstones of his mission after he was elected to the papacy in 1978. In numerous declarations and with highly publicized and highly significant acts, such as visits to Auschwitz in 1979 and to the great synagogue in Rome in 1986, the establishment of formal diplomatic relations between the Vatican and Israel in 1993, and the release in 1998 of an official (if controversial) Vatican document repenting for Catholic failings during the Holocaust, John Paul demonstrated a vivid appreciation of Jewish heritage, history, and values to the Catholic world and to the world at large. Jews, as he put it most famously, were Christianity's "older brothers"; they and their culture thus were worthy of respect, honor, and even love. His mission was crowned by an emotional visit to the Holy Land in March 2000.[28]

The role of Israel on the world stage and shifting attitudes toward the Jewish state in light of developments such as the Eichmann trial in 1961, the Six-Day War in 1967, the Israeli invasion of southern Lebanon and the Intifada in the 1980s, the Gulf War in 1991, and the ups and downs of the peace process also have focused attention on Jews and Things Jewish in general and have influenced European attitudes toward them, both on the governmental and personal planes. In much of Europe, as part of an anti-American, anti-imperialist political ideology that grew out of protests against the Vietnam war, many countercultural young leftists embraced a militant form of pacifism and sought to identify with all peoples and classes they saw as victims, including the Palestinians. Members of the influential left-wing intellectual community also frequently assumed a sharply pro-Arab, "anti-Zionist" position against Israel, America's close ally.

It took the waning and collapse of communism to make confrontation with history and the historical legacy the norm, in the East as well as the West. The growing interest in the Jewish phenomenon paralleled other trends across Europe when the end of the Cold War opened up idealistic new visions of an undivided continent and sparked general attempts to redefine, reexamine, reevaluate, and "fill in the blanks of" the past. Needless to say, these trends have had a dark side, too, with a growth not just of national pride and national curiosity but also of nationalism and of public, sometimes violent manifestations of racism, xenophobia, and anti-Semitism.

Jews themselves have not been immune to these changes. Parallel to the development of a non-Jewish embrace of Things Jewish in Europe has been an internal Jewish rediscovery of roots and heritage, particularly since the fall of communism. Indeed, the embrace of Jewish culture by mainstream society goes on side by side (and at times hand in hand) with efforts by Jews in various countries to recover or redefine personal Jewish identities and to revive or enrich Jewish communities, Jewish life, and internal Jewish culture. In this parallel process, the mainstream embrace may serve to nurture emerging new Jewish communities and stimulate debate and internal development—but it may, too, overwhelm or even alienate them.

There is, in fact, a very fine and dangerous line between appreciating Jews and their culture and mythologizing them. While welcoming the new openness, some Jews are acutely uncomfortable with the new role forced on them and their culture and history. They feel used and exploited. In the early 1990s Michael Alpert, of the American klezmer group Brave Old World, expressed this vividly. He wrote a song in Yiddish describing his sense of profound ambivalence as, during a period of increasingly open nationalism, xenophobia, and anti-Semitism after the fall of the Berlin Wall, he made a living touring Germany playing eastern European Jewish music before audiences of Germans. The song, "Berlin 1990," made the charts in Germany:

> I've played here in Germany many's the time . . .
> But I swear by my muse . . .
> That not once has it been easy to be here.
> I see you at night in smoky hangouts,
> Talking youthful talk of today,
> I'm proud of my heritage,
> Yet I envy you,
> Today's children of yesterday's enemy,
> Because yours is the future,
> One land and one language,
> While we are left here, speechless . . .
> My own heritage is ever on my mind
> Even as I traverse the bright present,
> Because if not for the wars,
> Pogroms, slaughter,
> I too would have been Europe's progeny.
> Our world has already
> Gone down in flames here,
> Branches severed from the Jewish tree,
> Yet again walls and fences are being built,
> And you persecute those poor souls seeking a home.
> You drive them anew from your gates,
> Hunting them through nights of broken glass.
> What chutzpah you have, to act like that—
> Are we supposed to forgive you? [29]

The Viennese Jewish author and filmmaker Ruth Beckermann was more blunt. "By playing Yiddish music and telling Jewish jokes the consensus of silence can be maintained," she wrote in an essay published in 1994. "The illusion that people have nothing against Jews is comforting. Most Jews find it incomprehensible that even flaming anti-Semites have a good time in a typically Viennese Jewish cabaret. They take this as the beginning of a dialogue and don't even notice that in doing so they accept the following conditions: to remain silent about the events during the Nazi period; to repress the humiliating experiences of postwar Austria; and to downplay the day-to-day anti-Semitism of the present." [30]

Some Jews, however, feel, or at least hope, that the interest among non-Jews in Jewish culture may signal a real change in attitudes toward Jews. During a session at a June 1997 conference in Strasbourg, "Strengthening Jewish Life in Europe," an Israeli professor angrily rejected the picture I presented of non-Jewish enthusiasm for Things Jewish as "self-delusion—a folkloric tour of a series of events that are not of much interest." At the same session, however, Jewish participants, particularly those from eastern Europe, expressed pleasure—and pride —that Jewish art, music, and performance have found an audience in the mainstream. Several of them thanked me for pointing out this new public recognition and what they perceived as the more open and tolerant climate that it represented. One man, a sad-eyed Yiddish singer from Chisinau (Kishinev), gave me his card and asked me to keep my ears open for festivals or other venues where he could perform.

Other Jews, such as Tullia Zevi, president of the Union of Italian Jewish Communities from 1983 to 1998, may cringe at what Zevi has termed a "morbid interest" among non-Jews in Things Jewish but feel nonetheless that Jews must seize the opportunity as something positive both for themselves and for non-Jewish society. "Why are Jews so 'visible'?" Zevi asked in 1998.

> Why are they so talked about and written about? Is it due to the Shoah? To the state of Israel? To the ethical and religious pregnancy of the biblical message? To their high-profile presence in the mass media, in the arts, in science? Whatever the reasons are, the fact remains that the Jewish minority has a weight that is higher than its numbers would indicate. Jews will obviously remain a minority, but they are not marginal. . . . Particularly in Europe, the Jewish minority has been given a new historic function, which does not consist only in bearing witness to the tragedy it has suffered. It is a function that imposes new obligations and responsibilities regarding racism, xenophobia, respect for human rights, holding out a hand to the "new" others. It is not a secondary role. It is a role that we will succeed in carrying out if we know how to deepen and transmit our ethical and religious values.[31]

"A Dim Puff of Star Dust"

In the following chapters I discuss dimensions of virtual Jewish worlds, ways in which they are created and issues involved in the process. I have tracked aspects of the phenomenon since the 1980s, both as an outside observer—a journalist—and as something of a protagonist, and it is from these two sometimes contradictory vantage points that I approach the subject. A Jew myself, I became associated in 1980 with the so-called Flying Jewish University in Warsaw, a semiclandestine group of young Polish Jews and non-Jews who were trying to teach themselves about Judaism and Jewish history, culture, and traditions. At the end of the 1980s I began documenting Jewish heritage sites in east central Europe and in 1992 published a Jewish heritage travel guide to the region aimed not just at encouraging Jewish-theme tourism but also, literally, at putting synagogues, Jewish cemeteries, old ghettos, and former Jewish quarters, long ignored or forgotten under communism, back on the map—at "filling in the blanks" and thus reintegrating Jewish history and memory into contemporary mind-sets. In this dual role, I, too, have frequently shared the ambivalence and discomfort expressed by many Jews about the "virtual Jewish" phenomenon. Yet I also support many of its manifestations and sympathize with the activities, emotions, and ideals of many people who are involved.

The phenomenon under discussion is real, and I appreciate its reality. Obviously, my use of the terms "virtual Jewish world" and "virtual Jews" relates to the cyberspace concept of virtual worlds and virtual communities. (Indeed, among the thousands of Jewish web sites, there are sites called "Virtual Jerusalem" and "The Virtual Shtetl.") People can enter, move around, and engage in cyberspace virtual worlds without physically leaving their desks or quitting their "real world" identities. On-line, however, they can assume other identities, play other roles, and be, or act *as if* they are, whoever they want. Like virtual worlds on the Internet, the various aspects of "virtual Jewry" are linked together and overlapping. One can approach them either passively, as a mere consumer, or "interactively," as a participant, through, for example, performance and interpretation. They may be enriched by input from contemporary Jewish communal, intellectual, institutional, or religious sources, or they may be self-contained within totally non-Jewish contexts.

Comparisons are often and inevitably made between the way Jews and Things Jewish are regarded in Europe and the way Native Americans and Things Native American are dealt with in the United States— and on many levels, from New Age fascination through the echoes of past injustice to stereotyping, performance, nostalgia, fantasy, role-playing, and schlock marketeering, the parallels are easy to see.[32] Elements of a majority culture's assumption of a minority culture's substance, of the appropriation or even usurpation of Jewish functions and pursuits, are also at play: a European equivalent, perhaps, of "blue-eyed soul," or white musicians playing the blues, jazz, soul, and gospel music.[33]

A 1995 exhibition by the American photographer Erica Lehrer on commercializing the Jewish past in Poland included images of Jewish dolls, posters advertising tours to Auschwitz and *Schindler's List* sites, and a museum display of a mannequin dressed as a Jew. Lehrer, like many Jewish visitors to Poland, clearly found the scenes she photographed disturbing. But in a pamphlet for the show she rightly made reference to the ways Americans, too, use similar stereotypes "of 'us' and 'them,' of what we remember and what we forget," when viewing the American past and American visions of some minority groups.[34] Lehrer specifically noted examples such as Red Man tobacco and Aunt Jemima pancake mix. Much has been written elsewhere about minstrel shows and blackface entertainment, including involvement by Jewish performers such as the most famous blackface artist of them all, Al Jolson.[35] And there has been an ongoing discussion over the name and mascot of the Cleveland Indians baseball team: comparisons have been made between the caricature "Indian" face of the mascot and anti-Semitic caricatures found in the vicious Nazi magazine *Der Stürmer* in the 1930s.[36] Even the rows of Indian dolls in fringed dresses lined up for sale in places like the Denver train station and Niagara Falls souvenir shops are remarkably reminiscent of the shelves of mass-produced Jewish dolls for sale in Poland.

Although the phenomenon of Jewish reintegration extends across Europe, east, west, north, and south, I confine my focus in this book primarily to several more or less contiguous countries in the heart of the continent, each representative of a different history and tradition, where both civic authorities and individuals have opened their arms to Jewish culture—or what is perceived as Jewish culture—in the absence of any numerically significant Jewish population. These are Germany, Austria, Poland, the Czech Republic, and Italy, although experience in other, neighboring countries will also be mentioned. I begin with a discussion of the virtual Jewish world as a whole and of some of the postwar developments that have contributed to its evolution. I then go on to a discussion of several specific aspects of the trend, all of which find cross-border expression in many countries. Among these are the physical recovery of the Jewish built environment; the display and commercial exploitation of Jewish heritage through tourism and Jewish museums; and the popularity of "Jewish cultural products," specifically eastern European Jewish music.

My principal focus is the relationship of non-Jews to the Jewish phenomenon from a popular, rather than scholarly, perspective. But I also touch on how this trend intersects with the revival of Jewish life in some countries and how local Jews and Jewish communities are affected by, participate in, influence, and interact with the non-Jewish interest. It is by no means my intention, however, to discuss here the entire scope of relations between Jews and local mainstream societies in various countries, nor do I focus on past and current anti-Semitism, except where it relates to the principal theme. Neither do I dwell on specific Holocaust commemoration, the construction of Holocaust monuments, or the preservation of Holocaust sites, such as death camps, except in the context of the broader reintegration of Jewish history, cultural heritage, and memory.[37]

Much of the discussion is open-ended; I explore issues rather than claim to have answers: Is there, indeed, an intrinsic "Jewish space" or Jewish component in Europe that exists whether or not Jews are there to physically define it? Where is the line between sincere desire to reintegrate the past and complacent self-congratulation for doing so? When does appreciation cross the line into appropriation, and, in any case, is mainstream appropriation of Things Jewish such a bad idea? Will the new public face and popularity of Things Jewish help to counter anti-Semitism or just contribute to entrenched stereotyping? Is there a saturation point for this type of integration?

The virtual Jewish phenomenon is fluid and constantly changing. It tends, in a sense, to "ebb" and "flow." Answers (or conditions) that were valid a decade or even a few years ago in one country may no longer hold true in that country but may have become pertinent elsewhere. The klezmer craze, for example, developed in Germany in the mid-1980s but did not develop in Italy until nearly a decade later. In some places the full force of some aspects of the phenomenon may have "peaked"—or at least become the province of a steady, more specialized niche rather than an exciting or provocative innovation. By necessity, then, I present snapshots in a process rather than the final word on the trend.

It is clear that questions raised by the virtual Jewish phenomenon take on particular import and exert a particular fascination amid today's post-Holocaust, and now, postcommunist, conditions in Europe along with the concrete reality of Israel as a Jewish anchor and homeland. But this is, of course, not the only time that non-Jews in Europe have evinced interest in, or even sympathy for, Jewish culture, customs, and history—interest and sympathy that often coexisted with hostility, suspicion, anti-Semitism, and contempt directed at living Jews. There is evidence for such interest already in ancient Roman times and also during the Renaissance and the early modern period, when Christian scholars, theologians, and others studied Hebrew texts, published books on Jewish ritual, and sometimes visited Jewish neighborhoods and attended Jewish services to hear the sermons.[38] This developed further after the outset of the Enlightenment and the Jewish Enlightenment (Haskalah) movements in the late eighteenth and early nineteenth century, when interaction between Jews and Gentiles became more prevalent and emancipated or assimilating Jews, too, began to exhibit, study, and rediscover Jewish art and traditions.[39]

A century ago Mark Twain evoked issues about the persistence of Jews, both as a living people and as a powerful image in popular perception, in his famous essay "Concerning the Jews," written in Vienna in 1898, at a time when he also wrote about Austrian anti-Semitism. To be sure, Twain was writing in conditions quite different from those of today. Still, I find his essay a particularly resonant articulation, as his words recall to a remarkable degree the questions raised exactly one hundred years later by Tullia Zevi in Rome. Twain wrote:

> If the statistics are right, the Jews constitute but *one per cent* of the human race. It suggests a nebulous dim puff of star dust lost in the blaze of the Milky Way. Properly the Jew ought hardly to be heard of; but he is heard of, has always been heard of. He is as prominent on the planet as any other people, and his commercial importance is extravagantly out of proportion to the smallness of his bulk. His contributions to the world's list of great names in literature, science, art, music, finance, medicine, and abstruse learning are also away out of proportion to the weakness of his numbers. He has made a marvelous fight in this world, in all ages; and has done it with his hands tied behind him. He could be vain of himself and be excused for it. The Egyptian, the Babylonian, and the Persian rose, filled the planet with sound and splendor, then faded to dream-stuff and passed away; the Greek and the Roman followed, and made a vast noise, and they are gone; other peoples have sprung up and held their torch high for a time, but it burned out, and they sit in twilight now, or have vanished. The Jew saw them all, beat them all, and is now what he always was, exhibiting no decadence, no infirmities of age, no weakening of his parts, no slowing of his energies, no dulling of his alert and aggressive mind. All things are mortal but the Jew; all other forces pass, but he remains. What is the secret of his immortality?[40]

2

A Virtual Jewish World

Shortly after the ouster of the Czechoslovak communist regime, Prague—a city with an acknowledged Jewish community of about fifteen hundred people—was awash with Czech teenagers sporting Stars of David around their necks and big, black paper yarmulkes on their heads. The teenagers had not converted en masse to Judaism, nor were they interested in Judaism, Jewish history, or even the Holocaust per se. They were fans of a local rock group called Shalom, a band whose music was described by critics as a cross between U2 and Depeche Mode. It was Shalom's gauntly handsome, non-Jewish leader, Petr Muk, who had declared an interest in Judaism, and that was enough for his followers. Muk wore a yarmulke onstage and off, claimed to be studying Judaism—I met him once at an informal Friday night Jewish study group—and called Israel his "spiritual home." "The symbols that Shalom . . . uses mean something to me," Muk told an interviewer in 1993. "I am an artist who uses as artifacts those things which reflect my personal feelings about Judaism. My trouble is how to express all of this because it is something that comes from my private life." Muk's biggest hit was "Rachel," an anthemlike song about a girl during the Holocaust, which was first recorded in the 1980s but was banned for three years by communist authorities because of its references to religious identity. His repertoire also included tracks called "Israel" and "Haifa," and Shalom CDs featured a menorah logo.

This was heady stuff in the wake of communism, which had repressed Jewish expressions for decades; Things Jewish were now recognized as potent symbols of new postcommunist freedoms—but often as nothing more. Shalom was the best-selling rock group in Czechoslovakia in 1992. It packed concert halls and sold more than 130,000 CDs, LPs, and cassettes. A twenty-five-minute documentary of a trip to Israel by the group was shown on Czech television. The band made it so big that fans sometimes spray-painted Stars of David on walls. The fad was intense but, in the way of many rock-and-roll trends, relatively short-lived. It had little to do with actual Jews and Judaism but a lot to do with the perceived significance of the Jewish phenomenon in mainstream society: Jews as metaphors for freedom, spirituality, antiestablishment counterculture, and so on. And it was also one of the most bizarre public demonstrations of how casualties of communist repression were taken up as postcommunist cults.[1]

Is It Jewish? Is It Culture?

Continuing debates over what makes something—or someone—"Jewish" take many forms and have been going on for centuries, among Jews and non-Jews alike. Similar debates apply, too, to the ways in which people define Jewish culture. Certainly, for some, Jewish culture means exclusively the religious and traditional teachings, texts, and customs that make up the internal world of observant Jewry or are carried out in Israel. Others feel that it also encompasses works of art, music, literature, and the like, produced by Jews, on Jewish themes, for a Jewish audience. Others broaden the definition still further, to embrace all or much of the intellectual and creative production of Jews, on whatever theme or subject, simply because they are Jews: making the identity of the producer, in effect, define the product. For still others, the definition is more tenuous, stretching to include cultural production of non-Jews on "Jewish" topics, or even on "non-Jewish topics which nonetheless express distinctive Jewish experiences, such as a Diaspora experience."[2] Some prefer to speak of various "Jewish cultures" rather than "Jewish culture."[3] Non-Jews create their own definitions, based on their outsiders' perceptions or understandings.

In *The Renaissance of Jewish Culture in Weimar Germany,* the German Jewish scholar Michael Brenner uses a definition of Jewish culture that encompasses "all literary, artistic, and scholarly expressions promoted by such institutions as schools and theaters, publishing houses, cultural associations, and clubs that consciously advanced a collective identity among German Jews, which differed from that of their non-Jewish surroundings." This does not mean, he goes on, "that all those educational projects, publications, and artifacts aimed at an exclusively Jewish audience; most of them, however, contained a specific message to their Jewish addressees."[4]

In the Weimar Republic, the brief interwar period before the rise of the Nazis, there was a large, varied, and vital Jewish population, nearly ten times the size of the Jewish population of Germany today and one hundred times bigger than that, say, in today's Czech Republic. But in the context of the discussion that follows, in the context of today's Europe, Brenner's definition still serves well, with some important modifications.

In a sense, Brenner's definition can be reversed. Today in Europe the public idea of Jewish culture—or what is "Jewish"—is shaped very much from outside as well as from within the Jewish community. Likewise, the wealth of performance, instruction, talk, and exhibition that today consciously advances an idea of collective Jewish identity as often as not ends up advancing it in the minds of a non-Jewish rather than a Jewish audience. Given the post-Holocaust lack of flesh-and-blood Jews and visible social, cultural, and religious Jewish environments in much of Europe, the resulting collective vision is quite frequently the product of literary imagination—"Jewish style," perhaps, rather than "Jewish." This virtual Jewishness or virtual Jewish world is a realm, thus, in which Jewish cultural products may take precedence over living Jewish culture; a realm in many senses constructed from desire rather than from memory or inherited tradition. "Jewish" thus can become a label with a life of its own, as people embark on what the Berlin-based American scholar Gary Smith has called a "search for the essence, the nature of Jewishness."[5]

Many of today's new "Jewish-style" restaurants, with their subdued lighting, tastefully arranged antique furniture, scattered menorahs, background klezmer music, and dark oil paintings of old-fashioned Jewish scenes, are meant to conjure up a vanished world, but they bear scant resemblance to what most real prewar Jewish eateries looked like. A suburban Berlin culture center's project to stage a musical evocation of an eastern European Jewish marketplace has little to do with any real aspect of its muddy, tumultuous model. The skill of the non-Jewish Italian composer Riccardo Moretti, who issued a CD of what he called "Jewish music," lies in "an insoluble blend of imitation, reminiscence, and invention."[6]

Dining tables laid for a Passover Seder or a festive Sabbath meal are centerpieces of Jewish museums under state, civic, or private non-Jewish administration—in Gorizia, Frankfurt, Bratislava, and the little village of Tykocin, in eastern Poland, to name but a few. In some ways these installations resemble the reconstructed old-fashioned Jewish living room, fully furnished for a traditional *Shabbes,* that was installed in 1899 in the museum of the Vienna Jewish community by the Jewish artist Isidor Kaufmann. Kaufmann, who was born in Transylvania, was known for affectionate evocations of traditional Jewish life in the shtetl communities of eastern Europe; he had gathered material on extensive travels to small Jewish outposts in the region. Kaufmann's Sabbath room installation appealed to nostalgic recollections of the urbanized (or urbanizing) Viennese public, for many of whom the twin image of the shtetl and traditional Jewish ways of life had already achieved mythic status. When they stepped into Kaufmann's installation, both Jewish and non-Jewish visitors felt that they were stepping into the past. It was a past they had discarded or outgrown or perhaps never known. But it was a past that had a direct link with the present—either via their own childhood memories of Grandma's house or via the "authentic" old-fashioned ways that still existed, like an endangered species, in some remaining eastern outposts.[7]

Today's "Seder table" installations are sometimes elaborate in every detail—the one in Tykocin, situated in the tower of the restored synagogue that houses the museum, re-creates an entire furnished room—but often they are demonstrative reconstructions, aimed at illustrating concepts rather than evoking real warmth or real memory. The china and glassware will never hold food and wine, and the chairs around the table will never seat living people; the plates, goblets, and cutlery may even have come from different cities and countries. Most, if not all, direct links are cut. Indeed, according to Ewa Wroczyńska, who established the Jewish Museum in Tykocin (a village whose physical appearance still fits the bygone image of a shtetl), not a single object connected with the Jews who once made up the majority of Tykocin's population has survived.[8] The impression is often given that the very practice displayed is extinct; the life-sized plaster figures in the Seder table installation in the city-run Jewish Museum in Frankfurt look like ghosts.

Konstanty Gebert, founding editor of the Warsaw Jewish magazine *Midrasz,* says, "The infusion of cultural contexts comes from the culture at large. I can easily imagine a novel written by a [non-Jewish] Pole today, about a young Hasid torn between his love for Torah and his love for a Gentile woman or for the communist revolution or whatever. But who the hell would be able to write a novel about the intellectual competition going on between yeshiva *bochers* [students], or the insatiable drive of digging in deeper and impressing everyone with insider knowledge? It would be boring to death. Nobody would be able to write it, and nobody would be willing to read it. Yet the second kind of situation was a basic staple of Jewish intellectual life; the first, a colorful exception. So, what is it we're dealing with here?"[9]

In many ways, in many parts of contemporary Europe, a literary ideal of Jewishness and Jewish culture is entrenched among Jews, too. Post-Holocaust Jews in Europe are also trying to forge identities based on a severed past. This sense of discontinuity is most palpably visible in post-communist countries, where Jewish communities and Jewish life are being reconstructed by people who often didn't know they were Jewish until yesterday. Gebert himself, born in the early 1950s and raised in a communist family with little knowledge of Jewish traditions, embraced Judaism only as an adult.[10] But the dilemma is also evident elsewhere.

In a 1980 autobiographical meditation on the postwar Jewish condition, the French Jewish critic Alain Finkielkraut, born in 1949 in France to Polish Holocaust survivors, used the term "Imaginary Jew" to describe a spectral singularity that haunts the relationship between postwar Jews and Jewish history, as well as between postwar non-Jews and their perception of Jewishness. Today many Jews, like himself, he argues, are "Imaginary Jews" because they—indeed, like non-Jews—draw their ideas of Judaism, Jewish culture, and even Jewish identity not from real-life situations but from their mental imagery, based on stories they've been told, books they've read, and films they've seen about the Holocaust and the world the Holocaust destroyed; from things that have been taught from the outside rather than experienced or organically passed on and for which there is frequently no on-site living model: "Jewishness doesn't come naturally: an uncrossable distance separates me from the Jewish past. With the Jewish community carried off in catastrophe, my homeland is gone. Memory's imperative springs from the painful awareness of this divide. Unquenchable nostalgia for the Jewish life of Central Europe is the entire legacy I have been left. Jewishness is what I miss, not what defines me, the base burning of an absence, not any triumphant, plentiful instinct."[11]

Finkielkraut's lament for a true Jewish legacy in Europe is a typical expression of second- and third-generation deracination. It is similar to that of his fellow baby boomers and other Jews, in North America as well as in Europe, who as adults seek to reclaim the lost culture of their parents or grandparents by turning to religious Judaism or by other means—through the study of the Yiddish language, for example, or by playing klezmer music, or through genealogical research. For American Jews, though, it is a cultural and religious heritage that was lost primarily through immigrant assimilation into American society rather than through the destruction of the Holocaust.

Such a perceived loss of roots dates to well before post-Holocaust conditions, becoming evident with the development of the Haskalah and the subsequent tensions inherent in the transformative process of Jewish emancipation. Before and after World War I, for example, young, assimilated, Westernized Jews in Europe voiced complaints almost identical to those of the post-Holocaust generations. They, too, felt cut off from their roots (and sometimes from a national identity)—not by disaster or transoceanic immigration, but by modernity. The most famous lament for a lost Jewish tradition denied by assimilating parents, Franz Kafka's *Letter to His Father*, written in 1919, bears striking similarities to Finkielkraut's long essay.[12] Against a background of mounting political anti-Semitism, Kafka and other young assimilated Jews, in both western and eastern Europe, felt cheated by what they perceived as empty or artificial "modern" Jewishness and became fascinated with what they viewed as the "authentic" Judaism of traditional eastern European communities. (The chord struck by Isidor Kaufmann's Sabbath room installation fits into this framework.) Writers Alfred Döblin and Joseph Roth embarked on journalistic fact-finding trips to eastern Europe in the 1920s. Others set off on true ethnographic expeditions to gather Jewish songs, stories, handicrafts, and folklore and to photograph far-flung Jewish communities and lifestyles. The most famous such expedition was that to the Ukraine led by the writer S. An-Ski in 1911. But already in 1897, inspired by contemporary nationalist debates to explore a Jewish national cultural identity, the Russian Jewish composer Joel Engel went into the field to gather melodies. He published these melodies and also used them in his own art music compositions, sparking a broader interest in Jewish music that culminated in the foundation of the officially sanctioned Society for Jewish Folk Music in St. Petersburg in 1908.[13]

Much of this activity to discover traditional Jewish culture and practices entailed clear-eyed collection and documentation, but a romanticized vision of the shtetl also found fertile ground. Some Western Jews traveled to eastern Europe on spiritual quests, seeking out Hasidic masters the way later twentieth-century youth sought out spiritual gurus much farther to the east.[14] Others, like Kafka or Martin Buber, plunged into the study of Jewish traditions and the Hebrew and Yiddish languages; Kafka became obsessed with a Yiddish theater troupe from Poland and its leader, Yitzhak Löwy. Jewish painters depicted, often in a sentimental fashion, a vanishing Jewish way of life, and Jewish authors captured traditions that were bygone or, sometimes painfully, by-going. A number of non-Jews also became fascinated with the romance of "authentic" Jewish ways and portrayed traditional Jews in a positive or sentimental way in literature and painting; some actively encouraged the scholarly study of Jewish art and culture.[15] Jewish community organizations, too, in the late nineteenth century, began to collect ceremonial objects, ethnographic finds, and other items and to conserve them in museums that amounted to shrines to past ways, "wax-works for [their] own history."[16]

Germany's Lehrhaus movement of the 1920s finds a particular echo today. Started by Franz Rosenzweig in Frankfurt, the Lehrhaus was an adult Jewish education movement that stressed "new Jewish learning." Its teachers were Jewish but not specialists or even religiously observant. They themselves were outsiders, Jews "in search of a lost Judaism," who thus had to learn about Judaism and Jewish culture while teaching similarly unknowledgeable students.[17]

The process of outsider discovery is reflected strikingly in contemporary Europe, with the signal difference that in a great many instances the outsiders are true outsiders, non-Jews exploring a "different" cultural tradition. The Westfalen Jewish Museum, opened in 1992 in the northern German town of Dorsten, for example, baldly declared that its program of lectures, films, seminars, and other events on Jewish topics was "conceived by non-Jews for non-Jews." It called this program a "Lehrhaus" and made the claim of following on as heir to that Jewish tradition. (Similarly, the non-Jewish German publisher Suhrkamp declared its new Jewish publications division, Jüdischer Verlag im Hause Suhrkamp, founded in 1992, the direct heir to Germany's first Jewish publisher, the Jüdischer Verlag, founded by Martin Buber and others in 1902.)[18] The prime mover of the Westfalen museum has been an elderly Ursuline nun whose name, Sister Johanna Eichmann, resounds with an irony that is almost too heavy for her role. The circumstances are more complex: Sister Johanna was raised from childhood as a devout Catholic, but she had a Jewish mother who was deported to a concentration camp. Johanna herself was enslaved as a forced laborer by the Nazis in 1944 and after the war was detained by the Russians because she was a German.[19]

Today's seekers of Jewish authenticity, nostalgic or not, do not have the option of running off to Belz or other remote shtetl communities in eastern Europe for inspiration. Real models of traditional Jewish life still exist, of course, in London, New York, Antwerp, Paris, Israel. . . . But today's Jewish models may be modernized to the point where they no longer fit the preconceived ideal of what traditional Jewish life encompasses: the coexistent reality of sidecurls and cell phones may not quite jibe. Moreover, enclaves of fervently orthodox Jews who still speak Yiddish and who physically preserve the "look of the past" may remain closed to the outsider, even hostile. And Israel's hard-line right-wing religious politics and street demonstrations by Haredi militants in beards and black hats can make the image of "authentic" Jewish ortho-doxy seem threatening rather than quaint. The models thus can end up being corrupted, so that what is regarded as "authentic" can take root in stereotype or even caricature. For example, in June 1993 I saw a re-markable exhibit of paintings at a Roman Catholic–run interfaith cen-ter located some five hundred yards from the Auschwitz I death camp.

The Auschwitz-Birkenau death camp complex has been a political and emotional battleground of memory since the end of the war. It is perhaps the best-known example of how, under communist regimes, the Holocaust and specific Jewish suffering in the Shoah were generally subsumed within the general suffering during World War II: what were 6 million Jews, after all, compared to 20 million Soviet dead? In Poland, a country whose population suffered heavily in the war, the general for-mulation described 6 million Polish citizens as victims, among them 3 million who were Jews.[20] Most Holocaust or war memorials in com-munist Europe thus were raised to honor generic "victims of nazism" or "victims of fascism."[21] To most of the world, Auschwitz-Birkenau, the biggest and most notorious Nazi death camp, has long been syn-onymous with the (Jewish) Holocaust. But the memorial-museum in-augurated there in 1947 by the Polish government was dedicated to "the martyrdom of the Polish nation and other peoples." That Jews from all over Europe made up 90 percent of Auschwitz victims was scarcely noted in museum guidebooks, information documents, exhibit cap-tions, or placards. Jews were listed as just one of more than two dozen "nationalities" who suffered and died there; an exhibition hall on Jew-ish suffering under the Nazis that opened in 1978 was given the same prominence as exhibits dedicated, for example, to the Austrians and East Germans. For Poles themselves, Auschwitz became the symbol of Polish suffering under the Nazis, a national shrine of Polish Catholic martyrdom. Painful conflicts between these visions flared up in the late 1980s and 1990s over, among other things, the establishment of a Carmelite convent in a building abutting the Auschwitz I camp, the commemorations staged in January 1995 to mark the fiftieth anniversary of the liberation of Auschwitz, and the erection of crosses at Auschwitz in the late 1990s by militant and sometimes vocally anti-Semitic Catholic fundamentalists. The interfaith center where the 1993 exhibition was held was established, in fact, in a newly constructed complex as part of the hard-fought deal whereby the Carmelite nuns quit their convent and moved into new premises.[22]

The paintings I saw in 1993 were the work of an amateur art group in Oświęcim, the town outside of which the Auschwitz camp is located. They represented prewar Jewish life in Oświęcim, known as Oshpitsin in Yiddish, more than 50 percent of whose pre-Holocaust population of twelve thousand was Jewish. I found the paintings bizarre and troubling, concocted from the conditioned imaginations of the painters. "Real" memory had little—if anything—to do with the representations. Today, Oświęcim boasts a population of more than fifty thousand, but the vast majority came from elsewhere, or were born after the war, and have no firsthand knowledge of local prewar conditions. The paintings undoubtedly were well intentioned, but they perpetuated a whole range of iconic stereotypes, from the saccharine to the sinister. There were doleful "portraits" of imaginary Jews fully equipped with beards, sidelocks, sad eyes, and long, crooked noses, and scenes of "characteristic" Jewish types haggling in shops and on the market square, studying, praying, walking on old-fashioned streets. There were imaginary landscapes studded with gesticulating "Jewish" figures. One painting was titled *Route to the Mikvah* (*Ritual Bath*). The images were caricaturish, but it seemed clear at the same time that the artists themselves had thought of them not as caricatures but as romantic—or maybe even "real," even loving—visions of the vanished past. Reproducing these scenes was meant to commemorate, to "bring back," to "repopulate."

Models of authenticity can change, too, of course. A telling example was seen in 1999, when the glossy Italian travel magazine *Gulliver* ran a special sixty-two-page section devoted to "Yiddishland," a mix of contemporary Jewish life, romantic recollection, and Jewish virtuality.

"From Berlin to Prague, from Budapest to Antwerp and Paris," it said. "In the bars, in the synagogues, in the cafés, in the streets. Everywhere, a world that seemed extinct is being reborn: that of the great Yiddish tradition." *Gulliver,* it said, had set out to discover "a language, a culture, a style of life and thought that today is more vital than ever. Between past and future, an itinerary in the heart of Old Europe." The article, amply illustrated with photographs, described Jewish tours of the five European cities listed above, plus long sections on New York and Italy. It provided lists of museums, restaurants, cafés, souvenir shops, kosher groceries, and even some synagogues, as well as a glossary, historical background, and books, films, jokes, recordings, recipes, Jewish holidays, Jewish personalities, and other resources.[23] In a sense the article turned everyday contemporary Jewish life into exotica but accessible exotica—a tourist attraction—and exotica closely linked, too, to past romantic or literary models:

> It is a land that is immense and real but doesn't appear in any atlas. Its borders blur, sliding over the eastern edge of the map of Europe. Like Peter Pan's Neverland, it does not appear at first sight, but it exists and is tangible. It was almost lost in the mists of time and history. It is Yiddishland, a land that does not have a capital but has a language, a history, a literature, cinema, music, poetry, and a style all its own of eating, laughing, crying, praying. That world, by now legendary, existing for a thousand years in east-central Europe, centered around the shtetl, the Jewish village at once crowded, chaotic, and quarrelsome, disheveled and joyful, a tangle of hovels and alleyways permeated by mysticism and human warmth. Of that all-consuming universe that studded the maps of Poland or Hungary, Russia or Romania with little communities before the Second World War, remain a few black and white clichés, the novels of Isaac Bashevis Singer or Shalom Aleichem, the films shot before the war. But if the physical universe of the shtetl was pulverized by the Shoah and its population reduced from 11 million human beings to less than half that number, Yiddishland still lives. Indeed, it is reviving, protagonist of an exceptional cultural and linguistic renaissance. But the most extraordinary thing is that this is happening in the original places, where the horrors and persecutions took place, and not in some far-off diaspora.[24]

The article's use of "diaspora" refers not to its usual meaning of the Jewish Diaspora from the Land of Israel but to a "diaspora" from the pre-Holocaust Jewish homelands of Europe—a diaspora from the Diaspora. Many aspects of the cultural and linguistic renaissance in Europe it speaks of, as well as many of the attractions it recommends—cafés,

shops, CDs, atmosphere—were elements, even commercially established elements, of the virtual Jewish world now filling physical, prewar Jewish space.

Mediators and Alter Egos

Postwar Italy has had an uneasy relationship with the Jewish phenomenon that reflects its uneasy relationship with its twentieth-
century history in general. The Italian Jewish writer and critic Guido
Fink, who survived the Holocaust as a child, hidden with his mother by
Italian peasants, recalls a "conspiracy of silence" about Things Jewish
that lasted for years after the war. "Fascism had vanished apparently, but
nobody talked about anything," he told me. Indeed, postwar Italian democracy was built on a sacrosanct foundation of antifascism that exalted
the wartime anti-Fascist resistance while minimizing the extent to
which many Italians had supported—and fought for—the Fascist regime of Il Duce, Benito Mussolini, which entered the war as Nazi Germany's closest ally. This created an emotional and political block both
between and within generations, an area for decades explored only
gingerly by historians, politicians, and individuals. Fascist Italy's relations with Italian Jewry were ambiguous, too. Jewish emancipation
came with the nineteenth-century Risorgimento movement that unified
Italy, and Italian Jews felt a profound Italian identity. Many Jews even
supported Mussolini's nationalist, law-and-order Fascist government after it took power in 1922: as many as ten thousand Jews became party
members.[25] Few Italian Jews indeed were prepared for the rigid anti-
Semitic laws imposed by Mussolini's government in 1938.[26] Italian Fas-
cists arrested Jews and interned thousands in prisons and concentration
camps, and about eight thousand Jews were deported to Nazi death
camps after the Germans occupied Italy in 1943. But Italians themselves
have won praise for their role in helping Jews to survive.

Italy's postwar intellectual elite was firmly grounded in the left
wing, which had deep roots in the anti-Fascist resistance but for decades
was dominated by the Italian Communist Party (PCI), Italy's second-
largest political force and the largest Communist Party in the West.
Sympathy existed for Jews as anti-Fascist freedom fighters, as part of the
historical vanguard of the prewar Left, as symbols of an idealist interna-
tionalism, and as a persecuted yet persisting people. But for years this

vision coexisted and sometimes bitterly struggled with prevailing pro-Palestinian and anti-Zionist political attitudes.

Against this background, the non-Jewish scholar Claudio Magris has played (and still plays) the role of an outside mediator who, in the manner of the assimilated Jewish teachers in Rosenzweig's Lehrhaus movement, learned about Jewish culture as he passed on his acquired knowledge to fellow outsiders. Magris's 1971 book, *Lontano da dove? Joseph Roth e la tradizione ebraico-orientale* (Far from Where? Joseph Roth and the Eastern Jewish Tradition), which explored the vanished world of eastern European Jewry through the writings and experiences of Joseph Roth, was one of the important early gateways through which the postwar generation in Italy gained awareness of the prewar Jewish world and began molding a particular image of Jewish experience.[27] Several of his other books, as well as numerous lectures, articles, and university courses, also deal with these topics. Moni Ovadia, a Jewish performer who himself became a leading mediator for Jewish culture in Italy in the 1990s, calls Magris his "master."

Born in 1894 in Brody, Galicia, on the eastern edge of the Austro-Hungarian Empire, Roth was an assimilated Jew, a brilliant, if erratic, journalist who traveled widely throughout Europe, including his voyage of discovery to eastern European Jewish shtetl communities in the 1920s. In addition to his journalistic reports, he wrote novels, essays, and short stories. His works were marked by a sense of exile, despair, and displacement in the wake of the empire's post–World War I disintegration, Jewish assimilation and loss of tradition, and, eventually, the looming specter of the Nazi rise to power. Dislocation and despair permeated his personal life as well. "I feel at home in myself, but otherwise I have no home," he wrote in a letter in 1930. "My fatherland is where I am unhappy. Happiness for me exists only outside it."[28] Roth moved to Paris when Hitler became chancellor of Germany in January 1933. Despondent and alcoholic and overcome by personal and political anguish, he attempted suicide and died in a Paris hospital for the poor in 1939 at the age of forty-four.

Magris used Roth as an alter ego. In his dense examination of a world, a culture, and an author that were little known to Italians, Magris—like Roth himself—dealt with the eastern European Jewish experience in metaphoric terms of absence and exile. Magris, however, looked backward, through the lens of the Shoah. Roth and his work became a symbol of the lost, mythic world of "Mitteleuropa," which included the lost, mythic world of eastern European Jewry. As Roth's writings powerfully conveyed, it was a world that was already disappearing before World War II but that was destroyed irrevocably by the Holocaust. The Iron Curtain put the very landscape itself out of reach. Eventually Roth's books, printed in translation by an influential Italian publisher, developed almost a cult readership in Italy among the intelligentsia.

"I wrote the book through the device of Joseph Roth because I didn't feel that I could directly confront this theme head-on," Magris told me in 1998. "I couldn't write directly about things that I knew very well from a lay point of view, but not from the inside; I needed a filter, a metaphor. And so Roth was a pretext—although Roth knew only a little bit more of that world than I did. It is not a book about Roth; a book about Roth became a way of speaking about these themes that I didn't want to deal with directly." Magris took the book's title from an old Jewish joke that itself can be seen as a metaphor for perception, absence, and exile. "You're going all the way there?" asks a man. "You'll be so far away." "Far from where?" is the reply. This signifies an identity that is far away from everything, without a rooted physical center, but also one that is not far away from anything, as it carries its own center with it.[29] This, for Magris, was a metaphor for the Jewish condition, a people "who have their homeland within them, rooted not in space but in time, in memory, in a book, in allegiances, in affection. Thus, to be in exile but also never to be uprooted, never to be only in exile."[30] It is a metaphor that became deeply entrenched among Italian readers and that persists in Italy today; it colors, for example, the lure of the Yiddish language and klezmer music that developed in the 1990s. One of the reasons the Neapolitan novelist Erri di Luca gave in 1998 for his personal fascination with Yiddish was that it was a language that "changed citizenships without changing the place where it was spoken."[31]

Magris himself approached the Jewish phenomenon as an outsider who was drawn to it, he says, irresistibly and somewhat inexplicably through a long, imperceptible process that grew out of his work as a scholar of Austrian-German literature, as well as through the historic connections of his native Trieste, the former Hapsburg port, family friends and connections, and correspondence and contact with the Yiddish writer Isaac Bashevis Singer. "[I]t certainly became fundamental in my work and, beyond my work, in my life," he wrote. "It was almost a spontaneous necessity; I got there without being aware of it. I did not choose it as a subject of interest the way one chooses a subject of study.

Somehow I ended up encountering a culture that made me understand—or at least gave me the impression of understanding—the
world and myself a little bit better: the disasters of the world, but also
the enchantments of the world. A culture that in some way helped me,
despite everything, to live—to feel myself more 'at home' in the
world—and it was precisely this culture that is so expert in tragedies, in
persecutions, in exclusions." [32]

Approaching the Jewish world, Magris told me, was like coming
across a landscape he felt he had always known. Nonetheless, despite the
familiarity and attraction, it is a landscape in which he does not actually
dwell, nor, he says, does he wish to dwell there. He feels an insider's
sympathy but seeks to maintain an outsider's perspective and identity.
He was touched and amused, he recalled, when a rabbi from Vienna
once asked him, "But you are not a Jew, are you?" After Magris replied
in the negative, the rabbi stretched out his hand in a gesture of reassur-
ance and added, "I was just asking." [33]

Magris, an erudite Western intellectual born in 1939, has deeply pon-
dered his attraction to Jewish culture and has worked in the field for
more than thirty years. Yet his description of how he was drawn irresistibly to Things Jewish is in some ways remarkably similar to the experience and emotions recounted by Marcin Kacprzak, a twenty-one-
year-old Polish law student in the town of Płock, northwest of Warsaw,
in a poignant letter to the Warsaw Jewish magazine *Midrasz* in 1997.
Both Magris and Kacprzak cite their inability to fully explain their attraction, and both cite the importance of Isaac Bashevis Singer and
his work as a catalyst. Indeed, Singer's work, particularly after he was
awarded the Nobel Prize for literature in 1978, has been an important
gateway to explorations and involvement in Things Jewish in various
countries. It may be significant that the bulk of Singer's work, including many stories that wove recollection, reality, and myth in a spirit-
haunted shtetl world, were written "in exile," after he emigrated to
New York in 1935.[34] Kacprzak writes:

> For a long time now, probably since elementary school, I have felt an
> indescribable bond to the Jews who existed and who are no more. There
> was something strange about this bond. Each time I passed the old Jew-
> ish cemetery or the old Jewish district I felt something . . . I do not know
> what to call it—nostalgia, curiosity, fascination? I tried to imagine what
> Jewish life used to be like here before the war (26.5 percent of the citi-
> zens of Płock were members of the Jewish community). I started asking
> my parents and grandparents if I had any Jewish ancestors. Alas, it turned

out that I did not. . . . I wonder why I have become so fascinated by the Jewish world. Maybe I wanted to find something that would make me different from my peers? Maybe I was feeling nostalgic about a world that no longer exists? Maybe it was compassion? After all, no other nation has passed through such terrible ordeals as the Jews. Maybe it was just curiosity and interest in a different culture, so mysterious, exactly because it has been forgotten. And maybe simply—"a Jewish dybbuk within me sings long-forgotten songs." Thus I started feeling a bond with Jews although I am not a Jew myself. On my eighteenth birthday I got my first cassette of Jewish music as a present. Later I got more and more, and today I have thirteen of them. . . . This music uplifts me when I am down. It puts me in a good mood. . . .

Later, I started reading I. B. Singer—I would like to read everything he wrote. It is a strange and fascinating world. It allows one—if only for a short while—to forget about reality and go back to those narrow streets from before the war, to the murmur of Friday prayers, to the joys, musings, High Holy Days and everyday life.

What is left in Płock from back then?

The Jewish cemetery is comprised of only a few *matzevas* [tombstones] and a monument commemorating those who were murdered. For three years now, I have been lighting candles there on All Saints' Day (apart from me two other people or so do it). The synagogue remains an empty building—for several years there was a carpenter's workshop and a warehouse there. Some time ago I climbed in through a broken window—I found nothing inside except for garbage and bricks. (A few days earlier a friend of mine had found several pages with texts in Hebrew.) Old Jewish houses, little shops in the basements, where Jews used to tend store also remain.

Memory—I am not sure if it has been kept alive. Hardly anybody remembers. People are always in a rush, they do not pay attention. It is easier to forget. It hurts to think that so many people are no more, that there is nothing left of such a magnificent culture. A few buildings, a cemetery overgrown with weeds. That is all. There is nobody to remember. That is why I try to keep the memory alive. To remember what my grandmother has told me and what I have read. I would like to somehow keep it all alive. I do not want to live just for myself, with no mission in life. I would like to somehow honor the millions of those who were murdered. It is too bad that I am alone here. What is encouraging is that I met a fellow student who like me also has this strange bond with Jews. I talk to him and recommend books. Another encouraging development was [a] demonstration against racism . . . which drew a crowd of eight hundred young people. It is very painful when one encounters anti-Semitism. In my city, where there are no Jews anymore, the word "Jew" remains the most offensive insult one can use.[35]

Phantom Pain

For two millennia Jews created a distinctive presence and played important, albeit shifting, roles in Europe. Jews were "different"; even in heterogeneous societies they were separated from other minorities, as well as from the majority culture, by religion, and both their religious faith and their religious practices made them the frequent object of prejudice and superstition. Jews in Europe were familiar yet foreign: near neighbors but the ultimate outsiders, the consummate other. Even after Jewish emancipation in the nineteenth century enabled Jews to integrate into mainstream society, the distinction often remained: Christian religious "anti-Judaism" and the political and racial anti-Semitism that developed in the late nineteenth century made this clear. The Holocaust made it definitive.

Yet the Jewish phenomenon was also characterized by the perception of Jews in the surrounding non-Jewish society. There was superstition, stigma, and stereotype, to be sure, but there was also a penetration and an awareness of Jewish customs, songs, jokes, foods, language, traditions, and creativity that lingers to this day.[36] The Adriatic port of Ancona, Italy, once had an important Jewish community, but only about one hundred Jews live there now. Many local people, though, still refer to a holiday as "Shabbà," from the Hebrew *Shabbat*. Tales about the sixteenth-century rabbi Judah Ben Bezalel Löw, the legendary creator of the Golem, were so intimately entwined with the folklore of Prague that the city fathers erected a statue of Rabbi Löw—recoiling from death, as in one of the legends—outside the new town hall built in 1910 a few steps away from the historic Old Town Square. Of course, with their transborder connections, ambiguous national allegiances and identities, and frequent, often forced migrations, Jews have been stigmatized as members of an "international conspiracy." But, in a more positive sense, they are also seen as representing the first "Europeans," or even Europe's first "multicultural entity."[37] This is often underscored today in our age of European Unionizing: nine years after its 1987 resolution recognizing the overall Jewish cultural contribution to Europe, the Parliamentary Assembly of the Council of Europe issued a recommendation that hailed Yiddish culture as "once a cross-national culture in Europe, a mediator for intellectual advance and also a component of local national cultures."[38] Jewry, Vera Giese, the German manager of the klezmer star Giora Feidman, told me in 1997, "is the only real multicultural society in the world. It gave to society and took from society. That's the most interesting thing about Jewish culture. It's like bees, taking pollen from flowers and giving birth to fruit."

In the aftermath of the Holocaust, most physical and economic European models of what was a Jew, what was Jewish, and what was Jewish culture were lost. Often, all that remained, even among many Jews, were lingering stereotypes, both positive and negative, snatches of stories and tunes, and iconized recollections.[39] Alain Finkielkraut wrote of "Imaginary Jews." But other images are also frequently utilized, by Jews and non-Jews, to describe the enduring effect: a "void," "vacuum," or "black hole" that is impossible to fill; or "memory lapses," "anti-matter," or an abiding "presence of absence"; a wound—like a stigmata—that "refuses to heal," or "phantom pain" from an amputated limb.[40] "It's like an afterlife," one Jewish woman who fled Germany for the United States in the 1930s told me. "It's the soul living on after the body is dead." The concept of the enduring presence of a Jewish void or Jewish absence is sometimes expressed by physical means. The American architect Daniel Libeskind's remarkable, highly symbolic design for the new Jewish Museum in Berlin, under construction in the 1990s, incorporated an actual physical void cutting through its structure, a "void [that] every participant in the museum will experience as his or her absent presence."[41]

Inherent in all these descriptions and representations is a sense of undefined, irremediable loss, of a present haunted by a Jewish specter looming out of history. A dybbuk, perhaps, as the Polish student Marcin Kacprzyk imagined: the wandering spirit of a dead person that takes possession of the living. Jews, of course, express this most poignantly. But non-Jews, too, have expressed a longing for the intangibles that characterized society "before the Jews went away." Humor is often recalled as more witty, literature and criticism as more profound, art and drama as more creative, entire cities as more vibrant and less provincial. Jews are remembered as the "leaven of society."[42] The Polish journalist Ewa Berberyusz, who was born in 1929, put it this way in 1987: "[T]he absence of Jews, whom I still remember but who are now gone, leaves me, for one, with a sense of irreplacable loss. I voice here not just a sentiment in which is enshrined an idealized memory of old Poland, but rather an awareness of the real, manifest impoverishment of Polish culture. Poland has lost a very important creative contribution."[43]

Hugo Bettauer anticipated this longing more than a decade before

Hitler came to power. His description in *Die Stadt ohne Juden* of how Vienna collapses into an intellectually, culturally, socially, and politically stagnant wasteland within months of the expulsion of its Jews exaggerated the issue to an almost farcical degree to hammer home a point, but it is a point well taken; the Jewish loss was—and remains—a loss for all of Europe, not just for surviving Jews.

In an influential 1984 article describing the "tragedy of central Europe" in post–World War II, Cold War conditions, the exiled Czech writer Milan Kundera included a list of what he called some of "the most representative figures" of several central European countries: Sigmund Freud, the philosopher Edmund Husserl, Gustav Mahler, the Czech poet Julius Zeyer, Franz Kafka, the Hungarian writer Tibor Déry, the Yugoslav writer Danilo Kiš, and Joseph Roth. "[A]ll of the names I've just mentioned are those of Jews," Kundera noted. "Indeed, no other part of the world has been so deeply marked by the influence of Jewish genius. Aliens everywhere and everywhere at home, lifted above national quarrels, the Jews in the twentieth century were the principal cosmopolitan, integrating element in Central Europe: they were its intellectual cement, a condensed version of its spirit, creators of its spiritual unity. That's why I love the Jewish heritage and cling to it with as much passion and nostalgia as though it were my own."[44]

Likewise, in *Germany without Jews,* a philo-Semitic litany of remorse written in 1979 whose title overtly harks back to Bettauer's original fantasy, the non-Jewish German author Bernt Engelmann listed page after page of prominent, prewar Jewish names and swamped the reader with detailed statistics on Jewish Nobel Prize winners, doctors, artists, scientists, mathematicians, and other intellectuals and professionals. One appendix ran to twenty pages of notable Jewish "men and women of medicine" of the late nineteenth and early twentieth centuries. "Now the German culture is to all intents and purposes 'cleansed of Jewish influence,' just as Goebbels and his friends had wished," he wrote. "At the same time, we must realize that the promised gains have eluded us; instead an indefinable loss seems to have set in—a loss at best only felt, possibly estimated. How could such loss ever be measured?"[45]

This feeling of cultural loss has found frequent expression, with the lost Jewish intellectual tradition and contribution in central Europe in particular celebrated, mourned, elaborated, and "retrospectively idealized."[46] But it is also all too easy to romanticize, to blame today's cultural paucities and failings on the absence of Jews—rather than on the absence of local talent. The late Ignatz Bubis, the pragmatic and politically savvy president of the Central Council of Jews in Germany in the

1990s, a Holocaust survivor who was well aware of the consequences of the Shoah, rejected an anguished, overblown vision of the past that put Jews on pedestals rather than regarded them as people. "A lot is being said in Germany about the loss resulting from Jewish artists, writers, and other creative people being killed; there is a yearning for days past, for lost intellectuals," Bubis said in 1997. "But the majority of Jews who were living in these countries before the war were [ordinary] people." In Germany, he said, obviously exaggerating to make his point, "it was not much different from East European shtetls." [47]

Bettauer himself stood the "Jews as the leaven of society" analogy on its head, presenting a mordant illustration of the double-edged way in which Jews can be regarded, even by a society that longs for their return. "The yeast that is used in the making of bread has a horrible taste—but bread cannot be made without it," Leo, his Jewish protagonist who is masquerading as a Christian, tells a meeting of disgruntled Viennese in *Die Stadt ohne Juden*. "We must look at the Jews in a similar light. Yeast—not very pleasant by itself, and harmful in excessive quantities—but indispensable, in the right proportion, for our daily bread." [48]

Tension between philo-Semitism and anti-Semitism still vividly colors present-day circumstances. As opinion polls, news reports, far-right political successes, and skinhead demonstrations make clear, the embrace of Things Jewish by some in the non-Jewish population is paralleled by overt anti-Semitism manifested by others. Some, indeed, consider anti-Semitism and extreme philo-Semitism as "two sides of the same coin." [49]

Virtual Jews

In the absence of "real" Jewish protagonists in much of Europe, "virtual Jews" often take on themselves the onus of filling the Jewish void, easing the phantom pain, stanching the bleeding wound, providing yeast to the baker. I met Gisella Blume at the gate to the Jewish cemetery in the Bavarian city of Fürth on a damp afternoon in November and followed her on a slow walk among the rows of tombstones. An elegant, stylishly dressed widow, Frau Blume told me she had been drawn to her city's Jewish history almost by chance. By the time I met her, her interest had become an obsession. "It changed my life," she told me. Frau Blume volunteered to help clean up and document

Fürth's historic Jewish cemetery in 1990, partly as a means of becoming active again after the death of her husband a decade earlier. At the time, only a few dozen Jews lived in Fürth. She plunged into the task and found herself drawn into an ever deeper involvement as she methodically mapped, cleaned, and photographed the 6,500 tombstones. Eventually she started documenting the lives of the people buried beneath them. The dead in the cemetery—and what they represented—became, in a sense, her life, her world. When I met her in 1997, Frau Blume had been to Israel seven times, she was in frequent contact with former Fürth Jews, and, although she had not been a churchgoing Christian, she frequently attended synagogue services. She was also on the board of a society of friends of a new municipal Jewish museum under preparation in Fürth. She had become a self-appointed—and to a large extent self-financed—guardian of the cemetery, an earnest "godmother" of a burial ground that was founded in the seventeenth century and contains the graves of ancestors of the publisher of the *New York Times* and the singer-songwriter Billy Joel.

"Keep to the pathways," Frau Blume admonished me as I swished through fallen leaves in an open part of the cemetery, an area where the Germans had uprooted the tombstones during the war, "we don't know just where all the burials are." Frau Blume acted as if she personally knew the people whose graves she was tending and whose lives she was studying. She identified with them and the Jewish world they lived in; she championed and protected them: they were "hers." She found purpose, too, in delving ever deeper into what was destroyed by her father's generation of Germans. Indeed, Germany's Nazi past cast long and lingering shadows on Frau Blume's personal history, shadows that also clearly colored the intensity of her interest. Her father died in a wartime POW camp in the Soviet Union, and she herself was born in November 1938—the same month in which Fürth's synagogues, like synagogues all over Germany and German-occupied lands, were destroyed in what is called the Kristallnacht pogrom, the fiery prologue to the vaster Holocaust to come. Did she, perhaps, thus balance her own birth with the death of European Jewry? Define her own identity through her identification with Jewish victims?

Frau Blume asked me if I was Jewish, and she seemed almost envious when I responded yes. *My* Jewish identity, *my* connection with the dead, was fully intact, whether I kept to the pathways or photographed or pulled weeds or went to synagogue or traveled seven times to Israel or not. At the end of our visit, she gave me her business card; so strongly did she feel one with the cemetery and its spectral community that its design incorporated a photograph of the carving of a flower—*blume* in German—from one of the graves.

Just as Gisella Blume's life came to revolve around the Jewish cemetery in Fürth, in Kraków Janusz Makuch's life revolves around the Festival of Jewish Culture he directs each summer in Kazimierz, the historic Jewish quarter of a city that today has a population of only about two hundred Jews. Makuch and another young, non-Jewish Kraków intellectual, Krzysztof Gierat, cofounded the festival in 1988, more than a year before Poland's negotiated "round table" settlement removed the communist regime from power. Since then, the event has become Makuch's all-consuming passion. "This is my world, this is my life," he tells me, in a voice so tight with emotion that it is almost a whisper.

Makuch and Gierat had independently become fascinated with Jewish culture in the early 1980s, at a time when the success of the anticommunist Solidarność movement opened up new cultural and intellectual freedoms in Poland and sparked a wave of interest in the problematic Jewish past. Academics began carrying out research and organizing courses on Jewish and other subjects that had been off-limits. The imposition of martial law in Poland in December 1981 could only partially stifle this movement. Under martial law, intellectual freedom flourished underground, amid the widely circulated clandestine media. Not only that. The pervasiveness of the underground networks—combined with the regime's quest for political legitimacy—forced some relaxation on official levels. From the early 1980s onward, with official sanction that at times verged on co-optation, books on Jewish topics were published, research on Jewish subjects was carried out, and exhibitions, concerts, and performances on Jewish themes were held with increasing frequency. In 1988 an officially sanctioned publication offered an extraordinary status report detailing Polish "Jewish" activities in the 1980s. It noted, among other things, that between 1980 and 1986 more than 170 "books on the Jewish question" were published legally in Poland, and it described conferences, ceremonies, exhibitions, performances, broadcasts, and the like, describing them as a "renaissance of . . . interest in the Jewish question among the Poles living in Poland, a sincere and authentic interest devoid to a considerable extent of any additional motives."[50]

In 1986—the same year in which a Jewish research center was established at Kraków's venerable Jagiellonian University—Gierat organized a successful art house festival of Polish films on Jewish themes. Two years later Gierat and Makuch joined forces to organize a broader festival, which included a more ambitious film series, scholarly lectures on

Jewish history and traditions, concerts, exhibits, and a guided tour of Jewish Kazimierz. The Israeli representative in Poland (communist Poland and Israel did not yet have full diplomatic relations) attended, but otherwise all participants were Polish, including a few of the young Polish Jews who had begun rediscovering Jewish identity and traditions in the late 1970s and early 1980s through the semiclandestine Flying Jewish University. The festival was a milestone in the public embrace of Jewish culture in Poland. Makuch and Gierat organized a second, much more ambitious festival in 1990, and eventually it became a regular biennial, then annual event on Kraków's summer calendar. Most participating artists each year are Jews from North America, Israel, and elsewhere, although Polish (non-Jewish but also Jewish) performers, scholars, actors, and artists also take part. "It is absolutely special and extraordinary," said the late singing rabbi Shlomo Carlebach, who performed at the 1992 festival and toured Poland on other occasions. "I came back to the place which fifty years ago belonged to a different world. This world is gone today. I can tell people: Look, there is life here, we live here, we are not gone!"[51]

Most festival events are staged in and around Kazimierz, central Europe's most important complex of Jewish historical monuments. Crowded home to sixty-five thousand Jews before the Holocaust, Kazimierz became a run-down slum after World War II. However, it still encompasses seven synagogues that date back centuries, nearly a score of former prayer houses, two Jewish cemeteries, marketplaces, and dwellings and other buildings. "Kazimierz [is] a special place and a special space, a Jewish space, where the Jewish nation created its own culture for six centuries and gave a big contribution to Polish culture as well," Makuch told me. Festival events draw hundreds, even thousands of spectators, most of them Polish Catholics—and so enthusiastic that the festival has been dubbed a "Jewish Woodstock."[52] The festival, too, has been a catalyst for the gentrification and overall revival of Kazimierz as a tourist quarter whose attraction is based on its Jewish and Jewish-style character.[53]

A measure of the festival's success was the development of an odd sort of turf war for both audience and credibility among non-Jews and non-Jewish organizations sponsoring Jewish culture initiatives. In 1994, for instance, a parallel Jewish culture festival sponsored by the Austrian consulate ran virtually at the same time as Makuch's; in the late 1990s the Austrians, along with the Gentile-run Center for Jewish Culture, began sponsoring an annual, monthlong Jewish culture program each autumn. A bewildering number of other Jewish-themed cultural events take place annually in the quarter.

Makuch first learned about Jews in the late 1970s, when he was a teenager, from an elderly Polish professor. "It was like a discovery of Atlantis that people lived here and created their own original culture and had such a deep influence on Polish culture," Makuch recalled. He started attending synagogue in 1980 as a means of commemorating the Jews killed in the Holocaust. By now, Makuch exudes a rich aura of Jewishness. His speech is rife with Jewish references and Hebrew and Yiddish expressions; he maintains close contacts with Jewish friends in Poland and abroad and sometimes speaks before Jewish audiences in the United States. His demeanor, too, is that of a classic Jewish intellectual—or the literary image thereof, and with his dark eyes, full black beard, and furrowed brow, he even looks the part.

Makuch sees no contradiction in his role as a non-Jew directing a Jewish culture festival for other non-Jews in a former Jewish neighborhood that today is a Jewish ghost town. He has been asked the question a million times, in a million tones of voice, ranging from awe to accusation. He feels that he has a mission to bring Jewish artists to perform in the country he describes as the world's biggest Jewish graveyard, as a means of both honoring the dead and demonstrating Jewish survival— survival in New York or Israel, if not in Kraków itself. "When we pray the Kaddish," he says, referring to the Jewish prayer for the dead and including himself in the "we," "there are no words about death. We are waiting for the Moshiach—the Messiah—we are waiting for Shalom, peace; there is no word about death. And if I may say so, the Jewish Culture Festival is a special kind of prayer; for me it's a Kaddish, which [like the Kaddish] you pray once a year." Indeed, Makuch feels that he is doing what a Jew—what he—would call a *mitzvah*, a good deed that is also a God-given commandment: "People sometimes say this is a Jewish culture festival, so it should be organized by Jewish people. But in every Jewish shtetl there was a *shammas*. Why? You know why. Because on *shabbes*, someone has to turn on the light, for instance. OK, I'm a *shammas*."[54] (In the traditional hierarchy of the shtetl community, however, the *shammas*, or *shammash*, the salaried sexton of the community or congregation, was always a Jew. The Yiddish expression Makuch meant was "*shabbes* goy.")

"Virtual Jews" can act in highly conscious ways, as exemplified by the efforts of Blume, Makuch, and others, whose motivations are shaped both by personal needs and by local and national histories. "Jewish history belongs to our history as a whole," the Czech historian Jiří Kuděla, who in 1993 published a coffee-table book on Prague Jews, told me. "It's not something separate. It's part of the global history of Bohemia, but under communism our people were in the dark about this for a long time."[55] Some go so far as to convert to Judaism or to assume a Jewish identity or attachment to such an extent that they "become" Jews, or— like Claudio Magris—are sometimes believed to be Jewish. Personal or institutional atonement for Nazi-mandated destruction is often a prime motivation for involvement, particularly in Germany, where non-Jews, as part of the *Vergangenheitsverarbeitung* process, often seek to identify with Nazi victims as a means of "feeling their pain" and making amends. Lea Rosh, a flamboyant West German talk show hostess who from 1988 spearheaded the tortured and tortuous drive to build a Holocaust memorial in Berlin, adopted a "Jewish-sounding" name as a "nom de guerre."[56]

Reconstructing and then entering Jewish worlds, however artificial or imaginary, can also help some people in personal searches for selfhood. In an epoch when defining one's identity has assumed personal, ethnic, and national importance, the widespread (if exaggerated) perception that Jews have maintained a strong and developing identity during two millennia of persecution and exile exerts a powerful attraction. "Why am I interested in Jewish culture?" says Riccardo Rosati, a non-Jewish Italian publisher of fine books, including lavishly illustrated volumes on the Rome ghetto and on Jewish art in Rome and its surrounding region, Lazio. "I think it's a question of finding my own identity, as a Roman. Wherever you look in Rome you find Jewish influence, in food, in the language. Jews have lived in Rome for two thousand years."

Many Christians, Roman Catholic and Protestant alike, actively seek the roots of their own beliefs in the heritage of the Jews. When the American musician Willy Schwarz presented a concert titled "Jewish Music around the World" in a liberal church in Bremen, Germany, in 1998, he expressed concern that bright lights during the concert could have negative effects on carefully tuned instruments. The church representative responded that the only spotlight would be trained on a large statue of Jesus Christ. "When I proffered that this might not be the most appropriate thing for a concert entitled 'Jewish Music around the World,'" Schwarz told me, "he pointed out that Jesus was also a Jew." Rosa Alessandra Cimmino, a non-Jewish Italian who studied Yiddish at Oxford University, sings in a Yiddish group called the Mame-loshn Trio, and taught Yiddish courses in Rome and Venice, told me, "For a Christian, Jewish culture is of great interest but is also full of contrasts. Delving into it is like learning a part of yourself that you didn't know. And there is also the effect of the Shoah, the desire to understand what happened and why."

But entry into the virtual Jewish world is often much less intentional, sometimes even incidental. Exhibit-goers, book buyers, and concert attendees also people virtual Jewry. They form a more transient population, but their casual interest nonetheless also serves to define the phenomenon.

Three thousand people, most of them young non-Jews, clap and dance past midnight each summer at the gala open-air concert of klezmer and other Jewish music in the main square of Kazimierz that concludes Janusz Makuch's annual Jewish Culture Festival. At one end of the square stands the Gothic-Renaissance Old Synagogue, now a Jewish museum, with its distinctive saw-toothed roof. At the other end is the sixteenth-century Remuh Synagogue—still in use by Kraków's few remaining Jews—and its historic cemetery, the resting place of sages. Around various corners stand other former synagogues and prayer houses; many doorposts thoughout the neighborhood bear the oblong scars where mezuzot were attached. A former ritual bath has been turned into an upscale "Jewish-style" restaurant, which, along with several other such establishments, including a combined Jewish bookshop-café, has become a popular hangout for local Krakovians and tourists. In 1997 a former priest presided over a souvenir stall that sold postcards and carved "Jewish" dolls, yarmulkes, and colorful T-shirts. I even bought a T-shirt there that showed a barbed-wire crown of thorns surrounding a railroad track and what looks like a shower head, plus the infamous Nazi slogan "Arbeit Macht Frei" and, in Polish, the words "Never Again/Auschwitz." The Holocaust reduced to a souvenir T-shirt!

In the early years of the festival, when it was seen as a groundbreaking event in the recovery of the Jewish past and memory in Poland, musicians sometimes made the Holocaust a reference point in their performances. During the five-hour final concert in 1992, for example, Alicia Svigals, the violinist of the U.S. group the Klezmatics, dedicated the rock- and jazz-tinged music to Kraków's Jewish Holocaust victims. Holocaust themes still find expression in festival exhibits and other presentations, of course. But by now few, if any, of the dancing, clapping, exuberant crowd of concert-goers who link arms and press up close beneath the floodlit stage at outdoor concerts—or for that matter, few of the hundreds of people who attend the klezmer festivals in Ancona or Amsterdam, or the popular "Jewish Culture Days" or "Jewish Culture Weeks" festivals in Berlin, Munich, or Vienna—are likely to be interested in anything but a good time and good music.

A Parallel Universe

In her discussion of the creation of a new European Jewish identity in the wake of the fall of communism, Diana Pinto has stressed that Jews must come to terms with the non-Jewish embrace and decide how to deal with it. "A key question facing Jews today is how to interact with this 'Jewish space,'" she writes. "Should they fill it, accompany it, complement it or distance themselves from it? It is crucial for the creation of a new European Jewish identity that such a space not be monopolized by Jews, that it be open and open-ended. Without living Jews, however, such a space could become a museum."[57]

Virtual Jewry can and sometimes does become its own separate, compartmentalized, parallel universe. Many non-Jews study, teach, perform, produce, and consume in a virtual Jewish world of their own creation. Their internal relationships with each other and with Jewish cultural products—texts, music, objects, ambience, and whatever else they perceive or define as Jewish—may become a substitute or surrogate for relationships with living Jews and Jewish environments, creating the sort of "museum Judaism" where Jews themselves need have no place, except perhaps as artifacts.

This lack of contact is not necessarily always voluntary. Some non-Jews complain that even in places where Jewish communities do exist, they may find it difficult to make contact or breach what they perceive as barriers put up by Jews. Contacts may even be hostile. It can be simpler for non-Jews to pursue their interest in Things Jewish on their own. More than a few may even find it more satisfying to fulfill or devise their own idea of what "Jewish" means rather than risk being contradicted by living sources: their own Jewish cultural products become more "real" than "real" Jewish life. "No, I don't know any Jewish people," Michael, a curly haired twenty-year-old working as a volunteer at the Westfalen Jewish Museum in Dorsten, told me in 1997. "There is no Jewish life here in Dorsten." Yet the aim of the museum, he told me, was to teach visitors about the everyday life of Jews. I asked if he had ever hopped on the commuter train to nearby Essen to meet with the actual Jewish community there and learn firsthand about their everyday life. "No," he replied. The only Jews he had ever met were the occasional visitors, like me, who turned up at the museum.

It is in Germany that the non-Jewish embrace is most widespread, entrenched, multifaceted, and complex and where it has been most self-contained. It is in Germany, too, where Jewish uneasiness about the phenomenon is particularly acute. For obvious reasons, it can be enormously disconcerting to think of the descendants of the Nazi generation opening Jewish museums; teaching each other courses on Jewish history, culture, and traditions; studying Yiddish; wearing Stars of David; attending synagogue services; and flocking to concerts by German klezmer groups sometimes dressed up like people of the shtetl. "Are the German friends of the Jews concerned about the well-being of their charges, or are they more concerned about relishing their own feelings of guilt?" wrote the German Jewish author Rafael Seligmann in the mid-1990s. "Don't many of the German philo-Semites resemble butterfly collectors, who have great affection for and a lively interest in the objects of their benevolence, and know a great deal about them, but can deal with them best when they are already preserved—dead, in other words?"[58]

So intimately did many Jews feel themselves part of German culture and society before the Nazi rise to power that the relationship was spoken of as a "German-Jewish symbiosis." Events proved this to have been an illusion. But, in a sense, a German-Jewish symbiosis still exists, one that the German Jewish historian Dan Diner has described as a "negative symbiosis."[59] It is, however, an uneasy and highly nuanced symbiosis not so much between Germans and Jews as between Germans, their own visions of Jews and Jewish matters, and themselves. Henryk Broder, a caustic Jewish writer and journalist in Germany today, likes to describe German-Jewish relations since the Holocaust as an endless quarry. "Everyone can go there and dig as much as he wants, and take away what he wants, and do with it what he wants: a little pebble or a huge boulder," he told me. The rock can be carved or sculpted or broken or whatever. And people can go back for more—and more. "All options are available. There is always material; you never get to the clay. And it's so big that a lot of people can work there without getting in each other's way."

The Federal Republic of Germany came into existence in 1949 with the official creation of two separate German states, and every step of its postwar transition into a Western democracy took place—and indeed, even a decade after German reunification was still taking place—under intense international scrutiny. West German public policy on Jewish issues became a bellwether for measuring the civic development of German society. Thus, on the official level, the institutionalized anti-Semitism of the Nazi era was replaced by overt philo-Semitic attitudes and institutionalized mea culpas. The approximately thirty thousand Jews who remained living in West Germany after the war, most of them displaced persons from eastern Europe, in a sense became "moral hostages" to the process of reconstructing Germany's respectability, their very presence hailed as proof that the process was succeeding.[60] Public anti-Semitism became officially taboo, but so, informally, did open reflection about the war, the Nazis, and German complicity in the Final Solution. An embarrassed and deliberate "wall of silence" grew up about the "Nazi Time," which persisted throughout the first postwar decades as the Federal Republic pressed forward with its rapid transformation into a Cold War NATO ally. It amounted to a collective amnesia, a popular negation of the past—or at least a popular distortion of it—which persisted for decades. *Jude*—Jew—became a word to be avoided.[61]

The Holocaust itself, meanwhile, tended to become universalized; the specific identities of perpetrators and victims became blurred, presented in such a way that Germans could identify with the victims. For example, the German translation of the diary of Anne Frank, issued in 1950, removed or softened Anne's hostile references to Germans and thus reduced the implications of Germans' responsibility for her fate. The book became a best-seller, and the American play based on it became a tremendous hit. But it was with the Jewish girl, Anne Frank, perhaps the most famous individual victim of the Holocaust, that German audiences identified—not with the Germans who killed her: her suffering became their suffering and the suffering of everyone in the war.[62]

A "prospering victim imagery" developed in German discourse, in which "[o]lder generations often say that they were victims of outer circumstances, of Hitler, the advancing Soviet army, the Allied bombing raids, or Jewish conspiracies. Younger generations claim to be victims of their country's past, their grandparents or parents, capitalism, or contemporary politics."[63] In this context, Jews came to be regarded as victims with an ambiguous identity: victims requiring sympathy and atonement but also reproachful victims who persecute the present with constant reminders of the past. "No young German could develop a normal relationship to you," the American Susan Neiman quotes a Berlin boyfriend as telling her in the 1980s. ". . . Every time I see you I think of Dachau."[64] (This tension engendered attraction. An American Jew who lived in Germany for most of the 1990s told me he had no problem dating: German women, he said, were eager to go out with a Jew.)

One event that proved a national catalyst in channeling an interest in the Jewish past was the broadcast of the U.S. miniseries *Holocaust* on West German television in 1979. This melodrama, couched in highly personal, viewer-friendly terms—Jews as "people," not statistics—brought the war and the Holocaust and its human implications into millions of living rooms. Though scorned as kitsch by some, it unleashed a well-publicized, intensely analyzed, emotional national debate. "*Holocaust* was more than a soap opera," the historian Walter Pehle recalled nearly twenty years later. "*Holocaust* told the story of nazism and the destruction of the Jews by using the concrete example of a family. At that time, historical discourse focused on the structure of history and not about its effects on people." Pehle experienced the impact of *Holocaust* in firsthand, concrete terms: he published an instant book on the *Holocaust* phenomenon in the Schwarze Reihe, or Black Series, of books on all aspects of the Nazi era, which he began editing for Frankfurt's Fischer Verlag in 1977. The book, *Holocaust—the TV Film: A Nation Feels Concern,* sold more than forty thousand copies in twelve weeks.[65]

In the 1980s the *Vergangenheitsverarbeitung* process dovetailed with a fashion in local history research in general, which saw the establishment of local history workshops, the opening of numerous local *Heimat* (hometown) and other museums and exhibits, and the publication of hundreds of books and articles on all aspects of prewar local history, including Jewish history. One of the most famous (or infamous) of these was an essay written in 1980 by a high school student, Anna Rosmus, about prewar conditions in her hometown, Passau. Rosmus came under attack for "outing" local Nazis and local prejudice, and her experiences resulted in a book and movie, *The Nasty Girl*. "No matter how hard I try, as a German of the second generation, I cannot undo a single one of those horrible memories," Rosmus recalled in September 1999. "I cannot heal the many hurt feelings. I cannot alter the course of history. All I can do is create little signs, small symbols of one individual's good will."[66]

Major anniversaries of wartime or Holocaust events in the 1980s, meanwhile, served as catalysts for local self-examination and historical scrutiny as well as for ritualized public commemoration. In a speech in May 1985 marking the fortieth anniversary of the end of World War II, German president Richard von Weizsacker told Germans that they had to "look truth straight in the eye" when confronting the past. The fiftieth anniversary of the Kristallnacht pogrom in 1988 in particular sparked a nationwide "commemorative epidemic" that encompassed as many as ten thousand individual acts of commemoration all over West Germany. The various "acts of commemoration" ran the gamut from synagogue and cemetery restorations to the opening of new Jewish museums and exhibitions to official atonement ceremonies to television shows, homecoming visits by former German Jews, lectures, vigils, study courses, concerts of klezmer and other Jewish music, and many other things in between. The 1988 events have been described as a "negative celebration" in which Germans, rather than Jews, "took control" of the mourning and memorializing of Jews killed by the Nazis and transformed the commemoration of Kristallnacht from a Jewish act of internal mourning to an institutionalized process of the German state.[67] (In East Germany, too, where the communist regime, eager to claim some sort of legitimacy as Europe's communist edifice began to crumble, allocated ample funding to Jewish cultural causes as a means of winning support in the West, "literally the entire population . . . was mobilized to commemorate the fiftieth anniversary of Kristallnacht.")[68]

Such efforts, however, were paralleled by a backlash, a growing sense among many Germans that it was time to draw a *Schlusstrich*, a "line under the past," and to define German identity in positive terms. An intense, public intellectual debate developed over the uniqueness of the Holocaust and Nazi crimes and the impact of the Nazi legacy on contemporary Germany.[69] Attempts to "revise" World War II and Holocaust history included efforts to relativize the Holocaust by comparing it to other atrocities, such as Pol Pot's genocide in Cambodia, as well as efforts to highlight normal aspects of life under nazism, to describe "the periphery instead of the core of fascism."[70] In the mid-1980s, for example, the German director Edgar Reitz produced a monumental twelve-hour television series called *Heimat* in direct response to the U.S. *Holocaust* miniseries. Beautifully filmed, written, and acted and portraying local history and values from a German point of view, *Heimat* told the generational saga of "ordinary Germans" in a mythical village. It became a media event in Germany second only to *Holocaust* itself. Like *Holocaust*, it presented history in highly personal terms: love and death; joy and pain. Politics, including the rise of nazism, are remote from the everyday concerns on which the story is focused. Scarcely a mention is made of Jews, persecution, or the Holocaust, and the only Nazi true believers are generally portrayed as dangerous buffoons.[71]

On November 9, 1989, one year to the day after the fiftieth anniversary of Kristallnacht, the Berlin Wall fell. The reunification of East and West Germany, dramatic symbol of the overall paradigm shifts in postcommunist Europe, proved to be an additional catalyst for the examination of history and historic attitudes, of nationhood and identity, particularly in the face of the xenophobic and sometimes anti-Semitic explosions and neo-Nazi movements that erupted in the early 1990s. The symbolic meaning of "Jews" and "Jewish culture" became crystallized. Just as several million Germans took part in street rallies protesting xenophobic violence in the early 1990s, many Germans used participation and demonstrative interest in Jewish culture as ways of making personal public statements against nationalism and neonazism. At the same time, however, many Germans deeply upset actual Jews by demonstrating in favor of Iraq during the Gulf War in 1991.[72] And throughout the 1990s ugly polemics over building the Holocaust memorial and the Jewish museum in Berlin shed light on the political and psychological aspects of what has been derided as "Shoah business."[73]

The changes that marked the period after unification also boosted the emergence of a new consciousness and self-confidence within Germany's Jewish community, particularly among Jews born and raised in postwar Germany who some years before had begun claiming a new "German Jewish" identity linked more to present conditions and not solely defined by Holocaust memory.[74] It was the collapse of communism, too, that enabled the immigration of Jews from the former Soviet Union who, if only by sheer physical presence, revitalized individual moribund communities. Aside from these recent immigrants, most Jews in Germany today are former eastern European displaced persons and their descendants, many of them long wracked by ambivalence about living in Germany. Germany's Jews were often vilified by other Jews for choosing to live there.[75] Indeed, as recently as 1996 Israeli president Ezer Weizman, during an official visit to Germany, told Israel Radio that he failed to understand how Jews (presumably including the more than 9,000 Israelis who had by then left Israel over the years to settle in Germany) could live there. "I am unable to understand that," he said, "but it is an independent world, so go ahead."

In a conversation in March 1997, just a few months before he was elected president of the Berlin Jewish community, the historian Andreas Nachama, born after the war to displaced persons, spoke bitterly of an "invisible glass window" between the virtual Jewry created by non-Jews and the real, living Jewish world in which he lived and which he tried to foster. Germans, he told me, "get in touch with the culture that [their] grandfathers tried to destroy, without meeting Jewish people. This is very hygienic—you don't have to touch those people that you wanted to make extinct, that you thought were rats, and so on. You don't have to touch them, you don't have to speak with them. But you get in touch with the culture. It's very entertaining."

In Poland, too, the proliferation of Things Jewish in recent years has often been viewed with shock and distrust, especially by foreign Jews who visit the country—most of them drawn as pilgrims to the Nazi death camps or to the small towns, now totally bereft of Jews, from which their ancestors were happy to escape. Poland, once the heartland of the Jewish Diaspora, represents more than just a country for most Jews. As many as 75 percent of North American Jews are descended from Polish Jewry, and the country, its landscape, its people, and its anti-Semitism loom large in Jewish myth and memory. "[M]y mind / is dreaming of poland stuffed with poland," the American poet Jerome Rothenberg wrote about the land of his immigrant parents years before he had ever visited the country. ". . . o poland o sweet resourceful restless poland / o poland of the saints unbuttoned poland repeating endlessly the triple names of mary / poland poland poland poland poland. . . ."[76]

Jews, who lived in Poland for a millennium and made up 10 percent of the country's population on the eve of World War II, loom equally large in Polish myth and memory.[77] The Holocaust and postwar communism created new layers of complexity and anguish in the intense, troubled relationship: layers of communist anti-Semitism, contradictory stereotypes (Jews as communist string-pullers; Jews as the capitalist rich), Christian anti-Semitism, and Holocaust destruction. As in other Soviet bloc states, Poles were denied what the British historian Timothy Garton Ash has called "normal access to the national past."[78] The postwar absence of Jews and their own memories and historical viewpoint coincided with and indeed aided the implementation of the official communist agenda. Everything unofficial was internalized or went underground, where it sometimes festered. Moreover, the distortions decreed by official ideology were often counterbalanced by memories, myths, rumors, and ambivalent feelings that themselves contributed to further distortion. Without Jewish input to influence discussion or contradict either the superstition or the general line, citizens of communist states in effect "were left alone with their own, now uncontested, memory of events."[79] The resulting vacuum in knowledge could be profound and could lend itself readily to manipulation.

Poles in general did not and do not suffer the guilt of Germans as perpetrators of the Holocaust; they suffer another kind of guilt, a guilt one Polish writer has called "guilt by neglect," the guilt of having been bystanders, of having been victims of the Nazis themselves but at the same time witnesses, often indifferent or even complacent witnesses, to genocide.[80] The Nobel Prize–winning poet Czesław Miłosz articulated this already in 1943 in two unforgettable poems, "Campo dei Fiori" and "A Poor Christian Looks at the Ghetto." In "Campo dei Fiori" he evokes the image of a merry-go-round outside the walls of the Warsaw Ghetto happily spinning as the ghetto went up in flames.

> The salvoes behind the ghetto walls
> were drowned in lively tunes,
> and vapors freely rose
> into the tranquil sky.

> Sometimes the wind from burning houses
> would bring the kites along,
> and people on the merry-go-round
> caught the flying charred bits.
> This wind from burning houses
> blew open the girls' skirts,
> and the happy throngs laughed
> on a beautiful Warsaw Sunday.[81]

In the postwar communist period—particularly after the regime's "anti-Zionist" campaign in 1968 forced more than twenty thousand remaining Jews to leave the country—lacerating self-examination of this type was repressed until taboos against exploring the Jewish past and objective analysis of the Holocaust and Jewish issues began to be broken in the 1970s, first by individuals, for whom "discovering the ruins of a synagogue or finding an old Jewish book could feel like a blow against the empire,"[82] and later by communist authorities who co-opted the trend in part, at least, to bolster their legitimacy. In April 1983, for example, less than a year and a half after he imposed martial law and crushed the Solidarność movement, the communist leader General

Wojciech Jaruzelski presided over unprecedented, highly publicized official ceremonies marking the fortieth anniversary of the Warsaw Ghetto Uprising.

Claude Lanzmann's epic film *Shoah*, which premiered in Paris in April 1985, sparked unprecedented discussion and generally outraged reaction after parts of it were shown on Polish television and Lanzmann made statements accusing Poles of involvement in the Holocaust. The Polish government issued an official protest to the French.[83] This debate was deepened in 1987, when the Kraków scholar Jan Błoński published an article in the liberal, Kraków-based Catholic weekly *Tygodnik Powszechny,* which declared that Poles indeed should feel some complicity in the Holocaust, if only because of their indifference. Titled "The Poor Poles Look at the Ghetto," it touched off what in 1990 was described as "the most profound discussion since 1945 of the Holocaust in Poland and, above all, of the vexed question of the Polish response to the mass murder of the Jews."[84] It was the first time that these highly charged issues, incorporating a full range of philo- and anti-Semitic views and rival visions of Poland and its past, were aired in a public forum. These issues remained unresolved and continued to color popular and political debate through the 1990s, with conflicting views of the meaning of Auschwitz a lightning rod for the tensions. A particularly important recent catalyst for this type of discussion was a book in 2000 by Jan T. Gross, *Sąsiedzi: Historia zagłady żydowskiego miasteczka (Neighbors: The History of the Destruction of a Jewish Shtetl),* detailing how the local population, and not the Germans, massacred almost all of the sixteen hundred local Jews in the small town of Jedwabne in northeastern Poland in 1941.[85]

A powerful exhibition mounted in Poland in 1996, and the remarkable response to it, demonstrated the many conflicting and highly charged levels of attraction, tension, and memory concerning Jews. The exhibition, "And I Still See Their Faces," displayed more than 450 photographs of Polish Jews, ranging from formal studio portraits to creased, faded snapshots of everyday life. They were culled from 8,000 photographs sent in—mainly by non-Jewish Poles from all over Poland—in response to an appeal issued by the show's organizers, the Shalom Foundation for the Promotion of Polish-Jewish Culture, a Jewish foundation based in Warsaw that was established by several Jews who were born in Łódź after the Holocaust, attended school together, and now live in various countries. The foundation has sponsored events such as high school essay competitions on Jewish topics, concerts, art exhibits,

Jewish film festivals, and Jewish song competitions. Its president, Gołda Tencer, is a Yiddish singer and actress who remained in Poland and for years has been the star of Warsaw's State Yiddish Theater.

"And I Still See Their Faces" in itself constituted a virtual Jewish world. A walk through it represented a walk through a crowd of Polish Jews that would be impossible to assemble today. The number of photographs sent in more or less approximated the number of people identifying as Jews in Poland today; the number of photographs hung in the show was more than twice the number of Jews living today in Kraków. Although some of the photographs show scenes from wartime ghettos and postwar pogroms, the vast majority date from before World War II, when Jews, as the phrase goes, were "part of the Polish landscape." The pictures show old people and babies; teenagers and adults; rich and poor; pious and secular. There are Jewish chefs and Jewish nursemaids; Jews haggling in crowded marketplaces and vacationing at posh resorts; a Jewish family dressed in kimonos during a visit to relatives who were living in Nagasaki for business. In one picture, two bearded orthodox Jews drink tea and play chess at an outdoor table; in another, from the 1920s, a jaunty middle-aged fellow in shorts, kneesocks, and a polka dot tie nonchalantly smokes a cigarette at an outdoor café while a woman in a bathing suit looks on, slightly startled, from behind. Many of the people in the pictures are anonymous: their names, their fates, have been lost in time and tragedy. Others are fully documented. Many who sent in pictures wrote out all they knew about the people and circumstances shown, as well as the fate of individuals. Some of these messages tell heartrending stories. One photograph, sent clandestinely by a Jewish girl in the Warsaw Ghetto to her non-Jewish best friend outside, still bears the inscription "Wandzia, remember Lola for as long as you can! A few hours before the departure for the unknown—from Lola."

The deluge of photographs sent after the appeal was launched in 1994 on television, in the press, and through advertisements stunned the Shalom Foundation organizers. So did the response to the exhibition. "We thought we would get maybe one hundred pictures," Gołda Tencer told me in 1997. More than a year and a half after the exhibition had been shown in Warsaw, photographs were still arriving from all over Poland. Tens of thousands of people visited the exhibition in Warsaw and later in Kraków, Frankfurt, and elsewhere. Four thousand people tried to get in to the Warsaw opening alone. The show received extensive press coverage and sparked a documentary film. A coffee-table book that lovingly reproduces every picture in the exhibition along with accompanying comments from the people who sent them in won a national prize.[86]

One reason the exhibition was so significant was that the collective image of Polish Jewry it presented was so diametrically opposed to the commonly diffused stereotypes. The photograph of a pensive young couple that was publicized in posters and dominates the cover of the exhibition book became a haunting image that crystallized the staggering dimensions of human loss, presenting a three-dimensional, human, "normal" identity of "the Jew." As Tencer points out in the introduction to the book, in most of the photographs, be they snapshots of everyday scenes or formal portraits, "the light falls on faces still free of terror and fear. We can see on them quiet reflection, the joy of family life, a smile that manifests belief in a friendly world."

Ironically, these images are in sharp contrast to those presented by the State Yiddish Theater, where Tencer has long performed. Directed since 1970 by Tencer's husband, Szymon Szurmiej, the theater was one of the few officially sanctioned institutions of public Jewish expression under communism—"the flagship of the Jewish community to the Polish public, as well as to world Jewry"[87]—and as such its productions played an important role in forming and maintaining an image of the Jew in Polish society. Szurmiej, who survived the 1968 anti-Semitic purges, was Poland's senior Jewish figure for years. He was president of the secular, state-allied Social and Cultural Association of Polish Jewry (TSKŻ) and served as a Jewish representative in Parliament in the 1980s. The theater, located in a modern building next to Warsaw's lone synagogue (long decrepit until a government-funded restoration in 1983), launched messages that were highly dubious. It staged pieces from the classic Yiddish repertoire of Goldfaden, An-Ski, Sholem Aleichem, Peretz, and others, but without the balance of living Jewish contexts, the slapstick, sentiment, and staginess of performance became self-contained and self-perpetuating surrogates. Revues that the theater brochures claimed brought back to life the "perished world" of the "fairy-like Jewish towns of old prewar Poland" as portrayed in Chagall's paintings employed—and reinforced—classic prewar stereotypes of the Jew as awkward, even ridiculous, other and used a crudity of caricature that, given the circumstances of postwar Poland, was devastating in its implications. The theater was criticized for being "composed of worn-out older Jewish actors and awkward young players, most of them non-Jews, trying pathetically to bring the images of Chagall to life. A case of art trying, unsuccessfully, to imitate art, . . . [of] moaning and swaying actors and actresses tying to ape Hasidim and other shtetl types, . . .

[of] [n]on-Jewish actors in a Jewish theater, transmitting anti-Semitic stereotypes—in Yiddish—to the young generation of Poles!"[88] Other messages were dubious in a different way: One production, *The Song of My Nation*, presented a communist version of Jewish history, culminating, as the theater's official brochure, published in the 1980s, put it, with "the period of People's Poland, the socialist country of all working people, irrespective of their origin and nationality, of which Poland and Jewish revolutionaries have been dreaming."

Culture or Cultural Products?

From July through December 1998, the city of Trieste, Italy, sponsored an elaborate festival of Jewish culture called "Shalom Trieste" that included more than half a dozen major exhibitions, plus guided tours, concerts, food tastings, and theatrical productions. I visited Shalom Trieste in October, so that I could attend the premiere of a musical theater piece about the Jewish history and associations of Trieste produced especially for the festival by the singer-actor Moni Ovadia, a Sephardic Jew who was born in Bulgaria in 1946 and grew up in Milan.

Ovadia draws rave reviews and standing-room audiences all over Italy with performances based on eastern European Jewish culture and often partly performed in Yiddish. A veteran folk singer and stage performer who began devoting the bulk of his work to Jewish, particularly Yiddish, themes in the late 1980s, Ovadia has been one of the chief catalysts in the vogue for Jewish culture that mushroomed in Italy in the 1990s. "I have the unpleasant sensation of becoming 'trendy,' a fashionable Jew," he confessed in 1995. "Until not long ago I had an audience that was almost esoteric; now everyone wants to come and see me. I'm not complaining, but it's wise to be wary. To be too popular is never good."[89]

Ovadia is an undeniably talented and charismatic performer, and much of his work, deeply influenced by the Polish director Tadeusz Kantor, is complex and often highly constructed. But, in the context of this discussion, my interest is more in the impact or message of his performances than in their mechanisms or merits as stage productions. And I admit that I am troubled by much of his work.

The premiere of Ovadia's Trieste piece took place at one of the city's leading theaters on the eve of the Jewish holiday Simchat Torah, a joyous festival that marks the conclusion of the yearlong cycle of the reading of the Torah. Before going to the theater, I attended services at Trieste's synagogue, a magnificent pile built in 1912, when Trieste was the main Hapsburg port and its Jewish community formed an influential, prosperous sector of its population. Only about seven hundred Jews live in Trieste today, and far fewer than that were in the congregation. Still, men paraded around the sanctuary carrying Torahs bedecked with jingling silver, and at least a score of young children marched behind them waving flags. Then half a dozen men danced with the Torahs in front of the Ark. Despite the small size of the congregation and the disrepair of the enormous temple, it was a scene that was redolent of Jewish life and tradition.

The theater, a few blocks from the synagogue, was sold out. The audience was several times larger than the congregation in the synagogue. The performance consisted largely of Ovadia reading excerpts from books about the Jewish experience in Trieste, interspersed with songs, music, and Jewish jokes. He cited Claudio Magris half a dozen times and referred repeatedly to Magris as his guide; Magris himself was sitting in the audience near the stage. Disembodied voices of Trieste Jews were broadcast through loudspeakers, telling stories of their prewar youth. But no mention at all was made that the premiere was taking place on a major Jewish holiday and that a synagogue service was going on at that very moment just a fifteen-minute walk away. As the final scene of the stage show, Ovadia turned off a light, plunging the theater into darkness and symbolically indicating that Triestine Jewish life was no more. It was a powerful demonstration of how the quality of self-containment can lead to the impression that the only "living" Jewish world exists in artificial reconstruction.

Ovadia's role in popularizing Jewish culture, particularly eastern European Jewish culture, and also what I call cultural products, in Italy in the 1990s cannot be overemphasized. Since his first specifically Jewish production, *Dalla sabbia dal tempo* (From Sand, from Time), produced with the Milanese Jewish stage director Mara Cantoni at a Jewish culture festival in Milan in 1987, Ovadia has become a national reference point for Jewish culture. Probably more than any other single influence, his work in this period has sparked the popularity in Italy—among Jews and non-Jews—for klezmer and other Jewish music and has inspired fans to read books by Jewish authors, study Jewish history, and even learn Yiddish. A woman who studied Yiddish in programs in Paris and Oxford and then began teaching Yiddish in the southern Italian city of Bari, for example, told me in 1998 that her interest in Yiddish dated from seeing a Moni Ovadia performance in 1990. "I was blown away," she said.

Ovadia has deliberately forced his audiences to confront the history of the Holocaust and the destruction of eastern European Jewry. At the same time, an immigrant himself, he has helped to promote and validate the image of the Jew as other and of the Yiddish language, Jewish humor, and Jews themselves as potent symbols of survival, self-irony, and identity maintained in exile. The embodiment of the "Wandering Jew," he tours all over Italy with elaborate theatrical productions that often address Holocaust themes and with what he calls "Yiddish Cabarets" of jokes and music, appearing in venues ranging from big-time theaters in major cities to open-air piazzas in the provinces to Jewish community–sponsored events. He appears on television, on radio, and in movies; he addresses high school groups and scholarly conferences; and he and his message have been written up repeatedly in the national media. In 1997 Ovadia was cited by a radio program as one of the six most popular cultural figures in Italy, and Ovadia told me in summer 1998 that his troupe, TheaterOrchestra, was one of Italy's top ten theater companies in terms of audience.

Like others, Ovadia says he feels he is carrying out a post-Holocaust mission, that he is "possessed" by a dybbuk. He performs in Yiddish, he says, as a deliberate homage to eastern European Jewry wiped out in the Holocaust, as a means of forcing his non-Jewish fans to confront their fate and reflect on the loss. "It doesn't matter that the audience doesn't understand the words. What's important is that they hear the sound and cadences of Yiddish, the language spoken by the overwhelming majority of Holocaust victims," he told me. Onstage, he frequently wears a long coat, battered hat, and tiny wire-rim glasses—conventionalized costume props used for more than a century to perform "the Jew."[90] Bearded and long-haired, he gesticulates and grimaces, and when he tells one of the Jewish jokes for which he is famous, he speaks Italian with a heavy Yiddish accent.

Ovadia is hailed by Italian Jews and non-Jews alike for, in the words of a non-Jewish commentator, "taking upon himself the tender and somehow terrible task of bringing back to life for us, for all of us, a reality practically canceled by criminal Nazi madness: the reality of the popular Jewish culture of eastern Europe, Yiddish culture, with its burden of pain, wisdom, and folly, with the heartbreaking, gut-wrenching enchantment of its music, with the painful, desperate, irresistible vitality of its humor."[91] But, in a country whose Jews historically did not speak

Yiddish, live in shtetls, or even eat gefilte fish, his charismatic, highly idiosyncratic performances in fact create a new reality, infused by contemporary symbolism and based on ideals, emotion, and literary reference, rather than re-create or restore a reality that once actually existed.[92] In Italy, Ovadia is working—Yiddishly—in a vacuum. But to a certain extent it is the vacuum of a tabula rasa, not a haunted vacuum such as that in Poland, where the State Yiddish Theater's stereotypes rattle like costumed skeletons. Ovadia, in a sense, recycles old stereotypes. He plays with them and reproposes them as theater to audiences who often seize on them, not just as theatrical, but as re-creations "brought back to life" of "what once really was."[93]

One of Ovadia's big theater productions, *Il caso Kafka* (*The Kafka Case*), which premiered in 1997, deals with how Franz Kafka, the quintessential assimilated "Jew in search of Judaism," became fascinated with the "authentic" eastern European Judaism of the Yiddish actor Yitzhak Löwy and his Yiddish theater. Ovadia plays Löwy, the quintessential, authentic, Jewish insider—a "hot Jew," as the program put it, full of passion and innate wisdom. This is a larger-than-life role that Ovadia plays in many of his stage appearances. During a 1997 performance of his Yiddish Cabaret in an open-air piazza in the central Italian town of Perugia, for example, he gestured broadly and shook his long, gray-streaked locks. He leaned back in a chair and, accompanied by guitar, accordion, and violin, belted out songs in a raucous voice that emphasized the sobs and *krekhts* of a cantor. Striding the stage, he told a stream of jokes in his Yiddish accent. The jokes dealt with "Yiddishe mamas" and the misadventures of characters named Moishele and Avroimele. They had punch lines centering, among other things, on Jewish greed and the shape of Jewish noses and brought roars of appreciative laughter from the standing-room audience. In monologues between jokes and songs, Ovadia mused about Jews, Judaism, and Yiddishkayt; what they are and what they mean, both to him personally and to the world in general. At one point he underscored that he was the only Jew on the stage: the musicians he works with, he told the crowd, are all goyim. Few, if any, of the audience were Jews: only a handful of Jewish families live in Perugia. For probably the majority of the audience, Ovadia was the only Jew they had ever knowingly encountered firsthand; his persona represented the closest they had knowingly come to the "real thing."

The irony is that Ovadia himself is an outsider to the Yiddish culture he is perceived as personifying. He was born in one country where Yiddish was not spoken and grew up and now performs in another country that for the most part has no recent Yiddish traditions; "the shtetl" is as much a literary experience for Italian Jews as it is for non-Jews. A committed leftist who at the end of the 1990s still professed himself an Italian-style Eurocommunist, Ovadia sang Yiddish songs when he attended Jewish school in Milan and later in the left-wing folk scene of the 1960s and 1970s. (One of his productions deals with historic Jewish experience in the Left.) But he only started learning Yiddish as an adult from a Chabad Lubavitch rabbi in Milan, after he wandered into a small prayer room there whose congregants were elderly Holocaust survivors from eastern Europe. "There in front of me, as if by magic, was the shtetl," he recalled. "I realized that this little synagogue was a theater. Yiddish was exploding in the air in all its variants, mixed with an Italian spoken in Yiddish; I felt like I was in the middle of a Jewish joke." He says that he models his stage gestures on the behavior of this rabbi and the elderly congregants—"stealing," as he puts it, their mannerisms, looks, speech cadences, and tics and "turning them into theater."[94]

Ovadia is thus creating, for both his non-Jewish and his Jewish Italian audience, a "virtual" image of the eastern European Jew and the mythic shtetl, based on an exaggerated stage version of the post-Holocaust immigrant experience in Milan rather than on the eastern European Jewish experience itself. Ovadia's books print many of the *w* sounds as *v*'s. This, as he put it, offers the reader "a crumb of the flavor of the language as spoken."[95] But the language is not Yiddish. Rather, it is the comic mispronunciation of a native Yiddish speaker clumsily trying to speak Italian: the Jew as outsider, exile, inexorable other.

For many Italians, ignorant even of Italian Jewish traditions and history, this image can serve as an image of Jews in general. It is not a dominant culture demarking this otherness but a Jew proclaiming it. It is an image, too, that relies heavily on tortured interrogations as to the true essence of "Jewishness." The program for *The Kafka Case* underscores this. It prints a photograph of Kafka next to a photograph of the real Yitzhak Löwy. Kafka is sleek, serious, and totally Western, with hair parted in the middle and high white collar and tie. Löwy, the "authentic Jew," is shown apparently in performance: wearing a blousy white shirt, he is on his knees, his face contorted in a grimace, his hands drawn up to his chest and hooked in clawlike, spastic gestures.

Ovadia insists that he is just a performer; he describes himself as a *saltimbanco*, an acrobat. "I am not a scholar in search of reality but a performer in search of feelings that stimulate an interest in that world," he told me. "I am trying to do my part in making Yiddish known, but in a personal way. What I do onstage is to explain the effect that the Yiddish world has had on me. . . . I hope I stimulate others. I hope that some will say that they started with me and went further." He is well aware, too, of the irony of himself, a newcomer to Yiddish culture, being regarded in Italy as that culture's most prominent representative. In program notes to *The Kafka Case* he described himself as an "East European Jewish actor who isn't; who really is a Sephardic Slav; a Levantine counterfeiter who 'speaks' Yiddish, a successful braggart." He and Roberto Andò, the non-Jewish Sicilian with whom he coauthored the production, Ovadia said, made "a great couple of rascals." He clearly recognizes, too, the inherent ambiguity of the jokes and stereotypes employed in his performance: in 1998 he told an audience at the Rome Jewish Community Center that he realized many of the jokes he uses onstage could sound anti-Semitic if told by a non-Jew. He did not, however, address the question of whether in telling such jokes before mainly non-Jewish audiences he, a Jew, could give the appearance of sanctioning or legitimizing such descriptions in the mainstream. "The merit of my success," Ovadia has said, "is in fact that I simultaneously satisfy vast categories of people: Jews who love to laugh at themselves; those who feel a sense of guilt for that which happened and finally can laugh at Jews along with a Jew; anti-Semites who see their stereotypes confirmed."[96]

And that, I feel, is the point. For, despite Ovadia's disclaimers, he represents in Italy much more than an actor who simply gets up onstage and performs. The world he creates in performance extends beyond the stage, forming a synthesis of "artistic representation and ethical teachings."[97] He himself has declared that in his work he "chose to forget the 'philology' to try another possibility by proclaiming that this music transcends its 'scientifically determined' space-time coordinates, to tell us about man's distances, his wounded soul, his absolute feelings, his relationship with natural and social worlds, his 'holy' being, his possibility of facing the universe, weak yet sublime."[98] For many of his fans, Ovadia has taken on the character of a guru as well as a gateway to a little-known culture—a culture that, as Claudio Magris has observed, can seem familiar, even universal.

"Moni Ovadia has succeeded in the miracle of gathering a crowd of us around his performances devoted to a language that was buried alive," Erri di Luca, the Neapolitan novelist, wrote in a front-page article in the left-wing newspaper *il manifesto*. Di Luca taught himself Hebrew and Yiddish and has had popular success in Italy with Italian translations of the Old Testament. He has also translated Yiddish songs into Neapolitan dialect and in 1999 jointly hosted a concert with Ovadia: di Luca introduced Neapolitan songs while Ovadia presented Yiddish ones. "He didn't receive [this language] from his parents, he went in search of it; he raised it like a daughter and now brings it into our midst," di Luca wrote. "And to us it sounds familiar, something of our own. I, for one, find shreds of Neapolitan in those miseries, hungry sisters of Pulcinella: in dances like tarantellas, in a fondness for stringed instruments; in a vocation to be a language of *mamma* and of the street, good for invective and for pet names, for screaming and for lullabies. And I feel that everyone finds, in the Yiddish of Moni Ovadia, a feature of his own intimacy with his homeland, and so that language becomes a compendium of others."[99]

Fans write Ovadia letters, send him books on Jewish themes, and turn to him with questions about Judaism and about life itself. After the show in Perugia, a teenaged girl knocked timidly at the door of his makeshift dressing room, accompanied by her beaming parents. She had a question for Ovadia: "I want to study Hebrew. Where shall I go?" An older woman approached him a few minutes later with outstretched arms. "Thank you for what you are doing," she said.

Ovadia sometimes seems taken aback, even overwhelmed, at his impact and at the role he has been assigned. But this reaction can appear disingenuous, given the obviously dramatic impact he enjoys. In 1995 he had expressed the fear that his popularity was a fad, but three years later he felt differently. "I think it's something deeper, something more serious," he told me. "Because too many people come to me, not to say, You are a good artist, but to tell me, I love you, you are important for me. There's a huge amount of affection for my work and my person. And I'm very moved because I couldn't realize that I could go so far. In a way things have become so incredible, it's a little utopia."

In early 1998 the northern Italian town of Pordenone paid homage to Ovadia with a five-week series of performances, lectures, and seminars in his honor. A book of essays by several prominent Jewish and non-Jewish intellectuals (including Magris) was produced for the occasion. Its cover and frontispiece were a pastel portrait of Ovadia. This time he is not wearing his "stage-Jewish" costume reminiscent of a poor immigrant or caricature Jewish peddler. Instead, he is portrayed in old-fashioned clothing; his features are elongated. Eyes sunk deep in their sockets look back over his shoulder under a wrinkled brow; beard and hair are flowing. He is depicted as an idealization of an old world Tzaddik, not a man born in the mid-twentieth century, after the Holocaust, who regularly uses a cell phone.[100]

The image Ovadia projects and his immense influence in Italy over the past decade illustrate another trap: the risk that Jews themselves can create or perpetuate Jewish worlds that are just as virtual or "absolutely fake" as those created by non-Jews. "I had a vision of Yiddishkayt, that one-word wrap-up of the folkways of eastern European Jews, awaking from its dormancy and discovering it was still in a nightmare—its past and essence could be shaped at will by strangers," was the reaction of the American ethnomusicologist Mark Slobin to a 1997 performance by Ovadia in Bologna.[101] The world presented by Ovadia, the most visible Jewish cultural figure in the public Italian arena, has little to do with either the physical image or the popular culture of Italy's largely accul-turated Jews. He deals only rarely, too, with his own, Sephardic Jewish traditions. Indeed, he told Slobin that this would be getting "too close."[102] Nor, in his frequent evocations of the Shoah, does he gener-ally address the role of Italian fascism or the persecution of Italian Jews.

Particularly where there is little or no powerful Jewish counterincentive, virtual worlds can have a powerful influence on internal Jewish aware-ness. Today's public rediscovery in Poland of the Jewish phenomenon is accompanied by internal efforts among Polish Jews to revive Jewish communal life. These efforts, like similar efforts among Jews in other postcommunist countries, have been sustained largely through pro-grams funded by foreign Jewish organizations such as the New York–based Ronald S. Lauder Foundation and the American Jewish Joint Dis-tribution Committee, whose representatives stepped in from the late 1980s to help newcomers to Judaism find their faith, their identity, or their communal affiliation and also to fill the local Jewish leadership vac-uum. By the end of the 1990s the Lauder Foundation sponsored a Jew-ish school in Warsaw, Jewish clubs and education groups in various cities, and *Midrasz*, the glossy monthly Jewish magazine that has a read-ership of several thousand. Fledgling local lay leaders, many of them "graduates" of the Flying Jewish University, struggled with identity questions, outreach and assimilation, funding shortfalls, financial scan-dals, battles over property restitution, conflicts between orthodox and reform, religious and secular, young and old—yawning problems, both quotidian and theoretical, that challenged Jewish communities world-wide, be they long established or just emerging.

This internal revival, though still precarious, has been dramatic in the Jewish context but not highly visible outside Jewish communal bound-aries. Indeed, though the number of self-identifying Jews in Poland has increased tremendously in the decade since the fall of communism, numbers are still very small, and also imprecise. It is a measure of the fragility of the community and its communal identity that estimates of the numbers of Jews in Poland range from five thousand to thirty thousand.

Visiting outsiders and probably even many Poles, however, often confound the vitality of the virtual Jewish world with the real thing, mistaking external Jewish style for internal, communal, Jewish substance. "Two months ago I went with my son to the most celebrated of the Jewish cafés in Kazimierz," the Polish-born writer Abraham Brumberg wrote in early 1998. "Two Poles were ladling out the café's *pièce de résistance, tsimes,* to enthusiastic young West Europeans who were attending a course on contemporary Poland in a castle near Warsaw. A few hours earlier I had delivered a talk on Polish Jews to this audience, gathered in the Center for Jewish Culture in Kazimierz. They were as appreciative of the spiritual nourishment as they were, a few hours later, of the *tsimes.* Yet I wondered, as I looked at the faces of the young men and women, to what extent they were conscious—as I could not help being—of the counterfeit atmosphere around us. There were no Jews in the café, and no one to tell them that *tsimes* had never actually been the fare in Jewish restaurants. What we were being treated to was a show—a useful show . . . but a show nevertheless." [103] (Indeed, the Center for Jewish Culture where Brumberg gave his lecture is the one run by non-Jews I mentioned earlier, which sponsored more than six hundred Jewish events in its first three years of operation.)

Jews, too, enjoy, partake, and relate to the new, fertile terrain. "This Gentile Jewish culture is shaping the perception of what is Jewish [in Poland]," Konstanty Gebert told me in 1997. "It is becoming a dominant trend. And it has one huge asset that no Jewish culture ever had—it's so easy to assimilate. To participate in Jewish culture took an effort. You had to be educated, culturally educated, religiously, secularly, whatever. And here you get the equivalent of McDonald's. It's not haute cuisine, it's McDonald's. And the problem is that it comes to the point that McDonald's is taken for being haute cuisine, especially when we speak of families with a low quotient of Jewish identity. If this is becoming acceptable, what is it that we have to oppose it? The real question is what are we Jews going to do about it. For most assimilated families, the McDonald's version probably is actually a step forward—or so they think."

Indeed, the dearth of what might be called "genuine" Jewish cultural values that can counter the torrent of popular artifice is a widespread concern among Jewish leaders in Europe—and not just, of course, in Europe. This is a pressing issue in countries where Jews already feel ambiguity about their identities and are uneasy about their roles both as

Jews and as full-fledged members of general society. For Jews and non-Jews alike, "buying a book, a journal, a record, or a CD, buying a ticket for the theater or a movie is undoubtedly easier than mastering the liturgy or learning Hebrew," writes Gábor T. Szántó, editor of the Hungarian Jewish monthly *Szombát*. ". . . Being part of an audience is an anonymous, impersonal relationship to culture, without responsibilities, which, by its very nature, contradicts traditional Jewish thought."[104]

These issues infuse recent internal Jewish discussions and strategy sessions on the role, direction, meaning, and definition of Jewish culture and Jewish cultural policy. Using and promoting Jewish culture is increasingly seen as a key to Jewish survival. The agenda for an international seminar on Jewish culture for the twenty-first century, held in Paris in February 1999, for example, included the following topics: What Is the Significance of Jewish Culture Today? Jewish Cultural Politics and the Challenge of a Global Society; The Role of Jewish Culture in Developing and Sustaining Jewish Life; A Jewish Public Space within Mainstream Cultures; The Channels of Transmission of Jewish Culture and the Marketplace (Jewish Museums, Mass Media, and Internet); and Jewish Culture in a Multicultural Europe.[105] Jewish strategists, concerned about how to reach out and attract the alienated or unaffiliated, recognize that easily assimilated cultural encounters can be a tool. At a meeting of European Jewish lay leaders held in Barcelona in May 2000, Lena Stanley-Clamp of the London-based Institute of Jewish Policy Research stressed the need to provide new avenues into Jewish involvement and to commit resources to the nurturing of Jewish creative artists. "According to British statistics, nine out of ten young people attend cultural events," she told a workshop on how to attract the "missing generation" of young adult Jews. "Jews, given the chance, might attend Jewish plays, exhibitions, concerts of Jewish music. They want to be part of a diverse and living Jewish culture which makes a distinct contribution to the wider society, a window on the world rather than a back garden."

An angry front-page article in the German Jewish newspaper *Allgemeine Jüdische Wochenzeitung* demonstrated sensitivities that in America, with its large, secure, multifaceted, and self-assured Jewish community, might seem highly exaggerated and even a little paranoid. Headlined "Jewish Culture in Germany: Inventory of Distress," the article decried the ascendancy of constructed Jewish culture and popular Jewish cultural products at the expense of ingrained or organic Jewish traditions. It was accompanied by a picture of two dancers on a stage during a "Jewish Culture Week" performance, dressed up like characters from a Chagall painting. "Not only the beard is false," ran the caption.

The article slammed a popular German-based klezmer group called Colalaila, whose leader, an Israeli-born woman, Irith Gabriely, calls herself the Queen of Klezmer and dresses up onstage like a Hasidic man in a long black jacket, black knee breeches, and white kneesocks, as long dark sidelocks flow from under her broad-brimmed black hat. "[Gabriely] is as little a Hasid as her pasted-on sidecurls are *pejes*," the newspaper scolded. "She is an Israeli, and her family comes from Yemen. The music, the whole concert, has mighty little to do with real Jewish culture, and almost nothing at all to do with German Jewry before 1933. What goes on onstage is linked to nothing, leads to nothing; it is a straightforward falsification." [106]

But Gabriely, who fronts an otherwise non-Jewish band, is a competent, engaging musician, and Colalaila was widely popular at the time. The group toured outside Germany as well as domestically (it played at the 1998 Shalom Trieste Jewish culture festival in Italy), and the CD that features her pseudo-Hasidic image on the cover is one of the better-quality German klezmer offerings. The music is fun and draws from a variety of Jewish sources. In America her gender-bending stage persona would be seen—by Jews—as what it is: simply another commercial gimmick to gain an audience, a theatrical play on stereotypes, like the Levy's Rye Bread ads, to be taken or left as the case may be. Even in countries like Poland or the Czech Republic or Italy, whose small Jewish communities tend to regard popularizations of the Jewish phenomenon as positive, most Jews would likely take a more relaxed view—after all, despite his shtetlesque stage persona, Moni Ovadia is not a Hasid, nor is he a Yiddish speaker. And when younger Polish Jews visit the former Jewish quarter of Kraków, they tend to patronize the atmospheric "Jewish-style" but nonkosher Klezmer Hois or Alef restaurant—where Abraham Brumberg ate *tsimes*. They rarely set foot in the Jewish-owned restaurant across the street whose food for a time was advertised as kosher but whose atmosphere was that of a second-rate business hotel in some anonymous provincial airport and whose glass and steel facade was an intrusive eyesore that, besides not fitting the local notion of what was Jewish, somehow seemed to have evaded the historic Kazimierz building code.

Tourist in Prague's Old Jewish Cemetery, probably the most famous and most visited Jewish heritage site in Europe, 1992. (Photo by Ruth Ellen Gruber.)

PART TWO

Jewish Archaeology

[T]he Jewish cemeteries are for the most part deserted, unattended, belonging to nobody. But these Jewish graves do belong to somebody. They belong to us! We have survived the Holocaust. . . . Taking care of the deserted graves should be an absolute duty for us.

Lidové Noviny newspaper, Prague

3

"There Is No Future
without Memory"

In 1955 the eighteenth-century former synagogue in the small town of Hohenems, in western Austria near the Swiss border, was converted into a fire station. Given the fiery end of so many other synagogues across Europe, this seems a particularly cynical conversion of the building, which had survived World War II with its barrel vault, double mansard roof, and distinctive nineteenth-century clock tower intact. City fathers proudly affixed a dedication plaque to the bright, modernized structure, but the plaque made no mention of the building's origin and history; it even implied that it had been newly constructed. "Fire station and infant welfare / erected 1954/55," it read. The plaque also bore the name of the town's then-mayor: "H. Amann." It was not until the late 1980s, when municipal authorities initiated a project to rehabilitate the town's Jewish quarter and create a local Jewish museum, that the irony of the mayor's name became apparent: it is almost identical to that of the biblical tyrant Haman, who in the Book of Esther vows to exterminate the Jews. In 1991 a new plaque was affixed to the former synagogue; this one denotes the building's history and bears the exhortation "Never forget."[1] In 2001 the building was again transformed, becoming Jewish museum exhibition space.

The rediscovery and recognition of brick and stone traces of Jews are among the key ways in which Europeans have embraced the Jewish phenomenon as their own. In scores of cities, villages, and towns like Hohenems, where few or no Jews live today, local Jewish history is being reclaimed, recognized, exhibited, and exploited as part of local heritage. The process, described by some as "Jewish archaeology," represents for

both individuals and national institutions a physical as well as an intellectual and emotional confrontation with the past. Documenting, restoring, rebuilding, and reconstructing ruined cemeteries and synagogues, ritual baths, and entire ghetto quarters represent concrete, but
at the same time highly symbolic, means of reversing oblivion, of "setting things right." This physical reclamation forms part of the broader
phenomenon of integration: in Germany, thus, it has become an almost
clichéd instrument of both personal and institutional *Vergangenheitsverarbeitung,* and in former Soviet bloc states it has been a conspicuous feature of postcommunist "filling in the blanks." But, stimulated by the overlapping influences of education, commemoration,
scholarly research, and the burgeoning tourist market, the process goes
on, too, in countries less overtly burdened by such heavy recent historical baggage.

Whereas even in 1990 information on Jewish heritage sites was hard
to obtain in many countries, little systematic documentation existed,
and few publications addressed the subject, by the end of the decade
Jewish heritage was on the agendas of national monuments authorities and local organizations, including tourist bureaus, in most European countries. The French culture minister, Catherine Trautmann,
succinctly voiced the new way of thinking in a speech to a government-
sponsored international conference on Jewish heritage in Europe held
in Paris in January 1999 on the premises of the newly opened Museum
of Art and History of Judaism, a state institution. "Jewish heritage in
France," she asserted, "is also the heritage of all the French people, just
as the cathedrals of France also belong to France's Jews." Even Pope
John Paul II, in a speech in Poland in June 1997, noted that "the Jewish
cemeteries, which are so numerous on Polish soil, speak of [the] common past [between Jews and Poles]. . . . These places are of particularly
deep spiritual, eschatological, and historical significance. Let these places
join Poles and Jews, as we are together awaiting the day of Judgment
and Redemption."

In many countries pioneering work by committed individuals pre-
ceded recognition by the establishment by many years and laid the
groundwork for changes in official (or commercial) mind-sets.[2] At the
same time, issues regarding Jewish built heritage were becoming of
growing concern to many Jewish organizations, communal bodies, and
individual Jews. This concern, spanning interests ranging from the emotional to the economic, also represented a radical change of mind-set.
What to do with this patrimony and how to do it became key policy is-

sues and at times explosive flashpoints. Such issues became particularly
acute in former communist states, where Jewish property seized during
and after the Holocaust was being returned in part to Jewish ownership,
in an uneven restitution process frequently fraught with legal, political,
financial, and even religious disputes.

Blank Spaces

The scope of the destruction of the Jewish-built sites
during the Holocaust was unprecedented. Thousands of Jewish cultural monuments—synagogues, cemeteries, even entire neighborhoods
—were desecrated, ransacked, or destroyed. Of the thousands of synagogues and prayer houses of various styles, ages, and dimensions that
stood in Germany and Poland alone, only a few hundred survive in
some form today.

In the first three decades after the war, only a few synagogues of recognized historic importance were reconstructed or restored in ways that
retained their Jewish identity, as Jewish museums or memorial sites, for
example. Among the most notable were the early medieval synagogue
in Worms, Germany, which was totally reconstructed from rubble between 1959 and 1961, and the Gothic Old Synagogue in Kraków, which
was restored in the late 1950s and opened as part of Kraków's Historical
Museum.[3] Several former synagogues served as exhibition halls for the
State Jewish Museum in Prague, and the Renaissance synagogue in the
Moravian town of Holešov was renovated in the early 1960s as a branch
of the Prague museum. Likewise, the seventeenth-century synagogue in
Tykocin, Poland, was renovated and opened as a museum of Judaism in
the 1970s, and in Sopron, Hungary, a tiny medieval synagogue discovered in the 1950s was restored as a Jewish museum. But these and other
examples were few and far between. In eastern Europe in particular, a
number of surviving synagogues, often the largest building in a town or
village, were given dignified conversions into local museums, libraries,
or concert halls—in Lesko in Poland, for example, or Szolnok in Hungary, or Kasejovice in what is now the Czech Republic. But often Jewish sites were left derelict, and often, too, the willful and widespread
Nazi destruction of Jewish monuments, as well as other destruction
wrought by World War II, was exacerbated by willful postwar cancellation—whether by tearing down abandoned synagogues or bulldozing

and building on top of cemeteries or by transforming distinctive Jewish structures and rededicating them to new functions that ignored or obscured their original identities. In the Czech Republic alone, at least eighty-five synagogues were razed during the communist regime—far more than were destroyed there during the war.[4]

Some of this process was simple (if that is the word) postwar cleanup. But frequently, as in Hohenems, there was a calculated cancellation of memory. In the transformation of synagogues for other uses, architectural or decorative elements that could bear witness to the building's former function—domes, Arks, arched ceilings and windows, Stars of David, inscriptions, and the like—often were deliberately masked, remodeled, or removed. Some postwar urban renewal projects blatantly targeted Jewish sites in a way that could only have been deliberate. In the early 1970s, for example, communist authorities in Bratislava, the Slovak capital, destroyed the city's former Jewish quarter, including a twin-towered synagogue of ornate, Moorish-style design, during construction of a showpiece bridge and highway complex that arched over the Danube and sliced through the city. The project was conceived in 1968—one year after the Six-Day War, in the wake of which almost all communist states broke relations with Israel and, in some countries, including Czechoslovakia, embarked on harsh new anti-Semitic (or anti-Zionist) policies. (In Prague that year, the communist regime closed down the Pinkas Synagogue, part of the State Jewish Museum, which in the 1950s had been turned into a Holocaust memorial with the names of the 77,297 Bohemian and Moravian victims of the Nazis inscribed on its inner walls. The official reason was to repair damage from groundwater seeping into the walls, but the closure was also clearly motivated by politics: the building remained barred to visitors for more than two decades, and all the inscribed names were removed.) It was as if obliterating the physical traces of where Jews once lived and worshiped would also cancel or reshape the past itself. Once the physical evidence of Jewish history was destroyed, who was to say that that history really existed?

In West Germany, writes the Bremen University scholar Sabine Offe, "[w]hatever traces bothered the 'conscience of the eye' after the end of the war were destroyed in the process of the so-called reconstruction during the 1950s. Neither the shape nor the outlines of their original sites were preserved as reminders of the large synagogues destroyed in 1938 or by bombs during the war. The remains were demolished, removed, and covered by parks, newly built roads, or new buildings. . . .

No building, street, or site was permitted to preserve the memory of the Jews who had once lived there[;] their former function and significance [were] forgotten. The memory of a history shared by Jews and Gentiles was hidden from the visual and physical consciousness of postwar Germans."[5]

While a number of Jewish cemeteries in West Germany were preserved as memorial sites or tended by local Jews, by 1987 in the state of Hesse alone, 63 of the 245 synagogue buildings still standing in 1945 had been torn down and almost all of the others had been "rededicated" for other use, the most widespread new use being apartment houses or other dwellings that blended in seamlessly with the surroundings.[6] The physical side to postwar negation in Germany did not apply simply to Jewish buildings but also at times to other uncomfortable structures with intense Nazi symbolism or connotations, which were likewise transformed or disguised. This happened, for example, to the enormous, distinctive grandstand and other surviving structures from the Nazi Reichsparteitagsgelände in Nuremberg—a gargantuan complex, scene of the ritualistic Nazi Party rallies of the 1930s—whose design was overseen by Hitler's chief architect, Albert Speer, and whose buildings were meant to express Nazi ideology in architectural terms.[7]

The postwar fate of the synagogue in the northern German city of Essen is an example of attempted negation as well as eventual metamorphosis. Originally called the New Synagogue, it was built in 1911–13: a splendid domed building of massive proportions that proclaimed the pride and prosperity of the acculturated local Jewish community, which at the time numbered forty-five hundred. That it was designed by a non-Jewish architect, Edmund Körner, emphasized the Jewish sense of belonging to the German whole. A Jewish commentator at the time noted that the "monumental edifice could no longer be a purely internal affair of the Jewish community."[8] Yet the synagogue was in use for only twenty-five years. The building was heavily damaged, but not destroyed, in the Kristallnacht pogrom and remained one of the few major buildings standing in downtown Essen at the end of the war. A haunting photograph from 1947 shows it looming amid a sea of rubble, "an admonitory ruin, huge and powerful," as a local brochure put it in 1990. But it was a ruin whose symbolism proved a bit too strong for local psyches. Municipal officials erected a memorial to Essen's slaughtered Jews on the synagogue steps in 1949, but its inscription reflected the deliberate amnesia of the time. "More than 2,500 Jews from Essen had to lose their lives," it noted, without mentioning who killed them, why, or how. A new memorial plaque erected in the 1950s still exuded ambivalence, calling the ruined synagogue "a silent witness of a terrible incident we all have to make good for."

The gutted structure was too big—and too ruined—for the two hundred Jews who reconstituted a community in Essen after the war. (Another eerie photograph shows a Sukkah inside the ravaged sanctuary.) Despite calls by local Jews and from Israel to restore it for use as a community or cultural center, or to turn it into a memorial to Jewish victims of the Holocaust, the building was left standing as a ruin until 1959, when it was sold to the city. In 1961 the city installed a museum of industrial design there, a spanking new showcase for all that was sleek, modern, and aimed directly at the future. The streamlined, functional interior obliterated all remaining Jewish elements; even the dome was hidden by a low-slung, false ceiling, floating staircases, and hanging fluorescent lights. Meanwhile, in 1959, Essen Jews demonstrated their faith in the new Federal Republic by building a new, much smaller synagogue for their use. Like the prewar synagogue, it was designed by non-Jewish architects. But it was a modest structure, shaped like a hemisphere pierced by small, circular windows, that contrasted sharply with the monumental display of the earlier building. In her landmark 1985 book on the synagogues of Europe, Carol Herselle Krinsky has noted the ironies offered by the two structures: "The massive [old] building, too solid to be blown up, revealed the firm confidence of a community that was in fact to be blown away. The thinner, delicate forms of the postwar construction . . . hints at the fragile nature of Jewish existence. On the other hand, the city has an officially benevolent policy toward Jews, who may well use the new synagogue for a long time."[9] And, indeed, it has already been in use much longer than the original synagogue.

An accidental fire in 1979 destroyed portions of the museum, and on November 9, 1980, the anniversary of Kristallnacht, the building took on yet another identity. The city rededicated it as a municipal memorial site and documentation center, now called the Old Synagogue. A commemorative plaque installed in 1981 finally acknowledged that twenty-five hundred Essen Jews had been "murdered by the Nazi regime in the years 1933–1945," but the center's permanent exhibition, "Resistance and Persecution in Essen, 1933–1945," portrayed the Jews as just one of many persecuted groups. Later in the 1980s, influenced by the evolving *Vergangenheitsverarbeitung* process and boosted by World War II and Holocaust anniversaries and by a new program under which former Essen Jews were invited back annually to visit the city, the synagogue's interior underwent yet another change—a costly renovation that brought it back to a semblance of its original prewar state. The renovation included the restoration or reconstruction of once-obliterated Jewish architectural and design elements. In 1988, as part of the nationwide commemorations of the fiftieth anniversary of Kristallnacht, the Old Synagogue was again rededicated in this form, with a new permanent historical exhibition, "Milestones of Jewish Life, from Emancipation to the Present," that was aimed at revealing the historical significance of the site "in an appropriate manner." Directed by an Israeli-born scholar, the Old Synagogue hosts lectures, exhibits, cultural and commemorative programs, and an archive. At the end of the 1990s its permanent exhibit was expanded and redesigned to portray German and local Jewish history from a Jewish perspective and also to deal with postwar Jewish renewal.

In eastern and central Europe, postwar communist suppression of Jewish practice, culture, and history for the most part extended to the surviving built heritage of Jews, too. Already by the early 1950s, communist regimes had reneged on promises that Jewish property seized by the Nazis would be returned to survivors and that Jews would be compensated for their suffering during the Holocaust. The communists considered the state to be the owner of all property in the nation; Jews who wanted their property back were branded as "looters of national property."[10]

From time to time, depending on the changing local political climate, some officially sanctioned initiatives to document, restore, or commemorate Jewish sites in communist countries took place, and some Jewish sites were listed as cultural or historic monuments by the state. In the 1950s, for example, the Polish architects Maria and Kazimierz Piechotka produced an exhaustive illustrated book on Poland's destroyed wooden synagogues; and over the decades various scholars published articles on specific synagogues and Jewish cemeteries in the bulletin of the Jewish Historical Institute.[11] Researchers at the State Jewish Museum in Prague, likewise, carried out scholarly work on Jewish cemeteries, synagogues, and ghettos, much of which, however, though published in the museum's bulletin, *Judaica Bohemiae,* was aimed at a foreign audience: *Judaica Bohemiae* appeared in foreign languages only. Local Jewish communities also published some documentary material. But this recognition was sporadic and desultory. In 1964 the official monuments list in Poland, consisting of more than 35,000 entries, included eight Jewish cemeteries and seventy-two synagogues, most of which were in disrepair.[12] In 1991 in Prague, a staff member of the Czechoslovak State Monuments Office showed a visitor from the World Monuments Fund "two thin folders" that contained information on 230 Jewish sites in what is now the Czech Republic and Slovakia. Most of the listings dated from 1988, and the sites were classified as having "low preservation value."[13] In the Czech town of Třebíč, site of one of central Europe's most extensive preserved ghettos, of the ghetto's more than 120 buildings, only three houses and the two seventeenth-century synagogues were listed as historic structures; one of the synagogues was transformed into a church, and the other was a ruined shell by 1990. In the 1980s communist town authorities had drawn up a plan that would have razed most of the area and erected modern apartment blocks in its place.

Across the region Jewish cemeteries lay forgotten, swallowed by forest undergrowth, or bulldozed to make way for urban construction, or even used as quarries.[14] Without the Jews, there was no one to care for them—or even to care. Jews from outside had little interest either. From time to time individual Jews from abroad would tend family graves or sponsor a Holocaust memorial in their ancestral town, and Hasidic Jews in particular cared for a number of cemeteries where important rabbis were buried. But, in general, Jews in the West wanted nothing to do with countries viewed as a mass graveyard, a closed chapter.

Unlike in West Germany, though, where the rush to rebuild, modernize, and surge forward as a new, democratic, western European economic power left little "unsightly" wartime wreckage standing, scores of abandoned synagogues in eastern Europe were simply left in place, even in the very hearts of towns and cities, along with other, non-Jewish, damaged or abandoned property.[15] This contrast was strikingly evident in Berlin, where two halves of the same city came under western and eastern domination. A Jewish community of several thousand people reconstituted itself in West Berlin after the war, and a state-funded, modern new building was erected as a community center in 1959 on the site of one of Berlin's destroyed synagogues; the ornate portal was salvaged from the ruins and incorporated into the design of the clean-lined new structure to link the past to what Jews hoped to build as a future. In East Berlin, the gutted shell of the New Synagogue on Oranienburger Strasse stood untouched for decades, looming over a derelict quarter, until restoration officially promoted by the communist regime began in the cathartic Kristallnacht anniversary year, 1988. Only a few hundred (or at most a few thousand) Jews lived in all of East Germany: unlike in the West, a Jewish future for them did not seem an option. In 1966, the one hundredth anniversary of the synagogue's construction, Jews in East Berlin placed a plaque on the ruin saying that the ravaged facade should "remain a site of admonition and remembrance."[16]

Entire former Jewish quarters became run-down neighborhoods or even slums in the shabby hearts of a number of eastern European towns and cities. Often only the scars on doorposts showing where mezuzot were once affixed bore witness to centuries of history, and in most cases these, too, were covered over by new residents. Younger generations, born after the war, might not, as I sometimes found, even know what was meant by the word "synagogue." In 1992 the only person I encountered who remembered the existence of the Jewish cemetery of Méra, a village in northern Hungary, was a malodorous old drunk, who got in the car and guided me there. I found the broken frame of a gate and a few eroded tombstones embedded in a thick wall of brush just off the side of the main road.

In communist countries, too, "Jewish" elements were sometimes retained despite the transformation of Jewish buildings: the brilliantly painted inner dome of a synagogue turned into a sports hall and fencing arena in Budapest; Hebrew inscriptions on the outer walls of synagogues used as warehouses in the Czech towns of Strážnice, Ivančice, and Velké Meziříčí; Stars of David atop the domes of a Moorish-style synagogue used as a school in Malacky, Slovakia. Inside the Malacky synagogue, colorful wall paintings and interior decorations were left intact, but flooring cut across the Ark and shelves full of art projects flanked the lower portion, while children had dance class in front of the arched top. Monika Krajewska, one of the pioneers of postwar Jewish monuments documentation in Poland, recalls visiting the Kupa Synagogue in Kraków's Kazimierz district in the 1970s, when it was used as a warehouse: "We stared at the walls, with their paintings: the lion, the deer, all the things that relate to Jewish biblical tradition of synagogue decoration. And there were workers who were just installing additional shelves; they were making holes in the lion's nose, in the instruments of the Levites painted on the ceiling. It seemed so inevitable that Kazimierz would crumble, brick by brick, that in a few years it simply would disappear." This may have represented an even crueler way to cancel memory than anonymous transformation: a casual statement that the symbols—the synagogues themselves—were meaningless in the wake of the destruction of the people who gave them meaning. Only occasionally were plaques affixed to identify the building or commemorate a destroyed Jewish community: a plaque on a neoclassical synagogue in Gyöngyös, Hungary, listed the structure as a historic monument and noted the architect, but it did not identify it as a former synagogue. When I visited, the building had been turned into a video game arcade.

Less calculated postwar neglect also took its toll. In Italy most sites of Jewish heritage survived the war (as did most of Italy's Jews). But Italy's disused synagogues, Jewish cemeteries, ghetto quarters, and other monuments—some dating back to ancient Roman times—shared in the legendary neglect that has long afflicted Italian cultural sites, from Roman ruins to Renaissance palazzi. In the early postwar years, Jews were so concerned about their inability to maintain their property that they dismantled the interior furnishings of a number of ornate provincial synagogues and shipped them to Israel. The buildings themselves, some still containing rich ornaments and ritual furnishings, were closed up and locked tight, out of sight, out of mind—even out of the consciousness of many of Italy's Jews, particularly from the 1970s onward, when thousands of immigrants from Libya and elsewhere in the Arab world changed the face and collective memory of Italy's Jewish community.

Annie Sacerdoti, a Jewish writer and editor who since the 1980s has become Italy's leading specialist in Jewish-built heritage, produced a documentary on the history of Jews in Lombardy for Italian television in 1983. "It was then that I discovered the synagogue of Rivarolo Mantovano, with a portrait of Garibaldi in place of the Ark, that of Viadana, which had been transformed into a sawmill, the grandiose and crumbling synagogue in Sabbioneta, deserted as was the town itself," she wrote three years later. "I realized thus that the history of Italian Judaism was not written solely in the big ghettos such as Rome and Venice, but also, just as richly, in many, many hidden places, little centers and villages almost totally unknown even to Jews." This revelation spurred Sacerdoti to seek out Jewish heritage sites all over Italy. She began writing about these rediscovered places in Italy's Jewish media and, in 1986, published a comprehensive guidebook to Jewish Italy. Her target audience, she wrote, included Italy's Jews as well as its non-Jews. This book, she hoped, would, as she herself had experienced, "give Jews a stimulus to rediscover the thread that links them to their past, and give non-Jews an instrument to discover, perhaps on a Sunday drive, how widespread are the roots of Judaism in the history of our country." [17]

At about the same time, the Italian region of Emilia-Romagna's Institute for Cultural Heritage conducted a detailed census of all items and sites of Jewish heritage in the region. The resulting seven-hundred-page book listed more than thirty towns where there were traces of old ghettos or Jewish quarters, two dozen Jewish cemeteries, a score of synagogue buildings or sites of former synagogues, and hundreds of ritual objects. In the preface to the volume, Bezalel Narkiss, director of the Center for Jewish Art at the Hebrew University in Jerusalem, expressed admiration for the unprecedented undertaking. The task, he wrote, was "so monumental, mainly because it had so few methodological examples [to] follow. [Researchers] had to develop methods of cataloguing, invent technical terms and adapt systems of description for the different objects. This in itself is a pioneering work." [18]

A Little-Known Legacy

The destruction of Jewish heritage sites during and after the Holocaust was unprecedented, but the ambivalent postwar attitudes had deep roots in traditional ways of thinking—and indeed still persist in many quarters. [19] This makes the recognition and recovery that we find today all the more dramatic. "The problem of Jewish heritage is a mental problem," says Valery Dymshits of the European University of St. Petersburg, who carried out documentation of Jewish sites in Ukraine, Moldova, and elsewhere in the 1990s in association with the Center for Jewish Art. "Jews and non-Jews think we are the 'people of the book' and no one has been interested in physical heritage."

Throughout history the fate of Jewish sites in Europe was routinely marked by ruin, neglect, and transformation. Each time Jews abandoned—or were expelled from—places where they had lived, they left synagogues, cemeteries, and, often, entire Jewish quarter complexes behind them, which frequently were demolished or taken over by the non-Jewish community. This paralleled a general ahistorical attitude toward stone: the Colosseum was used for centuries as a quarry; and Christians turned Roman temples into churches. European towns and cities, or individual buildings, are often palimpsests on which many levels of history and use can be seen. Jews themselves were not immune to reusing material: the medieval tombstone of a rabbi, conserved in a museum in Maribor, Slovenia, was clearly originally a Roman stone that still bears part of a Latin inscription. Often, thus, the only reminders today of historic Jewish presence or the original Jewish character of buildings are lingering street names, architectural conventions, and occasional archaeological finds. The oldest synagogue building still standing in Poland, for example, is a tiny brick structure in the Silesian town of Strzegom. Built in the 1300s, it already had been abandoned and converted into a church in the fifteenth century. Similarly, Jews were expelled from southern Italy five hundred years ago, yet a number of towns in the south and in Sicily conserve former Jewish ghettos and even synagogue buildings. Spain, too, is studded with such stone ghosts of the Jewish life that flourished there before 1492.

In more modern times, the civic equality granted to Jews in much of western and central Europe by the mid-nineteenth century spurred Jews to move almost en masse in some countries from small towns to big cities. They, too, left synagogues, cemeteries, and neighborhood infrastructure behind. The rush to the cities assumed such great proportions in Bohemia and Moravia that a law in 1890 formally abolished many local Jewish community organizations; by the 1930s more than half of the Jewish cemeteries in Bohemia were no longer in use.[20] Emancipation also enabled urban Jews to leave the old Jewish quarters where they had been forced to live and move into new suburbs and other more salubrious residential districts. (These demographic shifts continued into the twentieth century, and, in cities such as London, whose Jewish population was not destroyed in the Holocaust, they continued after World War II as well.)[21] Urban renewal projects in a number of cities at the end of the nineteenth century and the beginning of the twentieth century—in Prague, Florence, Frankfurt, and Rome, for example—razed all or part of the run-down former ghettos and replaced them with broad streets and modern new residential buildings. There was often little sense, even among Jews, that these places formed part of a specific Jewish heritage that should be preserved. On the contrary, the squalid old Jewish quarters symbolized centuries of Jewish inequality and persecution, and Jews were generally happy to leave them behind or see them disappear.[22] As in Essen, they built grandiose new temples to reflect the promise and prosperity of the postemancipation period. In Rome, where the ghetto was formally abolished only in 1870, the magnificent domed synagogue built in 1904, which has become a city landmark on the bank of the Tiber, replaced a demolished ghetto building that had housed five synagogues for nearly three hundred fifty years. A few years later, the Moorish-style Jubilee Synagogue was built to replace three seventeenth-century synagogues demolished in Prague.[23]

Aside from these modern landmarks and a few notable historic or artistic monuments such as the eleventh-century synagogue in Worms, or the Tránsito (Samuel ha-Levi) Synagogue in Toledo, Spain, or Prague's medieval Altneu Synagogue and Old Jewish Cemetery (admired for its picturesque air of mystery by nineteenth-century romantics), the Jewish built environment generally tended to be ignored, or at least overlooked, as part of the overall cultural patrimony not only by general society but also by Jews. To be sure, some synagogues and the occasional Jewish cemetery or Jewish quarter were portrayed on pre–World War II picture postcards, along with other Jewish scenes and subjects (including anti-Semitic caricatures).[24] And many synagogues, frequently among the standout buildings in some towns, were recognized as architecturally or locally important. Still, whether in use or abandoned, synagogues and cemeteries, ritual baths, and rabbis' houses were regarded, for the most part, as normal, generally unremarkable parts of Jewish everyday life, not showcases for tourists or subjects for scholars. The preservation that was undertaken was generally of a practical nature, and, as contemporary photographs and descriptions testify, many sites were left in poor condition. In 1894 the historic Jewish cemetery in Frankfurt was reported as having beautifully carved tombstones but as being "in a sad state of neglect; many of the stones have fallen to the ground, and lie in great confusion, and many are beginning to crumble."[25]

In eastern Europe, where some of the most extraordinary Jewish monuments were found, tourists interested in Jewish sites were generally former residents who, particularly after World War I, returned from their successful immigrant experience in America to visit relatives and former haunts—or they were curious secularized Jews, such as An-Ski, Döblin, or Roth, on ethnographic or journalistic expeditions. As the American travel writer Grace Humphrey noted in 1931, few tourists of any kind, Jewish or non-Jewish, went to Poland: "To my dismay I found no Baedeker for Poland, no Blue Guide. I went to half a dozen travel agencies, hoping their booklets and folders would give me numerous suggestions; nowhere could they give me anything on Poland. Oh, yes, plenty of literature on Czechoslovakia, on Norway, even one tour announced for Russia; but Poland? Nothing whatever. Why, nobody goes to Poland."[26] Relatively few scholars took a serious interest in the artistic aspects of eastern European Jewish sites either; there were exceptions, of course, but most of the documentation on cemeteries dealt with the personalities who were buried there rather than the elaborate carving and iconography.[27] Some scholars who sought to document and describe Jewish physical heritage, such as Majer Bałaban in Poland, bemoaned the poor state of synagogues and Jewish cemeteries even as they strove to bring their importance to public attention. The widespread destruction of Jewish monuments during World War I, though, triggered alarm bells. In 1923 scholars in Poland began an exhaustive inventory of synagogues under the auspices of the Institute of Polish Architecture of the Polytechnic of Warsaw amid concern that such monuments were endangered: it was the first attempt at such a comprehensive survey and resulted in thousands of photographs, measurements, drawings, and detailed descriptions. A number of synagogues, including many of Poland's unique, richly decorated, wooden synagogues, were listed as historical monuments by the state. But the main organizers of the inventory project, including its dynamic director, the Jewish art historian and photographer Szymon Zajczyk, were killed in the Holocaust, and much of the material they gathered was destroyed during the war; the surviving descriptions and photographs are in many cases the only evidence we have today of many destroyed, centuries-old structures, including the incomparable wooden synagogues.[28]

In 1933, the year that Hitler took power, the American Marvin Lowenthal published *A World Passed By,* a book he described as the first comprehensive guide to Jewish heritage in Europe and North Africa. He lamented the fact that "[t]he synagogues, as in Segovia, Cordova, or Lemberg [L'viv], often stand within a stone's throw . . . of a famed cathedral. The cemeteries, as in Pisa, often lie literally and figuratively in the shadow of a renowned historic pile. The ghettos . . . wait around the corner from a tourist postcard shop. But the average traveller knows nothing of their existence. Yet, like the cathedrals and castles of Christian Europe and the Moslem antiquities of Spain and North Africa, the Jewish monuments embody and perpetuate one of the oldest cultural forces of the Western World. They, too, are a part of Europe's past and the heritage of our common civilization."[29]

In his book, Lowenthal already referred to Nazi vandalism of Jewish cemeteries, but neither he nor any other observer at the time could dream of the deliberate wholesale destruction that would soon take place. Still, his words sound remarkably prescient from today's post-Holocaust, postcommunist vantage point. They could be repeated even more forcefully today as a credo for contemporary researchers, restorers, travel agents, tourists, civic, state, and religious leaders, monuments preservation authorities, and ordinary citizens. Sometimes, in so many words, they are: a brochure of the Warsaw-based Citizens Committee

for the Protection of Cemeteries and Monuments of Jewish Culture in
Poland, a grassroots organization founded in 1981, reads, "We appeal to
all men of goodwill, to the authorities, to all local groups—let us save
these monuments of Jewish culture! Let us not pass by without concern for them—they are part of our common history. Let us learn to
appreciate their unique beauty and let us preserve them for future
generations."

4

Touching the Past

Study, performance, research, and discussion of Jewish issues fill in metaphorical blanks. But documenting and restoring Jewish heritage sites and displaying Jewish relics are hands-on operations. The blank spaces they fill in can be delineated on maps, in landscapes, and on city streets. Results of even simple actions—cutting weeds, reerecting tombstones, listing sites, taking photographs—can be easily seen, demonstrated, and admired. For some, the interest may be primarily artistic or architectural: synagogues, cemeteries, and ghetto quarters provide a rich and fascinating array of styles and iconography that add to our knowledge of architecture and religious art and design. Many surviving synagogues feature vivid frescoes and other types of decoration dating back hundreds of years, and Jewish cemeteries in Poland, Romania, Ukraine, and elsewhere in eastern Europe are especially rich in vigorous carving inspired by religious and folk motifs. Many dilapidated synagogues in Hungary in particular are important examples of nineteenth- and early-twentieth-century architecture: for example, the Moorish-style synagogue on Rumbach Street in Budapest, long derelict, was an early work by Otto Wagner. Budapest's long-overgrown Jewish cemeteries, too, include grand mausoleums and stunning sculptural tombs by Ödön Lechner, the founder of Hungary's turn-of-the-century national art nouveau style, and his disciple Béla Lajta, whose work foreshadowed art deco, among others.[1]

But the emotional and political message of Jewish heritage sites is also clear. Physical Jewish traces are solid symbols, powerful evocations of a lost, destroyed reality, monuments to an annihilated people.

The process of discovery, recovery, documentation, and display imbues them with a broader cultural and emotional significance that transcends living memory. "Memories often cleave to the physical settings of events," Brian Ladd writes in a book about the changing architecture of Berlin.[2] Agata Tuszyńska describes the movie theater housed in a former synagogue in the Polish town of Kazimierz Dolny as "obviously wiser" than any ordinary movie cinema.[3] And Irene Benkhart, an official in the Bavarian village of Georgensgmünd, has a favorite spot in the restored and scrupulously maintained hilltop Jewish cemetery from which she likes to gaze down at her town. "From here the Jewish cemetery, the Catholic church, and the Protestant church are all in view, all at once," she tells me. "And standing here in summer, you can smell a wonderful fragrance in the air from the wild herbs."

In a sense, Jews and their physical traces become talismans that connect the present world to a "truer" world that existed before the catastrophe—"before communism" and "before the Nazi time." Or simply "before oblivion." This onetime world may be a nostalgic never-never land: a world that might have been or that one would have wished for. Restoring or identifying the physical relics of Jews creates tangible bridges that link "before" and "after," despite, or because of, what happened "in between." The process may be conscious or unconscious, and it often entails a physical act of discovery (or "uncovery"). Documentation and restoration of Jewish sites thus help to heal a "desecrated landscape." Sometimes the healing itself creates a scar: tumbled, uprooted, or scattered tombstones may be righted and rearranged in rows whose pristine neatness is reminiscent of the stitching on a wound.[4]

In Frankfurt in the 1980s, a civic alliance of churches, political parties, intellectuals, and cultural figures protested plans to build a public works center at Börneplatz, site of the medieval Frankfurt *Judengasse,* or Jewish street, when excavations for the new building uncovered the foundations of centuries-old *Judengasse* houses. Although most of the *Judengasse* had been razed in urban renewal projects well before the Nazis came to power, the protesters wanted the excavations to remain visible as a "stone witness" to Nazi crimes and an "open wound" in the city landscape. "The *Judengasse* became a symbol for Germans, and the area of the city where Jews had been forced to live from medieval times on became synonymous with the ghettos created by the Nazis in Eastern Europe," wrote Cilly Kugelmann, a prominent Jewish intellectual and then senior staff member at Frankfurt's Jewish Museum.[5] In the end, the public works center was built, partially atop the site of the

Börneplatz synagogue destroyed on Kristallnacht. But the excavated remains of the *Judengasse* were displayed, along with an exhibit on the Börneplatz protests, as a branch of the Jewish museum that was incorporated into the new building's structure: they remained visible and visitable as stone witnesses to the past, but the setting, as Kugelmann put it, created "a wound that had healed over." The new building abuts a Holocaust memorial in a plaza that separates it from Frankfurt's historic Jewish cemetery. The memorial includes a tracing of the outline of the Börneplatz synagogue, partially emerging from under the new public works center and clearly showing how the original site is now largely covered (crushed?) by the new structure.[6]

Acts such as these liberate history as they liberate stone. They may also embody a physical form of atonement, even a form of penance through physical labor; physical responses can serve as "commemorative rituals" that effect a symbolic transformation of guilt about the past into acts of salvation and protection.[7] A Christian volunteer organization in Germany, Aktion Sühnezeichen (Action Reconciliation), for example, takes Germans on trips to clean up abandoned Jewish cemeteries as part of its program of good works to help countries and people that were victims of Nazi terror.[8]

The physical act of recovery is of fundamental importance in this process, but at the same time, as in all archaeological research, Jewish history and culture are brought to light in less concrete ways. Epitaphs and carvings on tombstones name names and tell human stories; buildings and architectural spaces delineate human parameters within historical and artistic contexts. Guilt or nostalgia may influence the process, but the approach need not be emotional and often decidedly is not. Political expedience, commercial exploitation, and cynical (or superstitious) do-gooding can also play a role. As do, of course, unaffected scholarship and the basic desire to reverse historic and cultural negation.

The Hungarian architect Anikó Gazda, of the Hungarian Institute for Town and Regional Planning, led intensive documentation and research work on synagogues throughout the 1980s, a time when the Hungarian government had begun to relax its attitude toward Jews and Jewish memory.[9] The sensitive restoration of the synagogue in the town of Baja for use as a library won a Hungarian architecture prize in 1985, and a similarly sensitive restoration as a culture center of the synagogue in the village of Apostag received an international award, the Europa Nostra Prize, in 1988.[10] Gazda was Jewish, but she wrote that her interest in Hungarian synagogues was a scholarly outgrowth of her work in urban architecture.[11] Her research resulted in a lavishly illustrated book on Hungarian synagogues that was published in 1989 with an introduction by Hungary's chief rabbi.[12] Most of the synagogues she inventoried fit the general communist-era pattern: they were either derelict or had been transformed into sports halls, culture centers, stores, warehouses, and the like; there was, she noted, a "great danger" that many of them would disappear, and she wanted to gather information on the buildings before it was too late. But she also wanted her work to serve as a memorial to Hungary's Jews, and she cited a verse from Jeremiah that symbolized this goal: "My soul has them still in remembrance / and is humbled in me."[13]

Physical Jewish traces often seem haunted, sometimes literally. In Warsaw it was long rumored that a skyscraper being built on the spot where the city's destroyed Tłomackie Street Synagogue had stood was cursed and that years-long delays and problems in construction derived from that fact. I myself felt a visceral attraction to the forgotten markers and crumbling buildings I discovered when I started documenting Jewish monuments in 1989. One tombstone in particular, in a small cemetery in Transylvania, drew me in an almost mystical way; the stone stood upright, at a distance from others, and vaguely resembled a human figure. I felt very powerfully that it *was* human, or somehow tangibly represented the soul of a living being, a member of what the Polish writer Anna Kamieńska so evocatively described as "a tribe of stones, a people of stones, an obstinate tribe which is ever marching and ever shouting and calling voicelessly[,] . . . still talking about those who lived here and passed away. About righteous men, just and charitable, about God-fearing and loving women who toiled for others."[14]

"Rescuers of Atlantis"

In 1982 Tomasz Wiśniewski, a young journalist in the eastern Polish city of Białystok, was jailed for nine months by Poland's martial law regime for underground anticommunist activities. While in jail, Wiśniewski, who is not Jewish, read widely and discovered his region's rich Jewish history. Since his release from prison, he has devoted his time to documenting and bringing to public attention local Jewish heritage. He has written guidebooks to Jewish heritage in the Białystok region, published other material for both the Polish and the foreign

market, and put together a series of postcards based on prewar photographs of Jewish sites. Not far from Białystok, in the village of Brańsk,
Zbigniew Romaniuk became fascinated in the 1980s with the Jewish
tombstones he kept finding in barns and used as paving stones. Acting
on an impulse, he and some friends began "rescuing" these stones,
cleaning them, restoring them, and, eventually, returning them to what
had been the prewar Jewish cemetery. In order to read the inscriptions,
Romaniuk taught himself basic Hebrew; eventually he began sifting
through archives in a painstaking investigation of all aspects of Brańsk's
Jewish history. Romaniuk has disclaimed having more than a scholarly
interest in filling in the blanks in his hometown's past, but his work, the
difficulties and hostility he encountered, and the questions his activities
raised formed the centerpiece of a 1996 documentary film, *Shtetl*, and a
1997 book with the same title that was published in the United States.
(Some of the difficulties Romaniuk encountered came from the film
itself, which was shown on PBS. The filmmaker, Marian Marzyński,
questioned Romaniuk's motives and portrayed him as someone who,
despite everything, could not break out of anti-Semitic patterns.)[15]

In summer 1998 Wiśniewski, Romaniuk, and a score of other non-
Jewish Poles were honored by the state of Israel for their work. Israel's
ambassador to Poland, Yigal Antebi, handed out framed certificates at
a ceremony held in Kraków at the conclusion of the annual Festival of
Jewish Culture.[16] This recognition, which became an annual event, was
the brainchild of Michael Traison, a Jewish lawyer from Detroit who
during the 1990s spent much of his time in Poland doing legal work for
his firm. "These people," Traison told me, "are ordinary people who
have gone beyond the call of duty in making efforts to preserve Jewish
memory in Poland in one or more of a variety of ways including cemetery preservation, journals of history, creating homemade museums,
acting to protect Jewish sites, and the like. My idea was to say thanks to
the honorees and to encourage them in their work." He told me he
wanted to get across three messages: "First was to thank the people for
what they have done and are doing. But also, we want to tell the Jewish
world that there are Poles who are caring for Jewish places. And we also
want to tell Poles that there are Jews who appreciate it."

Despite some authorized or state-sponsored initiatives, the care of
and research on Jewish monuments under communism was frequently
the pastime of isolated individuals like the honorees, who, fired by personal passion or oddball academic interest, roamed through the coun-
tryside with bikes, backpacks, large-scale maps, and prewar documents

or doggedly assumed a proprietary interest in the Jewish history and physical heritage of their own towns, regions, or villages. Some were Jewish individuals tentatively reconnecting with their roots and identity; most were not. They generally received no help or encouragement from local or regional authorities.[17] On the contrary: the recovery of Jewish heritage sometimes became a subtle means of expressing opposition to the communist regime, particularly after 1968, when communist "anti-Zionist" campaigns increasingly made Jewish history and culture the stuff of samizdat and dissident study groups. Seeking out Jewish heritage sites "was part of our generation's interest in whatever was prohibited or object of a kind of a taboo in official education," recalls Monika Krajewska, who was born into a Catholic family a couple of years after the war and began seeking out and photographing Jewish sites in the 1970s. "In tourist guides you didn't see any mention of Jewish cemeteries in a given region," she told me. "It was all banned by the censorship; or if it was not always literally prohibited, whoever was making a tourist guidebook knew that these things simply shouldn't be mentioned. It didn't apply only to Jewish art, but to all minorities, such as the Ukrainians. They could only be presented during folk art festivals in a strictly limited and censored way without any possibility of going deeper, of seeing the difficult or tragic aspects of our common history."

Krajewska (who married a Jew and eventually converted to Judaism) and others crammed their personal photographic archives, notebooks, and related documents into cardboard boxes and onto crowded shelves in their tiny apartments and were able to publish infrequently, if at all. Few had contact with like-minded and similarly equipped people carrying out the same work in other countries, or even other towns. At times they ran afoul of the authorities for their interest, and sometimes, too, they were damned or harassed by local people suspicious of their motives and fearful of raising ghosts or disturbing the status quo. Some independent researchers rediscovered Jewish cemeteries that had been forgotten even by official local Jewish organizations. Wiśniewski recalls, "Almost no local historian wrote about the Jews or studied their history. Today, many do, but back then [the early 1980s] the political police called me in for questioning, asking: Why are you so interested in the Jews? Who is paying you for this?" Jiří Fiedler, a Prague-based editor of children's books, and Jaroslav Klenovský, a Brno-based architect, both of whom started documenting Jewish monuments in Bohemia and Moravia in the 1970s and early 1980s, also were warned by secret police about their activities. Fiedler recalls how officials even at the State Jewish Museum barred him from conducting research on Jewish sites in the museum's archives. Dariusz Waleriański, who was one of the 1998 honorees for his work in preserving Jewish heritage in Zabrze, Poland, "kissed a girl for the first time at an old Jewish cemetery, which he [had] found by accident. 'It was like the discovery of Atlantis,' he says, 'and the first kiss is something you never forget.' Waleriański unguardedly mentioned that kiss in an interview and since then he has been labeled not only a 'Jew' and a 'lunatic' but also a 'necrophiliac.'"[18]

Wiśniewski's personal experience is emblematic. Before the Holocaust, Jews made up more than half the population of Białystok, a prewar center of the textile industry northeast of Warsaw: in the early part of the twentieth century Białystok reportedly had the highest concentration of Jews of any city in the world, and in the 1920s as many as 90 percent of its businesses were run by Jews. The city was a center of the Haskalah as well as a focal point for Jewish labor union activities and the Bund Party. During World War II, tens of thousands of Jews were confined in the Białystok Ghetto; resistance fighters staged a valiant but abortive uprising against the Nazis in 1943. In June 1941 the Germans burned down a Białystok synagogue after herding at least one thousand Jews inside. This was secret, even guiltily secret, history to the postwar generation.

Wiśniewski, born in the 1950s, grew up unaware of this aspect of his hometown's past. Only three out of more than sixty prewar synagogues in Białystok survived the war, and all were put to other uses, one of them as a sports hall. The main surviving Jewish cemetery was an overgrown jungle; another had no stones left and was used as a public park. Wiśniewski's prison reading, especially a book about the wartime Białystok Ghetto, changed his understanding of both his hometown and his country and thus, in a sense, his own identity. "The book I read began with the outbreak of World War II on September 1, 1939, and ended with the Jews' almost total annihilation," he told me. "I wanted to know what there was before, when Jews lived in Białystok."

Once of out prison, Wiśniewski tried to complete the picture. But he found no books about the Jews of Białystok in the public library and nowhere to study Jewish history or Jewish subjects. He thus began his own investigations and located prewar guides and newspapers. Barred from many jobs because of his dissident politics, he managed to convince a local newspaper to let him publish "brief and innocuous" articles about Białystok's Jewish history. He called these articles "Postcards from Atlantis" and wrote more than one hundred of them. "At the beginning they were rather clumsy," he told me. "Without know-ing much, I tried to tell the story of what before the war was practically a Jewish city. But then elderly people and even a few Jews began to seek me out at the news office. I talked with them for hours, I taped these conversations, I roamed through the city; they showed me the build-ings of old prewar Jewish schools. At the same time, I read, read, read all that I could get my hands on about this subject. And so it began. I made contacts with Jews from Białystok in Israel, the United States, everywhere. They sent me their books, photocopies of documents, pho-tographs. I became an expert, even if for political reasons I couldn't work at the university."

Like Janusz Makuch in Kraków (who also used the Atlantis image), Wiśniewski describes feeling charged with an emotional obligation. "The history of the Jews of Białystok is not just history for me," he says. "It is also the present. The history of the Jews in Białystok, and of Pol-ish Jews in general, is a major part of Polish history. An honest history of Poland does not exist without the history of the Jews, just as the his-tory of the Jews does not exist, I think, without the history of Poland. I think that this is important, above all, for Poles—it is necessary to pre-sent the fate of the Polish Jews in an honest manner. Back in the early 1980s, few people wrote about Jews, so I considered what I did almost a duty. In addition, I felt that whoever could tell me the truth about earlier times would die soon; that year after year those who remem-ber the ghetto, who lived through the Holocaust, are always fewer. I wanted to talk to them myself, face to face, and not base my knowledge on what is written in books."

As official communist attitudes became increasingly more open to-ward Jewish issues throughout the 1980s, Wiśniewski was able to expand his operations, make contacts with other researchers, and eventually publish books on Jewish monuments and history. The significance of Jewish monuments, he said, began filtering into the local consciousness, even in his part of provincial Poland. Already, when he took me around Białystok in 1990, plaques were being put in place, and some restoration work was beginning. Sometimes groups of schoolchildren were taken to clean up cemeteries. In the mid-1980s Wiśniewski told me, the Jew-ish cemetery in the remote town of Krynki was used as a garbage dump; drunks would hang out there, blinding themselves on vodka; tomb-stones frequently were stolen. But in the late 1990s the situation had changed. Wiśniewski received a telephone call from someone in Krynki whom he did not know. This person was indignant because someone had dumped garbage in the Jewish cemetery. In fact, the townspeople found the culprit and made him clean up the mess. (This certainly marked a reversal: when I visited the Jewish sites in Krynki in 1990, I was hassled by a group of paralytic drunks who threatened to torch my car because I was Jewish.)[19]

In 1998 Wiśniewski told me that he considered the reintegration of the Jewish component in Poland a step on the way to a higher goal: constructing democracy and a tolerant civil society. "In Polish bookstores there are many, many books on Polish Jews now, and there is a big, authentic interest in the history of the Jews," he said. "This makes me happy because it is as if the Polish Jews 'had returned' in a metaphorical sense to Poland. Today, though, the main task is to unmask the many half truths and prejudices that uselessly divide Jews and Poles. This means a more general teaching, a teaching of democracy, of tolerance, and this for me as a journalist is more important on a broader scale, not only regarding Jews and Poles, but all human beings in general. If you understand what the words 'tolerance,' 'understanding,' [and] 'honesty' mean, you are a normal human being."

An Outpouring of Activity

In November 1990 a conference on the future of Jewish monuments was convened in New York by the Jewish Heritage Council (JHC) of the World Monuments Fund (WMF), a private, nonprofit organization that sponsors cultural heritage preservation projects. The WMF had established the Jewish Heritage Council two years earlier, after it had overseen the restoration of the sixteenth-century Scuola Canton Synagogue in Venice. At the time the JHC was the only program specifically dedicated to the preservation of sites and structures of Jewish artistic, historical, and cultural significance worldwide. My brother, Samuel D. Gruber, was its first director, and he chaired the 1990 meeting. It was the first international conference held specifically to address the issues inherent in the preservation of historic Jewish sites, and it aimed both to raise preservation priorities and to explore an agenda for the coming decade. Momentum was just building in the field, but the meeting drew some two hundred participants from fifteen countries. They included curators, historians, Jewish lay leaders, rabbis, government representatives, and private-sector donors, as well as several independent researchers from former communist states who had worked in isolation under communism. Most had questions rather than answers, and many presentations, particularly from eastern and central Europe, were little more than catalogs of desolation. The conference represented an unprecedented public, international statement that Jewish monuments were part of the global cultural heritage, not meaningful solely to Jews any more than Egyptian, Greek, and Roman monuments are meaningful solely to Egyptians, Greeks, and Italians. But at the time, Gruber has recalled, "how we would proceed, and what we would accomplish, remained very much a puzzle. There were relatively few success stories about the rescue of old synagogues and neglected cemeteries."

Nearly nine years later, at the January 1999 International Conference on Jewish Heritage in Europe, sponsored by the French government in Paris, a significantly different world was described. Although most Jewish heritage sites remained in perilous condition, the conference highlighted an array of activities, funded and sponsored by a wide range of public and private sources, that bore eloquent testimony to an awakened acknowledgment of Jewish built heritage. "There was much to cheer about," Gruber said afterward. "Information about new excavations revealing medieval remains; of new museums; and of new tourism initiatives were all evidence of how far the movement to save Jewish monuments [had] come in a decade. Nonetheless, it was also clear that we are still just scratching the surface. Unlike ten years ago, however, we seem to know where we are going; the outline of the puzzle is put together. We have developed successful methodologies, proven strategies, and produced credible and popular results."[20]

Some thirty speakers from a dozen countries addressed the conference. A sampling of their presentations gives an overview of the vast range of projects undertaken since the late 1980s: only a few of the projects described had been initiated at the time of the 1990 conference.

- Arno Pařík of the Prague Jewish Museum described at least twenty synagogues that were restored, dozens of Jewish cemeteries that were cleaned up or repaired, and former Jewish quarters in more than half a dozen provincial towns that became targets of development in the first eight years after the "Velvet Revolution" in the Czech Republic. In addition, he noted that more than a dozen new Jewish museums or museum departments had been opened or revamped, and more were planned.

- Otto Lohr, of the Landesstelle for nonstate museums, a service board of the Ministry of Culture in Bavaria, described the different

ways in which the nine Jewish museums in Bavaria—all of them publicly run, several of them situated in restored synagogues, and all of
them opened since 1988—dealt with Jewish heritage and the presentation of Jewish history and memory in Germany.

- Progress reports were given on high-profile synagogue restorations
  in Kraków, Poland, Hania and Veroia, Greece, and Toledo, Spain,
  which highlighted a diversity of funding sources, aesthetic approaches, technical procedures, and local attitudes.

- Reports detailed the methodology used in carrying out, funding, and
  collating ongoing surveys or inventories of Jewish cemeteries and
  synagogues in Romania, Ukraine, Great Britain, France, Moldova,
  and Germany. These reports highlighted widely varying conditions
  in countries whose Jewish heritage sites had been ignored, neglected,
  or abandoned as a result of both natural demographic shifts and
  Holocaust or communist-era damage. Comprehensive status reports
  on the condition of synagogues in Poland, Hungary, and parts of
  France were also presented.

- A report described cooperation since the mid-1990s between local
  tourist authorities and a local B'nai B'rith organization in the Alsace
  region of eastern France in an aggressive strategy of sponsoring Jewish cultural events and promoting tourism to some two hundred
  Jewish heritage sites, including cemeteries, synagogues, ancient *mikvaot,* and museums, most of which had long lain abandoned or in
  disrepair.

These activities were organized, funded, and executed by a wide range
of sponsors or participants, from local and state authorities to public,
private, and religious organizations and foundations, tourist bureaus,
and private individuals. (The full-scale survey of Jewish heritage sites
under way in Great Britain, for example, begun in the early 1990s by
a London-based registered charity called the Jewish Memorial Council, received £146,000 in funding from the National Lottery in 1997.)
Foreign-based or international bodies, such as the European Union,
and foreign-based foundations also funded or sponsored Jewish heritage activities. And Jewish organizations, institutions, and individuals
also played varying roles, as financial backers, fund-raisers, sponsors, advisers, or information gatherers on projects ranging from the erection
of Holocaust memorials to the cleanup of cemeteries to growing genealogy databases and inventories of sites.

In postcommunist Europe, the U.S. government has also been an important, if little-known, player in this process, through the activities of the U.S. Commission for the Preservation of America's Heritage Abroad, a federal body established in 1985. The commission's original function was primarily to provide nonfinancial backing for orthodox Jews seeking to protect cemeteries in communist countries where important rabbis were buried. With the fall of communism, its options broadened. Recognition of Jewish (and other minority culture) sites was promoted as a means of fostering civic values among emerging democracies. Starting in the early 1990s, the commission has sponsored detailed surveys of the location, condition, and threats—ranging from vandalism and urban sprawl to encroaching vegetation—to existing Jewish monuments in Poland, the Czech Republic, Slovenia, and other countries.[21] Published in book form and also made available via computer database and the Internet, these were the first such systematic global inventories of Jewish sites in the countries concerned since the end of World War II and probably the most extensive inventories ever taken of Jewish heritage sites in these countries. For example, the Czech survey provided information on more than seven hundred Jewish cemeteries and synagogues, and the Polish survey included more than one thousand sites. Significantly, these surveys were the result of official, government-to-government agreements between the various postcommunist European states and Washington, D.C. The researchers who oversaw the projects and carried out the survey fieldwork included a number of individuals who had sought out and documented Jewish monuments on their own under communism.[22]

The commission, which has a full-time staff of only two people, worked at times in cooperation with the JHC, which, along with several other institutions, organizations, and scholarly institutions in North America and Israel, took the lead in spearheading programs in the 1990s to document Jewish sites internationally or point out preservation priorities. In 1996 the WMF released its first "Watch List" of what it considered the one hundred most endangered cultural monuments worldwide. The list included four Jewish heritage sites. At the same time the WMF issued a separate "Preservation Priorities" list of ten endangered Jewish sites, most of them in Europe. These were chosen on the basis of preservation needs and historical, architectural, and artistic significance, which included financial as well as physical considerations.[23] By the end of 2000, restoration of five of these priority sites had been completed.

The Center for Jewish Art at the Hebrew University in Jerusalem became particularly active in documenting Jewish built heritage and related material. During the 1990s, it sent teams of architects, art historians, researchers, and photographers on expeditions to systematically survey and document synagogues and other Jewish sites in about twenty countries, mainly in east central Europe and the former Soviet Union. Foreign-born individuals (such as myself and the Israeli husband-and-wife team, Ben-Zion and Rivka Dorfman) also began to compile personal collections of photographic and other documentation.[24] As an outgrowth of his work with the Jewish Heritage Council, Samuel Gruber became president of the International Survey of Jewish Monuments; he revived an organization that had been inactive for some time and in 1997 established a quarterly journal, the *Jewish Heritage Report*, and later a related web site (www.isjm.org), to serve as clearinghouses for burgeoning information on Jewish heritage documentation and preservation issues worldwide.

5

What to Do?

The 1990 New York conference on the future of Jewish monuments identified at an early stage a range of practical as well as emotional questions that have remained crucial to the "Jewish archaeology" process and in many cases have remained unresolved. The 1999 follow-up conference in Paris added new dimensions to these questions, based on experience, more accurate evaluation of conditions, and fast-changing legal, economic, and political circumstances, particularly in former communist states. One overriding question emerged: Now that the importance (and in some cases the existence) of Jewish built heritage has become widely recognized and the historic preservation of Jewish monuments is on the Jewish agenda and the agendas of national monuments authorities, tourist bureaus, and other institutions, what do we do with these places, and how do we do it?

Thousands of Jewish heritage sites lie scattered across Europe, most of them still in perilous condition. Which sites should be chosen for protection or restoration? Once chosen, how should renovated Jewish sites fit into the surrounding urban fabric? Should they be reconstructed to their original condition or renovated into something new? What, in this context, is meant by "original" condition, particularly for a building hundreds of years old? Should a restored site appear pristine, or should evidence of historic damage be retained? The Holocaust and post-Holocaust decades created their own forms of damage, but prewar photographs and descriptions show that synagogues, cemeteries, and Jewish quarters were often in dilapidated states even when in active use by healthy Jewish populations. Synagogue interiors also were subject to frequent changes over the decades to fit contemporary styles. Stripping down to basic brick can thus erase centuries of history or historic patina. How, then, in a restoration should the building's history best be reflected?

Such technical and interpretive questions are, of course, commonly addressed during many historic preservation projects.[1] But the post-Holocaust Jewish context makes these issues particularly sensitive, imbuing them with political, psychological, historical, and religious significance: Jewish heritage sites may be "sites of glory," that is, magnificent examples of faith, community, and history, but they also often represent "sites of shame," physical reminders of the deliberate destruction of a people, which may have been carried out, supported, or witnessed by the local population. For whom, then, are the synagogues and ghettos being renovated? What should be the function of a restored synagogue, ritual bath, or Jewish quarter in towns where no Jews live? Who should finance such operations? Indeed, need all ruined Jewish structures be restored? And what should be done with Jewish monuments, such as the synagogue-turned-fire station in Hohenems or the synagogues-turned-apartment blocks in Germany, that have been already converted for other use? Not to mention the thousands of overgrown, desecrated, or otherwise abandoned cemeteries. Does each one need to be marked by a commemorative plaque, to have its history revealed, or, particularly in the case of cemeteries, to be treated as a sacred site? What role should the local Jewish communities play? What role should foreign Jews and Israel play? Is it possible — or necessary — to devise a coordinated, international strategy for Jewish monuments conservation and protection in Europe?

It is interesting to note that similar dilemmas have emerged in Bosnia-Hercegovina, where ethnic cleansing, like the Nazi genocide, targeted historic and cultural patrimony as well as people. In a 1998 article on this subject, Andrew Herscher describes how the "assault on cultural monuments" during the Bosnian War of the 1990s led to the coining of terms such as "warchitecture"—the deliberate destruction of architecture—and "urbicide"—the deliberate destruction of cities. He writes, "Bosnian Serbs and Croats attempted not only to conquer territory by vanquishing the Bosnian Muslim army that defended it, but also to legitimize their conquests by eliminating the evidence that called their claims into question: indigenous Muslim communities and the architectural environments they inhabited. . . . [In rebuilding,] what does it mean to reconstruct a damaged city in the absence of some or all of the people who inhabited, used, and identified with that city?"[2]

The manner in which Berlin's New Synagogue on Oranienburger Strasse was restored is a high-profile example of one solution. Built in 1866 and seating 3,200 people, it was once Europe's largest synagogue, not to mention one of the most ornate. It was damaged on Kristall-nacht, then severely hit by Allied bombing, and its ruined sanctuary was torn down in the 1960s. The front section of the building was left stand-ing in ruins, marked after 1966 with a memorial plaque, until 1988, the fiftieth anniversary of Kristallnacht, when the East German government put its multimillion-dollar restoration project into motion. The resto-ration was later completed by the newly united Federal Republic. The building was dedicated with a nationally televised, rain-soaked cere-mony attended by Chancellor Helmut Kohl, President Roman Herzog, and other dignitaries in May 1995, as part of events marking the fiftieth anniversary of the end of World War II.

"The damaged body of the building was felt to be a memorial," Robert Graefrath, an East Berlin monuments curator who worked on the restoration, wrote in an essay describing the dilemma of whether to "conserve or reconstruct" the hulking ruins. "[O]n the one hand, there were those who believed that the building should be restored to its orig-inal form, in its entirety. On the other hand, there was the view that any intrusion would be sacrilege, that the ruins should remain untouched, as a monument." It was not possible to follow either of these options. Instead, a compromise was reached "to restore the building as evidence of both phases of its history; to make the history of the building and its builders perceptible through a visible contrast between magnificent ar-chitecture and its violent destruction."[3]

The synagogue was restored as the Centrum Judaicum, a complex that includes a Jewish culture center and museum; its fifty-meter-high dome, glittering with gilded buttresses, is once again a landmark on the city skyline. But the ornate halls and exhibit displays end abruptly in a wall of glass that overlooks a vast, open plaza. This space is where the sanctuary once stood, with its rows of pews and its proudly prosperous congregation. Deliberately left empty according to Graefrath's com-promise vision, it is a conscious expression of absence that recalls not simply the destruction of the synagogue but the destruction of the Jew-ish congregation that once worshiped there and, by extension, the de-struction of millions of other European Jews and their world as well.

This is reflected, too, by the museum's "signature" exhibit: the *ner tamid*, or eternal lamp, from the original synagogue, which was discovered by construction workers clearing rubble in 1989. The lamp, which had hung in front of the Ark, had been mixed into concrete used for a reinforcing ceiling put up by the Nazis in 1943. It was thus saved—though heavily battered—by its would-be destroyers. Like the destroyed sanctuary itself, the lamp has not been restored. It is presented in a showcase at the entrance to the museum. It no longer has a ritual function in Jewish worship, but it clearly fulfills another, dual ritual: that of commemorating destruction and symbolizing survival and recovery.[4]

Postcommunist Challenges

In eastern and central European countries, the rapid economic, political, and social changes since the fall of communism have created new conditions and opportunities vis-à-vis Jewish heritage sites, as well as new challenges. This has been so whether hard-line communist regimes were ousted virtually overnight, as in Czechoslovakia, or whether the changeover was less abrupt, as in Poland, where it followed negotiations forced by years of widespread opposition struggle, or in Hungary, where it followed a gradual waning of official strictures. In part this process has been emotional; in part it has involved the construction of new social, political, legal, and economic structures.

With the final fall of communism, the uncovering of Jewish history and heritage became a counterpoint to the burying of the communist past. The toppling of monuments to Marx and Lenin, the renaming of streets, and the transformation of communist buildings for other uses were also seen as acts that reconsecrated a desecrated landscape. Historic town districts, palaces and manor houses, churches and other monuments that had been ignored or left untended under communism became objects of cleanup, paint-up, and fix-up campaigns. Both publicly and privately funded, they were conceived as reflections of new local pride and negation of communist-era neglect, as well as development schemes aimed at luring local business, foreign investment, and tourist dollars.

Recognition and recovery of Jewish heritage became part of this agenda of reversal: an increasingly, sometimes suddenly established matter of public policy rather than a private battle waged by individual iconoclasts. The government-to-government agreements signed with the U.S. Commission for the Preservation of America's Heritage Abroad were part of this pattern. Sometimes streets and squares bearing names from the communist era were renamed to reflect Jewish historical recovery. Broader postcommunist civic restoration projects in towns where few or no Jews still lived often were designed to include the specific redevelopment of neglected old Jewish quarters, the establishment of local Jewish museums and exhibits, the placing of commemorative or identification plaques, and the erection of new Holocaust monuments. (Significantly, if ironically, it was the economic stagnation and overall neglect of buildings during the communist period that left Jewish sites standing in easily identifiable, if ruined, condition.)

The speed, form, and content of this recovery has varied greatly, depending on local conditions—including, importantly, financial considerations. Ambitious plans launched in the heady aftermath of the fall of the Berlin Wall were frequently halted for lack of funding. The restoration of the magnificent, domed, nineteenth-century synagogue in Győr, Hungary, was a case in point. Within a year of a postcommunist local government taking power in Győr in 1990, the city set up a foundation headed by the mayor to oversee and raise money for the synagogue's restoration. The project eventually got under way thanks to a grant from the European Union, but it sputtered ahead slowly because of difficulty raising additional funds and in 1997 was still far from completed. The fate of Otto Wagner's Rumbach Street synagogue in Budapest, with its unique octagonal sanctuary, was even more disturbing. It was sold to the state by the Jewish community in 1988 and became the property of an agricultural association, which planned to restore the building and sell it for a profit. Work was halted when the building was 80 percent finished: money ran out, and no fixed function for the restored building had been established. A buyer could not be found, and throughout most of the 1990s the building stood empty. Decay and neglect negated much of the restoration work, leaving it, by the end of the decade, in a condition that was almost as bad as it had been in the first place.[5]

Official civic development plans were often augmented and sometimes overtaken, too, by the activities of private entrepreneurs. This happened in Kraków, where the unfettered private commercial development of Jewish-style shops, cafés, restaurants, tours, and the like, and the promotion of events such as the Jewish Culture Festival and the activities of the Center for Jewish Culture leapfrogged attempts by urban planners to manage development of the former Jewish quarter as part of a citywide restoration plan devised in the late 1980s. A municipal agency devoted to shaping a regeneration strategy for Kazimierz was set up in 1991. Two years later, under the sponsorship of the European Union, Kraków, Berlin, and Edinburgh initiated a joint project to produce a "Kazimierz action plan" aimed at providing "a strategy and clear policies" to revive the district. The resulting report of more than one hundred pages, published in 1994, offered specific recommendations on the development of tourism, trade, and urban spaces for visitors and local residents. But it already noted that organic private development was overtaking public planning and that some building restorations were being carried out in violation of city codes. Lack of clarity regarding property ownership also affected planning and development.

Even before the Kazimierz action plan was published, restoration work had begun on several synagogues and other Jewish buildings in and around Kazimierz, with funding from both public and private sources. At the request of the tiny Jewish community in Kraków, the World Monuments Fund targeted the ornate, nineteenth-century Tempel Synagogue (still consecrated as a house of worship) as one of its projects. Funded by private donors, the European Union, the Getty Grant Program, and other foundations, and with partnership participation by Kraków's municipal Committee to Protect Historic Monuments, the project was completed in 2000. During the years of restoration, the synagogue was used for religious services for Jewish tour groups and also served as a venue for concerts and cultural events, including concerts by the Kraków Philharmonic aimed at promoting ecumenical dialogue, with senior Roman Catholic clergy as guests in the audience.

Global government policy and high-profile projects did or did not find immediate echo in towns and villages where uncovering local Jewish history also meant reexamining, in a sometimes intimate manner, local attitudes to Jews before, during, and in the wake of the Holocaust. In the Czech Republic some of the dozens of Jewish monument restoration projects that had been completed or were under way by the late 1990s had the institutional backing of associations or foundations set up in the early 1990s by municipal authorities, sometimes in conjunction with private organizations. These drew up detailed development plans and attempted to raise funding from state, city, church, and international organizations as well as from corporate and private donors, benefit concerts, sales of posters and postcards, and the like.[6] In Třebíč and other places, in fact, the restoration of old ghettos assumed an almost assembly-line dynamic, each following a model that incorporated the restoration of a synagogue, the opening (or planned opening) of a little Jewish museum or exhibit in or near the synagogue, the placing of a Holocaust memorial, the refurbishment of ghetto houses, the publication of books or pamphlets on local Jewish history, and the encouragement of the boutique trade. In most cases this accompanied commercial and physical revitalization of the surrounding town, aimed both at drawing tourists and business investors and at creating better conditions for local residents.

The changes were dramatic. Between 1990 and 1997, for example, Třebíč and the central Moravian town of Boskovice, sites of two of the most extensive old Jewish quarters in central Europe, went from being shabby and run-down backwaters to poster towns for the market economy, and their Jewish quarters went through similar transformations. By 1997 Boskovice, a town of eleven thousand, was alleged to have more than thirty pubs and cafés. Many of its old ghetto buildings had been cleaned, painted, and fixed up, and the restoration of its seventeenth-century synagogue was nearing completion (though stalled by lack of funds). Elaborate frescoes discovered during the restoration process covered the interior walls.[7] A plaque on the wall of one house, affixed in 1993, marked where a turn-of-the-century Jewish author and playwright, Hermann Ungar, had been born. Next door was the Hermann Ungar Teahouse, where one could sip exotic infusions and buy New Age books. A little Jewish museum, displaying local Jewish ritual objects, historical information, photographs, and other relics, had been opened in a ghetto house in 1994. A video presentation—in several languages—recounted local Jewish history, and a small memorial listed the names of the more than four hundred Jews from Boskovice and its surrounding areas who were killed in the Holocaust. The guest book was signed by numerous Czech school groups as well as occasional visitors from Israel, Germany, and the Netherlands. A few steps away, a prominent sign with Hebrew lettering on it advertised the Makkabi restaurant. It was dark, noisy, and smoky, with a low, barrel-vaunted ceiling, and decorated with antique bottles, old pictures of the ghetto district, and a poster for the 1995 European Maccabee Games in Amsterdam. Its youthful clientele sported long hair and pierced noses and eyebrows. There was nothing remotely "Jewish" (much less kosher) on the menu.

A brochure given out by the local tourist office spelled out the symbolism accorded Jewish culture, history, and urban structure in the postcommunist context: "There are only few towns in Central Europe that can boast such a tradition of culture, past and present, as Boskovice. One unique aspect of this is the former Jewish Quarter. A few decades ago, this was one of the most remarkable urban expressions of Jewish culture in Europe—a little mysterious, and somewhat oriental. During the Communist years of 'elaborate plans and bright tomorrows,' the Quarter became dilapidated and depopulated; the valuable Jewish input into local culture faded away and people forgot it. Just like many other decaying historical monuments, the nearly empty Quarter, the abandoned synagogue, and the neglected Jewish cemetery turned into a true reflection of our society." An exhibit on Jewish Boskovice mounted in 1992, it said, had been conceived as part of the entire ghetto renovation plan "to remind the public of the Quarter's past glory, to emphasize its values both obvious and subtle, to readdress 'accepted' facts and to address irrational prejudice."

A New Jewish Dimension

At the end of the 1990s, the chance discovery of a medieval Jewish cemetery during excavations for an insurance company building in downtown Prague sparked an explosive dispute involving the Prague government, the insurance company, Czech Jews, and fervently orthodox (Haredi) Jewish groups from around the world. Work was halted on the multimillion-dollar project as the government, local Jews, and rabbis from Israel and other countries wrangled over what to do with the newly found graves, which had been buried deep under city buildings for five hundred years. An e-mail campaign falsely claiming that Prague's famed Old Jewish Cemetery was endangered stoked passions. Television news broadcasts in February 2000 showed scores of orthodox Jews weeping and praying on Prague streets demanding reburial of unearthed bones. And well into the summer, Prague police scuffled with orthodox Jews from abroad protesting as sacrilegious a solution accepted by Czech Jews under which the government agreed

to pay $1.2 million to change construction plans and leave the ceme-
tery site untouched but encased in concrete. Orthodox Jews also
staged protests outside Czech consulates in New York, London, and
elsewhere.

The opening up of former communist countries to Jewish interest—
and interests—from abroad and the awakening of Jewish consciousness on the local level have contributed new religious and legal dimensions to Jewish heritage issues that had been virtually nonexistent in the
communist period. Jews themselves, both inside and outside the countries in question, began recognizing the religious, historical, symbolic,
and economic significance of surviving Jewish monuments. Ownership
questions and the reclamation of lost or confiscated property became
dominant issues. As individuals, institutions, and religious communities, Jews began to offer, if not demand, a say in the fate of Jewish heritage sites. Among Jews in the West, too, the question of "why" to recover, preserve, document, or restore such monuments was giving way
by the end of the decade to questions of "how" to go about doing so—
and, though few disputes were as painful, costly, or well publicized as
the cemetery dispute in Prague, there were many different, sometimes
conflicting answers.

This new attitude marked a dramatic reversal. In the decades after
World War II, support from official Jewish bodies and most individual Jews for Jewish monuments preservation in Europe, particularly in
communist Europe, was minimal, other than maintenance of active synagogues and cemeteries or, in the East, occasional efforts by orthodox
Jews to refurbish the tombs of revered rabbis or by Holocaust survivors
to erect memorials in their hometowns. Jews living in the West and in
Israel often expressed open hostility to supporting such projects in
countries where Jews had been murdered. Jews living in communist
states generally had little possibility of staking claims or speaking up.

In postcommunist Europe, Jewish input has taken a variety of
forms. All postcommunist countries have witnessed the development of
emerging Jewish communities, often composed of Jews who had hidden or denied their Jewishness until religious freedom was instituted.
By the end of the 1990s the ultimate fate of these still-fragile communities was yet to be written. Nonetheless, backed by international bodies, they formed small but active and increasingly self-confident centers
able to voice actual local Jewish concerns on local Jewish-related issues, both at home and in international forums. The postcommunist
political climate also enabled international Jewish organizations and

Jews who had ancestral ties to the region to interest themselves in such matters.

Postcommunist authorities enlisted local Jewish communal bodies, institutions, and individuals as active advisers or at least titular partners in various civic projects, lending legitimacy to these initiatives. Important synagogues in several countries were targeted for restoration not as museums or monuments but, like the Tempel Synagogue in Kraków, as synagogues that would remain consecrated for worship as well as fulfill a public cultural use. The state provided the bulk of the funding for projects such as the restoration of the Dohany Street Synagogue in Budapest, Europe's largest synagogue, and the Great Synagogue in Sofia. Both projects were completed in 1996, and the synagogues were rededicated with gala ceremonies that demonstrated the aim of "making good" to the Jews as well as restoring important city landmarks. In the Czech Republic the Prague Jewish Museum, run by the state since 1950, assumed a high-profile public outreach role after it was returned to Jewish community management in 1994, and experts from the museum and from Czech Jewish communities have acted as close advisers in the redevelopment of provincial ghetto areas, the restoration of synagogues, the establishment of small provincial Jewish museums, and the planning of Jewish cultural programs associated with the museums.

The opening of eastern Europe enabled orthodox Jews from Israel and elsewhere to become more active in maintaining tombs of important rabbis through organizations such as the London-based Committee for the Preservation of Jewish Cemeteries in Europe. In 1999, for example, an agreement was reached among the Jewish community in Bratislava, Slovakia, the Bratislava municipality, and the New York–based International Committee for the Preservation of the Gravesites of Geonai Pressburg for the reconstruction of the tombs of the revered nineteenth-century sage Chatam Sofer and other rabbis. The tombs, remnants of an extensive cemetery destroyed during World War II, are located in an underground mausoleum, and the project entailed rerouting a major city tram line and building a prayer house.

Holocaust survivors or their descendants in Israel, the United States, and elsewhere also initiated numerous projects to clean up or fence Jewish cemeteries or erect memorial sites in their home- or ancestral towns. Sometimes these were individual efforts, but frequently they involved people in a variety of countries working in close cooperation with local town and sometimes church authorities. In a number of cases, the town hosted Jewish survivors and their children who returned for the dedication of monuments.

One example was the monument dedicated in September 1997 on the site of the Jewish cemetery in the Polish town of Wyszków, northeast of Warsaw. The monument's design incorporated scores of reclaimed tombstones and fragments that the Nazis had uprooted in 1939 and used as paving stones and construction material for the Gestapo headquarters. The $60,000 project was spearheaded by the families of several former Wyszków Jews and organized by the U.S. Commission for the Preservation of America's Heritage Abroad, which worked for more than four years in cooperation with Polish government and local Wyszków officials. The city returned the cemetery site to the Warsaw Jewish community, and Warsaw's Jewish Historical Institute served as general contractor. Financing came from private donors. Dozens of Jewish survivors from Wyszków and Jews who traced their ancestry to the town traveled to Wyszków from the United States, Israel, Latin America, and Germany for the dedication ceremonies. Polish, American, and local Roman Catholic dignitaries, as well as hundreds of local townspeople, also attended. The U.S. ambassador read a letter from President Bill Clinton praising Polish-American-Jewish cooperation in carrying out the project, and at a special, crowded Roman Catholic mass, a local priest spoke of the horrors of the Holocaust and the need for remembrance and led the congregation in prayers for peace, justice, and Jewish-Polish reconciliation.[8]

Restitution

The collapse of communist regimes opened up the possibility that property expropriated from Jewish communities and individual Jews by the Nazis or communists might be returned, and pressing for restitution of prewar Jewish property became a dominant motif throughout the 1990s. This did not happen in a vacuum or develop on its own but in the wake of general economic reforms and privatization programs aimed at clarifying title and enabling investment. In 1992 a number of international Jewish organizations and two Holocaust survivor groups established the World Jewish Restitution Organization (WJRO) to serve as a central body to coordinate efforts aimed at recovering or receiving compensation for communal and organizational Jewish assets seized by Nazi and communist governments. In 1995 the U.S. government appointed Stuart Eizenstat, then the U.S. ambassador to the European Union, the State Department's special envoy on property restitution in central and eastern Europe.

Hard-fought new laws and policies in a number of countries enabled the transfer of ownership of scores of synagogues, cemeteries, and other Jewish communal property, as well as other buildings, to Jewish hands and called into question the legal status of many other structures. But the process—still far from complete by 2000—has been tortuous, painful, at times bitter, and (as Eizenstat spelled out in testimony before a House committee in 1998) fraught with questions going beyond strictly legal parameters.[9] Specific legal difficulties, Eizenstat noted, included questions of ownership and jurisdiction. Some property designated by state laws for restitution was under municipal control, other property under private or state jurisdiction. Citizenship or residency requirements for regaining prewar assets or even owning real estate presented obstacles in some countries. Some countries distinguished between "religious" and "nonreligious" communal property. In addition, governments were well aware that restitution of property to individuals or to religious groups (including Christian churches) could involve extensive holdings. Changing postwar borders and population shifts also complicated matters, as did conflicting claims of ownership as a result of Nazi and communist confiscations and bureaucratic red tape. What was to be done, too, about people, businesses, or institutions that had occupied appropriated Jewish property? After, in some cases, fifty or sixty years, didn't they also have rights? New legislation not only had to establish legal frameworks for property restitution, it had to establish an oversight body that could adjudicate conflicting claims and enforce decisions.

In some cases a new sensitivity as to who owned or who might claim a certain building halted or delayed civic restoration (or sometimes demolition) plans. But the possibility that Jews could reclaim former property also could translate into hostility, prompted by fear that Jews would return and displace those who had moved in after the war. People confused laws regulating return of specific Jewish communal property with the potential claims of individual Jews or their descendants to family possessions. In late 1998 an alarmist report on Poland's main television news broadcast warned viewers nationwide to beware of spurious claims by Israelis and other foreign Jews who pretended to be descendants of property owners. The report deliberately played on local fears, guilt, and superstitious stereotype, stating, for example, that 40 percent of the real estate in Kraków and 60 percent in Tarnów had once belonged to Jews. The implication was clear. But Poland's 1997 restitution law covered only former community-owned property, not private claims, which were handled on a case-by-case basis. This type of fear was compounded by fears of potential claims by other people displaced during or after the war, in particular the millions of ethnic Germans expelled from Poland and Czechoslovakia. Christian churches, too, had had vast property nationalized by the communist state.

Properties returned to Jewish communities were mixed blessings. "In many cases," said Samuel Gruber, "it was like getting the ingredients for a soup but not a pot or fire to cook with." Some communities, such as those in Prague and Budapest, were able to realize income from regained properties or from payments in lieu of properties. But many properties slated for restitution were in need of expensive restoration, care, and maintenance—or were assessed for property tax payment—that far exceeded income-earning potential. And another major cost was compensation to current occupants who were being displaced. A large part of the prewar communal Jewish property eligible for restitution in Poland, for example, amounted to some one thousand cemeteries in various states of ruin. "These are priceless, but they will never generate money; rather it requires money for their upkeep," a member of the board of the Union of Jewish Religious Communities in Poland told me. "Even if the restitution is successful, there will not be enough money to take care of all of them." Polish Jewish leaders estimated, too, that it would cost at least $800,000 just to prepare documentation on sites in order to submit restitution claims.

Sometimes conflicting new Jewish interests clashed. As occurred in the Prague cemetery affair, they could clash over different views of religious responsibility toward cemeteries. The sanctity of burial and human remains is a basic tenet of Jewish law. Were all cemeteries sacred places that must remain untouched and inviolate? Or did local communities have the right to sell off parts of cemetery land to gain funds for today's communal needs? Jewish interests also clashed over which properties to pursue for restitution. And they clashed, too, over the ways in which restitution money from prewar Jewish property should be allocated and what should become of restituted property itself. Some felt that income from such property should be used only for social and religious purposes and dismissed "secular" attempts to care for Jewish sites and artifacts that were not in current ritual use.[10] Holocaust survivors and other Jews originating in eastern Europe, as well as some Israeli bodies, sometimes asserted that their concerns had more weight than decisions taken by tiny local communities living in the region. In Poland it was only after years of acrimonious negotiations, refereed by the U.S. government, that local Polish Jews and the WJRO came to an agreement in 2000 about how restituted communal property should be managed and cared for and how potential income from such properties should be divided.

Looking Ahead

A reawakening of Jewish interest in the fate of Jewish heritage sites in the 1990s was not limited to postcommunist Europe, but the increased awareness on the part of Jews was uneven and in some places remained low. The consensus that evolved at the 1999 International Conference on European Jewish Heritage in Paris, however, was that cooperation by Jews and Jewish bodies with civic and private institutions would be essential in future projects and planning, given changing political conditions, Jewish communal evolution, and limited financial resources. In addition, non-Jews and civic institutions had to be assured that Jews themselves were concerned about preserving Jewish heritage sites—both to reassure them of the validity of their own efforts and to break the barriers between the Jewish and the virtual Jewish worlds. The main point was to find meaningful solutions to suit the new understanding of the importance of Jewish heritage sites. Preservation of Jewish monuments, Samuel Gruber put it, "should always be done in the light of responsible dialogue, not as a clinical project by experts, but as a continuing cultural, educational process. A building in isolation is like a stamp in an album: it means nothing by itself. Restored in context, it vibrates."

Already in 1990 the Hungarian architect and synagogue researcher Anikó Gazda had stressed the view that surviving synagogue buildings in towns without Jewish populations should be used for cultural purposes. "It would be wise, however, to keep all symbols, inscriptions, Tablets of the Commandments, Stars of David and other memorials to preserve and commemorate the former Jewish communities for future times, as well as to document the function of the buildings," she wrote. "Nothing morally objectionable should be put in the buildings which could be considered 'unchaste'—for instance as has already been done in Hungary in recent years using synagogues as gyms, fencing, boxing or wrestling halls, swimming pools, savings banks, bazaars or shops, etc." [11] This would certainly be the ideal. But what about a case such as the city of Cluj, Romania. In 1991 four main synagogue buildings were standing, two unused and two still consecrated for worship, one of the latter designated a memorial to Holocaust victims. The Jewish community numbered five hundred, mainly elderly, people and was steadily dwindling. By 1999 one of the disused synagogues had been turned into offices. One, which had been in very dilapidated condition, was undergoing a sensitive restoration by a private organization for use as a culture center. One of the consecrated synagogues, though, had been "deactivated" and rented out by the Federation of Romanian Jewish Communities to obtain much-needed income for communal activities; almost all signs of its former identity had been stripped away or covered, and it was being used as a furniture store.

In 1999 several European Jewish organizations began a tentative exploration to formulate a global policy agenda on these matters, or at least to sketch guidelines, models, and suggestions that could serve as reference points in the future. A score of experts who had attended the Paris Jewish heritage conference stayed on an extra day for an informal strategy session organized by Ruth Zilkha, then chair of the European Council of Jewish Communities. The aim was to define long-term, Europe-wide priorities regarding the Jewish built heritage and to explore areas in which Jews, Jewish organizations, state, local, and Europe-wide bodies, institutions, and preservation organizations could coordinate efforts, including fund-raising. This meeting drew up a preliminary list of recommendations, which included accelerating the inventory and documentation of heritage sites to determine what actually existed; creating a coodinating body to serve as a clearing-house for information on projects and funding; involvement of young people in the awareness, preservation, and promotion of Jewish heritage; organization of training programs in the field; organization of a European Day of Jewish Culture to promote Jewish sites, on the model of the Alsace program that had been outlined during the Paris meeting. Except for this last recommendation (discussed in chapter 7), the proposals remained under discussion but still pending by the middle of 2001.

In October 1997 I attended a strange little ceremony in the Slovenian city of Maribor at which many of the issues I cited above converged. It centered on the symbolism inherent in an eight-hundred-year-old building that once was a synagogue and on how that symbolism, and the symbolism of Jews, was perceived and used by both individuals and civic authorities in a newly independent postcommunist country trying to define its identity. It also entailed new relations between emerging Jewish communities and mainstream societies, as well as the ways in which outside Jewish interests interacted with local conditions.

The ceremony was held to affix a mezuzah on the doorpost of Maribor's medieval synagogue, a full five hundred years after the Jews were expelled from Maribor and from most of the rest of what today is Slovenia. The country, with a population of two million, became independent in 1991, after it seceded from Yugoslavia, touching off the Balkan wars of the 1990s. It marked the first time in history that Slovenians had formed an independent state.

The Maribor synagogue dates back to the thirteenth century and is one of the oldest buildings in what is a charming university town and Slovenia's second-largest city. It is thus one of the oldest buildings in Slovenia. The much-rebuilt structure is located at the site of the old Jewish quarter, an area just inside the town walls above the Drava River that for years was run-down and neglected but which even during the communist period was known as "Jewish street." Jews flourished in Maribor in the Middle Ages, and Maribor rabbi Israel Isserlein was renowned throughout central Europe in the fifteenth century. But Jews were expelled from Maribor in 1497, and few Jews have lived in the city since then. Already by 1501 the synagogue had been turned into a church. In the nineteenth century it was used as a warehouse, and later it was converted into a dwelling. By 1997 there had not been an organized Jewish community in Maribor for five hundred years.

Renovation work got under way on the building, which is owned by the city, in the 1990s. Factions in the municipal administration, however, clashed over what use should be made of the structure: some wanted to see it converted into a youth center, or even a pub or discotheque, that would anchor commercial and touristic development of the surrounding old quarter. Others wanted it for use by the city as an archive. Others insisted that the building be restored as closely as possible to its "original" appearance and used for a more dignified cultural purpose that underscored its original Jewish religious identity. By 1997 it seemed clear that the synagogue would ultimately be restored as a cultural center that would contain information on local Jewish history. Restoration would be of wider significance as well, as it is one of the few medieval synagogues still known to be standing in Europe. But practical as well as political problems also dogged the project. City monuments authorities said they wanted to restore the building according to what they believed was its original appearance, but this was impossible to determine. Some of the initial work was carried out hurriedly and incorrectly, in accordance with local, uninformed ideas of what was Jewish and how a synagogue should look, and was going to have to be removed: this included a women's gallery installed as a partial upper floor of the sanctuary. By 1997 there was still little idea of what the final form and function of the building would be. Nor was a program of activities or a plan for exhibition space drawn up. Lack of funds was another problem. Work on the building seemed stalled indefinitely.

The mezuzah was nailed to the synagogue doorpost during a small ceremony that followed a two-day international symposium on medieval Jewish communities in central Europe and their cultural heritage. Sponsored by the city of Maribor, the University of Maribor, and the Maribor Regional Archives, the symposium was the first full-scale international conference on a Jewish topic to be held in the town and was considered a prestigious event. Slovenia's president, Maribor's mayor, and other Slovenian dignitaries, as well as the U.S. ambassador, a representative of the Israeli ambassador, and the secretary-general of the Council of Europe, attended the opening ceremony. Scholars and experts from Slovenia, Israel, Italy, Germany, Austria, Hungary, and the United States presented papers.

Neither the symposium nor the synagogue restoration had anything much to do with Jews per se. Few of the symposium participants were Jewish, and the fact that the symposium opened on the second night of the Jewish holiday of Sukkot caused at least one scheduled Jewish speaker to cancel. The events instead had to do with Slovenians and their perception of Jews as symbols—and of their drive to foster a sense of specific national history for the newly independent country. Peter Pavel Klasinc, deputy mayor of Maribor in the mid-1990s, who spearheaded the move to ensure that the synagogue's original character would be recognized in any restoration, told me, "After we became independent, Slovenians began to pay attention to their own history.

Before independence, our identity was subordinated as a part of Yugoslavia. Now we are on our own. In the past, Jews played an important role here, particularly in Maribor. We realize now that this is part of our national history." A survey of Jewish monuments in Slovenia that I had carried out a year earlier, thanks to an agreement between the Slovenian and U.S. governments, served the same end.[12] "Slovenia is a relatively small country with a very picturesque history," the director of the Cultural Heritage Office of Slovenia told me at the time. "Slovenia was always multicultural, so it is therefore interested in all cultural, material, and humanistic traces."

The mezuzah did not come from Slovenia, however. It was brought to Maribor by Mark Cohen, a Washington-based lawyer who had taught law at Maribor University several years earlier and was associated with the U.S. Commission for the Preservation of America's Heritage Abroad. Cohen attached it to the doorpost of the synagogue, and blessings were recited; it was the first time a Jewish religious symbol was associated with the building in half a millennium. Then the mezuzah was taken down. "It's just temporary and symbolic for now, as the synagogue is currently undergoing restoration, but we hope that when the work is complete the mezuzah will be affixed here permanently," Cohen said. No rabbi was in attendance; at the time there was none in Slovenia. Instead, Géza Komoróczy, a Hungarian Judaica scholar who had attended the symposium, recited blessings in Hebrew. Komoróczy heads the Center for Jewish Studies that was established at the Hungarian Academy of Sciences in 1988. He looks like a classic Jewish sage, with a long flowing beard—but he's not Jewish. Nonetheless, during the meals provided at the symposium, he was one of the few to choose prepackaged kosher food. He did so, he told me, to demonstrate "warm sympathy" for the Jewish people.

Also taking part in the ceremony was Mladen Svarc, at the time the coordinator of the Slovene Jewish community, which was then an unstructured organization that numbered fewer than one hundred members and carried out almost no religious or social communal function. Like almost all Jews in Slovenia, Svarc was secular and assimilated, and his family roots were not local. "In the name of the Jewish community of Slovenia," he said, "I want to express thanks that we have lived to see this day and that we will work together with the city of Maribor and all people who are trying to preserve this synagogue as a living monument. We will cooperate in the future so that this will be a living memorial to Slovenian Jews." Svarc was ousted from his position not long afterward.

Three years after the conference and the mezuzah ceremony, most of the outer restoration work on the synagogue had been completed, but it still had no exhibit inside, nor had a final plan been decided. In the meantime, a rabbi had taken up a part-time post in Slovenia, and religious sensibilities had begun to revive. Local Jewish leaders were insisting that the final restoration of the synagogue must include a prayer room.

Visitors walk among life-size cutout figures of photographs of prewar Jews, arranged inside the restored Izaak Synagogue in the former Jewish quarter of Kraków, 1997. (Photo by Ruth Ellen Gruber.)

PART THREE

Museum Judaism?

Representing Jewish Culture

Participants in these special tours should dress respectfully due to the nature of these sites, and men must cover their heads when visiting the synagogues, cemetery, and Terezín.

Brochure, Precious Legacy Tours, Prague

It is perhaps the ultimate absurdity that the remains of the history of a people that hardly ever enjoyed a secure place, sheltered against prosecution and assault, are housed in the protected rooms of a museum—accessible only at certain times, safe-guarded against trespassing and human touch.

Sabine Offe, "Sites of Remembrance?"

6

Seeing Is Believing

In a 1995 article on the Holocaust Memorial Museum in Washington, D.C., Philip Gourevitch wrote that he felt the Holocaust maxim "Remember" may be acquiring a new meaning with the passage of time. "What we cannot remember directly," he wrote, "we must imagine through representation, and our response is less immediately to the event than to the medium that has conveyed it to us."[1] Gourevitch was writing specifically about how the Holocaust is remembered and represented, but his observation extends to the entire sweep of Jewish heritage and historical experience.

The dilemmas involved in presenting—and representing—the Jewish phenomenon to, for, and by the mainstream public, and the philosophical, practical, and artistic questions that accompany this process, become especially acute when theory is put into practice and discovery or recovery makes the transition to display. The exploitation and marketing of Jewish sites and culture as tourist attractions and the contemporary proliferation of Jewish museums in places where few, sometimes no, Jews might live are two closely related areas in which these questions become particularly nuanced. Both are closely entwined with the overall recovery of the Jewish component by individuals and institutions. And both are obvious, opportune, often income-earning responses to the many still open questions regarding what to do with and how to manage newly recognized Jewish heritage sites.

Both, too, mediate the Jewish phenomenon physically as well as intellectually. They express, even define, in concrete visual, aural, spatial, tactile, and even gustatory terms what is, or what is considered to be,

"Jewish" or part of the Jewish experience. In setting these parameters, they can exoticize Jews and the Jewish world or delineate them as forming part of the national or local whole; they can represent Jews and their traditions as a living part of today's society, or they can consign them to a bygone era. They can also commodify the Jewish phenomenon by boiling it down to specific things to see and to hear, things to buy, things to eat and drink, things to do, personalities to admire. In doing so, they can end up reinforcing stereotypes, even if unwittingly.

The definitions and modes of representation depend on who does the defining and presenting—scholars, tour operators, civic culture authorities, commercial entrepreneurs, enthusiastic amateurs, religious leaders, Jewish communal structures, or whoever. The process often involves the marketing of associations or products of negative history in a positive way without seeming to be perverse or to trivialize tragedy.[2] How this is done is influenced and conditioned by markets, finances and funding sources, and local politics, as well as by the needs, knowledge, and expectations of widely varied target audiences that encompass Jewish roots seekers, pilgrims to Holocaust sites and Hasidic tombs, local schoolchildren and foreign study groups, mainstream and "Jewish Heritage" package tours, local residents looking for nostalgia (or expiation), and casual Jewish and non-Jewish observers. What works for some targets may deeply offend or alienate others.

The market can be as vast as it is varied, far outstripping the size of local Jewish populations and bulldozing minority sensitivities under the monster moneymaking press of mass appeal. Each year, more than 600,000 visitors, most of them foreign tourists, tour the Jewish Museum in Prague, and more than one million visitors walk more casually around Prague's former Jewish quarter: as much as the Old Town Square and Charles Bridge, a few minutes' walk away, the quarter is a "must-see" sight on any tourist itinerary of the city. Likewise, more than 200,000 people visit the Sephardi Museum in Toledo, Spain; as many as 70,000 or more visit the Jewish museums in Venice and Vienna. Some 10,000 visit the Jewish museum in out-of-the-way Hohenems annually; and 5,000 visited the Jewish museum in the quaint Bavarian market village of Schnaittach in the first nine months after it opened in 1996. Figures like these dwarf not only current Jewish populations. In quite a few instances they most likely outstrip the numbers of Jews who ever lived in these places.

Jewish museums, which often serve as anchors for broader Jewish tourism itineraries, are among the most significant tools with which Europeans seek to "fill in the blanks" regarding the Jewish phenomenon. As institutions that can easily be visited by the public, Jewish museums play an educational role that is of particular importance. They often become the public face of Judaism. Often, as in Hohenems and Schnaittach, or in Gorizia or Tykocin, they are the only visible, visitable, active "Jewish" presence for miles around, even if they are run by and were conceived by non-Jews; that the museums in Schnaittach, Gorizia, Tykocin, and Łańcut, Poland (among many others), are all located in old synagogue buildings reinforces this impression. "We are building museums where there is no longer Jewish life," the Italian Jewish scholar and communal leader Amos Luzzatto told a conference on Jewish museums held in Bologna in 1996. "It seems as if we are witnessing two phenomena that are parallel but go in opposite directions: the number of museums is growing; the communities disappear."[3]

Both the tourism and the museum experience entail the creation or promotion of Jewish virtualities: physical spheres and representations that are often complemented by publications, lecture programs, classes, festivals, and other activities. Bulletin boards, walls, and hoardings in neighborhoods or at or near sites delineated as "Jewish" bear prominent notices and posters for these events. Tourists, many of them Jews, "repopulate" old Jewish quarters and onetime shtetls. Jewish culture festivals draw crowds. Signs bear Jewish symbols, Hebrew lettering, or Latin lettering made to look like Hebrew. Jewish music—klezmer or cantorial—serves as a background score for Jewish museums, exhibitions, and restaurants. All this may give the impression of a living "Jewish" entity, a "collective impression" of Jewish life, history, or reality that in fact dwarfs or is quite unconnected with "real" Jewish populations or communal activities and is sometimes a dramatic mixture of fact, fiction, and fantasy. Even the physical parameters of these virtual Jewish worlds can be quite skewed.

I experienced this vividly one summer day in 1994, when I found myself sitting in a shiny, German-built minivan as it drove down a road paved with Jewish gravestones. The stones were fake—and I knew it. They were concrete casts of real tombstones, and they led into a fenced enclosure of crumbling barracks and rusting barbed wire that were also, I knew, simply stage sets. I was on a guided tour around Kraków of sites related to *Schindler's List*, Steven Spielberg's 1993 movie about the German industrialist who saved Jews during the Holocaust, which had opened in Europe several months before. Winner of seven Academy Awards, *Schindler's List* had already become an extraordinary tool for spreading Holocaust awareness—including awareness of the Holocaust and, by extension, the Jewish history of Kraków. Visitors who had once come to Kraków to enjoy the city's medieval Old Town and history-steeped castle, churches, and other attractions were now, thanks to the movie, adding sites of Jewish, Holocaust, and Schindler (or Spielberg) interest to what they wanted to see.

Local tourist agencies had quickly stepped in to serve this new market. The tour I went on was run by Jordan Tours, a private travel agency located in the Jewish quarter, Kazimierz, which had been offering tours of Jewish sites for several years. The route encompassed a mixture of celluloid and reality that I found deeply disconcerting. For nearly two hours we followed the sometimes tangled footsteps of Oskar Schindler and Steven Spielberg, visiting not only historical places from the Holocaust tragedy of Kraków's Jews but also various places in Kraków where Spielberg had shot scenes from his film: alleyways in Kazimierz, which had formed the backdrop of certain scenes in the movie, the district's untouched architecture standing in for the real site of the Kraków ghetto; the ghetto museum in the neighborhood across the river where the actual wartime ghetto had been located; points from which actors in the movie had looked down over the city (or at least had appeared, on film, to do so). We even were taken to see the factory where Schindler used Jewish labor to make enamelware. The factory, where some of the scenes from the movie were shot, still stood, though it now made electronic components—and in the wake of the movie's success, the factory staff had recently put up a small monument to Schindler in the courtyard.

Our guide, slightly cinematic himself in dark glasses with acid green earpieces, stumbled into confusion as he attempted to separate our Hollywood and Holocaust experience. "This," he said more than once, "existed in reality *and* in the film." Each site was given equal weight. The two-hundred-yard-long road of concrete tombstones and the fencing and barracks with fake tile roofs made out of now-tattered plastic were all that remained of Spielberg's set representing the Płaszów concentration camp. The Nazis built the real Płaszów on the site of a Jewish cemetery and really did build a road paved with tombstones through the camp. The film set, though, was situated not where Płaszów actually had existed but a couple miles away at the site of what had been a Nazi labor camp for non-Jewish Poles, dramatically located in an old quarry. The area now belonged to the Kraków sanitation department, and after the movie was shot, sanitation department trucks actually did rumble over the trail of fake tombstones taking loads of rubble and building material to a sort of dump at its end, just as Nazi trucks had done on the real road of tombstones half a century earlier. Our tour ended at the site of the real Płaszów camp. Nothing was there except for a bare windswept hill, two monuments to the camp's victims, one or two standing gravestones from the destroyed cemetery, and the house where the SS camp commander, Amon Goeth, had lived. The balcony from which Goeth really had played target practice with living prisoners, as shown in the film, was still there—complete with the satellite television antenna of its present residents.[4]

I spent the rest of the afternoon in Kazimierz. Browsing in the Jewish bookstore, I thumbed through postcards of Jewish sites, and I bought a little guidebook called *Retracing "Schindler's List"* whose front cover featured a photo of the fake but dramatic road paved with tombstones at the stage-set Płaszów camp and whose back cover featured a photo of the real but modest monument to Jewish victims that stands at the site of the real Płaszów. The text, too, followed the footsteps of both Spielberg and Schindler. "I am looking at [Kraków] as if it were a stage," it quoted Spielberg as saying. "A stage we didn't have to build. . . . [W]e are using ready scenes, we are filming authentic places where events depicted in *Schindler's List* really happened. Kraków has presented us with its history and opened its history handbooks for us so that we could dance on their pages."[5]

I wandered into a Jewish art gallery and visited the Jewish museum located in the Gothic Old Synagogue, a display of ritual objects and other material whose overwhelming message is that of absence: "A large synagogue empty of worshipers, containing books that will not be read and menorahs that will not be lit [and] objects that once belonged in every Jewish home that have here become precious artifacts, displayed behind glass, the exotic remnants of a lost civilization."[6] Tour groups and casual visitors like me made up a new kind of "congregation," some rapt and reverent, some footsore and ready to move on after seeing yet another sight. I had dinner at one of the Jewish-style restaurants, a pleasant place run by friendly people serving good food, a place where, in the summer, I have spent long hours sitting at an outdoor table watching passersby and meeting friends, including foreign tourists, professors and students at American university Jewish study programs held each summer at the nearby Center for Jewish Culture, performers and audiences at the Jewish Culture Festival, and even one or two local Kraków Jews. In the evenings, house klezmer and other Jewish music bands often play. On the wall, among the framed mirrors, wood panels, and dark paintings (including a retro-style painting of a shtetl scene by a contemporary Polish artist), hang framed autographs of Steven Spielberg and actors from *Schindler's List,* even a New Year's card from the entire smiling Spielberg family. (These, too, became attractions in themselves: a few years after my Schindler tour, I overheard a Polish guide urging a camera-draped American tourist in a safari vest, hat, and sunglasses to enter the restaurant. "Come in here," she urged him, "you can see Steven Spielberg's autographs.")

Before 1990 little of this upfront "Jewish-style" touristic infrastructure had existed. I was aware that there was another market of visitors to Jewish Kraków for whom much of it still had little, or indeed no, charm: Hasidic and other religious Jews who came to the city by the hundreds to pray in the Remuh Synagogue and venerate the tombs of ancestors and sages, above all the great sixteenth-century Talmudic scholar Moses ben Israel Isserles, known as Remuh, who is buried in the Old Jewish Cemetery. Once, such pilgrims were practically the only foreign Jews (and among the few foreigners at all) who visited the Jewish quarter. They pile memorial pebbles on tombstone ledges and stuff crevices with petitions on folded scraps of paper; when they are in town, the squares and alleyways—and the synagogue, too—are peopled by the bearded, sidelocked, caftaned, black-hatted figures whose iconized images stare out from photo books, pastiche paintings on restaurant and gallery walls, postcards, and kitschy wooden carvings. Other visitors, tourists and locals in their shorts and T-shirts, pull out their cameras and immortalize the scene.[7] For the fervently orthodox Jews, whose main purpose is prayer, and for the numerous Jewish groups and individuals whose overriding purpose in Poland is to consciously mourn the victims of the Holocaust, the commercial presence can seem an irrelevant, even sacrilegious, intrusion; a souvenir shop in a cemetery. It represents, however, an important transition: rather than sanctify Jewish Kazimierz as a place of mourning and remembrance, it signifies it instead as a place that can be "enjoyed."

7

The Tourist Track

Tourism has played a chicken-and-the-egg role in the Jewish archaeology process. This has been so especially since the waning and end of the Cold War enabled easy access to ancestral Jewish homelands, as well as the possibility for entrepreneurs to capitalize on new tourist trends. "Berlin walls fall, iron curtains rise and suddenly the vast expanses of Eastern Europe are open to view for increasing numbers of travelers eager to explore its riches and/or to investigate their own specific roots in the area," Gabe Levenson, travel writer for the New York *Jewish Week,* wrote as early as February 1990. "Tour operators are developing programs to satisfy a pent-up hunger for general information, and others are creating itineraries whose very particularity makes them exciting and newsworthy."[1]

But the boom in tourism to Jewish sites, both by Jews and by the mainstream public, has had an impact in other countries as well. Tourist interest and fulfilling tourist needs have become part and parcel of the recovery of Jewish heritage in Europe, a major part of why Jewish sites are preserved and presented. Once-neglected old Jewish quarters in Prague, Venice, and Berlin, as well as in Kraków, with their cafés, bookstores, and boutiques, figure by now as major stops on regular tourist itineraries and as popular hangouts for local people, too, while numerous new tourist guidebooks and Jewish travel agencies help foreign visitors and local people alike to find their way to once-forgotten Jewish sites that, like Boskovice, Třebíč, Hohenems, and Győr, are much farther off the beaten track.

Locally produced Jewish guidebooks exploded off the presses in the first years after the ouster of the communists. Jiří Fiedler's work was published as a guidebook in 1991; Jaroslav Klenovský began publishing a series of monographs on the Jewish history and sites of individual towns in Moravia at the same time and also produced a poster and post-cards of Moravian synagogues. A dozen or more guidebooks to Jewish sites in Polish towns and regions were published, in Polish and English, from the late 1980s onward.[2] *Jewish Heritage Travel,* my own guidebook to Jewish heritage sites in east central Europe, was first published in 1992. After she cowrote the first comprehensive Jewish guidebook to Italy in 1986, the Jewish writer and editor Annie Sacerdoti began edit-ing a series of detailed Jewish guidebooks to individual Italian regions in 1992. A guidebook to Jewish sites in Germany was published in Mu-nich in 1993, and another came out in 1997. Many mainstream general travel guides to various countries also added Jewish heritage sites to their entries. And state and local tourist organizations in Germany, Poland, the Czech Republic, Austria, and other countries also issued brochures, pamphlets, maps, and other information on Jewish heritage. In addition, hundreds of other new books, brochures, pamphlets, CD-ROMs, and web sites describe individual synagogues and cemeteries, catalog monuments, and detail the specific Jewish history of individual towns and regions in countries across the continent.

But in light of history and in the absence of Jews, an underlying question lingered amid all this activity. Can or should a Jewish heritage site or Jewish museum be treated the same way as any other tourist at-traction? Or must there be a balance between display and remembrance? Must commercialization be coupled with at least token commemora-tion? And what about Jews? Sometimes, as in Kraków, Jews themselves can be treated as museum pieces. Eli Valley, a young American who lived for several years in Prague, made this clear in an angry essay: "In the five summers since communism's collapse, [Prague's] Jewish Quar-ter has become a veritable Jurassic Park of Judaism, a Williamsburg for the conscience of Europe," he wrote in early 1995. ". . . On the street you can purchase a Jewish doll, complete with black robe and jumbo nose, for $50. In the eyes of the tourists, Jewish Prague is a circus of the dead. On the infrequent occasions that a Hasidic family visits the area, visitors abandon the dead religious objects and take out their cameras. They swarm even on an aged man, to capture him on film. And when I stand outside the Old-New Synagogue, wearing my yarmulke, I too am gawked at by the bemused mobs."[3]

In his book *Vanishing Diaspora,* Bernard Wasserstein pessimistically posited a Europe in which Jews remain but here and there, in small remnant groups, like the Amish in the United States. I have spent years trying to encourage visitors to east central Europe to include Jewish heritage sites on their tourist itineraries; one of the reasons I set out in 1989 to document Jewish sites and write a Jewish guidebook to east central Europe was my anger at the fact that Jewish sites were not on the tourist map. Echoing Marvin Lowenthal's concerns of nearly seventy years ago, I am convinced that Jewish heritage sites have their own intrinsic historic, artistic, and architectural value, in addition to their symbolic status as post-Holocaust survivors, as the legacy of a lost world.

But I am haunted by an image from childhood, a huge caricature of a bearded Amish man, looming at the side of the Pennsylvania Turnpike, advertising a Pennsylvania Dutch restaurant. As far as I know, there are not yet any billboards featuring happy Hasids pointing the way to a restored synagogue or Jewish museum.[4] But in Kraków's Kazimierz, a huge illuminated iron menorah flanked by rearing lions towers over the entrance to one of the several Jewish-style restaurants, luring in the tour bus trade. In Bavaria's Georgensgmünd the same signpost points the way to the restored synagogue and Jewish cemetery as well as to the train station and a waterwheel; in a poor choice of words a pamphlet for Jewish travelers in Germany, issued by the German National Tourist Office in about 1989, notes that "[o]ne of the best features for tourists in Germany is the rail network." Outside the rust-colored Tuscan hilltown of Pitigliano, a billboard advertises the Jewish cemetery and recently rebuilt sixteenth-century synagogue as major sights of the town. By 1998 the old Jewish quarter of Třebíč, where no Jews live, boasted Jacob's Snack Bar, the Synagogue Guest House, the Jewish Grocery, and Rachel's Wine Cellar. Tourists who tired of the Jewish sites in Boskovice could drive a few miles out of town to Wild West City, a cowboys-and-Indians theme park of corrals, saloons, and stage-set "High Noon" streets set up in an abandoned quarry. Will Things Jewish become the roadside attractions of the twenty-first century?

Routes

Modern tourism has been compared to the religious pilgrimages of old, with today's travelers substituting "secular saints" for former religious heroes and creating secular tourist pilgrimage itineraries around sites and places linked with these people.[5] Ideas, eras, events, and even entire geographies also engender sites that must be visited, history that must be "entered," and realities that must be "established." Wars and the Holocaust itself have generated their own powerful itineraries of commemoration. Cultures—or their trappings—are promoted and marketed within this framework as part of what is described as the "heritage industry."[6] Jewish theme travel and tourism (aside from specific Holocaust commemoration) now increasingly enters this commercial and highly marketed mainstream, as the Jewish component as a whole is welcomed into the European fold. Schindler's Kraków, Henry Kissinger's Fürth, "Budapest Through Jewish Eyes," complete with a klezmer concert, "In the Footsteps of the Jews of Tarnów," and so forth, take their place as valid, if still somewhat off-the-beaten-track, itineraries, alongside Mozart's Salzburg, Shakespeare's Stratford-upon-Avon, Battlefields of the Ardennes, and the Wineries of Chianti. "Place promotion has become an important actor on the stage of local and regional economic regeneration over the years," writes the Haifa University scholar Stanley Waterman. "Selling a place to the wider world, or selling the culture as an inseparable part of the place, rapidly becomes a significant facet of many forms of Jewish culture. If the selling is successful, then the culture becomes an important image-maker in its own right."[7] Synagogues and Jewish museums; ghetto areas and Jewish cemeteries; Holocaust memorials and Jewish Heritage Trails: marked now by plaques, designated on tourist street maps, pictured in brochures and tourist handouts, listed in Jewish heritage and mainstream guidebooks, and advertised on the Internet, they are part of the official tourist landscape, complemented by the array of cultural events, commerce, and visitors that make them "come alive."

The sites have always been there, but they were ignored or presented in a different guise: aside from a few major attractions, most promotion of Jewish sites after World War II was limited and aimed at an internal Jewish market.[8] Tourism providers, entrepreneurs, and local boosters now recognize that Jewish sites and personalities can define the identity or atmosphere of a town or neighborhood as much as do churches, kings, and city halls. The same non-Jewish (or nonreligious Jewish) tourists who take souvenir pictures of pious Jews at prayer in Prague or Kraków will often themselves place a pebble on a tombstone, without knowing who is buried there or why the pebble is placed: it is part of the "Jewish cemetery" experience. This change in mind-set, in a broad sense, places visits to Jewish sites within the framework of "tourism" rather than that of "travel."

"Discovery" is an initial key. For Jews, many of whom grew up believing that nothing was left in the old country after the Shoah, it is the discovery of the tangible evidence of their own heritage, in the general as well as personal sense—and the discovery that they can actually go to see it, touch it, and photograph it and even send a picture postcard home or buy a trinket to remember the experience. This concept is particularly powerful in regard to eastern Europe. The American Jewish genealogist Miriam Weiner, who in 1990 led the first organized group of Jewish genealogists to work in Polish archives, wrote, "How often have you heard someone say 'my ancestral shtetl was wiped off the map during the Holocaust and all the records were destroyed'? It is simply not true."[9] But it is a discovery, too, of the instrinsic value of this heritage, and of history, as Sacerdoti put it, that flourished not just in famous major centers but also in small towns and out-of-the-way villages—where it left traces that edify and astonish.

For mainstream tourists, the experience may represent the discovery of a drowned or hidden world, a "heritage worth getting to know, exceptionally rich and varied," as one French tourist board slogan puts it; the world is next door and now increasingly accessible but still somewhat exotic—and, in some representations, as remote from today's realities as the Renaissance or ancient Romans.[10] For seasoned travelers, it may also be, more simply, the discovery of new or different sights to see, alongside the time-honored old standbys. For first-time visitors, the Jewish sites that are increasingly included as integral parts of mainstream itineraries or listed as regular sights in mainstream guidebooks represent part of the overall discovery of a town or country or region.

Whereas the changes vis-à-vis Jewish-theme tourism have been most dramatic in postcommunist east central Europe, three travel brochures on France vividly illustrate shifting approaches regarding even one of the world's great, long-established tourist markets. They demonstrate overt global changes in the concept of what a Jewish attraction is and what kind of visitors they are expected—or aimed—to attract. Jews and non-Jews alike travel to France for a complex of experiences: the scenery, the history, the art and architecture, the food, the romance. There have long been remarkable collections of Judaica and Jewish historical material in several museums, including the Louvre and the Cluny.[11] But until recently Jewish historical and heritage sites figured little either in tourist promotion or in national monuments preservation policy: while only a dozen Jewish sites were listed as historic monuments in France in 1980, for example, some fifty were on the list by 1994.[12]

A booklet titled *France for the Jewish Traveler,* printed in the United States in the 1980s and issued in cooperation with the French Government Tourist Office, was aimed at "the Jewish traveler who may also desire to meet his co-religionists." [13] Its cover pictures include typical French tourist shots—the Eiffel Tower, a château, a wine-tasting— as well as photographs of kosher restaurants and the entrance to a synagogue. The text stresses living Jewish communities in a country of (as the brochure estimated) seven hundred thousand Jews; France's Jewish attractions are its active synagogues, kosher eateries, Jewish community centers, and bustling life. The brochure sketches in Jewish history in some locations and notes a few major Jewish historical sites or museum collections, but its main purpose is to provide a link to Jewish social and religious infrastructure for Jewish tourists on conventional sight-seeing trips: where to pray, where to eat, where to shop, where to meet other Jews between visits to châteaus and cathedrals. It is indicative that in describing the historic synagogues in Carpentras and Cavaillon, now more museums than active houses of worship, hours for religious services are given.

The Road to Jewish Heritage in the South of France, an English-language booklet issued in 1993 by the Tourist Office of Vaucluse, on the other hand, and *A la découverte du judaïsme alsacien,* a multilingual brochure printed in 1998 by the Alsace tourist board, take a completely different approach. They are aimed at mainstream tourists, Jewish and non-Jewish alike, and Jewish heritage sites, not contemporary Jewish contexts, are the main and indeed practically the only attraction. They—and the thinking behind them—thus are products of the new Jewish archaeology process.

Jews flourished in the south of France in the Middle Ages. Despite expulsion in 1394, they were able to remain in several towns in the Comtat Venaissin, which was ruled by the popes, living in quarters or Jewish streets called *carrières.* Among these towns were Carpentras and Cavaillon. Jews also flourished in Alsace in medieval times; after persecution in the mid-fourteenth century, they lived mainly in dozens of rural communities, maintaining this pattern after Alsace was annexed by France in 1675. The communities prospered after emancipation—some 176 synagogues were built in Alsace between 1791 and 1914—but began to die out in the latter part of the nineteenth century. About one quarter of the Alsatian Jews were killed in the Holocaust, and after the war most rural communities disappeared as survivors moved to big cities. Abandoned village synagogues and other sites shared the same fate of neglect and transformation that occurred in other countries whose postwar Jewish population was radically diminished.

The cover of the Alsace tourist brochure features photographs of synagogue exteriors and interiors, evocative old Jewish tombstones, an ancient *mikvah,* and embroidered synagogue textiles. That of the south of France booklet shows a painting of a menorah. Inside photographs in both booklets feature museums, artifacts, ancient *mikvaot,* picturesque cemeteries and synagogues, and beautiful items of Judaica. Both brochures provide historical text and maps tracing routes or pinpointing sites; in Alsace, France's richest region for Jewish heritage sites, more than two hundred places are noted, none of which was mentioned in the earlier *France for the Jewish Traveler* booklet.

Not one contemporary living person, however, is portrayed in either the Alsace or the south of France brochure. The latter includes a 1913 photograph of a man standing by the Ark of the Cavaillon Synagogue, with the caption, "Old [view] of the Cavaillon Synagogue in use." Otherwise, the only human figures to be seen are in old paintings and drawings and, in the Alsace brochure, which includes a summary of Jewish communal and family religious traditions, costumed effigies of a family at a Seder table in the newly opened Alsatian Jewish Museum in Bouxwiller. Addresses are listed for two kosher wineries and two matzo bakeries in Alsace, which can be toured, but there are no addresses in either booklet for any kosher restaurants. For people who want to visit "synagogues in use," the Alsace booklet provides the contact numbers of the two Alsatian Consistoires (regional Jewish communal organizations), but otherwise no addresses for active Jewish communities or communal organizations are provided in either brochure. Both brochures instead list numbers for local tourism boards and tourist offices in various towns.

Even for Marseilles—one of the main Jewish centers in France today, with two dozen active synagogues and a Jewish population of more than seventy thousand—the south of France brochure listing reads: "All the old aspects of the Jewish community have disappeared. However, one can still admire the 19th century main synagogue." The accompanying photograph shows a huge, ornate sanctuary lit by glowing chandeliers. A worn prayer book lies open in the foreground, but the synagogue is totally empty; it is listed as being closed on Saturday. The implied message is that the Jewish chapter in this part of France belongs to the past. The brochure text expounds this point; its references to Jews are all in the past tense, as if Jewish life, culture, and development stopped long ago and never revived: "The historic road we propose aims to provide better knowledge of several of the largest and most important Jewish communities in Southern France through the visit of the 'carrières,' synagogues and museums. This road offers a panoramic view of a different world, adding a special dimension to the usual touristic itineraries. Encountering the Carrière means taking a journey back to the past." Each photograph in the brochure is presented in a frame: the impression is that they hang, enshrined, as museum exhibits.

This approach is a striking form of recognizing Jewish history as national history, part of the French historic whole. The sites are presented not so much as specific "Jewish heritage" but as "the heritage of Jews" who once lived in France—not, by implication, heritage that had anything to do with the Jewish immigrants from North Africa who make up a large segment of French Jewry today and worship in at least some of the old synagogues. As in brochures describing historic castles, churches, and cathedrals, the sites are depicted in architectural, historical, liturgical, and art-historical terms only: that is, for outside visitors rather than for actual "users."

At least in the case of Alsace, I was told, the choice not to include contact information for contemporary Jewish communities, kosher restaurants, and the like was a political decision, based on France's strict laws separating church and state. The authorities, including the tourist board, refused to fund any published material that might have been viewed as promoting a specific religion or religious operation.[14] Nevertheless, in their lack of information on Jewish contemporary contexts, these French brochures differ strikingly from similar brochures promoting Jewish heritage that were published in the 1990s by, or in association with, the national tourist authorities in Austria and Hungary. *Jewish Vienna & Austria: Heritage and Mission* and *Shalom: Jewish Relics in Hungary* focus on illustrations of and information on cemeteries, abandoned or transformed synagogues, artifacts, Judaica objects, and Jewish museums.[15] But they also feature photographs of today's living Jewish communities and provide long lists of addresses and telephone numbers of Jewish institutions and communal offices, kosher restaurants, and Jewish schools. Both brochures thus present today's local Jewish communities as attractions in themselves. Tourists need not actually visit Jewish communal institutions, but knowledge of their existence is deemed important as providing context.

The Austria brochure openly places the recognition of Jewish heritage within the process of "coming to terms with the past" that was sparked by the campaign and election of Kurt Waldheim as president in 1986, despite revelations that he had (and had hidden) a Nazi past: "Recent events in Austrian politics have triggered probing discussions about the country's past throughout Austria. As a result, during the past few years, Austrians have dealt extensively with the Jewish heritage in their country's history. . . . It was not until the eighties that a large segment of the Austrian population began to realize that Austrians were implicated in the crimes of the Nazi dictatorship and not merely its victims." The Hungary brochure is a conspicuous example of the embrace of the Jewish phenomenon as part of the postcommunist effort to fill in the blanks: "This publication commemorates the 600,000 deported, the ones who never returned, and the few that were saved, presenting the heritage, the historical values, culture and present of Hungarian Jewry. This is not only the confontation of the survivors with the ancient past, but also a part of Hungarian history and Hungarian culture."

Despite its omissions, the Alsace brochure was prepared in an exemplary collaboration between public tourist authorities and local Jewish institutions and individuals, primarily the Jewish B'nai B'rith association in Strasbourg. The collaboration, whose evolution was described at the January 1999 Paris conference on European Jewish heritage, represents an approach to promotion of Jewish heritage sites that is intensive, innovative, and even aggressive in its scope and methodology. It goes far beyond the simple tracing of Jewish heritage routes or the presentation of Jewish sites and Jewish history in guidebook form— whether by official national travel boards or by private publishing houses or Jewish communities. And it goes far beyond the organic or localized type of promotion, development, and exploitation that has grown up in individual places. Rather, the Alsatian plan entails a formidable interconnected and strategically coordinated series of initiatives that encompass the complete path of Jewish heritage rediscovery, recovery, exploitation, and display. Success of this model has led to additional, professionally coordinated cross-border projects involving Jewish and non-Jewish bodies in more than a dozen countries. It is worth describing in some detail.

The partnership coalesced in the 1990s as the result of convergent objectives that neither the tourism authorities nor Alsatian Jews could attain independently. A slowly ripening internal Jewish concern with saving neglected Jewish heritage dovetailed with the tourist board's aim of developing novel, income-earning itineraries that would draw new tourists to the region. The tourist board had the financial, organizational, and marketing resources to put such a plan into action, but it needed the sanction and support of the Jewish body before going ahead. Most synagogues, for example, even those that had long stood abandoned, still belong to the Jewish community. Also, noted Claude Bloch, director of the Heritage Commission of B'nai B'rith in Strasbourg, "[t]here was a lack of knowledge, a fear of encroaching on sacred territory."[16]

Among Jews, new recognition of the value of the hundreds of Jewish heritage sites began dawning in Alsace, as elsewhere, in the mid-1980s. In 1984 committed individuals founded a lobbying group with the specific aim of saving the derelict synagogue in Bouxwiller from demolition and establishing a museum there dedicated to Alsatian Jewry. Their object was to foster self-knowledge of Jewish heritage among Jews themselves as well as to spread knowledge among the mainstream. This group, together with the Heritage Commission, eventually expanded its focus to include the preservation of Alsatian Jewish heritage in general. Their activities, however, were frustrated by obstacles ranging from a lack of finances to a lack of concern on the part of public authorities. "In 1984 the problem of abandoned and derelict synagogues in villages was a taboo subject," said Gilbert Weil, president of the Association of Friends of the Jewish Museum at Bouxwiller and a prime mover behind these activities. Local authorities, he said, felt that any action regarding these places was solely the responsibility of local Jews— but Jewish officialdom at the time had little interest either.

Formal partnership with the tourism authorities began about a decade later, in large part in response to the growing trend in "heritage tourism." Catherine Lehmann, of the Bas-Rhin Tourist Development Agency (ADT) in Strasbourg, said, "Developing cultural tourism, fostering memory-building sites, was fashionable at the time. Also a type of pilgrimage tourism based on religious curiosity, as well as roots tourism. Tourists are finding new elements to discover." (Lehman's own Jewish identity also piqued her own personal interest.) The ADT provided an organizational framework and direction and worked with the B'nai B'rith to plot a detailed planning program and step-by-step marketing strategy aimed at making Jewish heritage a major tourist attraction in Alsace while remaining responsive to Jewish sensibilities.

The process was a coordinated, unsentimental battle plan incorporating everything from regionwide on-site surveys to in-depth market feasibility studies. First, a detailed inventory of sites was undertaken to ascertain what was there and to assess tourism potential. Working groups were set up, and sites were selected for promotion as key attractions that could anchor interconnected tourist routes. Researchers discovered that isolated local initiatives in the reuse of synagogues and other buildings for cultural purposes were already under way. These, it was decided, could be encouraged, advised, supported, and incorporated into the global scheme. Besides Weil's project for the transformation of the synagogue of Bouxwiller into a Jewish museum (which eventually opened in 1997), these included the restoration of the disused synagogue in Pfaffenhoffen, which was built in 1791. The French government had recently listed this synagogue as a national historic monument, and the World Monuments Fund had included it on its 1996 list of ten Jewish site preservation priorities. The synagogue was totally restored, with regional and national monuments authorities contributing 70 percent of the total funds, and by 1998 it was opened to the public.

Meanwhile, the B'nai B'rith organized a training program for Jewish heritage tour guides and interpreters, which attracted about forty people. As work progressed, concerted efforts were made to prepare the market by raising the issue of Jewish heritage and its value in the minds of the local public. Crucial in this was the orchestration and promotion of "Open Days" of Jewish culture, events during which selected Jewish sites were opened to the public. The events were experiments to test public interest and were publicized primarily on the local level. Local people (but also tourists) were invited to visit Jewish sites and participate in a coordinated series of cultural programs, guided tours, and other initiatives. The first example took place in summer 1996, when some five thousand people visited eighteen Jewish heritage sites. The second Open Day was organized in June 1997, when thirty sites—most in Alsace but a few over the border in Germany—welcomed about ten thousand visitors. Both years about 90 percent of the visitors were non-Jewish local residents.

The success of these two experiments encouraged the ADT and the B'nai B'rith to launch a full-scale promotion of Jewish heritage tourism in Alsace and to plan a much more elaborate Open Day for 1998. That summer, a number of new sites were opened to the public for the first time. Many were kept open throughout the summer. Meanwhile, between June and September, some 130 events—concerts, lectures, guided tours—were staged on thirteen individual Open Days. Marketing and public relations were carried out for the first time on a national, even international scale with extensive media coverage and some two thousand promotional posters. The events drew approximately twenty thousand visitors, far more than had been anticipated. ADT officials said they were particularly pleased on two counts: the events had made many towns aware of the importance of local Jewish heritage, and they had fostered collaboration between Jewish communities and local municipalities. For example, the municipality repainted the facade of the eighteenth-century synagogue in Mutzig, which is owned but rarely used by Jews. The Jewish Consistoire did some repairs on the disused synagogue in Westhoffen. The B'nai B'rith, meanwhile, mobilized about fifty volunteers to serve as guides and provide information to visitors.

The publication of the Alsace brochure in 1998 took the promotional campaign into a new, more commercial and concentrated stage. At the Paris conference on European Jewish heritage, the ADT's Catherine Lehmann and the B'nai B'rith's Claude Bloch outlined a comprehensive planning program for the coming year. Their presentation seemed almost relentless in its dynamism and demonstrated a new type of professional polish in the selling of Jewish sites as destinations. The agenda they outlined included lobbying efforts to have Jewish heritage programmed on general package tours of Alsace, creation of a web site, and extensive marketing activities. Lehmann said talks had been initiated with Michelin and other publishers to have Alsatian Jewish heritage sites incorporated in general travel guidebooks. And there were plans to present Jewish Heritage in Alsace itineraries to the thousands of participants at the annual American Society of Travel Agents convention, to be held in Strasbourg at the end of the year. Plans for the 1999 Open Day of Jewish Heritage, she said, were to focus on just one date, August 29. Local Jewish authorities would be more closely and actively involved in the endeavor, and for the first time all two hundred Jewish heritage sites in the region, including those that to date had been closed to the public, would open their doors to visitors. She also outlined a wide array of Jewish-theme concerts, exhibitions, lectures, and other cultural events to be held throughout the summer. A new, English-language edition of the Alsace brochure, issued in June 1999, included more information on contemporary Jewish life.

Lehmann and Bloch's presentation caught the imagination of several people associated with Jewish organizations and institutions who already had begun working on Jewish heritage agendas. The newly formed Jewish Heritage Committee of the European Council of Jewish Communities (ECJC) joined forces with the Alsace activists, with the result that August 29 served as a hastily coordinated international

Open Day involving some seventy-five sites in Spain, Switzerland, Italy, France, and Germany. This led to even more ambitious plans for a European Day of Jewish Culture on September 3, 2000. Coordinated by the Alsace ADT, in cooperation with B'nai B'rith Europe and the ECJC, planning started well in advance, and by May 2000 sites in more than a dozen countries were on the list. The ADT prepared detailed instruction guidelines directed to participants, including Jewish communities, Jewish museums, tourist agencies, and municipalities. It also prepared coordinated slogans, logos, and poster designs, which were made available print-ready on CD-ROMs. The initiative was also listed under a Council of Europe program promoting multiculturalism, "Europe, a Common Heritage." In the end, September 3 events involved hundreds of sites in sixteen countries and drew more than 150,000 visitors, 47,000 in Italy alone. Associated events ranged from concerts to Jewish food tastings.

Roots

If the Alsace example was a proactive search to attract, indeed, to create, tourist markets, the experience in postcommunist eastern and central Europe was, at least initially, a reactive response as millions rushed in eager to visit places that the Iron Curtain had made either off-limits or off the beaten track for many decades. The new tourist influx paralleled the burst of taboo-busting, local interest in the Jewish phenomenon. The display, representation, and exploitation of Jewish heritage and heritage sites, as well as infrastructure and services by tourism providers and facilitators, had to fulfill the needs and expectations of very diverse markets, ranging from people with a casual, primarily abstract or literary interest in Things Jewish to those for whom every town, building, and square inch of earth had a hallowed place in personal or collective memory. The transition from "travel" to "tourism" has thus taken different forms and guises.

These differences can be seen in the Czech Republic and Poland, the two countries in the region where Jewish culture and heritage have been put to the broadest and most cultivated touristic use. In each, different approaches were mandated by specific history, historic memory, Holocaust experience, and the emotional centrality of the Jewish phenomenon, as well as by new commercial interests, opportunities, and markets and by the number and type of tourists. In short, although nearly eighty thousand Czech Jews were killed by the Nazis, encountering the Jewish experience and relics in the Czech Republic can be, for Jews and non-Jews, a relatively detached, quite positive experience and is promoted as such, whereas in Poland, even positive experiences such as pleasant evenings in Kraków's Jewish-style cafés are inevitably underlain by thick, emotional layers of uneasiness and sharp whiffs of the grave. Indeed, people engaged in Jewish-theme tourism in Poland, like those engaged in related endeavors, often describe their activities as part of a broader mission. "This is a special place, Kazimierz," the proprietor of the Jordan Jewish bookstore there told me in 1997. "People who are working here are trying to do something. More hotels, restaurants, cafés, and businesses in Kazimierz make it more alive—and this place should be alive! From the beginning, we knew our shop should be a special place—after all, we're not selling shoes! We created a special place, and we are happy that people know where they can get help. It is more comfortable for Poles, and Jews, to come here to find out information on Jews, because here we sell only Jewish books—some people are not comfortable about buying books on Jewish topics in a big bookstore; there is still something in the air in Poland about these things, I wouldn't call it anti-Semitism, but a strange feeling in the air." Said Kazik Kuc, the former Catholic priest who at the time ran a Jewish souvenir stand in front of the bookstore, "There are barriers between Poles and Jews, between Catholics and Jews. I want to break them down." Barbara Olszowy, a non-Jewish woman in the central Polish city of Kielce, even opened a travel agency in the building that was the center of the infamous 1946 pogrom that killed forty-two Jews and became an emblem of Polish anti-Semitism. Its interior was decorated with modern Jewish art, and in a 1994 interview she said she chose that location for her business because "it was [her] moral obligation to preserve the memory of what happened here."[17]

It is in the Czech Republic, particularly in Prague, that the representation and "selling" of the Jewish component as an integral part of the mainstream—and to a mainstream, not necessarily Jewish, public—has been most diligent, organized, and universal.[18] Captivated by the night-to-day drama of the so-called Velvet Revolution as well as by the city's physical charms, tourists flocked to Prague in unprecedented numbers and from all social and economic categories. This engendered a fierce and sudden market competition among entrepreneurs and tourism providers, as well as a rush to muster adequate infrastructure to accommodate the new wave of visitors.[19] All of Prague's glorious architecture, charming cobbled alleyways, and richly fascinating history became an attraction—including its important Jewish component. Just as Rabbi Löw and the Golem were reinforced as symbols of Prague the magic and mysterious, Franz Kafka, the Czech Jew who wrote in German, whose sisters died at Auschwitz, whose work was discouraged if not outright banned under communism, became the symbol of the multicultural "Mitteleuropean" ideal, so diametrically opposed to the monolithic imprint of the ousted regime.

The headlong tourist influx produced a market for Jewish souvenirs, postcards, books, T-shirts, and other tourist items. But this exuberant exploitation was not confined to Jewish Prague. Virtually *all* of historic Prague attracted swarms of tourists and generated similar kitsch; for most visitors, Prague's Jewish sites became simply parts of a kaleidoscopic whole. Specific discomfiture associated with the staggering tourist exploitation of Prague's Jewish heritage—Eli Valley's "Jurassic Park" of Judaism—is associated with the fact that it has turned Jewish history, particularly the tragic recent history of Jews there, into just another of the city's many draws. On the other hand, Jewish entrepreneurs and the Jewish community itself eagerly embraced the trend. The tourist influx generates much-needed income for the 1,500-member Prague Jewish community, which has its seat in the old Jewish quarter. The Jewish community draws rents from some of the souvenir stands and other commercial spaces, and local Jews (and some Israelis) are among the entrepreneurs cashing in on the crowds. The Jewish Museum was scolded by some for hiking admission prices after it was returned to Jewish management, but museum directors say this was a deliberate means of raising funds after state subsidies were withdrawn.[20] One of the three Jewish-run travel agencies located in the quarter and specializing in Jewish heritage tours is run under Jewish communal auspices—and has a souvenir shop featuring the same sort of kitsch, including caricature "Jewish" marionettes—as do privately run commercial kiosks. "On the one hand, we hate [the commercialization] because it's terrible in its essence, its substance," Tomas Kraus, secretary of the Federation of Jewish Communities in the Czech Republic, told me in 1997. "On the other hand, it enables us to live. Because this is a big financial tool, an engine of income."

In this milieu, new Jewish-run tour agencies compete for business with mainstream agencies by paradoxically offering tours of Jewish Prague that, arranged and guided by Jews, set Jewish sites *apart* from the rest of the city and aim to provide a more "authentic" or meaning-ful experience with a personalized Jewish touch. Guides employed by Jewish tour agencies for visits to Terezín frequently include survivors of the wartime Terezín ghetto; they are advertised as such, becoming "sights" themselves. In April 1997 I joined three other people on a walk-ing tour of Jewish Prague run by one of these agencies, Precious Legacy Tours, which was founded and operated by Ljuba Poleva, a young Jew-ish woman who became a tour guide in 1993, several years after she and her family emigrated to Prague from then-Soviet Ukraine. She named her agency after the famous "Precious Legacy" exhibit of objects from the State Jewish Museum that toured the United States and other coun-tries to widespread success in the 1980s. "I wanted it to have a Jewish-associated name but not a name that would keep non-Jewish clients away," she told me. "Precious Legacy is a name people remember."

Our guide was a retired teacher named Susanna, who was a Holo-caust survivor. Our small group threaded its way in and around big groups of restive teenagers from Italy, France, and Germany who were on school trips to Prague during spring break. In the Maisel Synagogue, where the Jewish Museum displays a historical exhibit, at least five of these groups came and went during the time that Susanna moved us slowly from one display case to the next. Susanna spoke slowly and softly and made every step personal, detailing her own recollections and experiences. Her stories were so compelling that other people drifted over to listen. When we looked at the Jewish Museum's famous exhibit of drawings by children who were prisoners at Terezín, she gathered us around her in a tight knot as she dramatically pulled a folded piece of manilla paper out of her bag. It was a drawing of a menorah, with birth-day greetings to "Auntie" from a boy, she told us, who died in Terezín in 1944. Holding the paper, she quietly recounted her own experiences at Terezín, telling how she worked in the garden and stole vegetables to give to three children and describing the transport that took her hus-band away to his death. Susanna may have told the same stories in the same way to every group she led, but it was a spellbinding moment nonetheless. Later, she told me she had started working as a guide to the Jewish Museum after she retired in the early 1980s, when the mu-seum was run by the communist state and there were relatively few vis-itors. For her, she said, it marked a reconnection with the Jewish culture and world she had rejected after the Holocaust: after returning from Terezín, she had become an idealistic communist until the anti-Jewish show trials in the 1950s—during which she was compelled to vote for false, rubber stamp condemnations of Jews—left her bereft of political as well as religious beliefs.

Precious Legacy competed head to head with Wittmann Tours, founded in 1990 by Sylvie Wittmann, a Czech Jew, born in 1956, who was involved in clandestine Jewish study groups in the 1980s and pioneered organized Jewish tourism in the Czech Republic after the fall of communism.[21] Her original program featured Prague walking tours and one weekly trip to Terezín. By 1997 Wittmann Tours had grown to have a fleet of two minivans, a seventeen-seat bus, and other, rented vehicles at its disposal, featured daily trips to Terezín—where Wittmann and four partners opened a Jewish-style restaurant called Sabra—and ran several different Prague tours. From the beginning, however, Wittmann offered more than just the opportunity to tour Jewish sites with a Jewish guide or to tour Terezín with a Holocaust surivor. She offered visitors—and also local Czechs—the possibility of participating in informal Jewish religious services, discussions, and study sessions as part of a group called Bejt Simcha that she established and operated, along with the travel agency, out of her apartment. In addition to tourists, Bejt Simcha, modeled after communist-era Jewish study groups, was designed to attract non-Orthodox Jews, local people with Jewish ancestry who wanted to explore their Jewish identity but were not Jewish according to Halakhah—and thus could not join the official Prague Jewish community—and non-Jewish Czechs who were interested in Judaism. Peter Muk, the leader of the Shalom rock group, attended. Wittmann trained other members of the group to work as guides for Wittmann Tours. Bejt Simcha eventually affiliated with the reform Jewish movement, and one member, a Czech woman whose father was Jewish, converted formally to Judaism and undertook rabbinical training at the Leo Baeck College in London.

"There are people who identify themselves with Jews through the chimneys of Auschwitz," Wittmann told me in 1995, describing people who attended Bejt Simcha or who manifested interest in Things Jewish in other ways. "Some of them have ancestors who suffered in the Holocaust. Then there are people who feel like outsiders within local society. They are oversensitive, intellectual, and so on. Somehow, somewhere they find a Jewish ancestor. That qualifies their 'otherness.' There are a lot of people like this. There are people who do not have a Jewish ancestor, and are not searching for a Jewish ancestor, but for whom it is interesting to be connected with mysticism, something spiritual that is not necessarily Christianity. They don't want to be *part* of Jewish life and culture but to be *in touch* with it. Then, too, there are Christians, aged forty and up. Deeply believing Christians. They can be called Christian Zionists. They associate with Jews, help Jews, and believe that when all Jews are back in Sinai, then Jesus Christ will reappear."

The evolution of Jewish and Jewish-theme tourism in Poland had quite a different dynamic. It was linked to the gradual public opening to the Jewish component throughout the 1980s and to a more gradual growth in tourism after the fall of communism—but above all to the powerful, special place held by Poland in Jewish history and memory, both for Jews and for local Poles. For Jewish visitors, as for local Poles, the Holocaust, and dense, divided, and contested memory over the prelude to and destruction of Polish Jewry, provided a deep and inescapable matrix for any and all such activities. Jewish travelers went to Poland for highly specific reasons and with concrete expectations that—unlike in Prague—had nothing to do with conventional tourism. Few Jews visited Poland simply to sight-see, and even fewer went to have a good time. Jews went to Poland to remember, and many conquered deeply ingrained fears to make the trip. The anthropologist Jack Kugelmass wrote in 1993, "[T]here is something unique about Jewish tourism in Poland. Jewish tourists see nothing quaint about the local culture either Jewish or non-Jewish; their interest is the dead rather than the living. They go as antiquarians rather than ethnographers; consequently, they bring back with them no experiences that deepen their knowledge of the local culture. The experiences they remember are likely to be those that enhance an already existing negative opinion. Indeed, they are the experiences they expect to have in Poland, and because they confirm deeply held convictions, they are almost a desired part of the trip."[22]

Aside from religious pilgrims, Jews who traveled to Poland during the first few postwar decades tended to be survivors returning to their hometowns, sometimes to maintain contact with friends and neighbors who aided them during the war. Jews began traveling to Poland in greater and continually growing numbers in the 1980s, after the short-lived success of the Solidarność movement. Indeed, tourism by Jews was encouraged as part of the calculated political line of the communist regime. This policy intensified particularly after low-level relations between Poland and Israel were established in 1986 (full diplomatic relations were established after the ouster of the communists) and opened the country to Israeli visitors. The vast majority of this new wave of Jewish visitors came in organized tour groups, often sponsored as fund-raising missions by organizations such as the United Jewish Appeal. The trips took on the guise of pilgrimages: for the majority, this meant a pilgrimage to Auschwitz-Birkenau and other death camps. Many such "Holocaust" tours continued from Poland to Israel, accentuating their message of destruction and redemption. Such trips became standard for Israeli high school students in the late 1980s and were also programmed by synagogues and other Jewish organizations for North American Jewish teenagers. The aim was to combat a perceived crisis in Jewish continuity by what amounted to shock therapy and to strengthen Jewish identity by promoting Zionism. The teens would be shown Holocaust sites in Poland and then be taken immediately to Israel to celebrate the rebirth of the Jewish nation.

The biggest of these Holocaust youth pilgrimages was founded in 1988 as the March of the Living. Each edition of the March (originally held every two years but later changed to an annual event) has taken thousands of Jewish teens from many countries, all of them dressed in identical blue jackets with a big Star of David on the back, on a rapid tour of the site of the Warsaw Ghetto, Auschwitz and other death camps such as Treblinka and Majdanek, and sometimes a small town, like Tykocin, that still has the look of a prewar shtetl and thus emphasizes today's Jewish vacuum. The culmination is a mass march from Auschwitz to Birkenau on Holocaust Remembrance Day (Yom haShoah), generally in April, after which the teens are flown to Israel to celebrate Israel's Independence Day.[23]

I accompanied the March of the Living in 1994. It seemed clear to me how organizers used the Holocaust to manipulate the emotions of the young travelers and nudge them toward a "take no prisoners" form of Zionism. Poland lived up to negative preconceptions. The weather was terrible: bitterly cold, wet, and even snowy; the landscape gray and dead. It was a perfect backdrop for the trip, incarnating an image of Poland as bleak, forbidding, unfriendly, and anti-Semitic. The teens were rushed from one site of horror to the next on tour buses, and accommodations were often unpleasant (when several buses made a pit stop at a roadside restaurant, it turned out that there was only one bathroom—dozens of teens, boys and girls alike, fanned out into the forest). Contact with local Poles was discouraged or prevented; even most of the food was imported from Israel. Security was heavy; Israeli plainclothesmen carrying walkie-talkies accompanied each bus, giving the pervasive impression that the country was dangerous. An incident or two when drunken hooligans heckled the group underscored expectations that all Poles were anti-Semites, contributing to a siegelike sense of "us" against "them": when an elderly woman in Warsaw smiled at some of the young people, the interpretation was that she was laughing at them. The themes of destruction and redemption were hammered firmly home, along with a sense of what could only be described as Jewish triumphalism. Contempory Poles were branded responsible for Nazi crimes and sometimes held up to derision.[24] Poland was represented as a vast Jewish graveyard—and nothing more; a place to weep, mourn, disdain, and then leave: some of the teens expressed concern that they were not crying enough. One said his grandmother would be spinning in her grave if she knew he was there. One girl flatly announced to me, two days after we had visited Kraków, with its complex of medieval architecture, that Poland "did not have a rich history." They could not wait to get on the plane out. A vast infrastructure was put into operation, meanwhile, to handle the March: hundreds and hundreds of buses; thousands of hotel rooms; vast shipments of kosher food. At crossroads and highway rest stops all over eastern and southern Poland, Polish army units manned huge cauldrons of boiling water that the March groups ladled out into tens of thousands of plastic cups of kosher instant noodles from Israel.[25]

The Jewish "roots tourists" who began coming in greater numbers to Poland in the 1980s changed the overall equation. The Holocaust and memory also played a big role in their itineraries, and many still went to Poland with reluctance. But these travelers came with other expectations and other needs, too, as they sought family roots by visiting ancestral towns, finding family graves, and doing genealogical research on the spot.

Like many related trends, Jewish genealogy took off as the baby boomer generation came of age. *Finding Our Fathers,* by Dan Rottenberg, the first "how-to" book on tracing Jewish family roots, was published in 1977, the same year in which the first Jewish genealogy society was founded. *Toledot,* the first periodical specializing in Jewish genealogy, appeared at about the same time. So did Irving Howe's immensely popular evocation of Jewish immigrant life, *World of Our Fathers,* as well as *Image Before My Eyes,* the landmark 1976 photographic exhibition on prewar Polish Jews at the Jewish Museum in New York, which also resulted in a coffee-table book. *Roots,* Alex Haley's sweeping account of tracing his own African lineage, which won tremendous popularity as a book and as a miniseries in the late 1970s, was also very important in showing the children and grandchildren of eastern European Jewish immigrants who had fled pogroms, prejudice, and the Holocaust that even the descendants of black slaves brutally severed from their homeland and history could recover their heritage. By 1979 a brochure titled "Exploring the Jewish Heritage of Spain," put out by the Spanish National Tourist Board, could state, "In recent years, travel abroad has acquired a new and exciting dimension—a search for roots—an encounter with history. For Jews, Spain is one of the richest sources of their people's history."

Most North American Jews, however, trace their roots to eastern Europe, not Spain, perhaps 75 percent of them to historic Polish lands. "Most people who travel to their ancestral towns want to experience a walk in the footsteps of their ancestors," says the Jewish genealogist Miriam Weiner. "They want to see what remains of the old life: original buildings, Jewish sites [such as] cemeteries, synagogues, and Holocaust memorials." But until the waning of communist rule, which opened archives in addition to easing travel, few people researching family history could do this. Jewish genealogy grew exponentially during the 1990s. In 1990 there were 39 Jewish genealogy societies worldwide. By 1999 there were 75, with 8,000 registered members. They represented only a fraction of Jews interested in tracing their roots, however—some 30,000 people were registered with a "family finder" service on the leading Jewish genealogy web site, www.JewishGen.org.

Roots trips became powerful and emotional experiences. Many travelers videotape their journeys or take detailed notes. Once home, they write lengthy accounts, which they circulate among family members and friends, publish privately or in Jewish genealogy magazines and newsletters, or post on the Internet. Some roots travelers publish accounts of their personal searches as books or magazine or newspaper articles for the broader public market.[26] In an article recounting a trip back to his father's hometown, the American-born Israeli essayist and translator Hillel Halkin described this vast new genre as "the shtetl-ogue," complete with what he called its "stock scenes and situations." These included "the successful or disappointed hunt for the family house and graves—the forlornly untended Jewish cemetery—the old synagogue turned into a pizzeria or discotheque—the elderly Gentile recalling Jewish neighbors—the visit to the field, ravine, or ditch in which the town's Jews were shot—the last Jew of Dobroslavka or Podorosk: when so little is left, it cannot but repeat itself."[27] I myself experienced most of these tropes on a 1999 visit to my great-grandfather's hometown in Lithuania. But these elements, too, partly because they are so universal, become engrained in the perception of what is "Jewish" or a "Jewish travel experience." For local people, in their turn, the foreign visitors and how they look and behave become new, sometimes intimidating, models. Many Jews on such trips weep; they want to touch physical objects, to talk. Many recite the Kaddish, the prayer for the dead, bringing Jewish religious ritual to onetime Jewish population centers for the first time in decades; local old-timers will often reach back into their memories to address visitors in rusty Yiddish learned to communicate with prewar Jewish neighbors and will recount tales of times when the streets were full of people they still often refer to as *Żydki,* little Jews, a common pejorative.

Jews often express forceful feelings of discovery on these trips. Geographies and even types of trees or flowers evoke intense and surprising feelings of familiarity. The physical difficulties of travel in remote places —bad roads, crowded buses, difficult border crossings, wrong turns, lost luggage, horses and carts—frequently become a compelling part of the narrative, too, fostering a sense of contact with somewhere so far away and so hard to get to that it must be the past; almost as if two— or three—time periods are being lived at once: the present, the prewar past of ancestors, and the horror of the Holocaust. Halkin expressed this in his article; he entered the eastern European world through the medium of the Yiddish literature he translates, describing buildings, animals, boats, and rivers as literary images come alive. Yet he ends up, like any other traveler, smiling through tears, digging up soil from where his father's childhood home had stood to take back with him, "roots and all," to America.

"We sought to experience whatever remains in a geographic form of the places from which [our family] came," one American woman wrote at the end of a twenty-eight-page account of a roots trip to Poland, Lithuania, and Belarus in 1996. ". . . I realized[,] as the young Belarussians stood in the icy air of the Kuznitza border crossing and took in my answers to their myriad questions about America[,] that America, which they learn about chiefly from bits of television, radio and music, exists mostly in a contemporary form of myth; clearly, they have no expectation that it will ever become a real part of their lives. In a similar way, the Kuznitza of my Grandfather's youth existed for me largely as a place of myth."

In Poland and other countries, Jewish roots seekers tailored their itineraries to their own genealogical research and retracing of localized family memory. But many also had, or developed, an expanded interest in visiting general Jewish heritage and other historical sights to fill out the picture. As the region opened up, they were joined by an increasing flow of other tourists, for whom travel to these places was tourism and not a voyage of personal discovery.

Harriet Poland, a retired teacher from Philadelphia, had traveled several times to Europe before she went on a package trip to Warsaw, Kraków, Budapest, and Prague in 1996. It was not a specific "Jewish heritage tour," nor was seeing Jewish sights her principal motive for making the trip, though her grandparents were Jewish immigrants from Poland and Russia. Still, she was influenced by curiosity about this part of the world because of its Jewish (and also Holocaust) history. The conventional sight-seeing itinerary gave her enough free time to visit Jewish sites on her own. "I didn't experience feelings of anxiety or trepidation before I went on the trip," she wrote me later. "But at times, when I stopped and realized where I really was in the 'Old World,' it caused an unusual sensation. It almost felt like being a part of History. Maybe it's a little corny, but I felt different in Budapest, Prague, Warsaw, etc., than I ever did in London, Paris, or Rome. Maybe this was the Jewishness in me that I felt was aroused. I don't really know. I was not raised in an especially religious home. We never belonged to a synagogue and though I recently attended High Holiday services a few times, I never felt the emotional high that several others seemed to feel. But all in all, being Jewish is a feeling all its own. And you never can tell when something, a sight or sound, will trigger a memory or longing for all those who went before and suffered those centuries ago."

Changing conditions and changing mind-sets through the 1990s built Jewish heritage tourism into a solid niche market whose itineraries spanned the region. Personal ancestral roots and Holocaust commemoration remained part of the appeal but no longer were prerequisites. Package "Jewish heritage tours" to eastern and central Europe multiplied through the decade, translating travel into tourism on a wider mass-market scale. Typically, such tours to the region take in several major cities or sites in two or more countries—variations of the Prague-Vienna-Budapest-Kraków quadrangle—and often they are led or informed by a prominent personality: a Holocaust survivor, for example, or a rabbi, or an author or scholar. The tours often combine specific Jewish sight-seeing with conventional itineraries. Frequently, but not always, Holocaust commemoration sites are included, but as integral parts of broad Jewish heritage routes rather than as the primary focus for the travel.

Such tours became more diversified with market competition. People who had already walked through "Kafka's Prague" could attempt something more exotic, such as the "Yiddish Literary Walking Tour" that was sponsored in 1996 by the Oxford Institute for Yiddish Studies and led by the prominent Yiddish scholar Chone Shmeruk, a newspaper advertisement for which promised that "[t]his excursion will bring you to the surviving landmarks of Yiddish literature and will explore the last remains of Jewish life in today's Poland. The participants will be provided with a specially prepared selection of Yiddish texts on both the history of Yiddish culture and literature and Jewish life in pre-war Poland." Throughout the decade, too, the recognition of reviving local Jewish communities played a prominent role in structuring the tourist experience. In addition to visiting heritage sites and enjoying atmospheric "Jewish-style" cafés, visitors were encouraged to interact, attend synagogue, and view the local Jewish experience in terms of living culture rather than as relics, museums, and monuments of a closed chapter. This strategy was forcefully demonstrated in the brochures published in Austria and Hungary. Still, as I experienced so vividly during my *Schindler's List* tour of Kraków, the clashes among Jews and "virtual Jews," current realities and the past, commercial representation and collective memory, frequently remain fraught with perplexity and contradiction.

8

Structuring Memory

Jewish museums in Europe are a fulcrum for converging issues of presentation, representation, and interpretation of the Jewish phenomenon.[1] They are local institutions serving a local public and addressing or reflecting local attitudes and concerns but also focal points for incoming tourists, concrete "destinations" whose exhibits may provide a narrative structure to more complex itineraries within a physical and sometimes mental "virtual" geography of Jewish past, present, and future.[2]

Like all museums, Jewish museums in Europe today fulfill many functions, ranging from instruction to entertainment, from enlightenment to aesthetic enjoyment. Like other museums, they gather, preserve, and display the cultural artifacts of a civilization as an affirmative representation of identity and tradition.[3] Jewish museums in Europe, however, must also address and interpret that civilization's persecution and destruction, including questions of local responsibility, complicity, and guilt. Centuries of Jewish history are involved—not just the Shoah. Still, the Holocaust experience lies at the crux of this problem. Indeed, in today's Europe all Jewish museums are—to one degree or another—Holocaust museums of a sort; what is presented is inevitably viewed through the backward lens of the Shoah. In parts of Europe, every pre-war object on display is a "survivor"—as are the synagogues in which some Jewish museums are located. Some museums display items that actually bear the physical marks of their survival: fire-blackened silver from a local synagogue destroyed on Kristallnacht in the Jewish Museum in Vienna; the battered eternal lamp of the New Synagogue in

Berlin, discovered under rubble during reconstruction work and ritually displayed now as a symbol of salvation and rescue, survival and recovery, in the restored part of the building. The establishment of a Jewish museum can in itself serve as a ritual, be it a meaningful rite or a mechanical means of doing (or being perceived as doing) the right thing.[4] Visiting such museums may serve a similar purpose. Comments written by visitors in Jewish museum guest books, regardless of the orientation of the exhibition, frequently refer to the Holocaust or include exhortations such as "Remember" or "Never again."

Jewish museums in Europe evoke absence and provoke memory. Whether traditional displays of ritual art or dense presentations of local or global Jewish history, their exhibits may trigger personal memories in older individuals, but they also form a concrete structure on which collective memory can be built. They are public, often political places of memory; indeed, through their exhibits they provide an institutional definition of memory, just as their exhibitions may, in turn, define "Jewish culture." They designate what should—or must—be remembered, as well as the ways in which, and why, these designated objects of memory (and the past itself) should be represented and recalled.[5]

But who is to make these designations, and how is it to be accomplished? What should Jewish museums in Europe show, teach, or represent? How? To whom? By whom? From what perspective? Where should they be located? Who should set them up? Should they be set up in the first place? Indeed, does Europe need so many Jewish museums? These are questions that each Jewish museum and its creators must consider, whether in the planning stage of operation or in reevaluations of existing exhibitions and direction. They fall, clearly, within the framework of questions raised in the overall process of Jewish archaeology, but they are also specific to broader debates on museums, their design and their function in general.[6] Other questions are raised, too. Are Jewish museum exhibits to be shown from the point of view of the (albeit repentant) perpetrator or the victim? Can the Jewish religion and historic Jewish relations with the Church be presented in an unbiased way from a Catholic theological perspective? Should Jewish history and culture be portrayed as something special, separate from the local mainstream, or an integral part of it? These and other issues are the frequent topic of articles, studies, and national and international conferences and are sometimes subject to intense public and political debate.[7] In Germany, where the establishment of Jewish museums has been a pillar of the *Vergangenheitsverarbeitung* process, these issues have particular resonance. But the pattern is general.

The lofty terms in which Sicily's assessor of culture, Salvatore Morinello, announced that the Sicilian regional government intended to establish a Jewish museum in Palermo made clear that such a museum would embody a contemporary significance well beyond its historical or artistic content. Morinello made the announcement at the January 1999 international conference on European Jewish heritage in Paris. "When the Jews were expelled from the Spanish domains in 1492," he said, "the Sicilian Parliament was alone in opposing their departure. But, despite this painful separation, relations between Sicily and the Jews never totally ceased, and in their places of exile they continued, until recent years, to call themselves 'Sicilian Jews.' The regional government of Sicily means to pay homage to this ancient fealty, to this fruitful living together, with the establishment of a Sicilian Jewish Museum in Palermo which will safeguard and highlight a unique and priceless patrimony. It is intended to be a museum that for future generations can serve as a reminder of the values of tolerance, spirituality and research, and for all the Jews of the world can provide a welcoming home in Sicily and a monument to the original contribution of Sicilian Jews to Jewish culture." It was an ambitious project, he said, "aimed at restoring to Sicily, on the threshold of the new millennium, its dimension as a land of encounter and dialogue among the different religions and civilizations of the Mediterranean."

The variety of Jewish museums in Europe is tremendous, as are the variety of ways in which they confront the questions cited above. Writing in 1997 about the dozens of Jewish museums in Germany alone, the Bremen University scholar Sabine Offe remarked that their "multitude and diversity" were their "most striking aspects."[8] This holds somewhat less true in other countries, where Jewish museums are less numerous and tend to be much more similar in scope than in Germany. (Indeed, there are probably more Jewish museums in Germany than in the rest of Europe combined.) But Offe's description certainly holds true when Jewish museums in various European countries are viewed together.

The differences lie in their institutional orientation as well as in their size, style, concept, and physical setting. Some are publicly run, some are private; some are run by, or in association with, Jewish institutions or communal structures; many, if not most, are not. Some, like the important, publicly established Museum of the Art and History of Judaism that opened in Paris in December 1998, are "national" Jewish museums that serve as reference points for a state's new recognition and representation of the Jewish phenomenon; others are the fruit of the labors of zealous individuals. Their exhibits may thus be designed and curated by phalanxes of professional museologists and scholars or put together by well-meaning amateurs. Some are little more than displays of Jewish ritual objects; others employ innovative design concepts or are ambitious, even overly ambitious, multimedia complexes. Some strive to give a historical picture of local Jewish life within a didactic framework; others aim to portray Jewish history within the broader context of European, national, or local development; some try to illustrate the basic traditions of Judaism. For some, commemoration of a community destroyed by the Holocaust is a raison d'être; others make scant direct reference at all to the Shoah.

Many Jewish museums are housed in former synagogue buildings, and many other former synagogues have been restored and renovated to serve as exhibits in themselves. Still other museums are located in buildings that have a Jewish history or association, even if oblique. Some stand in isolation; some, like the small Jewish museums in a dozen or so Czech towns, were established as integral parts of the revitalization of Jewish quarters or entire historic town districts. The presence of some designate newly built structures or other buildings without a specific Jewish history as "Jewish."

Amid this proliferation, yet another question has been raised: how does one define a "Jewish museum" at all? Must use of the adjective "Jewish" mean that Jewish communal structures or institutions be involved in its establishment and organization? That, as the English scholar David Clark put it, it must be a museum "initiated by Jews, as Jews, for both Jews and non-Jews"? Or that "alliances—both within the Jewish community and with institutions of the wider host society— are necessary"?[9] Or can the adjective be used in the broader sense —defining content and orientation rather than creator or mode of creation?

"We, and when I say 'we' I mean the Jewish community, say you can't make Jewish culture without the Jews," Georg Haber, the general manager of the Jewish Museum in Vienna told me in 1996. "You can't make a Jewish museum without involving the Jewish community. It is not enough if you take some Jew from anyplace as an 'alibi Jew.' You have to involve the Jewish community, which is difficult, which means a lot of discussions and so on, but there is no other way." In Vienna, with an active Jewish community of 9,000 to 10,000, cooperation with municipal authorities in the establishment and operation of the city's Jew-

ish museum has been possible. Yet Haber's own daughter served as director of the municipal Jewish museum in Hohenems, located in a region where, the Nazi-hunter Simon Wiesenthal has been quoted as saying, "you have 50 times more chance of being hit by a car . . . than of
meeting a Jew." [10]

In this discussion, as throughout this book, I use the term "Jewish
museum" in its broadest possible sense, to encompass the wide and varied range, from large formal institutions to amateur permanent displays
and including museums that are perceived as or define themselves as
"Jewish" regardless of their organizational structure and history or their
links to Jewish communities or institutions. Contested perceptions and
definitions of what is "Jewish" are, after all, at the heart of dilemmas regarding display, interpretation, and representation of Jews and Jewish
culture and thus are central to any consideration of Jewish museums,
their nature, their form, and their impact. Below I discuss how these
and related issues are confronted by certain individuals and certain museums, in several countries and of several types.

Roles and Role Models

A number of Jewish museums existed in Europe before
World War II, in addition to a few collections of Judaica or individual
relics in mainstream museums (such as that displayed in the Cluny Museum in Paris, exhibits in the Alsatian Museum in Strasbourg, and museums in Bamberg and Würzburg, Germany, each of which preserved
an old, timber synagogue painted with murals). Among these were the
Jewish museums in Vienna (the first, founded in 1895), Prague (1906),
Worms (1912), Budapest (1916), Frankfurt (1922), and Berlin (founded
in 1933, just days before Hitler came to power). Although non-Jews
were instrumental in collecting Jewish art and in creating some prewar
Jewish museums, virtually all prewar Jewish museums were established
by or associated with official Jewish communal structures. One can thus
argue that aside from museums such as that in Budapest, still run (or,
in Prague, again run) by Jewish communal bodies or institutions, most
of today's Jewish museums, even those in cities that had Jewish museums before the Holocaust and whose prewar collections may form part
of current exhibits, cannot claim to be direct legitimate heirs of the prewar institutions.

A century ago, modern acculturated, even secular Jews had sought
to preserve and present the treasures of a religious tradition from which
they had grown distant. On the one hand, the display of Jewish creativity helped to foster a sense of Jewish national consciousness. But the ritual art and ceremonial objects also served as touchstones, assertions of
an old-fashioned Jewish identity, idealized, perhaps, as "authentic" but
implicitly acknowledged as out of date; family mementos preserved like
treasured photographs of beloved, but strangely attired, ancestors in a
family album. Some Jews were already uncomfortable with the attitude
of detachment and veneration regarding these relics. In *A World Passed
By*, Marvin Lowenthal described the collection of Judaica in the Prague
Jewish Museum, most of it salvaged from the three ancient synagogues
destroyed in the late-nineteenth-century urban renewal plan that demolished the medieval ghetto, as "unhappy dibbukim, things impris-
oned between life and death, demanding either release into the grave,
or back into the world where their beauty may be used again." [11]

In a sense those museums were nonreligious Jewish shrines to pious
Jewish tradition. Today's museums, particularly those run by Jewish
community organizations, still may fulfill this function in part, but often, too, they and their exhibits are enshrined as sacred relics of a destroyed civilization, "salvaged from the graveyard of destroyed Jewish
life." [12] Even everyday objects—coffeepots, cups, plates, clothing—
may be elevated to the status of artifact. The exhibits in many small Jewish museums, particularly in Germany, include objects that really were
salvaged—or exhumed—from what had been intended by Jews themselves to have been their graves: material found in *genizot,* caches of
worn-out books, textiles, and other material that were hidden away in
synagogue wall spaces and ceilings and found during synagogue restoration work.

In many museums, the ritual objects on display, beautiful in themselves, constitute treasures put together in an artificial context, objects
"out of function." Sometimes their provenance and history are unknown; they are objects in themselves, which could be viewed just as
easily by browsing in an auction showroom. (The catalog of the Westfalen Jewish Museum in Dorsten, Germany, the museum that declared
itself devised "by non-Jews for non-Jews," details how museum staffers
set about purchasing material for the new collection and includes photographs of museum personnel bidding for Judaica at Christie's in Amsterdam and, after the auction, standing at the door with a carton of
what they purchased underneath the Christie's sign.) [13] Some such mu-

seums set aside one section or room or corner to deal specifically with the Holocaust, either as an exhibit or as a memorial or a combination of the two, but others make no specific mention of the Holocaust or other Jewish historical experience. In fact, though, the very presence of the objects, on display as out of context museum pieces, provides a powerful subtext, concealing "a hidden history of terror." [14]

Many museums make sections of their exhibitions primers on Judaism, explaining customs and traditions, holidays and life cycles to accommodate the interest of a non-Jewish public as well as, sometimes, secular or assimilated Jews reluctant to affiliate with formal Jewish community religious structures. Reflecting traditional ways of laying out Jewish exhibits that date back to the early Jewish museums in the late nineteenth century and to temporary Judaica exhibitions of the same era and earlier, ritual objects are often set up as installations that aim to explain Judaism and Jewish practice by simulating scenes of Jewish life. [15] These installations may be as simple as an open prayer book and a kiddush cup placed next to Sabbath candlesticks with candles ready to be lit or as elaborate as fully laid Sabbath or Seder tables—though the significance and symbolism of these meals and their table settings may not be fully explained. The mannequins or cutout figures employed in some installations to set the scene are often shown dressed in "Jewish" attire of centuries ago.

Some Jewish museums, increasingly, make explicit narrative retelling of history a focal point, or even the focal point, of their presentations. Indeed, some (such as the museum in Gorizia, Italy, or the state-run Sephardi Museum in Toledo, Spain, located in the Tránsito Synagogue) have changed their orientation in recent years to reflect a more critical historical approach, aimed at demystifying Jews and their world. [16] Some have established special educational programs for schoolchildren and their teachers, as well as public lectures, film series, library resources, and classes. Some provide extensive informational panels, multimedia access points, or earphone guides.

Yet what history do they present? What interpretation? The message depends on the choice of material, and on who does the choosing and telling. In some Jewish museums, the Jewish experience is treated *only* as history; as a finite experience, relegated to the past. Ambiguous circumstances and conflict may be edited out; exhibits that focus on the the millennial course of Jewish history, or on the Holocaust in general, for example, may skip over local ramifications or, told from an "outsider" perspective, may unintentionally embrace stereotypes.

Even exhibits that represent Judaism and Jewish practice often end up exoticizing it, giving the impression of something far removed from present-day reality, of strange customs of a strange people who suffered a strange and horrible fate. As in some travel brochures, informational material may be written in the past tense or otherwise give the impression that ritual objects such as those on display are no longer used by Jews. And if the only figurative representations of Jews are old pictures or mannequins (sometimes faceless and featureless) in odd—sometimes discriminatory—historical costume, or representations of Jews as skeletal Holocaust victims or death camp inmates, what does that say about Jews, Judaism, and the Jewish phenomenon?

Eva Grabherr, the first director of the Hohenems Jewish Museum in western Austria and a thoughtful commentator on these issues, has recalled how sporadic attempts in the 1960s and 1970s to "incorporate Jewish history into the canon of local history" in the town of fifteen thousand people coalesced in the 1980s into a civic movement that resulted in the establishment of the museum and other permanent projects. The museum, which opened in 1991, soon became the most important attraction for visitors in Hohenems; projects involving the Jewish quarter included the placement of plaques (such as that on the synagogue–fire station), educational programs for schoolchildren, and occasional installations during which slides of prewar scenes were projected on the existing buildings.[17]

Jews settled in Hohenems in the seventeenth century and were important in the development of the town. At its peak in the nineteenth century, the Jewish community numbered some 500 of Hohenems' population of 4,000, and the two main streets were known simply as Jewish Street and Christian Street. Local Jews were merchants, craftsmen, livestock traders, and industrialists—and one local Jewish son, Salomon Sulzer, was a renowned nineteenth-century liturgical composer, the elegant, long-haired chief cantor of the main synagogue in Vienna, who became the lionized object of a personality cult.[18] In the late nineteenth century, following the typical pattern, most Jews moved away from Hohenems to seek their fortunes in bigger towns, and on the eve of World War II only a dozen or so Jews remained. All fled or were deported to their deaths; none returned to live in Hohenems after the war, although several hundred Jewish displaced persons lived in the town until 1954 amid conditions of "considerable friction" with local people and local officials—including the mayor, the same H. Amann who proudly signed the plaque dedicating the firehouse transformation of the synagogue.[19]

"[The] rediscovery process did not take place without controversy," Grabherr, who is not Jewish, has written.[20] Indeed, the process was part of the urgent confrontation with history in Austria sparked by the Kurt Waldheim affair. Austria was annexed by Nazi Germany in 1938, but though hundreds of thousands of Viennese cheered Hitler when he made a triumphant entry into the city, and though many Austrians were among the most enthusiastic Nazis, the victorious World War II Allies declared Austria "the first free country to fall victim to Hitlerite aggression."[21] This officially certified victimhood was adamantly maintained throughout the postwar period. It was only in the early 1990s that Chancellor Franz Vranitzky publicly admitted that Austria had been a willing servant of the Nazis.

The Waldheim affair split the country. Reaction to the critics (who included the World Jewish Congress) who publicized Waldheim's lies coalesced in a nationalistic, right-wing political force, the Freiheitspartei, or Freedom Party, led by the charismatic populist Jörg Haider, which by 1999 had grown to become the country's second-largest party (and in February 2000 entered the ruling coalition). At the same time, however, the affair also stimulated a desire to redress historic omissions. It also prompted a reactive wave of sometimes cloying philo-Semitism. An upbeat booklet about Jews in Austria, published by the Austrian government in 1994 (and updated in 1998), stated, "The desire for an opportunity to meet Jewish people was as great as the diversity of ingenious tactics adopted. For example, a group of young Austrians waited outside Vienna's City Temple for the congregation to leave, whereupon they handed them roses, saying, 'We are glad that you are with us.'"[22] Groups performing Yiddish music found that their bookings suddenly soared. "Right up to 1986 and the Waldheim election controversy, we were regarded as a bit exotic—like two blacks getting up on the stage and singing," Edward (Edek) Bartz, who for years played in a duo called Geduldig un Thimann, said in 1991. "For a lot of people in those days, we were the first Jews they'd even come across. But, after Waldheim, every appearance one made tended to be a statement in itself—a demonstration for or against something—though all we really wanted to do was sing."[23] Bartz's partner, Albert Misak, later told me how a woman once sat in the front row at a concert and cried all the way through the performance. "Edek had a strong reaction," Misak said. "He said, 'They are using us. They come to our concerts seeking absolution, maybe because their parents or grandparents were Nazis.' He didn't like this and ultimately left the group."

These conflicting elements were sharply evident in the way people in

Hohenems viewed the past and in the way the museum was set up. "It was not solely a question of whether room would indeed be made for Jewish history in the cultural memories of the town," Grabherr wrote. "From at least 1988 onwards, the principal issue was what kind of Jewish history was to be remembered—should it be only the history of important and famous members of the former community, or should it include the traditions of the community and its social structure including peddlers and the proprietors of groceries and general stores? Should the past be presented as a time of harmonious coexistence or should the narrative also include the expulsions of the 17th century, the anti-Semitic agitation of the 19th and 20th centuries and the destruction of the community and murder of its remaining members after 1938 in which the Nazi municipal administration had been involved?"[24]

The Hohenems museum in fact does present a well-researched, "warts and all" picture of local Jewish life and history, including documentation and exhibits on prewar anti-Semitism, the Holocaust period, and postwar tensions. Yet my perception was that its exhibits glossed over the fact that Judaism is a still-living phenomenon. It is true that no Jews live in Hohenems, but there are still thriving Jewish communities elsewhere in Austria and in neighboring Switzerland (as well as elsewhere, of course). I felt uncomfortable that the pictures used to illustrate Jewish religious traditions were from previous centuries, and even a photo of a Swiss synagogue was dated. I thought this could leave the impression that these traditions were no longer current. I raised my concerns with Grabherr. She told me this had been a conscious decision taken when devising the museum. The guiding principle, she said, had been to place all permanent exhibits within the site-specific historical context of the town itself and not within the global context of Judaism. Contemporary Jewish life, she said, was represented and demonstrated in others ways—through temporary exhibits, concerts, lectures, and other programs held at the museum, as well as through the range of contemporary Jewish newspapers available in the museum café.

When Grabherr left Hohenems after five years as director, she was replaced by Esther Haber, who served as director in 1996–98. Until Haber's arrival there was no Jew on the museum's staff (although one of the handful of Jewish residents of the Vorarlberg region served for a time on its board). In fact, Haber's Jewishness—the filling of this perceived gap—apparently helped her to get the job. During her tenure, Haber complained of feeling as if she were exposed as an exhibit—"the Jew"—herself. "It's like a striptease in a way," she told me.

Physical Constructs

The ways in which synagogues are restored or reconstructed to house Jewish museums or as exhibits in themselves can give physical shape to radically different modes of memory as well as to the historical and other messages that are conveyed. The mere fact that a synagogue stands empty of Jews, used as an exhibit or housing an exhibit, may end up being the principal means of conveying a sense of loss: palpable absence may be the most important "exhibit" on the Holocaust and post-Holocaust period. The Jewish Museum located in the former synagogue of the Polish village of Tykocin is a compelling example of this. The massive, seventeenth-century synagogue towers over the village, and its lonely and unexpected splendor in an out-of-the-way location lends haunting power to its message of emptiness, absence, and magnificent loss. Inside, brilliantly colored frescoes, including wall texts of prayers, cover the soaring walls and central *bimah,* and cantorial music plays from tapes. Ritual objects are displayed in a few scattered glass cases, with little contextual explanation. Jews once made up a majority of Tykocin's population and about half the population on the eve of World War II. A model of the village in the museum shows how life was grouped around two poles: the church and Christian marketplace at one end and the synagogue and Jewish marketplace at the other. No Jews live in Tykocin now, and the only physical traces of the prewar population are the synagogue, the abandoned cemetery, and one or two decorative window frames incorporating a Star of David. Ironically, though, in recent years it is the synagogue and its message that have become the focal point of the sleepy little town. The Jewish Museum draws some forty thousand tourists a year—mostly on package tours or "missions" such as the March of the Living. The interest has prompted new services around the synagogue, such as a café serving Jewish-style dishes and a bed-and-breakfast.

Some reconstructions attempt to reproduce the exact way a synagogue—regardless of what happened to it during or after World War II—appeared before the Holocaust, often the way it appeared at the height of the activity of a Jewish community that may no longer exist. In this way, post-1938 Jewish history may end up being "extensively undone."[25] Such, for example, was the case with the eighteenth-century synagogue at Veitschöchheim, near Würzburg in Bavaria, which was turned into a fire station in 1940. The synagogue complex, including the cantor's rooms and a *mikvah,* was restored and opened as a museum in 1994. It was restored to how it looked in the 1920s, with even the interior furniture of the sanctuary reconstructed from photographs. The only element that hints at the destruction of the local Jewish community and the "destructive new function as a fire station" is a memorial plaque, put together from fragments, that honors Jewish soldiers who died fighting for Germany in World War I.[26]

Quite a different model was attempted in the transformation of the synagogue complex in another Bavarian village, Schnaittach, into a Jewish museum. In this restoration, the museum director, Bernhard Purin (who previously worked at the Jewish museums in Hohenems and Vienna), wanted to demonstrate the ambiguity of local Jewish history—the desecration and destruction of the Nazi era and the neglect of postwar times, as well as the town's long and distinguished prewar Jewish past. Schnaittach's complex of Jewish buildings, unique in Germany, as well as the objects that are the basis of the museum, survived the war thanks to circumstances that demonstrated both the integration of Jews in the local mainstream and the precariousness of this integration. Jews settled in Schnaittach at the end of the fifteenth century, and at its peak in the seventeenth and eighteenth centuries, the community was the principal Jewish center in the surrounding territory, home to the chief rabbi of the district and a yeshiva. The Jewish population dwindled so much in the nineteenth century, however, that the local rabbinate was dissolved in 1883.

In 1932, before the rise of the Nazis, local Jews approved the loan of objects for inclusion in the village's local heritage (*Heimat*) museum. Even after the Nazis came to power, local Jews continued to loan or donate items. During the Kristallnacht pogrom in November 1938, the Schnaittach synagogue was desecrated and the few Jews who still lived in the village were arrested and eventually dispersed or murdered. The synagogue complex, however, was saved from destruction by one Gottfried Stammler, the honorary chairman of the *Heimat* museum, who secured the building as a new home for his museum: it was already operating as such by 1939 and continued in this function after the war. The sanctuary of the synagogue was whitewashed and served as an exhibition room for, among other things, Christian religious artifacts, including a dozen crosses. A statue of the Madonna was placed in the niche of the Ark, and a big hole was chopped into one of the walls in 1956 to make room for a massive baroque altar. Stammler also "annexed" numerous books, ritual objects, and other material used in the synagogue or confiscated from local Jews. These acquisitions, according to Purin, "are firmly anchored in the town's collective memory as having been 'rescued.'" Indeed, in 1945 surviving Jews, too, thanked Stammler for his actions: Stammler himself at that time handed over some objects from the collection to the surviving Jewish community in Nuremberg. Nonetheless, the ambiguity of his motives has since become clear: documents show that already in 1937, when he was looking for new premises for the *Heimat* museum, Stammler had put the synagogue complex high on his list and wondered, in a note, "When will we get the Jews out?"[27]

Purin's original plan was to leave the sanctuary looking essentially as it had been in 1995, "to show the vicissitudes through which it had passed." This would have included retaining the hole cut for the altar display and other damage caused by its use as a *Heimat* museum. But, he told me, the town council couldn't stomach this. Following "heated discussions," it ruled that the opening cut for the baroque altar would have to be covered up, and "other traces of the synagogue's history" would also be "partially concealed" during the restoration. Still, no attempt was made to reconstruct the Schnaittach synagogue into a facsimile of its prewar appearance. The visitor now sees a bare room with cream-colored walls, a blue ceiling, and some delicate frescoes above the small Ark. It is obviously a synagogue out of use, to which something drastic has happened. Written material describes the building's history, and the museum catalog includes a picture of it in use as the *Heimat* museum, crosses and all. Many of the objects on display at Schnaittach are those that were donated by Jewish families to the *Heimat* museum in the 1930s; they include ceremonial objects as well as items used in everyday Jewish life. The personal story behind each object and how it became part of the museum collection is known and illustrated; the life stories of the people who donated objects are recounted in detail, too, including, for some of them, their murder during the Holocaust.[28]

For Purin, items on display, and the ways in which they are displayed, must not just illustrate a vacuum; they must actively address issues of memory, how that vacuum came to be: "Only objects with stories are able to open windows to the past." All items used in the Schnaittach museum, he says, are place-specific objects that stimulate a presentation of place-specific history and Jewish experience, both positive and negative. If a Jewish museum does not have its own objects, related somehow to local Jewish communal life, Purin says, it should use other means to convey the Jewish experience—archival material, photographs, documents, personal history—rather than purchase "anonymous" objects at auction. Whatever aspects of Jewish practice are illustrated at Schnaittach thus do not constitute a general description of Judaism or Jewish traditions. Rather, they are limited to descriptions of Jewish practice directly associated with the individual objects on show.[29] No exhibit at the Schnaittach museum commemorates or specifically deals with the broad concept of the Holocaust either, but the Shoah and the fate of the Jews of the village underlie the presentation. Indeed, the Shoah and its effects provide the very matrix of the museum. The underlying premise, says Purin, is that "the difficult history of the collection and of the museum building itself must be one of the topics covered by the exhibition. Thus the exhibits are interpreted in their various dimensions as memorial objects, keeping memories alive." All the labels and informational material incorporated in the exhibits were designed to make clear that the objects on display "were forcibly removed from the tradition to which they belonged."

Purin told me that the museum design had prompted complaints. One woman objected that she could not "see the happiness of Jewish life." And some visitors objected to the use of a quotation by the American Jewish scholar Arthur Hertzberg, which Purin placed on a translucent panel at the entry to the museum as a motto: "It is important for us to remember—but what do we need to remember? Only how six million Jews died? Or how they lived?" People, said Purin, complained about the word "only."

The Insider Perspective

The organizers of Jewish museums run by Jewish communities or as Jewish institutions within or closely associated with Jewish communal structures have a quite different relationship to the objects on display and what they represent. As conscious representatives of living Jewish entities, they often voice a responsibility to educate the mainstream public from the "insider" perspective. Anna Blayer, the director of the museum run by the Jewish community in Rome, feels that only living Jews can tell the Jewish story correctly, from a living Jewish context. "Our museum is the calling card of our community," she told me.

Founded in the 1960s, the Rome museum is situated in the complex housing the ornate, domed synagogue, built in 1904, that towers over the Tiber. One of its aims is to educate a public, particularly a young public, that is often woefully ignorant, despite the recent proliferation of books, articles, films, performances, and broadcasts on Jewish topics in Italy. "In the course of a morning we sometimes have two hundred high school pupils visit here on school trips," Blayer told me. "We see that even young people eighteen or twenty years old don't know what they are coming to see. Sometimes they look at me with blank eyes, as if I am telling them about things they had never heard of before." The museum possesses a large and precious collection of ritual objects, textiles, and documents dating back many centuries, but as of 1999 little explanatory historical or background material accompanied the exhibits. Blayer told me this was deliberate: for tourists as well as for school groups, the museum encouraged guided tours led by museum staff, all of whom are members of the Jewish community. She and others associated with the museum stressed that the ritual objects on display were not simply "exhibits" but were still objects in active, if periodic, use by Roman Jews in synagogue ceremonies; the museum, thus, was a "living" museum, a "living storage space" for the synagogue, whose sanctuary was also shown to visitors as part of the tour.[30] At the entrance to the sanctuary, baskets held skullcaps for male visitors and scarves for women; having visitors wear them emphasized that the synagogue was still primarily a house of worship. "When we show visitors Hanukkah menorahs and explain Hanukkah, for example, we explain the symbolism in all details, elaborating similarities and differences with Christianity," Blayer told me. "But you can only do this through the voice of a person who can make these comparisons. I don't think you can do it with information panels—for one thing, not everybody reads the panels. A museum is multiform. It is one thing to describe something to someone, another thing to read a panel. With panels, you just get sterile information—I think you need a living person to explain things properly."[31]

Overreliance on information panels and other "do-it-yourself" material was in fact one of the criticisms leveled at the Jewish Museum in Bologna, Italy, which opened in May 1999 in a transformed palazzo in the heart of the city's medieval ghetto neighborhood. Jews were expelled from Bologna in 1593 and did not reestablish a real presence until the nineteenth century. About two hundred Jews live in Bologna today. The new museum, sponsored by the Emilia-Romagna region and administered by a semiprivate foundation that includes Jewish and public representatives, is the first major Jewish museum in Italy established outside of Jewish communal structures and also the first major Jewish museum in Italy to emphasize a didactic presentation of Jewish history. (The only similar example is the much less ambitious little Jewish museum in Gorizia.)

The Bologna museum is a "resource center" rather than a traditional museum. Its permanent exhibition has very few objects; instead it is based on information panels, videos, databanks, and computer hyperlinks that describe Judaism and global and local Jewish history and also note historic Jewish presence and surviving Jewish monuments in more than thirty towns in the Emilia-Romagna region. The museum was, in fact, deliberately conceived as a high-tech "virtual museum," directed primarily at a non-Jewish public. Its stated aim was to link visitors with regional Jewish heritage sites, including a Holocaust memorial at the site of the World War II labor-transit camp at Fossoli, near Carpi, and small museums in two nearby towns that are operated by Jewish communities and display collections of ritual objects and other local material. These are the museum in Ferrara, located in the centuries-old palazzo that houses Jewish community offices and three synagogue sanctuaries, and that in the small town of Soragna. Visitors to the Ferrara museum must be guided personally by a representative of the contemporary local Jewish community, who explains the objects and their history. No Jews live in Soragna anymore, but a small collection of ritual objects and memorabilia, put together by a local Jew, is displayed in the restored old synagogue complex, which is administered by the tiny Jewish community of nearby Parma. "The idea is that people can visit Bologna to orient themselves, discover the history, and use the resources," Bologna museum director Franco Bonilauri told me before the museum opened, "and then go out to see the objects and synagogues in situ, following organized or suggested itineraries. In doing so, they will pass from a sort of small 'virtual museum' in Bologna to a big 'real museum' comprising other museums and exhibitions, which will encompass the entire Emilia-Romagna region." [32] These itineraries are illustrated in the Bologna museum. The Bologna museum plan also entailed lectures and concerts and, eventually, temporary exhibits.

Although this novel approach, including its description as a "virtual museum," was made public well before the Bologna museum opened, it came as a shock to visitors expecting to find a more traditional presentation. The initial response was decidedly mixed. Within weeks of the opening, complaints surfaced about the museum's "virtual" quality. And although Jewish scholars, institutions, and communal representatives had been consulted during museum preparations and worked on the texts, criticism was raised by some Jews that the local Jewish community as a whole had not been adequately involved in the project and that Jewish sensibilities and perspectives were not taken into account in preparing some of the exhibits. (Much of this represented teething problems that died down as the museum became established. By 2000 the museum's cultural events were well attended, and organizers said as many as five thousand people visited the Jewish book fair and other events held at the museum on the European Day of Jewish Culture, September 3, 2000. The Association of European Jewish Museums, an organization that links Jewish museums in more than a dozen European countries, chose the Bologna museum as the site of its 2001 annual conference and, given the orientation of the Bologna museum, chose as the main conference theme the use of new information and media technology in museum work and new systems of documenting museum collections.)

Symbol and Transformation

The dramatic transformations undergone by the Jewish Museum in Prague illustrate a wide range of roles and functions. In its more than ninety years of operation, the Prague museum has undergone more transformations than any other Jewish museum in Europe. In many ways it has served as a symbol both for the changing position and image of Jews in mainstream society throughout Europe and for the changing character and significance of Jewish museums in the European context.[33]

The Jewish Museum founded in 1906 by the Prague Jewish community, like other Jewish museums of the time in their own milieus, initially represented a symbol of Czech Jewish "modernization," by which Czech Jews were preserving and presenting their own past. During World War II, the museum became a symbol of the Holocaust and the destruction of European Jewry. The Nazis took it over and in 1942 founded the Jüdisches Zentralmuseum (Central Jewish Museum); it was the first museum dedicated to displaying the relics of a murdered people—but its aim was triumphal rather than commemorative, in the ancient Roman tradition of piling up the spoils of conquest and dedicating them to victory.[34] "The museum was supposed to be a victory memorial, for the objects displayed here belonged to a race scheduled for annihilation. Nothing would remain of that race but these dead things." [35] The original Prague collections were expanded by a treasure trove of objects seized by the Nazis from 153 destroyed provincial Jewish communities in Bohemia and Moravia. The tragic irony is that leaders of the Prague Jewish community worked with the Nazis in the formation of this museum. Helpless to save their fellow Jews, their aim was to preserve at least the physical relics of Jewish culture. These were brought to Prague, where Jewish scholars—themselves doomed to deportation and death—cataloged them and arranged exhibitions. During the war, some of the material was displayed for the private viewing of senior SS officials in ancient Prague synagogues whose congregations had been deported and killed. Indeed, the accumulation and expansion of the museum collection of objects graphically paralleled the destruction of Jewish life. On the eve of World War II, when some 118,000 Jews lived in Bohemia and Moravia, the inventory of the Jewish Museum numbered about 1,000 pieces. At the war's end, the museum inventory far exceeded 100,000 articles, and 80,000 Czech Jews had been murdered. In Prague, "the scrolls of the Holy Scriptures were piled high, as was hair in Auschwitz. In Prague grew piles of temple curtains, and in the East, just outside the hell of the gas chambers, piles of wooden legs. In Prague were heaped silver goblets and there, in the death camps, gold wrenched from victims' mouths." [36]

Under communism, the museum, taken over by the state in 1950, became the symbol of the constraints placed on and around Jews, Judaism, and the Jewish phenomenon by the communist regime. Thanks to the work the Nazis had carried out in amassing the artifacts of destroyed Czech Jewry, the State Jewish Museum contained what is generally considered to be the richest collection of Judaica in Europe. The collection was displayed in several centuries-old synagogues and also comprised the famous Old Jewish Cemetery. But these Jewish collections were owned, managed, and exhibited by the communist state—primarily for the enjoyment and edification of foreigners, not for local Czechs or even for the few thousand surviving Czech Jews. [37] I have already noted that the museum's bulletin, *Judaica Bohemiae,* was not published in Czech and that the independent researcher Jiří Fiedler was barred from using museum archives in his work on Jewish heritage sites. As late as November 1989, one week before the "Velvet Revolution," the Jewish intellectual Desider Galský was insistent that I not quote his criticism of mired government plans to restore the Holocaust memorial in the Pinkas Synagogue, which formed part of the museum: even discussion of how a Holocaust monument should be reconstructed was a taboo subject. One of the museum curators recalled in 1990 how, under the communist regime, "We had to get authorization from the authorities to speak with foreign visitors, and then, afterward, we had to write out reports on our conversations, whether they had been with visiting scholars, journalists, or whoever. It was the pressure of a totalitarian regime." Thus, for more than forty years, the State Jewish Museum symbolized both the dead past and the stifled present.

The situation was reversed after the fall of communism, when the museum became a symbol of the postcommunist changes and Jewish revival. The Jewish Museum was returned by the state to Jewish community control in 1994, and it immediately took on a new function and role. It honors the past, to be sure, and the "tainted" or "bloodstained" origin of most of its priceless collections still remains disturbing to some observers.[38] But from the beginning its new director, Leo Pavlát, a former anticommunist dissident Jewish activist, embarked on a program of renovation, diversification, and expansion aimed at making the museum a living symbol of a renewed, reinvigorated, and reintegrated Jewish presence in the city.

Pavlát's personal history paralleled that of the museum. He was born in 1950 to a non-Jewish father and a Jewish mother who lost all of her family in the Holocaust. As he grew up under communism, he recalled, his Jewish identity was "a family secret."[39] His sense of identity became consolidated in 1967, when, as in other communist states, the Six-Day War sparked a wave of anti-Semitic and anti-Israel propaganda and policy by the communist authorities. The short-lived reforms during the Prague Spring in 1968 were another catalyst in his exploration of Jewish identity; the hard-line regime imposed after the Soviet-led invasion of Czechoslovakia in August 1968 intensified both his sense of Jewish identity and his anticommunist dissent.

Pavlát's projects have aimed at transforming the Jewish Museum from its passive display of objects during its incarnation as the State Jewish Museum under communism into an interactive participant in postcommunist development, a cultural and research institution of importance not just for Jews but also for society at large. The new strategy radically altered the look and presentation of exhibits. No longer are objects displayed, as they were in the communist period, in sterile isolation, simply as objects in themselves behind glass: "Here is a textile; here is another textile; here is a candlestick; here is book." Instead, Jewish items are displayed in the context of broad Jewish religious traditions, local Jewish customs within those traditions, and local Jewish and Czech history. The goal is to teach local people and tourists alike about the place, role, and importance of Jewish heritage in Czech history while at the same time exposing them to the magnificence of Jewish ritual art. Under Pavlát's direction the museum established tough standards for licensed tour guides who wanted authorization to lead groups around the museum. It also opened an education center for visiting groups, began a lecture series, started publishing a quarterly newsletter about events and activities, and established a web site. It sent staff members to advise people restoring synagogues and setting up Jewish museums in small towns, as well as to conduct seminars, lectures, and teacher training sessions in the provinces.

The museum collections are, as they were during communism, still displayed in several former synagogue buildings, but all the individual exhibitions have been totally revamped as elaborations of local Jewish history or practice, and major restoration work has been carried out on the synagogues themselves, including a complete restoration of the nineteenth-century Spanish Synagogue, which was reopened as the site of a permanent exhibit on Jewish history in Bohemia and Moravia. Moreover, the High Synagogue, previously used to display the museum's textile exhibit, was returned to the Jewish community for religious use. The Altneu Synagogue was also withdrawn from museum administration and returned to direct control by the religious community, which uses it for services but also exhibits it to visitors.

Meanwhile, the museum, cut off from state subsidies, also became actively engaged as a moneymaking operation. Ticket sales and tourist itineraries for the museum were coordinated so as to better handle the huge crowds as well as to maximize income, and quality souvenir shops and bookstores were opened. Pavlát personally came under fire for sharply raising the price of museum tickets to a level that some considered prohibitive. He told me that one reason for this was, in fact, to limit the numbers of visitors; the Jewish community, following suit, also raised the entrance fee for the Altneu Synagogue. In 1998 a combined ticket for access to all museum sites and the synagogue came to about $15.

Mnemonic Devices

Perhaps in no major Jewish museum in Europe by the end of the 1990s had the questions, theories, and dilemmas embodied in Jewish representation and the Jewish museum experience been translated into the actual practice of exhibition so consciously and to such a degree as in Vienna.[40] The Jewish Museum of the City of Vienna was opened in 1993 in a downtown mansion that local tradition associated with a prominent Jewish family and thus designated, however tenuously, as "Jewish."[41] Its establishment was very much a political as well as a cultural move, a pet project of the city's then mayor, Helmut Zilk, who championed the concept for years and has spoken frequently of the museum as his "child." Zilk first announced plans to establish a Jewish museum in 1986, amid the intense and bitter debate over Austria's role in the Holocaust sparked by the Waldheim affair. The museum was thus born as an overt means of demonstrating a progressive attitude that sought to acknowledge and make up for a dirty past.

Some officials of the Vienna Jewish community initially opposed the project, preferring to see public funding spent on education and social welfare. Other Jews expressed concern that the new institution might promote "Museum Judaism," memorializing the dead to overshadow the living Jewish community. Nonetheless, there was close contact among the political forces behind the museum, the city government, and the Vienna Jewish community on how the project should evolve and what kind of museum should emerge. Representatives of the Jewish community were allotted three of the seven places on the museum advisory board, and its first director was a prominent German-Jewish scholar, Julius H. Schoeps. Though a municipal institution, the museum coordinates its activities with the Jewish community and has ended up fulfilling some of the functions of an American-style Jewish community center: there is a well-stocked Jewish bookshop and a comfortable vegetarian café with racks filled with Jewish newspapers from several countries; museum premises are used for Jewish community functions such as Purim or Hanukkah parties, and the museum cooperates with the Jewish community in sponsoring an annual Jewish Culture Week festival.

Visitors to the museum's permanent historic exhibition, though, are not confronted by traditional display cases presenting documents, Torah scrolls, Holocaust memorabilia, or Jewish ritual objects, nor do they find dioramas or didactic installations. Missing, too, is a commemorative section or memorial dedicated specifically to the Holocaust. Instead, they step inside a bare room housing twenty-one holograms: ghostly three-dimensional images of ritual objects, paintings, photographs, documents, and architectural models rather than the real thing.

Each hologram represents a specific stage, facet, or theme associated with Austrian Jewish history and the relationship between Jews and Austrian society: for example, "Out of the Ghetto," "Houses of God," "Zionism," "Anti-Semitism," "Loyalty and Patriotism," "From Historicism to Modernism," "Shoah," "Vienna Today." Most of the images are holographic still lifes that combine groupings of various source materials, some of which are easily understood objects in themselves, while others are defined by context or elaborate back stories recounted in the ample information notes that accompany each piece. The hologram titled "Banishments," for example, shows what is described as a seventeenth-century Torah curtain that a Viennese couple took with them to Prague when they were expelled from Vienna in 1670, along with a pile of film canisters described as containing a copy of the classic movie *Some Like It Hot,* which was directed by Billy Wilder, who was born in Vienna and fled Berlin after the Nazis took power in 1933. The hologram representing the "Fin de Siècle" contains images of an array of artifacts described as having been owned, used, or associated with turn-of-the-century Jewish cultural figures: writer Karl Kraus's glasses, a candlestick from a music stand used by Gustav Mahler, a book by Arthur Schnitzler with a flyleaf dedication to Theodore Herzl, Sigmund Freud's bookplate, playing cards designed and used by Arnold Schönberg.

Eerily glowing red and green and yellow, the images are captured on sheets of plexiglass that look totally transparent until the visitor stands directly before them; unless the panels are approached, the room looks empty: even in the coffee-table museum catalog, the photograph captioned "The Historical Exhibition" shows a room that seems to have nothing in it but windows, lights, a parquet floor, and scattered, three-meter-tall transparent sheets. The hologram images appear, move, and shift with changed angles of vision; the objects seen are virtual objects; the scenes are glimpses of a virtual reality—one even includes a holographic film clip; they are seemingly three-dimensional images that exist but don't exist, a "real" virtual Jewish world.

"Holography could prosper only in America, a country obsessed with realism, where, if a reconstruction is to be credible, it must be absolutely iconic, a perfect likeness, a 'real' copy of the reality being represented," wrote Umberto Eco in the mid-1970s.[42] Yet the curators of the Vienna exhibit had the opposite in mind. Their aim was precisely to reject any attempt to present a "real" image of Austrian Jewish history and experience through the conventional use of the objects, documents, and displays typical of museum exhibits. The incorporeal holograms are attempts to show the imprecise nature of memory and the role played by imagination and interpretation in viewing and presenting the past. History is not an absolute; physical objects represent the historical meaning that we ourselves assign to them. Even what is "carved in stone" is subject to interpretation. The use of holographic objects and scenes that are "there" but "not there" at the same time is also, obviously, a striking means of elaborating a sense of Jewish absence and the continuing impact of the Jewish past on the present. The exhibit, which opened in 1996, is called a "place of remembering." We see the objects, but we see *through* them, too. The holograms are nothing—but many things altogether, "mnemonic devices" or "memory aids in the form of abbreviations." [43]

"A historical exhibition cannot show or explain everything," the museum's then chief curator Felicitas Heimann-Jelinek, who designed the hologram installation, told me in 1997. "So why not say from the beginning that, in principle, we cannot do it. Perhaps it makes more sense to think about the relativity of history and historical presentations than to say this object means this, and this year was that, and this event meant such and such, and so on—because it's not true. We cannot reconstruct history; we should openly say that we are only its interpreters and nothing else."

The Jewish Museum of Vienna thus offers a radical and highly sophisticated approach to the problem of dealing with history, memory, and absence. For Heimann-Jelinek, the function of the exhibit is to force its audience to think and reflect about the Jewish experience and the impact of the Holocaust on the present. "This installation gives people the opportunity to think about what would have been possible, what could have happened, what could be different today," she told me. "The hologram room is a very peaceful surrounding. It is a bit like a prayer room because on the one hand it is so spacious and on the other it is very calm. People don't talk loudly; they read the information panels and look at the holograms. There is a very contemplative atmosphere."

The Vienna museum, like any post-Holocaust Jewish museum, she believes, should "motivate its visitors to ask themselves the right questions and not only consume prepared answers to questions which they have never learned to articulate." [44] The holograms thus should serve as guideposts, a table of possible contents for future reference. The museum supplements the permanent hologram installation with frequent, thought-provoking, but more traditionally arranged temporary exhibitions on individual themes, but each theme chosen is somehow related to those embodied by the holographic images. The holograms are aimed at stimulating interest on the part of the visitor, either to learn more about a topic on his or her own or to return to the museum to visit a temporary exhibit linked to it.

The Vienna museum, though, is not just holograms and temporary exhibits. It does display ritual objects and other Judaica but, again, deliberately not in a traditional manner. Its ground floor lecture room contains glass cases displaying arrangements of exquisite ceremonial art, and some of the pieces, as in many other museums, are set up to represent the observance of Jewish festivals. But to dispel the impression of looking at Jewish ritual objects separated by glass from present-day contexts, the curators covered the front of the glass cases with German-language texts taken from translations of the Bible, the Talmud, and Jewish liturgy. The objects, thus, are viewed—physically as well as symbolically—through the filter of prayers and readings still used today in local Jewish practice rather than simply through the isolating medium of museum case glass.

Most of the museum's very rich collection of material, however, is exhibited as a "viewable storage area," a crowded mass of concrete objects that is in stark contrast to the holographic historical exhibition in which no "real" object is included. Its concept is quite the opposite from the Rome museum's "living storage area." The Vienna museum's entire stock of silver Torah shields, crowns, pointers, *rimmonim* (Torah scroll ornaments), spice boxes, candlesticks, Hanukkah menorahs, shofars, textiles, and other items are displayed, en masse, shelf upon shelf, in clear glass storage cabinets. This material includes the remains of the collection of the original, prewar Jewish museum, which was shut down by force after the German annexation of Austria in 1938, as well as objects salvaged from synagogues and prayer houses destroyed or desecrated on Kristallnacht and kept safe in hiding during the war. The material also includes postwar donations and purchases. There is no attempt to single out individual prize pieces or arrange illustrative holiday tableaus. The power and effect of presenting the objects in storage is precisely to show them, item upon item, out of context, thus emphasizing that they were often torn by force from their appropriate settings—synagogues, homes, schools, prayer houses, the old museum itself—to become, eventually, museum exhibits. Like the hologram installation, the "viewable storage area" also aims to raise questions among visitors and to prompt reflection. Massed together, the objects demonstrate the onetime prestige, prosperity, and integration of Jews in Austrian society; relegated to museum inventory, they demonstrate the marginalization, persecution, and destruction.[45]

Vienna museum organizers thus strove consciously to break out of old models in discussing or presenting the Holocaust as well as general Jewish history and also Jewish ritual art. "In dealing with the Holocaust, one finds always the same metaphors, the same pictures," Julius Schoeps told me. "They become devalued." The Holocaust and its effects, he said, permeate everything in the Vienna museum. "You only have to look. It's not necessary to use a hammer."

But visitors may be uncomfortable with museums whose style and exhibits do not meet their expectations. As we saw in Schnaittach and Bologna, the intended impact of the Vienna museum, too, is lost on some of the public. A New York rabbi returned to his congregation after a visit to the museum and gave a High Holy Day sermon in which he expressed anger and distress that, as he saw it, the museum did not touch on Holocaust themes.[46] Felicitas Heimann-Jelinek admitted to me that, according to surveys, only about half of the Vienna museum's visitors really appreciated the hologram exhibit; she said she found it frustrating that many visitors, locked into literal expectations, did not get the point. "I don't know why people don't see it, but it's there in everything, and also the viewable storage area," she said. "It's a documentation, but a documentation of what? Of what is left, and that actually means a documentation about the Holocaust."

Large carved wooden figure of a Jewish musician stands in front of a souvenir stand that sells Jewish theme keepsakes in Kraków's former Jewish quarter, Kazimierz, 1997. (Photo by Ruth Ellen Gruber.)

Klezmer in the Wilderness

If you can have anti-Semitism without Jews, why not Jewish music?

Rudi Assuntino, Rome

Klezmer in the Wilderness

If you can have anti-Semitism without Jews, why not Jewish music?

Rudi Assuntino, Rome

9

Making (and Remaking) Jewish Music

The Gothic tower of St. Marien Church looms over Flensburg, a quaint, pastel port some eighty miles north of Hamburg at the narrow tip of a fjord opening eastward into the Baltic Sea. On a wet winter night the church is aglow, and enticing strains of music waft out into the glistening streets. The music isn't a Gregorian chant, however, or a tenor singing Bach. It's electronically amplified eastern European Jewish music. Inside the church, in front of a massive sixteenth-century altar whose carved and gilded woodwork flamboyantly frames a painting of the Last Supper, the American klezmer group Brave Old World entrances a capacity audience of three hundred people who fill neat rows of chairs set up in the pillared nave. Brave Old World is no stranger to Germany. The group cuts its CDs in Hamburg and has earned much of its income over the past decade touring in all parts of the country. They had played in Flensburg three years before, during a monthlong "Anne Frank weeks" program promoting multicultural brotherhood. This concert now, one stop on an eight-city tour of Germany and the Netherlands in February 1997, is a follow-up, sponsored by local church organizations, the city itself, and a society for "testimony and service among Jews and Christians." Flensburg has no Jewish community, but it is a sister city to Ashdod in Israel; exchange groups go back and forth between the two cities each year. A man from the church youth organization introduces the concert with a brief speech. "Music," he tells the audience, "helps us discover the soul of others." Wearing a wine-colored shirt that perfectly matches the draperies in the painted Last Supper behind him, Brave Old World's front man, Michael Alpert, joshes with the crowd in Yiddish, regardless of whether they are able to understand it: aside from the disciples in the painting, he says, and from the Jesus nailed to an enormous fifteenth-century crucifix suspended from the vaulted ceiling, members of the band are probably the only Jews in the hall. The band launches into a fast-moving song about Bessarabia. Next to me, a young woman in her twenties bobs and jives to the music. She certainly has nothing as weighty as reconciliation on her mind. I ask her whether she thinks it's strange to hear this kind of music—I mean Jewish music—performed in a church. "Yes, it *is* sort of funny to hear a concert like this in a church," she agrees. "You feel that you can't really get up and dance."

Of all the ways in which non-Jewish Europeans have opened their arms to make Things Jewish their own, the embrace of klezmer and other music based on eastern European Yiddish traditions has become one of the most widespread. At the same time, the participatory and interpretive aspects inherent in musical involvement have made it one of the most debatable—and to some, one of the most vexing. No matter that the music is most broadly popular in countries where few Jews live today and where before World War II it was scarcely, if ever, heard or was even scorned. American neoklezmer revival groups such as Brave Old World and the Klezmatics and Israeli stars such as the Argentine-born clarinetist Giora Feidman draw enthusiastic crowds on their frequent tours of the continent, and they are emulated by an increasing number of homegrown European bands eager to construct their own variations of the genre.[1]

In Germany, the bittersweet wail of the klezmer clarinet has provided an iconized sound track for coming to terms with the past. There are scores of klezmer and Yiddish music groups around the country, and in 1997 it was estimated that between twenty and thirty groups played on a professional, semiprofessional, or amateur basis in Berlin alone. More than half a dozen klezmer or Yiddish music groups are based in Austria, and there are others in the Netherlands, Switzerland, Scandinavia, Hungary, Poland, Italy, and elsewhere. The interest has spawned klezmer workshops, klezmer festivals, and klezmer societies; local bands put out CDs and mount web sites. One cross-border Jewish music festival in November 1997 featured forty-eight performances by artists from half a dozen countries in venues scattered around Belgium, Germany, and the Netherlands.[2] Popularity, as it will, has produced competing styles and competing egos as well, not to mention competition for funding (public as well as private) for klezmer-related events.

Outside countries such as France, Britain, and Russia, however, where there is a Jewish music scene within the relatively large Jewish population, relatively few Jews are members of European klezmer groups—or, for that matter, of their audiences. The Gojim in Austria and the Netherlands and the Klezgoyim in Germany consciously point this out in their very names. Klezmer and Yiddish music (even more so than other Jewish music) is the quintessential Jewish cultural product. Involvement with Jewish music is one of the most universal access routes to an emotional, even physical encounter with "the rhythms of Jewish life," an easy ticket into the virtual Jewish world. For fans as well as musicians, it is a hands-on, hip-swaying way of undergoing a "Jewish" (or "Jewish-style") experience: musicians playing klezmer tunes can shape that experience, too, to reflect their own understanding of what is "Jewish." Non-Jewish musicians presenting their interpretations of klezmer in closed-circuit contact with non-Jewish audiences can easily diffuse a virtual sense of "Jewishness" that fits their own definitions.

The very sound of klezmer, with its capacity to express a dance and a dirge in the same breath, has become an immediate symbol of Jewish tragedy and survival in the Diaspora. It is an auditory Star of David that, like the Star, can be used in any desired context in which Jews or the Holocaust are to be evoked. Codified kitsch can hover close to the surface. And Jews, too, in places where few Jews live and where klezmer may not have been part of local Jewish tradition, may also wave the klezmer flag as a self-identifying banner.

On the first night of Hanukkah in December 1997, for example, an Israeli clarinetist, costumed in a blousy white shirt, black hat, and bright red hatband, pointed his instrument skyward with a piercing klezmer cadenza to open an extraordinary menorah lighting ceremony in the heart of Rome, a city where Jews have lived for more than two thousand years—longer than anywhere else in Europe—but where klezmer and the Yiddish of eastern European Jewish experience have no part in local Jewish tradition. Italy's president, prime minister, and other VIPs, as well as high-ranking Israelis and Rome's elderly chief rabbi, took part in the event, which kicked off celebrations marking the fiftieth anniversary of the founding of the Jewish state. The clarinetist's klezmer—eastern European Jewish music channeled via Israel—fluttered over the ceremony like a flag. The touch of melancholy in the notes tempered the joyousness of the celebration with hinted, easily accessed memory of the Holocaust and earlier centuries of persecution. It lent intensity to a scene that was already a powerful evocation of the Jewish Diaspora experience, contrasted with that of Israel's half century of statehood. The spotlit ceremony was staged in the ancient Roman Forum. Aided by the chief rabbi, Italy's seventy-nine-year-old president, Oscar Luigi Scalfaro, lit the first candle of a huge menorah dramatically set up in front of the Arch of Titus, the triumphal arch built after the Romans sacked Jerusalem and destroyed the Temple in the year 70. The inside of the arch displays a vivid carving of the Temple's looted menorah. For centuries the arch symbolized the Diaspora to such an extent that Jews refused to walk under it; the carving of the menorah provided the model for the menorah symbol of Israel. "This evening a circle closes," the Israeli ambassador told the audience in a moment charged with emotional and historical as well as political significance. "We are here at the arch not as slaves but as representatives of the independent, free state of Israel."

The klezmer phenomenon in Europe has a sound for all seasons; it is a complex, at times hodgepodge, mixture of good time music and—as in Rome—conscious use of Jewish motifs to make a political or emotional point. Some musicians and fans alike use involvement in the music as a means of seeking or clarifying their musical or personal identities. As a quintessential Jewish symbol, some make playing, promoting, or even just listening to the music a conscious means of remembering the world of eastern European Jewry that was destroyed in the Holocaust, or, creating a symbol out of a symbol, of taking a stand against contemporary racism. In some countries klezmer and Yiddish song are almost ritual components of Kristallnacht anniversary and other official Holocaust memorial ceremonies, as well as more general brotherhood events sponsored by civic, state, church, and interfaith organizations. By now, in some places, the image of a klezmer clarinet "laughing and crying at the same time" has become so hackneyed a metaphor for recalling the rocky Jewish experience that the New York–born fiddler Bob Cohen, who leads a klezmer group based in Budapest, describes playing klezmer for commemoration as getting "gelt for guilt."

Increasingly, however, as the past recedes, new audiences and new, younger, performers emphatically reject metaphoric overtones and claim fulfillment simply in the music itself. European klezmer and Yiddish music bands run the gamut of styles, competence, and awareness—or desire for awareness—of Jewish cultural or historical contexts. Their approaches to the music range from serious scholarly reproduction of sound or sophisticated experiments with innovative techniques to a naive, garage band eagerness simply to play fun tunes. Some—including music industry promotors picking up on new markets—seek consciously to integrate specifically "Jewish" culture and forms of culture into a broad, more universal European mainstream composed of many ethnic inputs: klezmer as the latest incarnation of world music, a model for a new, multicultural European identity. Others find in klezmer, with its historical confluence of many musical roots, a well-suited matrix for their own efforts at contemporary fusion or use traditional Yiddish or klezmer motifs to launch jazz or rock improvisation. For others, it's simply the music of the moment, an alternative music that carries the distinct cachet of "Jewish chic," as if contact with it represented, by association, connection with a hip, slightly exotic, somewhat countercultulture elite. This was vividly illustrated in October 1997, when *Glamour* magazine's Italian edition ran a flashy two-page feature on klezmer in its "Trend Monitor" slot.[3]

The notes to the 1995 compact disc *Shtil, di nacht is ojsgeschternt,* by the Austrian klezmer trio Gebrider Moischele, quote group member Hansjörg Schmid as saying, "We want to make music that touches. Music that inspires us to laugh, dream and cry. Music that grew out of the feelings, longings and dreams of ordinary people. Simply [Y]iddish folk music!" The cover shows three sturdily handsome young musicians wearing vaguely old-fashioned, vaguely folk-style black-and-white clothing; they cradle their instruments and look pensive against a bleak, wintry landscape. Gebrider Moischele, founded in the mid-1980s, is from Vorarlberg, the small, westernmost region of Austria near the Swiss border where Hohenems is located. The CD was recorded in a studio in the Austrian Tyrol; the music, a dozen more or less traditional eastern European Jewish songs, sung in Yiddish, is infused with the oompah flavor of a Germanic Alpine dance band.[4]

Far to the south, on a sultry summer night in the ancient Italian Adriatic port of Ancona, an eleven-member band from Florence called the T.E.S.T. Orchestra lets loose at the four-day International Festival of Klezmer Music. Band leader Luca Di Volo, a wiry man with a crisp brown beard, sends his saxophone on flights of wild jazz flavored by "Jewish"-sounding intonations. He bounces his riffs off Claudia Bombardella, a young blond woman in a bright red, skintight outfit, who hefts a bass sax almost as big as she is. "We don't try to do traditional things," Bombardella tells me after the show. "But just to recognize the spirit of klezmer—its strength and great energy. That's all that remains." What is this spirit? Di Volo, who has a background in both classical and folk music, says that in Jewish music he found "the correct degree of equilibrium between fingers and heart." Jewish music, he asserts, "is the best therapy against aging."[5]

The popularity of klezmer in all its incarnations does not approach that of some other forms of ethnic and traditional music in Europe, but the heavy historical baggage in at least some of the countries where the klezmer phenomenon is most widespread gives its development political and social resonances that have set it apart from, say, contemporary tango, Celtic, or country-western crazes—as well as from related trends, such as the penchant among some Europeans to dress up as cowboys and Indians and spend weekends in the forest pretending to live in the Wild West.

"I think you still can't perform klezmer music in Germany without making a statement," Christian Dawid, the clarinetist of the Klezgoyim, told me in 1997. "It's automatically a statement. . . . That's also why we decided to put that 'goyim' in the name of the group. Because we just wanted to make it clear that we're not copying something or that we don't think we own this music. We just wanted to say, OK, we like this music and we do this music and we want to play it as naturally as possible for us as musicians. But we also want to say, OK, this is not our music."

A Little Background

The Yiddish word *klezmer* derives from the Hebrew *kĕlēy zemer,* meaning "vessels of song," or musical instruments. *Klezmer* (pl. *klezmorim*) referred to the professional musicians who played the instruments. Only in the past few decades has the term *klezmer* come to mean not only the musicians but also the music itself. Scholars define a historic klezmer style and repertoire. By now, though, "klezmer music" is often used to describe the entire genre of music based on Yiddish traditional and popular motifs—be it note-for-note reproductions of tunes found on old records, contemporary interpretations of old material, new presentations of songs still played in eastern European villages, or rock and jazz improvisations based on klezmer sources.[6]

In the eastern European Jewish social structure, klezmorim historically formed a tightly knit caste on the fringes of polite society. The profession of klezmer was usually hereditary, and families of klezmorim sometimes intermarried to forge veritable klezmer dynasties. Klezmorim often traveled from town to city to village; their music was an essential component of festivities, especially wedding celebrations. They played for Jewish and non-Jewish audiences alike, and non-Jewish musicians sometimes played in klezmer bands. (The last scene of *Pan Tadeusz*, the nineteenth-century Polish national epic by Adam Mickiewicz, describes the Jewish tavern keeper, Jankiel—one of the most famous characters in Polish literature—playing Polish patriotic music on his cymbalom at a noble Polish betrothal party.)

The music of the klezmorim was the product of converging influences that reflected the cultural mix of the eastern European ethnic groups among which Jews lived; in a sense, it traced a symbolic road map of the Jewish Diaspora. Yiddish folk song, Jewish liturgical chants, Hasidic *nigunim* (wordless tunes), and the local folk music traditions of neighboring cultures—Gypsies, Romanians, Ukrainians, Poles—as well as popular songs and dances and even operatic arias all had their impact. Eventually, the shape of the music was further elaborated by the experience of the vast Jewish immigration to North America beginning in the 1880s. Until the Holocaust, there were continuing mutual influences between the music played by Jewish klezmorim who remained in eastern Europe and that played by those who made their way to the New World, where their repertoire was enriched by exposure to the American Yiddish theater and vaudeville, not to mention show tunes, radio broadcasts, jazz forms, and other realities of life in America. Technology also had an impact. From the late 1890s, the new recording industry enabled a further diffusion of the music and of local or individual musical styles. But the new technology forced klezmorim to cut and shape their performances to accommodate the strict time constraints of early recording techniques. And far-flung music fans could hear these recorded tunes and demand that local musicians play them exactly the same way. Many klezmer motifs played by bands today were learned from prewar recordings made in America by klezmer musicians who were born and trained in eastern Europe and continued their careers after immigration.[7]

The Holocaust put an end to the klezmer tradition in eastern Europe. Assimilation exiled it (as it exiled the Yiddish language) from upwardly mobile Jewish society in America; it did not disappear totally, but what remained was frequently considered a quaint holdover of little interest to modern young Jews, who usually rejected it wholesale. Even in Israel it was submerged in the struggle of the Jewish state to create its own, new cultural identity.

Giora Feidman, a fourth-generation klezmer who in 1957, at the age of twenty-one, moved from his native Argentina to Israel to play in the Israeli Philharmonic, was among the first to introduce klezmer music to

a new postwar generation of listeners. "I got this education from my father and my father from his father," Feidman told me. "But when I
went to Israel in 1957 there was nothing [there] about what we know
about Jewish music. It was a process. One day in 1960 or 1961, I went
to Kol Israel, the radio station, to record songs, and somebody gave me
something klezmer to play. I recorded it normally. But when I finished,
I said to him that if he wanted, I could play this in a style that I knew
he didn't know. So I recorded [it as] what we call klezmer. And in
twenty-four hours, this became a boom. It started this movement of
klezmer." Feidman eventually developed an almost mystical vision of
klezmer as a universal language that could unite peoples and has been
one of the most important influences in popularizing klezmer music in
Europe, particularly in Germany. But the European klezmer phenomenon also has direct links with the neoklezmer movement or klezmer revival, which emerged in North America in the 1970s with the coming of
age of Jews born in America after the Holocaust and often far removed
from their eastern European origins.[8]

This new interest among young American Jewish musicians in the
music of their ancestors took off at the same time that American Jews
started to become interested in rediscovering their roots, in both the
old country and the immigrant experience. By the late 1990s Jewish
genealogy, for example, had developed into an entire, self-generating
business, with scores of publications, genealogy societies, professional
genealogists, and Internet web sites. The revival of interest in klezmer
was the musical side of this coin. Many of the young American musicians who pioneered the neoklezmer movement were already involved
in playing or researching other forms of ethnic music, in particular Balkan or other eastern European music, but also American folk traditions.
Henry Sapoznik, who grew up in a Yiddish-speaking Hasidic home and
whose father was a cantor, played American folk music and bluegrass
and spent time in North Carolina learning Appalachian music from an
elderly fiddler. This fiddler "had always known that there was an extra-
ordinarily high percentage of young Jews playing old time music,"
Sapoznik has written. "He didn't understand it; but he accepted it. One
day he asked me in all candor: 'Hank, don't your people got none of
your own music?'" This, according to Sapoznik, is what spurred him
into beginning his research into Jewish traditional music.[9] He and other
young Jewish musicians sought out old 78 rpm records, yellowing sheet
music, and elderly immigrant musicians, such as clarinetist Dave Tarras
and the fiddler Leon Schwartz, to learn from. Some eventually made

field trips to eastern Europe—like Sapoznik's forays into the Appalachians—to interview, record, and learn from the few elderly Jewish musicians still living there.

In 1983 the ethnomusicologist Mark Slobin, who has written extensively about the early years of the klezmer boom in the United States, identified three categories of people responsible for the "remarkable rise" of the movement: "the historian/researcher types," "the elder statesman/repository of traditional repertoire" (for example, Dave Tarras, now dubbed "King Klezmer"), and "a handful of performance acolytes and band-creators . . . who re-articulate acquired skills and repertoire gained from researchers and vintage performers and recordings."[10] Slobin also noted how the klezmer sound had an immediate appeal for younger Jews: "[T]here has been no real musical symbol for college-age Jewish-Americans outside the Zionist movement. For this generation, the immigrant era is the Old World. To them, perhaps, Europe means only the Holocaust, death instead of life. The *klezmer* sound has the advantage of recalling two vanished Jewish worlds simultaneously, Europe and the Lower East Side of New York. . . . For the young, *klezmer* music is a musical surprise package to be unwrapped and enjoyed."[11]

By the late 1990s there were hundreds—if not thousands—of klezmer musicians of all levels of skill and dedication playing in scores—if not hundreds—of klezmer bands across the United States and Canada. The music hit mainstream audiences with the high-profile involvement of Itzhak Perlman, who took part in a 1995 PBS "Great Performances" documentary on klezmer, *In the Fiddler's House,* that was shot partly in New York and partly in Kraków, Poland, during Kraków's annual summer Festival of Jewish Culture. Perlman was filmed with Leopold Kozłowski, a squat, heavy-featured man with bushy sideburns who is one of the few prewar klezmorim still performing in eastern Europe.[12] But it was a "roots" program in more than a musical sense: Perlman was filmed walking through Kazimierz with his father, who had emigrated from Poland in the 1930s and was making his first trip back. "Klezmer becomes the lens through which we see something wider and deeper," the documentary's cowriter and producer Sara Lukinson told me during the filming. "Klezmer has given us the chance to open up to tradition, to what was here, and to what is not here anymore. The music becomes something that's more than just musical notes." Along with Perlman, the program featured five leading klezmer revival groups: Brave Old World, the Klezmatics, the Klezmer Conservatory Band,

Kapelye, and Andy Statman. Perlman and four of these groups later toured the United States, giving concerts before immense crowds at leading venues ranging from Radio City Music Hall to Ravinia. The two CD spin-offs from the PBS program and tour sold nearly two hundred thousand copies by the latter part of 1997, reaching a vast and varied public that otherwise would never have heard, much less heard of, this type of music and at the same time defining it as "art" as well as "folk."

The Old Country

The development of the klezmer craze in Europe has in many ways mirrored the American model and indeed was strongly influenced by it. All the same elements identified by Slobin are there, from the researchers to the elder statesmen to the early "acolyte" bands picking up on the craze. Rather than old-timers like Dave Tarras and Leon Schwartz, however, the "elder statesman/repository" figures for European klezmer fans and musicians as often as not tend to be contemporary personalities such as Giora Feidman (whose publicity, reminiscent of earlier references to Dave Tarras, calls him the "King of Klezmer") and the five groups featured in the Itzhak Perlman documentary, all of which frequently tour in Europe.[13]

Liner notes to the 1997 CD of the young Berlin group la'om, for example, describe how the group's clarinetist learned one song, "originally a Jewish folksong from pre-revolutionary Russia," from two of the American movement's most prominent clarinetists, Kurt Bjorling and Joel Rubin.[14] In Italy Moni Ovadia—who got his own introduction to klezmer from recordings by American neoklezmer performers such as the Klezmorim and Andy Statman—was a primary gateway to the music for locals. The avant-garde musician John Zorn, who developed an experimental music label called Tzadik that included a series devoted to "Radical Jewish Culture," has also been a powerful influence, particularly among younger Europeans. Many Europeans have told me that they only discovered the old prewar klezmer recordings (many of which have been reissued on CD or cassette) after becoming interested in klezmer through the modern sources: Andrea Pandolfo of the Rome-based group Klezroym compared listening to these recordings to listening to Dixieland; they are of archival interest but little more. "Is a klezmer group one that reproduces old sound," he said, "or one that takes it further?"

As in America, too, the European development has been in many ways a third-generation phenomenon—a desire to explore lost or forgotten traditions. Even the sense of klezmer music as a musical reference point that fills an emotional or spiritual vacuum is widespread. But the mirror in Europe is distorted by an inescapable dimension that did not and does not exist in America. In Europe the klezmer movement has been taking place in the countries where the Holocaust actually happened. Unlike in America (Perlman's mass audiences apart), in Europe concert-goers, CD buyers, and local musicians are overwhelmingly non-Jewish. The lost or forgotten traditions they seek to explore and interpret are not those of their own parents or grandparents but those of Jews wiped out by the Nazis, in some countries with the active participation of their parents' or grandparents' generation.

This poses questions about the music and its meaning that scarcely exist in the American context. The sociology often becomes as significant as the music itself. Although this has been changing rapidly, few European klezmer groups in the late 1990s were yet relaxed enough about the Jewish experience in Europe to engage in the irreverence and parody often evident in American bands.[15] Some groups appeared to feel the need to justify their involvement by citing, in their public relations, CD notes, or web sites, the historical participation of non-Jews in klezmer bands. Even groups that *have* pushed the limits—with their names or costumes or packaging, for example—will have thought long and hard about the effect. In 1991, three years after she cofounded the Vienna-based klezmer group Gojim, the actress Caroline Koczan recalled, "Austrian culture was so xenophobic that it was an open provocation just to sing what we sang, let alone call ourselves Gojim. It's an ugly word with an element of self-condemnation. But it's an honorable name with no false pretense that we're Jews. We speak the truth. We are Gentiles who sing Jewish music."[16] Members of Rome's Klezroym told me they used a blue background for the cover of their 1998 debut CD to stress the group's Mediterranean origin—blue evoking the sea. They also said that the cover logo, a mazelike composition based on a kabbalistic symbol, aimed at being "a Jewish symbol, but not aggressively so. We didn't want to use the usual Jewish symbols like Chagall paintings and Stars of David."

"If you are in America and talk about the Six Million and if you are in Europe and talk about the Six Million, it's different," Albert Misak emphasized to me over steaming cups of coffee in a smoky coffeehouse on Vienna's Ring. Misak was born in Vienna in 1949 and started playing Yiddish folk music as a teenager in the 1960s. He pioneered Yiddish and klezmer performance in Austria and has long been one of the relatively few Jewish musicians in today's European klezmer scene. "In America it's easy," he went on. "Nowadays people here [in Austria]—the third generation after the war—are trying to understand what happened in the Holocaust. People were killed. They were Jews. But who is a Jew? What is a Jew? They are trying to find out more about it. Our music helps them—or I hope it helps them—understand. But, of course, I don't believe you can understand the Holocaust. As a performer in this scene, do you want to be a performer or a storyteller—an admonishing storyteller?" He put down his cup. "You have to be very sensitive to the audience. Not be too heavy."

"Gelt for Guilt" or Good Time Music?

For many non-Jewish Europeans, the shadow of the Holocaust hangs heavy over every note and chord of even the liveliest klezmer tunes. "Personally," a German woman of about fifty, who plays cello in an amateur klezmer band in Berlin told me in 1997, "I like the meeting of melancholy and very gay music—most people feel it in their hearts. Sometimes I'm even a bit sad when I remember that the Germans did away with the culture of the Jews and destroyed the Jewish people. This is a tragedy for us. For us as a group, playing the music is a little bit thinking of the people who died because of our fathers—it allows the music to live again, prevents these wonderful songs from being lost." For this woman and others like her, playing or listening to klezmer and Yiddish music represents a symbolic attempt to right wrongs: to reconstitute Jewish culture destroyed in the Holocaust, to "bring back," to "resurrect," to "heal." Embrace of the music, too, allows at least momentary identification with Jews and their fate, enabling a sense of sharing the burden of the past.

In summer 1996 the Austrian violinist Herwig Strobl carried out a project with just this object quite evidently in mind. Strobl has specialized in Yiddish and klezmer music since the early 1980s. The project entailed collaboration with Bernard Offen, a Kraków-born Jewish Holocaust survivor who now lives in San Francisco, on a CD recorded in Kraków's seventeenth-century Izaak Synagogue.[17] The synagogue, which stood empty and dilapidated in the heart of Kraków's former Jewish quarter, Kazimierz, for decades after the war, had recently been restored; delicate frescoes of Hebrew texts and Jewish symbols were now revealed on the walls beneath its soaring vaulted ceiling. Collaboration between Strobl and Offen, the CD booklet says, represented "[t]wo people of different historical and cultural descent [coming] into contact." It doesn't, however, say just how different this background was. Offen survived Auschwitz and four other Nazi camps as a teenager. With his silver beard, long silver ponytail, and laid-back California style, he became a familiar figure in Kazimierz in the 1990s. By 1996 he had spent five summers lecturing in Kraków on his Holocaust experiences and conducting groups of tourists to sites related to his own and his family's suffering. He calls these tours "journeys and pilgrimages . . . of witnessing and healing" and advertises them on posters and handbills.

Strobl, born in 1940, is the son of a man who was an active Nazi. *Born Guilty: Children of Nazi Families,* a 1986 book based on interviews with Germans and Austrians whose parents (or sometimes grandparents) had been Nazis, cites a letter written by Strobl's father in 1965 counseling young Herwig in strong terms against getting involved with a Jewish girl, of bringing "someone of Jewish descent into our clan." [18] Strobl ended up dedicating himself to Jewish music; he founded the Linz-based band 10 Saiten 1 Boden in 1982 and became known in Austria for his interpretations of Yiddish songs.

What he produced with Offen is quite different from the feel-good presentation of Yiddish folk standards on his other recordings. It is a series of meandering solo violin improvisations, based mostly on the songs of Mordechai Gebirtig, the Kraków Yiddish bard who was killed by the Germans in 1942. The music echoes in the cavernous synagogue and is interspersed with brief cuts of Offen's voice singing in Yiddish or talking about a project to research and, as he put it, "re-create" the congregation that once worshiped there.

In this corner of the virtual Jewish world, Strobl, the Nazi's son, playing his own interpretations of the music of a murdered Jew, assumes the dual role of both Jew and resurrector. Offen, the "real" victim, at one point takes on the role of the Nazis: one of the tracks, based on Gebirtig's famous song "S'brent"—"Our Shtetl Is Burning"—evokes the wartime destruction of a Jewish ghetto. Strobl's playing interacts with accoustic effects produced by Offen: the thrum of marching boots and a hammering on the door to the German cry "Aufmachen!" (Open up!). "I felt you tremble while you cried out, taking up the oppressors' role, then marching. How could you creep into German boots?" Strobl says in a letter to Offen that is reprinted in the CD booklet. The recording session took place late at night, after Offen had set the emotional scene by guiding Strobl on a tour through the former Kraków ghetto, in the footsteps of his murdered family. "You were so weak, but strong at the same moment," Strobl's letter goes on. "Having overcome all the humiliation, having taken up the task of healing and without accusations showing: I am human, therefore I'm witnessing."

When I visited the Izaak Synagogue a little more than a year after the midnight session of musical communion that produced this CD, I was shocked to find that the sanctuary had been "peopled" by Jews brought back from the dead: creepy cutouts from prewar photographs of Jews in caftans and sidelocks, blown up to life size and positioned standing around the otherwise empty hall. The supposed aim of this, I read, was to "make it possible to 'travel in time' and experience the atmosphere of Kraków many years ago." [19] I found it the atmosphere of a sideshow, the roadside attraction of my nightmares.

Herwig Strobl's family background makes his involvement stand out among the masses of Germans—and other Austrians—who confront the crimes of their parents' generation. But European klezmer and Yiddish groups ostensibly far removed from the actual fact of the Shoah may also express profound ambiguities about the music. This comes through in the sometimes gingerly way they approach it—and even in the physical ways that groups sometimes present themselves. The Italian group Dire Gelt is a case in point.

The klezmer wave hit Italy in the early to mid-1990s, some years after it washed over parts of Europe farther north. Although a few Italian musicians, such as the Rimini-based Roberto Paci Dalò, had begun playing klezmer on a local level by the late 1980s, it was Moni Ovadia's performances that introduced the music to a wider public. Dire Gelt, which takes its name from the title of a Yiddish song popularized by Ovadia in his widely performed "Yiddish cabaret" production *Oylem Goylem,* was founded in Bologna in 1994, and its 1996 CD, *Klezmer Music, Yiddish Songs,* was one of the first released by an Italian klezmer group. The liner notes read as if the musicians had been almost afraid to play the music lest they somehow defile it. "The fact is," they say, "that Klezmer is a delicate subject, and it was not easy to clarify our relationship to this music and to the culture that generated it. These songs communicate a highly evocative force in their treatment of real life situations often tied to dramatic moments: the poverty of the ghetto, the persecutions, the death camps. We have striven to avoid any rhetorical temptation, while trying to preserve the consciousness and the historical memory." [20]

On the one hand, the uneasiness reflects the novelty of the experience (as does singer Sabina Meyer's mispronunciation of "klezmer" as
"kletzmer"). On the other hand, it reflects trepidation in choosing the
proper approach to anything having to do with Jews and the Holocaust—as if the group felt compelled to pay some sort of tribute to
Jews as a way of excusing their "trespass." But the uneasiness also is
grounded in the contradictory ways that Jews, Jewish culture, and Israel
have been regarded by the Italian Left. As underscored in the liner
notes, Dire Gelt was formed within an alternative, radical left-wing
political environment, an environment long characterized in an almost schizophrenic way by staunch "anti-Zionism" complemented frequently by a fascination with European Jewish culture and especially the
Jewish contribution to the intellectual world of prewar central Europe.

The Dire Gelt liner notes resolutely describe the group as a "Gojim
Klezmer Ensemble." The finely produced CD package as a whole aims
at creating a nostalgic sense of "virtual" Jewishness or resurrected Yiddishkayt. The CD comes in a dull green and khaki metal box rather than
the usual plastic or cardboard. It's like a ready-made heirloom, an "absolute fake" relic of the past, complete with the patina of age. The cover
design includes a high-contrast picture of the profile of a bearded man
wearing a hat. It employs writing in Hebrew-Yiddish calligraphy that is
so crude it is scarcely legible. The main group photo in the CD booklet
is a grainy black-and-white shot of the six Dire Gelt members dressed in
slightly old-fashioned clothing that suggests that they could be immigrants (or at least poor shtetl dwellers). Staring somberly and directly at
the camera, they thus assume that role, confronting the present-day
viewer with this virtual image of an earlier (imagined) time. Another
photo shows a black-hatted, black-bearded figure laden with suitcases:
the Wandering Jew.

At the start of a 1997 concert by Dire Gelt and the Klezroym in the
central Italian city of Terni (where few, if any, Jews have lived since the
Middle Ages), one of the Dire Gelt musicians took a moment to pay a
brief homage to Holocaust victims. The implication was clear: this
would be reanimated music, rescued from the dead. He did not appear
to be aware, however, that the concert was being held on the Jewish festival of Purim, a joyous holiday still celebrated with great festivities
by millions of living Jews worldwide—including in Rome, just sixty
miles away, where at that very moment the holiday was the occasion
for a crowded street fair near the city's ornate, domed Great Synagogue in the old ghetto neighborhood on the bank of the Tiber.[21]
(Three years later, members of Dire Gelt had re-formed into another

band and were featured as performers at, among other things, an art event hosted by the Israeli embassy.)

In recent years, as audiences and musicians have grown more knowledgeable and the market for klezmer music has become more commercial, "gelt for guilt" has given way to (or been joined by) other forms of appeal. A sophisticated public has evolved that seeks out quality and innovation in the music rather than an opportunity to wallow in nostalgia. "I don't want the music to be a political statement; I don't want to go onstage and to feel solidarity," Alexei Biz, a Jewish violinist from Russia who immigated to Vienna in the 1990s and played with various Jewish music groups in Austria, complained to me in 1997. "I want to go onstage and hear 'Yeah! You play great, man!' That's it. I make music, I don't make politics."

The influence of John Zorn, the Klezmatics, and other musicians who cultivate an avant-garde, blatantly "anti-shtetl" Jewish image has made klezmer music part of the young, hip, alternative music scene. In summer 1997 I met a tall, blond, athletic young man from Naples named Alessandro who had skipped out on his job to make the 250-mile trip to Ancona expressly to see the Klezmatics, who were headlining the second Ancona International Klezmer Festival. The festival, publicly funded, was organized by Fahrenheit 451, a local cultural association of young adults whose aim was to bring minority artists and cultures to public attention. The driving force behind it was Giovanni Seneca, a jazz and classical musician. "Ancona has a Jewish community that is very strongly rooted, so it made particular sense to us to develop something that took off from this specific historical characteristic of our city," Fahrenheit 451's president, Andrea Nobile, told me. That eastern European klezmer music was not part of the local Jewish tradition in Ancona was a minor point: klezmer was seen as a symbol of all Things Jewish and thus a legitimate means of celebrating or demonstrating the important Jewish contribution to a town whose Jewish population by the late 1990s numbered only about one hundred. "Because of its strong links with Jewish culture, klezmer represents a means of creating a cultural event that has a particular relationship with this city," Nobile said. Silvio Sacerdoti, a member of the Ancona Jewish community, agreed. "To me, klezmer represents the overall heritage of Jews, not only in Italy, but in all of Europe, and so it's a part of us," he told me. "It's a way to find your roots. To understand better who you are and where you come from." Festival organizers enjoyed the enthusiastic cooperation of Sacerdoti and other members of the local Jewish community leadership, who saw it as a way to raise the Jewish profile among Jews as well as the mainstream community. Each year the Jewish community has sponsored a lecture on various aspects of Jewish music, held in the ornate synagogue, as part of the festival events.[22]

Alessandro, the klezmer fan from Naples, was twenty-three when I met him and wore his hair very short except for a long braid hanging down his back. He excitedly told everyone he spoke to that he was starting up a klezmer band in Naples: he had discovered klezmer music about a year earlier and was galvanized by its "power and energy." He knew little about the music, other than its sound. Klezmer, he told me, was "music that was played on the street, passed from musician to musician." He possessed some tapes of klezmer music, but the only group whose name he knew was the Klezmatics. "I just had to hear the Klezmatics!" he repeated. "They fascinate me. That's why I came all this distance."

With songs about marijuana, gay rights, and the plight of refugees, the Klezmatics infuse their music with counterculture political activism that also enhances their following. The Klezmatics violinist, Alicia Svigals, who is a lesbian, recounted to me that the group received a "wildly enthusiastic" welcome by a sellout audience when they played their first concert in the southern Italian port city of Bari in 1996. "It seemed that the whole alternative/artistic population of Bari showed up for our show," she said. "It was really moving. At the end of the concert we talked to a lot of audience members; I was especially touched by a group of gay men and lesbians who came to talk to me. They told us how difficult things are still for them in southern Italy and how closet-y they often have to be."

10

Klezmer in Germany

Throughout the 1990s Germany had Europe's largest, most diverse, and most complex klezmer-Yiddish music scene: scores of klezmer and Yiddish groups of all types and of all levels of skill were performing around the country, and klezmer was a fixture at numerous Jewish music and Jewish culture festivals; klezmer CDs won national prizes, and klezmer songs hit German pop charts. Some U.S. klezmer musicians, including the Klezmatics, Brave Old World, and the Berlin-based clarinetist Joel Rubin, recorded their CDs in Germany and sometimes found broader distribution there than in the United States. From the start non-Jewish German interest in klezmer and Yiddish music was enmeshed in the tangled web of working through the past. Among the other ways that Germans have manifested their uneasy relationship with historical legacy, music became for many the most readily accessible Jewish icon. Approaches run the gamut from alternative chic to a mystical search for universal healing—and they often overlap. They involve stereotypes or idealized visions of what Jews were, what they are, and what they represent. They involve the use of Things Jewish as unconscious surrogates. And, increasingly today, they entail the integration of "Jewish" culture and space into the broad German mainstream. "Klezmer is a language between human people, from me to you, from soul to soul," Cecille Kossmann, a middle-aged psychologist and clarinet player who in 1990 helped found an organization called the Klezmer Gesellschaft (Klezmer Society), told me in 1997. "It speaks about the most important themes of life—love, death, and sadness—but also dancing and enjoyment."

Klezmer music and Yiddish song were never, ever, so widely popular in Germany as they are today, but the iconic image of Jews and Jewish culture embodied in klezmer is well removed from the prewar world of German Jewry. Klezmer music was not played (or to a large extent even enjoyed) by Germany's mainly assimilated, prewar Jewish community —much less by its prewar non-Jewish population. What we today call klezmer was the music—as Yiddish was the language—of the *Ostjuden,* the often impoverished, orthodox Jews of eastern Europe. To be sure, younger German Jews seeking their roots or rebelling against their bourgeois, assimilated parents a century ago may have romanticized the *Ostjuden* as an ideal of purity, piety, and authenticity and may have collected and played their music as an ethnographic exercise or a link to a discarded past. But generally Jews, Jewish practice, and Jewish cultural trappings from the East, including the Yiddish language itself, were scorned or derided or proved an embarrassment to prosperous, Westernized German Jews anxious to affirm a modern, "civilized" identity and forget or bury the fact that they themselves were often only a generation or less removed from sidelocks and shtetl. This anxiety became especially acute after 1880, when tens of thousands of *Ostjuden* settled in Germany; by 1910 some 20 percent of Berlin's Jewish population were immigrants from the East, living mainly in one section of the city, the Scheunenviertel, which many of the bourgeois Jewish majority considered an alien medieval ghetto in their midst.[1]

One exception, albeit a very early one, of an eastern European klezmer making it big in the West was the short, sensationally successful career of Michael Joseph Gusikov. Gusikov was born into a family of Hasidic musicians in Shklov, Belorussia, in about 1806. In the 1830s he invented a xylophone-like instrument made with wooden staves resting on a bed of straw. On it he produced music that one critic called "painful and tender," full of "deep melancholy [and] profound emotion." With his dangling earlocks and typical Hasidic attire of caftan and yarmulke a visible—and possibly deliberately contrived—part of his mystique, Gusikov toured Russia and then Austria, Germany, and France, taking audiences by storm before his death from tuberculosis in 1837. So popular did he become in his brief career that his orthodox sidecurls sparked a fashionable hairstyle among society women— the *coiffure à la Gusikov.* After attending a Gusikov concert in Leipzig in 1836, Felix Mendelssohn—the Christian grandson of the Jewish Enlightenment founder Moses Mendelssohn—wrote to his mother, "[Gusikov is] quite a phenomenon, a famous fellow, inferior to no virtuoso in the world, both in execution and facility. He, therefore, delights me more with his instrument of wood and straw than many with their pianofortes, just because it is such a thankless kind of instrument. . . . It is a long time since I so much enjoyed any concert as this, for the man is a true genius."[2]

Today Berlin is Germany's klezmer capital, and no other city in Europe—and possibly the world—may have as many and as varied klezmer and Yiddish music dates on its calendar. In March 1997 one notice board in Berlin's funky, now fashionable former Jewish quarter, which during the Cold War was in East Berlin, sported posters for individual and joint concerts by about a dozen Jewish music groups—foreign and local, experimental and traditional—in venues ranging from one of Berlin's most prestigious concert halls to a parish church to several nightspots to the Berlin Jewish Community Center. Around the corner, the Hackesches Hof-Theater, a popular club for the young, alternative set, featured what it called "Jiddische Musik am historischen Ort" (Yiddish music in a historic place), regular Jewish music nights twice a week by local and foreign artists, plus frequent other klezmer or Jewish music performances. Throughout the entire month of March in 1997, the club presented some sort of Jewish music on two out of three nights. Performers included several local non-Jewish klezmer groups and non-Jewish Yiddish singers, Bob Cohen's Die Naye Kapelye, on tour from Budapest, and a musical play—acted in German and sung in Yiddish—starring two well-known local Jewish performers, one of them, Mark Aizikowitch, an immigrant from the former Soviet Union. Aizikowitch also hosted a Russian-Yiddish night featuring fellow immigrant performers.

That spring another Berlin club held a regular weekly klezmer night featuring the local non-Jewish Berlin group Harry's Freilach. And klezmer music had yet another regular Berlin venue in the affluent suburb of Lübars, where a local community culture center, the LabSaal, hosted klezmer concerts by foreign or local bands at least once a month. The LabSaal hosted klezmer workshops as well and had its own amateur klezmer band, Klezmischpoche, whose members played together once a week and also staged occasional public events. These included two elaborate musical revues on Jewish themes: the 1994 Masl [sic] Tov, based on a Jewish wedding, and the 1995 Oifn Jorid, in which band members dressed up in Fiddler on the Roof–style costumes and pretended they were singing in a shtetl marketplace.

The klezmer craze in Germany began to develop in the mid-1980s and exploded a few years later after the fall of the Berlin Wall. It got its start on the heels of the international and political folk music scene that grew up in Germany, as in Italy and other countries, amid the countercultural movement of the 1960s and 1970s. Clubs, pubs, folk festivals, and campuses across Europe—as in the United States—resounded with shaggy-haired young musicians strumming guitars and singing Irish music, bluegrass, left-wing political anthems, protest songs, and Balkan dances as the baby boom generation began to come of age.

Many young countercultural West Germans joined young people of other countries in rejecting local mainstream popular music. Indeed, postwar West German pop music had degenerated into a slick, sugary, manufactured hybrid of oompah and lounge music that came to be known as *schlager,* or hits, whose banal, aggressively upbeat lyrics and lush arrangements aimed at creating a comfortable, escapist cocoon for a mass market middle class anxious to "forget and rebuild." [3] West German stabs at rock music, too, were often highly derivative. Young Germans had special reasons for embracing music of other cultures and other times rather than engaging in an exploration of their own national folk roots, as became popular in various other countries. For the generation that started questioning their parents about the wartime past, German folk music was indelibly tainted by the Nazi era. For many young people, innocuous folk tunes and even childhood lullabies conjured up shameful images.

In 1997 I spoke with Harry Timmermann, a non-Jewish clarinetist who was born in 1952 and leads Harry's Freilach. He told me, "Sometimes I have the feeling that people who listen to us, mostly people our age, between forty and fifty, thirty and sixty, remember what they lost in their own childhood because of this fascist history. For Germans, for people who are now fifty years old, that means that they had no songs to sing when they were children. When I go to other countries, to Turkey or France or Greece, and so on, they all have their songs to sing, songs that they have from their childhood. But in my generation, we cannot sing these songs." Even nursery rhymes sung to him by his parents, he told me, were poisoned. "They taught us these songs, but when we were fourteen and fifteen years old we didn't want to sing the songs that our parents sang in Fascist times. Maybe it wasn't always right, and maybe there are very beautiful songs from this time and older songs and so on. But we felt that they only sang us songs from their fascistic childhood. We didn't want this; there was an emotional distance from our parents." And as for German pop songs, "They were real German *schlager*—we didn't want that."

Young Germans looked elsewhere to find a musical language. For most, it was the Anglo-American rock filling the airwaves of Armed Forces Radio and other outlets. "For my generation," said Timmermann, "the history of our emotions began with the Beatles."[4] Christian Dawid, clarinetist for the Klezgoyim, who is a dozen years younger than Timmermann, told me a similar story of musical and other kinds of deracination: "The problem with my generation, this second generation after the war is that we actually grew up without a culture of our own. What was left after the Nazi time was just really definitely cut off: so."

Young Germans turned off by the emptiness of mainstream pop and the embarrassing dirndl-clad, beer stein–clanking, goose-stepping associations of German folk music sought refuge not just in the Beatles and other Anglo-American rock groups but also in other, more exotic musical traditions. This search coincided with the blossoming of the national obsession with the legacy of the Holocaust. Already in 1968 student protesters on the barricades sang Yiddish songs to symbolize their rejection of their parents' values, at the same time self-consciously aligning themselves with the victims of their parents' generation. Several leftist German folk performers in the 1960s and 1970s added Yiddish and Israeli songs to their repertoires and issued recordings of Yiddish music. One of the best known of these groups was called Zupfgeigenhansel. Its 1979 LP, *Jiddische Lieder,* was a well-timed landmark in the marketing of Yiddish songs. The album came out the same year that West German television aired the American mini-series *Holocaust,* bringing the Shoah into millions of living rooms and touching off a nationwide wave of soul-searching and "memory work." *Jiddische Lieder* was more than just a record. It came complete with an elaborate information booklet that contained photographs, lyrics, tunes, historical descriptions, and a bibliography—a veritable pop culture guide to the world of eastern European Jewry destroyed, as seen now on television, by Germans themselves.[5] Foreshadowing, meanwhile, the ritual commemorative use of Jewish music that has persisted to this day, Yiddish song performances often became hushed, almost spiritual encounters drenched in Holocaust imagery. "People would come and think, this will be two very sad hours, because it's Yiddish and a lot of the songs talk of the Holocaust," recalls Uwe Sauerwein, a Berlin journalist and musician familiar with the folk scene of the 1970s who plays in a klezmer–folk band called Kasbek.

The Yiddish folk scene expanded throughout the 1970s and 1980s, and not just in Germany. In Vienna, for example, Albert Misak and his friend Edek Bartz, who began performing as Geduldig und Thimann in the 1960s, issued their first recording of Yiddish music, *Kum Aher du Filosof,* in 1975, followed by releases in 1980, 1986, 1989, and into the 1990s. Their music began with Yiddish folk songs but increasingly incorporated elements of klezmer, Hasidic, and experimental, jazz-tinged Jewish music played by some of the leading international performers in these fields. Misak and Bartz became interested in Yiddish music as boys, thanks to the concerts of the charismatic performer Shlomo Carlebach, the late "singing rabbi" who began touring Austria and elsewhere in Europe in the early 1960s. "He grew up in Baden, near Vienna, and really had an audience in Austria," Misak told me. "Edek and I founded our group in 1962 after going to a Carlebach concert. We started singing his songs without knowing what the words meant. Our first concert was in 1964 in a Christian culture center! Then we started getting invited to play at orthodox Jewish weddings—though at the time Hasidism had the same status for me as some tribe in Africa. We were very surprised that this was part of the Jewish world, but it caught us up. And since we loved the music we felt we had to share it. It took us six years to make our first record and another two years to find a record company! But it sold well. People liked it." One of their songs hit the Austrian radio charts in 1979.

In West Germany, a key catalyst of the Yiddish song movement was Manfred Lemm, who became involved with the music in the early 1980s and devoted himself to resurrecting the songs of the Kraków carpenter Mordechai Gebirtig, the self-taught Yiddish bard who wrote hundreds of Yiddish songs before he was killed by the Nazis in 1942. Lemm, who set some of Gebirtig's lyrics to his own music, formed a Yiddish music group in Wuppertal, West Germany, in 1984 and began recording Gebirtig's work, touring, and conducting music workshops. His recordings won prizes, and in 1986 the title song of Lemm's second LP of Gebirtig's songs, *Der Singer fun Nojt,* hit the top of the charts of the Southwest German Broadcast Corporation in Baden-Baden.

Yiddish songs became staples at folk festivals and eventually generated festivals of their own: a Yiddish music festival was held in Zurich in 1984, for example. The interest in Yiddish music coincided with other currents of *Vergangenheitsverarbeitung*. In 1988 the first biennial International Festival of Yiddish Music in Fürth, sponsored by the city, coincided with the avalanche of commemorative activity marking the fiftieth anniversary of Kristallnacht. Lemm performed widely in various Yiddish music festivals and in 1993 organized a three-day European Yiddish music festival in Leverkusen that drew performers from ten countries. This festival, according to Lemm, was aimed at more than just enjoyment of music: it sought to develop a "spirit of agreement and understanding between people and to place before the public examples of an ancient culture that was for so long ignored." It won sponsorship from the city, the German UNESCO Commission, the German foreign ministry, and regional culture authorities in North Rhine Westphalia. The president of the Federal German Parliament, Rita Süssmuth, spoke at the opening.[6]

Yiddish songs also found a niche in East Germany, although the contexts were very different. In East Germany, as in other communist states, cultural matters were controlled by the communist regime. Folk clubs could feature international music, but the permitted repertoire was heavy on revolutionary propaganda and songs about fighting fascism. Official East German policy, like that in almost all communist states, was strongly anti-Israel and by extension anti-Jewish, but East German censors allowed some Yiddish songs because they were anti-Fascist: these could be heard, for example, on government-approved records by the leftist African-American singer Paul Robeson. Zupfgeigenhansel, which recorded on a West German leftist label, also performed at political song festivals in East Berlin, and it was possible to obtain copies of the group's Yiddish LP. Political constraints, however, hampered unfettered development of the Yiddish music scene until the late 1980s, when glasnost began taking effect throughout the communist world ahead of the final collapse of communism. Nonetheless, several non-Jewish groups or performers—including the group Aufwind and the singer Karsten Troyke—became interested in klezmer and Yiddish music in the early and mid-1980s. Indeed, one compelling attraction of such nonsanctioned music was that playing it was a way to express opposition to the communist regime. Some East German musicians gravitated to Yiddish sounds the same way other young East Germans coalesced in other "alternative" movements ranging from punk rock to pseudo-dada poetry to Christianity. Aufwind, which was founded in East Berlin in 1984, was one of the first groups in either Germany that was devoted to klezmer as well as Yiddish song, but until the Berlin Wall fell, the group was isolated from both the neoklezmer revival in the United States and the new interest in the music in West Germany.[7]

In the 1980s many of the few Jews in East Germany, most of whom grew up as believing communists in what called itself an "anti-Fascist" state, turned to an exploration of Yiddish music and other elements of Jewish culture, as well as religious traditions, as a way of clarifying their troubled identities as communists, Jews, and Germans. For some, this constituted an assertion of an alternative, or opposition, identity in the waning days of communist rule. Meanwhile, the East German regime, eager to claim some sort of legitimacy as the entire communist edifice began to crumble, allocated ample funding to Jewish cultural causes— such as the restoration of the Oranienburger Strasse synagogue—as a means of winning support in the West. The East Berlin Jewish folk-singer Jalda Rebling, daughter of a Dutch Jewish communist who settled in East Germany after surviving Auschwitz and gave concerts of Yid-dish songs in the 1950s and 1960s, began performing Yiddish songs as part of her own reconnection with Judaism. On January 27, 1987— the forty-second anniversary of the liberation of Auschwitz—she orga-nized a Yiddish culture festival in East Berlin. It received funding from UNESCO and took place annually into the 1990s. Holocaust remem-brance was integral to Rebling's presentation: an intense, dark-eyed woman with long hair, she would stand onstage, eyes closed, and sing songs of Jews murdered by the Nazis—and also, sometimes, songs by Jews murdered under Soviet Stalinism. "For me," she has said, "Yiddish songs and literature are the *heimishkeit* [homey feeling] I will always be searching for in vain, since it was lost with my family in Auschwitz. Only five people came back."[8] Rebling, Troyke, and Aufwind eventually be-came among the best-known Yiddish or klezmer performers in post-Wall united Germany.

The American Invasion

Into the fertile musical mix of generational angst, Holo-caust obsession, identity seeking, and unfocused philo-Semitism came klezmer: a sound closely related to traditional Yiddish folk songs but different enough—and dynamic enough—to excite a wave of popular-ity that spread the Jewish sound well beyond the limits of acoustic folk-dom. The phenomenon took off in the mid-1980s, when foreign klez-mer performers first began to tour. The lively European folk scene, with its notable Yiddish component, was ripe for this new input. The North

American neoklezmer movement was well established by then, and bands were beginning to tour widely. For their entrée into Europe, promoters initially presented the groups simply as representatives of another folk or popular music tradition. Such was the case with the first American klezmer revival band to tour Europe, Henry Sapoznik's Kapelye, which played at folk festivals and small traditional music clubs in Great Britain, France, Belgium, Switzerland, and West Germany in 1984.[9]

Besides a new music form, these groups brought something else that was new: a contemporary "real live" Jewish component. Kapelye and the other American groups were composed of young, hip-looking musicians who put on lively, upbeat shows with onstage patter and hard-driving, sometimes jazzy klezmer dance music that was the opposite of the sentimental, nostalgic, or Holocaust-tinged songs that made up much of the folk scene's Yiddish repertoire. Up to that time the occasional Jewish performer (local or foreign) of Jewish music generally fell into the solitary folksinger model.

For a German public yearning to come to terms with the past but unable or afraid to interact with living Jews in their own cities, the new groups proffered a new image of Jews and Jewish music. It was a vision, even if an onstage vision, of vigorous Jewish contemporary life, not a picture of Jews as antique shtetl dwellers or as prison-striped victims in a history book or on grainy black-and-white film. Nor did it fit other common philo-Semitic stereotypes: noble souls to be put on a pedestal, or baleful, reproachful witnesses constantly reminding German audiences of the sins of their fathers. Living Jewish musicians onstage created the illusion of real interaction with Jews. Audiences responded enthusiastically, and there was extensive media coverage of musicians and tours. "We were suddenly culture heroes, to some people at least, with a lot of the cachet black American blues-jazz musicians had enjoyed in Europe in an earlier era," recalls Brave Old World front man Michael Alpert, who played with Kapelye on its first 1984 tour and has toured frequently in Germany and elsewhere in Europe since that time.[10] "Certainly with Kapelye, and probably Andy Statman, too [who was touring around the same time], we didn't even mention the Holocaust in the [early] concerts," Alpert told me. "It was interesting to watch audiences and promoters and the press deal with that dynamic. I think one of the things they were delighted with about it, or very interested in— and in some ways not sure how to deal with—can be summed up in the response, 'You speak English together, we expected that you would speak Yiddish.' . . . But we were doing all this happy stuff, and jokes, and fooling around, and it was obvious that they were trying to process it, [saying] wait a second, this is a whole new thing—they're Jews, but they're Americans, but they're Jews, but they're Americans."

The mixture of Jewishness and Americanness became a potent symbol, vis-à-vis both the powerful role long played by American rock music and performers as points of musical reference in Germany and the importance of New York and the immigrant experience to klezmer itself. Indeed, when Kapelye toured West Germany in June 1986, the tour was marketed under the title "A Yiddish Ragtime." The German promoters put out a thick souvenir program that stressed the American–eastern European angle of the music and scarcely mentioned specifics of the Holocaust. The program cover showcased the name of the group, Kapelye, in big red letters, with the prominent subtitles "New York" and "A Yiddish Ragtime." [11] In one corner was a small photograph of an old, wooden, obviously eastern European house with the legend, "from the shtetl to America." The eighteen-page booklet, lavishly illustrated with prewar black-and-white photographs, presented a detailed, thousand-year history of Jewish life in prewar eastern Europe and New York, describing shtetl communities, big-city Jewish quarters (quoting a description of Jewish Warsaw from Alfred Döblin's 1926 book, *A Journey to Poland*), Yiddish (language, literature, and theater), klezmer, the pre–World War II immigrant experience in the United States, and even the "third generation" rediscovery of Yiddish and klezmer traditions. Among the illustrations were an 1880 map of Manhattan showing the Lower East Side and a map showing Jewish migrations in Europe from the Middle Ages to the seventeenth century. Almost in passing (and with some inaccuracies) it noted that while more than three million Jews had lived in Poland and while Warsaw had had Europe's biggest Jewish community, "today in all of Poland live 3,000 Jews." And it continued, "From 400,000 Jews in Warsaw live only 400. From the 50,000 Jews in Lublin twelve remain. In Kraków, the city where there was the first Jewish printing house, there are only six Jews. The Yiddish world from Warsaw and Vitebsk, Kraków and Kishinev, was wiped out."

The American groups, though, had a problem. At first, it was the very notion of being Jews playing Jewish music in Germany. For some of them, as for many American Jews, just setting foot in the country was a trauma. Henry Sapoznik recalls that his response to the audience the first time Kapelye played in Germany was "a kind of ghoulish feeling, some kind of freak show—'come see the live Jews.' Very creepy and weird." David Licht of the Klezmatics, a group that has toured Germany regularly since 1988 and has also recorded there, recalls being traumatized the first time he played in the country. "It was with a rock band in 1983," he told me. "I couldn't speak for twenty-four hours, just from hearing the language. It blindsided me." For Michael Alpert, the whole notion of performing Yiddish music and presenting Yiddish culture in Germany initially took on an "almost missionary significance, an idealistic, bridge-building cachet." It also meant making a taunting statement: "Yeah—you didn't get us all."

Later, as klezmer grew more popular in Germany, the American groups realized that if they wanted to make a living, Germany was where they would have to play, regardless of the paradoxes. The combination of German guilt, cultural curiosity, and philo-Semitism meant full houses, frequent tour bookings, and appreciative audiences, more often than not without a single Jew in the room. This, too, weighed on many of the musicians, particularly in the early years of the craze and later, in the early 1990s, when newly reunified Germany was swept by a wave of neo-Nazi xenophobic violence. Brave Old World underscored this ambivalence in the notes to their 1994 CD, *Beyond the Pale,* and, as I noted earlier, also transformed it into a powerful song, "Berlin 1990," which became the group's signature. "Berlin 1990" was more than just a song; it represented a firsthand social document describing a Jew's reaction to the virtual Jewish scene he found himself helping to create: "I've played here in Germany many's the time. . . . But I swear by my muse . . . [t]hat not once has it been easy to be here."

The Feidman Factor

Giora Feidman, too, made his first impact in Germany in 1984, through his role in the musical play about the Holocaust, *Ghetto,* by the Israeli playwright Joshua Sobol, which, produced by Peter Zadek, a German Jew, had its European premiere that year in West Berlin. The play is set in the Vilnius Ghetto during World War II. It engendered controversy by focusing on the agonizing decisions the ghetto's Jewish Council was forced to make in order to attempt survival—among them, having to choose which people should be selected for deportation so that others might be saved. These were decisions that could be seen as having forced Jewish victims to become "guiltlessly

guilty" accessories to the Nazi crimes, in a certain sense placing some of the responsibility for Holocaust deaths on Jews themselves. Jews and Nazis could thus appear to be distorted mirror images of each other; there was a blurring between victim and perpetrator.[12] *Ghetto* garnered extensive publicity in the press and broadcast media. The prominence of Feidman and his music not only brought Feidman himself and the klezmer sound to a wide audience but also firmly associated Feidman and his music with Holocaust themes and Holocaust memory.

Feidman's approach soon made him the single most important klezmer influence in the country, a musical star whose name alone on a poster was capable of selling out large concert halls. His work, name, and sound became synonymous with both "healing" and Holocaust remembrance, the musical embodiment of reconciliation. And Feidman, during tireless tours of the country, became a veritable guru for some of his fans.

It is illustrative, if not indicative, of Feidman's focus and message that in November 1992, one year after German reunification, a souvenir program for a major tour by Feidman to eastern Germany used a historical text that was almost identical to that used in the souvenir program of Kapelye's "Yiddish Ragtime" tour six years earlier. Vera Giese, Feidman's manager and the designer of the program, had also promoted Kapelye's tour and had designed the "Yiddish Ragtime" brochure. Unlike the Kapelye program, however, the program for Feidman's tour, which was organized under the patronage of the Central Council of Jews in Germany, included page after page of material on the Holocaust and on the rise of nazism in Germany—including an average figure for how many Jews were killed a day from 1941 to 1944, quotations from *Mein Kampf* and other texts, a rundown on Hitler's rise to power, and photographs from concentration camps. It also made mention of the attempts at Jewish revival taking place in former communist states, ending with the reassuring message: "We, the non-Jews, surely did not expect this prospect and perhaps we didn't deserve it, but we have it: We can begin from the beginning. The history of East European Jews is not over."

Feidman made klezmer a metaphor for universal personal expression uniting all peoples and all things. Although his quasi-mystical use of music has deep roots in Jewish tradition, particularly Hasidic and kabbalistic tradition, this approach was also clearly a deliberate strategy on his part and also ensured him a full touring schedule.[13] "Through the music of what I call klezmer," he told me, "I have been successful in

infiltrating myself into the healing process between Germans and Jews."
The role of klezmer, he went on, using the mystical language typical of
his approach, is to be "the holy glue to bring society to what we were
born to be—one human family." Feidman, in fact, goes so far as to reject a use of the term *klezmer* to indicate music with specific historical Jewish roots or repertoire or specific musical language. For him,
klezmer means something completely different. It is not a musical style;
it is more of a philosophical idea that denotes the "how," not the
"what," of the music, "a conception, not music," that reveals a person's
"inner still voice." "Klezmer music doesn't exist," he asserts, "because
klezmer is the instrument and music is the language." For Feidman,
even the songs that mothers sing to their babies are klezmer.

Feidman spread his message through incessant tours, workshops,
school visits, television appearances, and recordings. He tells his audiences, "Klezmer comes from two Hebrew words, *kli* [*sic*] *zemer,* meaning 'instrument of song.' Everyone born is a singer. God gave to us an
instrument of song, our body. *This* is klezmer. . . . Klezmer is not Jewish music. It has nothing to do with it. It is a conception the Jewish
people used to communicate with God." As an illustration, he plays a
range of music, including Ave Maria, the Scott Joplin theme from the
movie *The Sting,* and the Gershwin songs "Somebody Loves Me" and
"Swanee," intermixed with fragments and medleys of Yiddish folk songs
and *freylekhs* and *doinas* from the traditional klezmer repertoire. He
demonstrates the similarity between the first few notes of Gershwin's
"It Ain't Necessarily So" from *Porgy and Bess* and the melody for the
blessing over the Torah. Feidman blows kisses to the audience and
spreads his arms wide in a symbolic embrace. "We are confused because
we are educated that this is mine, this is yours," he tells them. "Music
doesn't have borders. If you think *this* music has borders, send me a fax
and tell me!"[14] (In 1996, I was told, Feidman took this to a further extreme, playing the music used as Germany's national anthem as one of
his examples of "klezmer.")[15]

Feidman drew a large and devoted following, both fans (he estimates
that 90 to 99 percent of his audience is not Jewish) and musicians. A
stocky, rumpled man with flowing hair and a salt-and-pepper beard that
frames a gap-toothed smile, he is an unlikely looking guru. But his universalist message held a powerful attraction. "He opened the door for
Germans to participate in the culture," says Heiko Lehmann, former
bass player of Aufwind. "This was the chance for a lot of Germans to receive absolution for the extinction of the Jews, even young Germans.

Feidman offered them a chance to do penance by adopting the music; the idea seemed to be 'first we killed, now we heal.'" It is impossible to reckon how much the market determined Feidman's ideology—and his ideology the market. But, not surprisingly, critics accuse him of virtually turning klezmer into feel-good cult by manipulating both the music and the memory of the Jewish heritage from which it came.

"Feidman has been selling a version of German-Jewish relationships via klezmer music that is extremely appealing to Germans for all kinds of reasons," Alan Bern, the musical director of Brave Old World, told me in 1995.

> In Feidman's ideology, the music doesn't have a specific content. It's entirely a question of the attitude of the musician. Feidman's message is sort of a universal message where the term "klezmer" comes to stand for a universal musical language, like musicality itself. There are obvious reasons why that has tremendous appeal in this country. I feel that people's feelings of guilt and need for forgiveness and desire for dialogue and all of these things are getting loaded on to a sort of a contentless idea. For me what's a problem, too, is that the entire [Jewish] culture is being made to disappear along with that. It's as if Jews didn't have anything to do with klezmer music. To approach it that way, it's like a second destruction of the culture.

Harry Timmermann, the clarinetist who leads the Berlin klezmer group Harry's Freilach, became interested in klezmer music in the early 1990s through Feidman recordings and workshops. When we spoke in 1997, he endorsed Feidman's view that the feelings and unspoken message of the music, rather than its historical identity or specifically Jewish cultural contexts, are what is important to convey. A pale, soft-spoken man with graying hair and wire-rim glasses, Timmermann was born in East Germany but raised in West Germany from the age of three. He played clarinet as a teenager but gave it up and later became a student of literature, philosophy, and theology. Timmermann says that his encounter with Feidman's music spurred him to pick up his clarinet again after twenty years. He started playing klezmer music with a Christian minister friend who was a guitarist. They would play klezmer in the minister's church and soon began attracting an audience. Part of the attraction of the music, Timmermann told me, was, in fact, a sort of Christian spirituality: "I sometimes have the feeling that I study the roots of Christian society with the help of Jewish melodies, but it's very personal and very emotional." Following Feidman's lead, Timmermann's performance style is heavy on personal interpretation, relying on intonation, phrasing, and evocation of mood. He makes his clarinet "talk" and "sing" and "laugh" and "cry" and aims to achieve a direct emotional connection with his audience, in a way that he feels approaches that of the original eastern European klezmorim. "Jewish" has something—but not much—to do with it.

"I do not transform klezmer into jazz, as many people do," Timmermann told me.

> I do not take these melodies and make improvisations. I take these melodies as they are. And I really think we play this music like the klezmer musicians did over the centuries, . . . though it's not my main purpose to conserve a special style from the nineteenth century. I call what I play klezmer because I'm very thankful to these roots, to these melodies; I respect these melodies very much and I don't want to change anything in them. I only work on expression, and I try to find an expression that of course sounds "Jewish"—but only "Jewish" in that I think that "Jewish" is the most intense feeling. You can also say that this has nothing to do with Jewish culture, that it could have been tango or something else. But for me, it was "Jewish" that I felt I could work on my feelings with these old melodies and that I can come very far. . . . I've tried to be respectful and thankful toward these klezmer melodies.

I spoke to Timmermann at the launch party and concert introducing a new CD by his group. It was an event that demonstrated the persisting Holocaust associations with Jewish and Yiddish music and the emotional-political symbolism associated with the genre—even when it was not being used as part of a commemoration. The concert, a non-Jewish group playing for a non-Jewish audience, was held in a venue simply called Die Ruine, The Ruins, a war-damaged nineteenth-century building deep inside the vast complex of the old Charité Hospital in former East Berlin. Before the war, the building housed the hospital's Pathology Museum, established in 1899 with a renowned collection of more than 23,000 anatomical and pathological specimens. World War II bombing destroyed most of the collection and left the large hall on the building's upper floor an open ruin that was covered by a makeshift cement roof only in the 1960s. In the 1990s, after German reunification, the building became a medical history museum: lower floors now house displays of diseased organs floating in formaldehyde as well as other gruesomely fascinating exhibits. The top floor was left partially ruined as an atmospheric venue for concerts and other events.

Here, then, Harry's Freilach presented a klezmer concert in a setting created by the actual physical destruction of World War II. The concert celebrated the release of a CD whose title, *Klezmer Tov!* was meant to express joy and whose packaging bore no reference to the Holocaust or Jewish trauma. But it took place in a cavernous, war-damaged hall with scarred brick walls, where rough brick internal structures stood in almost sculptural ruin and broken iron beams hung suspended from the lofty prefab concrete ceiling. Most of the eighty to one hundred people in the audience looked to be in their forties or fifties, although there were some older and younger people there, too. One woman told me the ruined setting was just right for the music. "I first heard about klezmer about three years ago," she said. "I can't say what is so special about this music. It seems as if it's something old coming back. Some old feelings somehow . . . about time gone by. If I see this building here, it's all broken down—and the music just fits in it. Most music nowadays is all the same, so normal, you can listen to it or you can just turn off the radio. But if I heard something like this [klezmer], I wouldn't turn off the radio—if I was in the car, I would sit in the car and wait until it was over. I have no ideas about music at all, I can just say I like it or not, and it makes something move inside of me. I can't say what it is."

Jewish Style, Jewish Chic

The fall of the Berlin Wall in November 1989 and the subsequent reunification of Germany galvanized the country—and the continent—on the widest possible range of cultural, social, political, and emotional levels. The exhilarating inception of the "new Germany" as a part of a "new Europe" was a watershed for the klezmer movement, too. The German klezmer scene shifted sharply and rapidly from passivity—mainly West German audiences, however enthusiastic, listening primarily to foreign groups—to more active participation. Eastern Germany quickly opened up as a market, particularly for young people who flocked to hear and then play an exciting new music from a virtually unknown and thus exotic culture that had been largely suppressed under communism.

Klezmer became a hip new fashion amid the general cultural explosion of the moment. Aufwind, the East German band, was invited to appear at the annual klezmer festival in Safed, Israel, in June 1990 through Feidman's intercession. Heiko Lehmann, then the group's bassist, recalls that when Aufwind returned to Germany it was bombarded with invitations to tour both in western and eastern parts of the country: "We toured West Germany so extensively that we had to turn down tours after a while."[16] In both east and west, workshops by Feidman, Brave Old World, and other foreign musicians (and the publication and ready availability of song sheets and crib books) spurred Germans to form dozens of their own klezmer groups. Most were resolutely informal amateur bands that played for their own pleasure. A few had professional aspirations, if not professional skill. Local musicians, too, took on the role of experts who held their own workshops.

The shabby heart of East Berlin, meanwhile—the Mitte district that was the center of the prewar city and was still composed of crumbling, prewar architecture and seedy Old World flavor—opened up to West Berliners for the first time in decades; the onetime Jewish neighborhood under the gilded dome of the former New Synagogue on Oranienburger Strasse, under reconstruction in the early 1990s as a Jewish museum and culture center, became a popular Bohemian quarter of boutiques and bookshops, music clubs, cafés, and thriving studios of counterculture artists, filmmakers, and performers. For many, the post-Wall rediscovery and revitalization of this part of East Berlin incorporated a rediscovery of the Jewish history and associations of the neighborhood, frequently a romanticized image of the former *Ostjuden* immigrant quarter, the Scheunenviertel. The "real" Scheunenviertel was a run-down district farther to the east, much of which had been razed in an urban renewal project as long ago as 1906–8. Today, broadened to include the Oranienburger Strasse area, which in fact had been a prosperous Jewish neighborhood of the rigorously bourgeois, the name conjures up images of the prewar Jewish world in general.[17] Klezmer music, the ultimate, easily accessible Jewish symbol, found an eager audience here. The Hackesches Hof-Theater opened its doors in the early 1990s and with its claim to present "Yiddish music in a historic place" overtly capitalized on the romanticization of the Scheunenviertel. "It's really quite a feeling to go there and to hear all these people playing," Arno Bachman, one of the developers of the Hackesches Hof-Theater, whom I met at Harry Timmermann's CD launch concert, told me. "You can smell the atmosphere from former decades, and you can think that this kind of music could have been born there."

As the klezmer vogue developed, more and more foreign groups, of all types, made German venues regular stops on their tours, exposing local musicians and audiences to a wide range of styles and attitudes and influencing the German scene firsthand. Many foreign musicians simply played their concerts and left. But some American neoklezmer musicians spent much of the year in Germany; some recorded their CDs in Germany and copyrighted their compositions there; some took apartments, opened bank accounts, and married or became involved with local women. These musicians and groups in effect became part of the German music scene themselves and responded to the German market. Some became better known, and to a wider public, in Germany than they were back home in the United States. They also played out professional and personal rivalries similar to those in any competitive cultural environment. (At the same time, a few American klezmer musicians settled also in other countries—New York–born Bob Cohen in Budapest, for example, where he formed Die Naye Kapelye, and Joshua Horowitz in Austria, where he formed Budowitz.)

Alan Bern, who has lived and performed in Germany since 1988, told me in 1995,

> Groups like Brave Old World and the Klezmatics work more over here than they do in America, so it is increasingly becoming a story of something that exists in between American culture and German culture, not really here and also not really there. When we play a concert in the United States, I feel relieved in one sense to play for an American or an American Jewish audience, yet in another part of me I'm always disappointed. And when I come back to Germany, there's a converse sense of relief and disappointment—the relief in the U.S. is that it's not such a big deal to be playing this music. In Germany, everything that one does connected to Jewish music is a big deal, there's no such thing as normalcy. One the one hand, it's wonderful in the United States to be normal, in a way. But just because one is normal, then part of one's work as an artist isn't taken as seriously. And here, in Germany, since the condition itself is one of unnormalcy or abnormalcy, then everything that one does is taken seriously, whether you want it to be or not.[18]

The German Jewish community also became involved with efforts to promote Jewish culture, including Jewish music. The goal ostensibly was to raise the level of Jewish cultural consciousness among local Jews, but in fact the concerts and festivals run by Jewish communities played to an audience that was largely non-Jewish. One of the first major events was in 1987, when, in association with celebrations marking the 750th anniversary of Berlin, the West Berlin Jewish community sponsored a "Jewish Culture Days" festival that included concerts of all types of Jewish music, performed by Jewish musicians, as well as other performances and exhibits. The festival became an annual event, attracting thousands of people. Jewish culture festivals sprang up in other towns and cities, too, sometimes sponsored by local Jewish communities, sometimes by city authorities. The New York avant-garde musician John Zorn organized a "Radical Jewish Culture" festival in Munich in 1992 showcasing experimental Jewish music. A concert series featuring traditional and popular Jewish music, performed by Jewish musicians from the United States, Israel, and Europe, formed part of the enormous Jüdische Lebenswelten (Patterns of Jewish Life) exhibition in Berlin in the first four months of 1992 and resulted in a double CD featuring klezmer, Yiddish song, liturgical chants, and Sephardic music.

Broadcast media and record producers, meanwhile, picked up on the market for klezmer and also began to influence the direction and scope of the trend, as did promoters of recordings and bands, as klezmer music became incorporated into the hip, world music circuit. "You don't need to know much to be hip like this, but at least it pulled klezmer out of the framework of the German bad conscience and put it into a musical context," says Heiko Lehmann. Christian Dawid told me that he felt like a real provincial once when he went backstage after a Kapelye concert in Berlin. "I had the feeling that this small klezmer world could be a parody of the big music world," he said. "Backstage after the concert there were a lot of people from the local radio station, and a lot of people who came in with free tickets. They all stood around—it was like, here they are, musicians, producers, and groupies."

At the same time, the sudden outbreak of xenophobic and anti-Jewish violence after the fall of the Wall, along with the rise of the ultra-right wing in general, lent a new urgency and significance to the klezmer scene. For some, the music took on a more overtly political meaning: Giora Feidman's vision of klezmer as a catalyst for reconciliation between Germans and Jews became transformed into a vision of klezmer as a broader symbol expressing opposition to xenophobia and racism in general. This, too, jibed with the aura of "alternative" multiculturalism already associated with the music, as well as with the concurrent view of Jews as the quintessential symbol of the other and persecution of Jews as a symbol for the persecution of all minorities.

Cecille Kossmann's Klezmer Gesellschaft was formed in 1990 as a spin-off of workshops run by Feidman. Its aim, according to a brochure, was not only "the care and development of klezmer music" but also "the fostering of tolerance and international understanding." Members of the society told me they felt it was important for Germans to play klezmer music, as a means of remembering the Nazi past, but also as a statement against any resurgence of the radical right. In 1997 the society numbered one hundred fifty members in thirteen countries and sponsored concerts, workshops, and other events, among them a happening in June of that year, which they called a "klezmer net." Early one morning that month, some two dozen society members walked through the gate into the former Nazi concentration camp at Sachsenhausen, not far from Berlin, carrying their musical instruments. They spread out throughout the grounds and played music for seven hours, each in his or her own spot and each deciding his or her own themes and improvisations. Every hour they met up at the camp gates and played one long sound together, then again spread out individually. "It was very moving to be there with my feet on the place where thousands died and to play their music—their music survived," Kossmann recalled. "It was a very joyful and deep experience. We played for seven hours because seven is a holy number. And when we met each hour at the camp entrance to play one sound together, we gave each tone a characteristic—sadness or happiness, or anger, hope, peace, and the like. The director of the camp said that for the people who were working there that day, it was a new atmosphere, an atmosphere that he found very touching. On that very day, he showed the camp to a man who had been a prisoner there as a child, and this man, too, found it very moving that the younger generation is doing something."

I spoke with Kossmann and her husband, Klaus, who also helped found the society, late one Sunday night in November 1997. They were exhausted and exhilarated after a Klezmer Gesellschaft–sponsored commemorative endeavor: a three-hour concert to mark the anniversary of Kristallnacht. Band after band had gotten up on a bare stage at a community culture center in eastern Berlin's Prenzlauer Berg district, a neighborhood that even before the fall of the Berlin Wall had gained a reputation as an "alternative" haunt of artists and other creative types. The show culminated with a mass jam session by all the groups, which had the capacity crowd clapping for more. The day before, the society had organized a similar concert to raise money for the memorial museum at Sachsenhausen. This event was cosponsored by the Sachsenhausen memorial itself, the Brandenburg Memorial Foundation, and an association of Sachsenhausen camp victims. The lineup for both concerts included seven local Berlin klezmer bands or individual performers and one ensemble from Denmark. The multicolored poster featured a yellow Star of David against a purple background and advertised the pair of concerts as "Klezmer against Forgetting." Klezmer music, it declared, was music "in which sorrow and hope, pain and joy are closely juxtaposed"—thus a fitting means to express commemoration.

Indeed, these concerts were only two of a number of klezmer and Yiddish music concerts, sponsored by non-Jewish organizations or local authorities, that annually mark an anniversary that increasingly has come to serve as a "festival" against racism, xenophobia, and right-wing extremism in general.[19] The irony was that the weekend commemoration concerts sponsored by the Klezmer Gesellschaft coincided with the annual Jewish Culture Days festival run by the Berlin Jewish community, which included numerous klezmer, Yiddish, and other Jewish music concerts, by Jewish performers. There was crossover among the audiences for the Klezmer Gesellschaft and the Jewish Culture Days concerts, but otherwise they had nothing to do with each other: the events sponsored by the Klezmer Gesellschaft were part of the "Yiddish scene," a virtual Jewish world of non-Jews performing for other non-Jews—and in this case, non-Jews performing for non-Jews in order to commemorate the Holocaust perpetrated by Germans against Jews. "I'm not in competition with the so-called klezmer scene," Andreas Nachama, the historian who in 1997 became head of the Berlin Jewish community and who at the time was the principal organizer of Jewish community cultural events, told me. "The so-called Yiddish scene in my opinion has no Jewish contexts at all."

Klezmer New Wave

By the late 1990s the local klezmer movement in Germany had more or less coalesced into several coexisting and overlapping schools or trends: there was klezmer as a political statement; klezmer as a means of healing; klezmer as a structured music derived from specific eastern European Jewish cultural contexts; klezmer as a facet of modish world music; klezmer as a springboard for the musical avant-garde; klezmer as a "laughing and crying" Jewish cliché; and klezmer as simply a fun way for amateurs to get together and make music. There was another, still fairly narrow current beginning to develop as well: klezmer as roots music, that is, klezmer and Yiddish music that was played by local Jews, mainly new immigrants from the former Soviet Union who—like the Jewish neoklezmer pioneers in North America in the 1970s—

were using music as a means of reconnecting with their own, often long-lost traditions.

The borderlines between most of these currents were often blurred. It's enough to think back to the Brave Old World concert in Flensburg: held in a church in a town with a sister city relationship with a town in Israel but no Jewish community, sponsored by church and city organizations to foster brotherhood, it attracted a capacity audience—many of whose members, younger members in particular, were mainly there to have fun. Some musicians who became involved in klezmer through Giora Feidman and his touchy-feely workshops moved on to explore the specific Jewish cultural contexts that had produced the music while still recognizing the music's political symbolism and emotional message.

The Berlin group la'om, a quintet of young musicians from eastern Berlin, fits the latter pattern. Three of the group's five members were turned on to klezmer in about 1993 after hearing Feidman and later attended Feidman workshops, where they met. They eventually found his approach unsatisfying, however, and came under the influence of Brave Old World and other American bands. They even attended Klezkamp, an intensive annual workshop on Yiddish music, language, and culture held each December in the United States. When I met them in 1997, the group was firmly part of the "hip" rather than "healing" wing of the local klezmer scene in Berlin. They played at Hackesches Hof-Theater and at the LabSaal in Lübars and were about to release their first CD. The group's name was a word they made up to "sound" Hebrew. The CD's main title is . . . *spielt!* Its subtitle, *Klezmer musik von Chicago bis Odessa,* aims to emphasize that the music, as interpreted by this group, is coming from "Chicago to Odessa"—not the other way around; that is, it seeks to pay homage to and to stress the influences of the contemporary American neoklezmer revival. There is deliberately nothing overtly "Jewish" or old-fashioned about the CD design. The photographs of the young musicians are as quirky (and self-indulgent) as those of any twenty-something rock band—accordionist Franka Lampe's nose stud is clearly visible. And in the information booklet, the band brashly disassociates itself from any "gelt for guilt" approach to the music: "It is difficult to explain why klezmer music finds such a resonance in Germany. During a visit to America, we were often confronted by Jews curious about this. They would ask us, 'Is it because Germans have a bad conscience about the past?' The reason we play klezmer music is because we enjoy it. And we also like to think that our audience listens to us because they enjoy it and not to compensate for their bad consciences. To do otherwise serves neither the music nor the attempt to come to terms with the German-Jewish history." [20]

Nonetheless, the group also plays at Holocaust commemorations: a few months after we first met, they were on the lineup of the big Kristallnacht commemoration and Sachsenhausen benefit concerts sponsored by the Klezmer Gesellschaft. They arranged one piece using elements of Mordechai Gebirtig's song "S'Brent" especially to "make a statement with [their] music." It was clear, too, that despite their interest and despite their friendship with American Jewish klezmer musicians, they operated in considerable isolation from any living Jewish traditions: the original date for their CD launch was scheduled for the first night of Passover, a night when any Jew would be home or at a Jewish community center celebrating the Seder.

Late one night I sat in a trendy, wood-paneled Prenzlauerberg pub where la'om was improvising with some visiting American musicians, drinking beer, and talking with members of the group about how they—young East Berliners in their twenties—got interested in klezmer. I had seen them perform a couple nights earlier at the Hackesches Hof-Theater. The recently renovated theater opened off a courtyard; it was a smallish, dark place with rows of seats rising steeply in front of the stage. The audience was standing room only, mainly younger "alternative"-looking people: beards, shaggy hair, heavy knit sweaters, and no makeup. Before the concert I had heard mixed views about la'om's music. Some friends described them as among the best young groups in the scene. But one German klezmer fan I met told me they were "not very brilliant." He said he thought they were playing klezmer because it was trendy. I had found the concert somewhat pedestrian. The group's repertoire was mainly klezmer standards from old records. They technically reproduced the notes but carefully, almost timidly, at a dragging pace. The performance seemed to lack passion: I didn't think the music would have encouraged many people to get up and dance at a wedding.

The musicians were engagingly open, however, and I found their description of their involvement in the music and their changing perceptions of klezmer a fascinating mirror of the changing scene and its varied attractions. The discussion also revealed how foreign Jews and experiences, rather than direct contact with the local Jewish community, became the gateways and reference points for their understanding of Jewish culture.

Stefan Litsche, la'om's red-haired, red-bearded clarinetist, told me,

"When I first heard Feidman in concert, I was very much impressed with his playing. Also [with] the way he dealt with the people, how he worked the audience. I was deeply impressed by how the audience left the concert hall singing the last song he played. But later his workshop was a problem. It was interesting, but they taught us Feidman's understanding of playing music, not much about klezmer music in the sense of Jewish music—and this is what I wanted to learn, how to play this different kind of music, this special style. But he didn't teach much at all about this technique."

"A few months later," Litsche went on, "I went to a Brave Old World workshop, and there I learned a lot of style and playing techniques, how to make a melody sound like klezmer music. I found it very, very interesting. I feel I have to deal with Jewish culture. I can't play klezmer music without understanding Jewish culture. It was very interesting to learn more about a completely different culture. I'm from East Germany, and I had only heard in school about Jews in connection with the Holocaust."

Mattias Groh, la'om's owlish, classically trained violinist, was less displeased by Feidman's approach. He came into contact with Things Jewish firsthand when he studied Hebrew in Israel for three months in preparation for theology studies, which he later abandoned for psychology. Back in Berlin, he played Israeli folk dances with friends and attended a Feidman workshop. "His philosophy gave me a lot of freedom to experiment with music," Groh said. "Feidman didn't say much about what to do with this freedom, but he organized the freedom. And for me, people who don't discover how to deal with freedom don't learn anything new."

la'om's long-haired accordion player, Franka Lampe, told me she had been dragged into klezmer more or less against her will. She had found the klezmer fad in the early 1990s amusing but had had no desire to join "the umpteenth klezmer band" in Berlin. Still, once she started playing, she said, she found a deep attraction: "I didn't expect it, but the music has led me very deeply into the culture around it. I've been reading books, learning about Jewish history, and I'm thinking about studying Yiddish, too. Also, before I played this music, I never went to Sachsenhausen [on my own]. When I had to go there as a child on a school trip, I said it was a horrible place and I didn't want to go. But now, with the music, I'm interested in things like this. And if there is an article to read about Jewish culture or an exhibition to go to, I'm interested and I do it."

Stefan Kühne, the Klezgoyim guitarist, is somewhat older than the la'om musicians and comes from West Germany, not the former communist East. But he, too, told me that his involvement in klezmer music had led unexpectedly to a deeper interest in Jewish culture that coincided with an exploration of his own personal identity. His introduction to klezmer was not Giora Feidman but a concert in Berlin in 1988 by the rock-and-jazz-tinged Klezmatics. "It gave me the feeling of the power of the music; a joyful sound that I hadn't heard before," he said. "I started to search for what this culture is, and what this culture meant to me, and why I am interested in this culture." This was a question that he still couldn't answer. Kühne, who was thirty-five when we spoke in 1995, said that he had learned in school about the Holocaust and the destruction of European Jewry, but he didn't know what it was to be a Jew. "*This* is the point I'm interested in now. I want to know what we lost during [the Holocaust]. Of course, klezmer music is not the Jewish culture of the German Jews. But some Jews have come here now from [the former Soviet Union], after living without any religious traditions for generations. I take great interest in the discussions in Jewish groups about living with a tradition and living without a tradition, finding out what it means to be a Jew. For me, it reflects questions such as what does it mean to be a Christian who grew up German—what does it mean to be me! It's like a mirror, but it is a mirror for me to look at what made someone a Jew and what made someone a Christian and what made someone an agnostic, and so on."

II

Whose Music?

When the non-Jewish klezmer band Kroke from Kraków
(Kroke is the Yiddish name for Kraków) made its debut appearance in
Berlin in 1997 it was advertised as "KlezMORE from Poland." "Klez-
MORE" because the group came from a more "authentic" place than
most other European (i.e., Dutch, German, Swiss, Italian . . .) non-
Jewish klezmer bands: a genuine eastern European country whose prewar Yiddish-speaking, shtetl-dwelling Jews actually played the music
and where—unlike in some other countries—local folk music traditions, which in the past influenced and were influenced by Yiddish music, are still strong. It was a sort of "authenticity by association." (This
contiguity of cultures was illustrated during the final concert of the annual Festival of Jewish Culture in Kraków in 1995, which featured Kroke
along with American Jewish klezmer groups. A Polish highlander folk
band from the Tatra Mountains south of Kraków, dressed in their distinctive white costumes and brimmed black hats, also joined various
klezmer ensembles onstage for several numbers. The most startling moment of this cross-cultural collaboration was when the highlanders
launched into a twangy version of "Hava Nagila." The Polish musicians inserted tone shifts that took the famous hora into a totally different musical dimension.)[1] Subsequently, two members of Kroke discovered that they had Jewish family roots, which made them even more
authentic.

The question of authenticity and cultural authority vis-à-vis klezmer
and Yiddish music has been a recurring one in the mainly non-Jewish
European klezmer scene. It parallels, of course, debates on appropria-

tion and authenticity in other spheres of Jewish culture (who should mount Jewish museums, who should teach Jewish studies courses, etc). And it also reflects similar long-standing debates inherent in other musical movements, from ethnic and folk music of all sorts to jazz, soul, rap, and other music whose sound and even subject matter are identified with a specific cultural tradition, be it that of the Bulgarian village or that of the urban American ghetto.[2] In the debate over klezmer, the old question, Can a white man play the blues? becomes, so to speak, Can a goy play the Jews'?

Ari Davidow, one of the leading American klezmer critics, who runs www.klezmershack.com, the most exhaustive klezmer site on the World Wide Web, dismisses the whole debate as "silliness." He is emphatic in asserting that klezmer in the late 1990s can be considered "revived, alive, and well" in Germany and elsewhere.[3] "Nowadays, the revival is over—klezmer is a popular music form that is no longer exclusively Jewish, and other forms of Jewish music are also gaining in popularity," he states on the klezmershack.com home page. "And no one questions the place of klezmer in both Jewish and popular cultures. Well, no one we care about. Meanwhile, the edges of musical and cultural boundaries continue to change, expand, and morph onward, fueled by the imperatives to explore new music on the one hand, and by the shifting sense of Jewish identity on another, not always related, hand."

On a certain level that is true (and becomes truer as time goes on). But German musicians involved in the klezmer movement, like it or not, even in the late 1990s, were themselves still trying to come to terms with the issue. And many Jews and others, locals as well as visitors, still could not countenance the idea of Germans, however sincere or however enamored of the music, soulfully singing about burning shtetls or Yiddishe mamas, particularly when they did it in front of an audience and particularly when they "made the music their own." The American journalist Margaret Talbot, writing in 1995 in the *New Republic,* described an example of how such use of the music was taken to extraordinary extremes. "[T]he German ice-dancing team[,] Jennifer Goolsbee and Hendryk Schamberger, who competed in the Lillehammer Olympics, chose to choreograph their routine to the strains of Klezmer music," she wrote. "She wore light blue and he wore a prayer shawl and—what was it wrapped around his arm? Could it be . . . ? Yes, it could. Phylacteries. The couple's coach explained that Goolsbee and Schamberger, neither of whom is Jewish, wanted to 'give the message that we feel for the Jewish people.'"[4]

Such flamboyant philo-Semitic motives breed embarrassment, distrust, and anger among many Jews (and non-Jews). Some Jews deride non-Jewish klezmer as nothing more than kitsch that perpetrates offenses reminiscent of blackface minstrel shows. Numerous non-Jewish bands, in Germany and elsewhere, dress up in pseudo-shtetl attire, for example, and one non-Jewish Polish musician in Kraków ostentatiously dons a yarmulke before each gig in a Jewish-style restaurant—whether as a means of demonstrating respect for Jewish sensibilities or simply as part of his act is not clear. Some Jews particularly resent what they feel is a non-Jewish theft of Jewish music and profiteering on the culture and ideas of a murdered people.

Organizers of Jewish culture festivals run by Jewish communities sometimes try to invite only groups with Jewish performers. "I feel sometimes very strange if I hear non-Jews performing synagogue music or klezmer music," Andreas Nachama confided in 1997 in Berlin. "Most of these people do it without knowing Jews, and some of them do it with the consciousness that they do it better than the Jews would have done it." In setting up the Berlin community's annual Jewish Culture Days programs, Nachama said, "I try to show how Jewish culture, even East European Jewish culture, looks in Paris or California or elsewhere." Nachama's goal was specifically to develop the Jewish cultural consciousness of Berlin Jews—regardless of the fact that the majority of the audience for festival concerts may often be composed of non-Jews. And, in fact, it is the low level of contemporary Jewish cultural consciousness—regarding religious as well as secular Jewish traditions—that has made some German and other Jews so sensitive to what they perceive as cultural appropriation or usurpation, not just of music but of other aspects of the Jewish phenomenon. Jewish community leaders, too, often have bristled over the amount of public funding that goes for festivals showcasing klezmer and other easily accessible aspects of "Jewish style" rather than Jewish substance. "You stuff an Indian and put him on show," Robert Liska of the Vienna Jewish community complained to me in 1996. "You will find very often more readiness on the part of public officials to support such retro-oriented glorifications than when you need Jewish schools, for example. To present the stuffed Indian is very often considered more appropriate than to fill something with life. And of course I am more interested in real life than in stuffed Indians even though they are part of the heritage."

The question of whether non-Jews in the genre, regardless of their skill and knowledge, must defer perforce to Jewish musicians, simply because they have the "right" religion, is not just a philosophical issue, however. It is a powerful, market-influenced commercial debate, and responses to it have changed and are changing the shape of the music. The question of who—if anyone—"owns" Jewish music has led at times to friction between bands with no Jewish members competing for gigs and recognition with bands that have Jewish musicians. Yet many Jews involved in klezmer—in America as well as in Europe—are as far removed from the destroyed eastern European Jewish culture as are their non-Jewish colleagues. Not only that. "There are plenty of non-Jewish musicians playing this music better than Jewish musicians who count among the leaders of the revival," Alan Bern pointed out. "What happens when you have a non-Jewish group from Germany that plays better than its teachers who are Jews from America? Who owns the music at that point? If you have an ideology that the Jews own the music no matter what, because it's Jewish music, then the teachers maintain control of the development of the revival."

A good part of Giora Feidman's appeal to non-Jews—not to mention his crossover marketability—indeed rests in his comforting assertion that it doesn't matter who you are or even what you play to make you a klezmer and involve you in klezmer music. Klezmer, the "universal language," can be played and understood by anyone; no translation is needed, no contact with Jews. All you have to do to be a klezmer musician, he says, is to have feeling and make music that comes from your feeling. Feidman states point blank that klezmer has nothing to do with Jewishness. The problem is that, despite this redefinition of klezmer to exclude its specific Jewish cultural origin, Feidman and some of his followers still appeal to a desire to connect with Things Jewish, to use the music as a ticket into the virtual Jewish world. The contradictory message is that a contextless universalist attitude toward the music is, in fact, the real, "authentic," true Jewish way.

But Feidman's vision is only one version of klezmer authenticity in the competitive marketplace. Indeed, as early as the 1970s authenticity was a byword of the American neoklezmer movement. By the late 1990s various European klezmer groups—or the marketing departments of their record companies—claimed a long list of authenticities as a means of promoting and validating their music and, in fact, making the limited klezmer market as wide as possible.

According to the notes to its CD *Live in Prag,* the Vienna-based Ensemble Klesmer, founded in 1989 and including both Jewish and non-Jewish musicians from Ukraine, Bulgaria, and Austria, "seeks to achieve maximum authenticity in the interpretation of traditional Jewish folk music. The interpretation of Klezmer music in its original spirit clearly sets Ensemble Klesmer apart from a number of other popular groups today."[5] The group Budowitz, which is based in Graz, Austria, and whose Jewish and non-Jewish musicians come from the United States, Austria, and Hungary, calls itself an "early music" klezmer ensemble and presents its music as being as close as possible to an authentic repertoire and the authentic way klezmer was played in previous centuries. Its 1997 CD, *Mother Tongue,* is subtitled *Music of the 19th-Century Klezmorim on Original Instruments,* and the notes booklet nearly collapses with the weight of its densely detailed information on sources, style, history, pedigree, and ethnographic approach. The repertoire, according to the notes, comes from "field recordings of Jews, Gypsies and folk musicians from eastern Europe, from early manuscripts, collections and musicological transcriptions, and from 78 r.p.m. discs recorded in Europe and the U.S. between ca. 1905 and 1929." Every step of the archival process is recounted. "Our European collection," the notes state, "stems from Bucharest, Warsaw, Lvov, Kiev and Moscow, which, although recorded in the early part of this century, gives us a very good insight into nineteenth-century style, due to the fact that musical change at that time occurred at a slower rate than it does now."[6]

Bob Cohen is the only Jewish member of his Budapest-based group Die Naye Kapelye, which includes two Hungarians and another American. But for him, this mixture, too, is authentic, as are the musical training, skills, and sensitivities of his musicians. The band, he says, is following in the tradition of early klezmer bands whose composition included Jews and non-Jews. For Cohen, authenticity means earthy, down and dirty, eastern Europe. "The band is playing klezmer because I asked them to, and they are capable of playing klezmer because they are all really good east European musicians," he told me in 1997. "They all have very good ears; they've been listening to it now for about four years. That is much different from being jazz musicians and trying to play klezmer. Or German classical musicians trying to play klezmer by listening to Giora Feidman records. All of us have gone down to Transylvania, we all know how a traditional band there plays. . . . There used to be a kind of klezmer band like ours [there], a small one, not commercial, which played in villages. The people in the band have learned a lot about Yiddishkayt just being in a band and hanging out with people who know more, [and also] taking courses in Holocaust studies and things like that."

Cohen has no use for klezmer in the popular guise of contemporary "fusion" music. "What you often hear is a mishmash," he sniffed. "This is OK locally, but people don't really need Norwegian klezmer fusion, touched with jazz or whatever—I don't think they really need it, although it's going to be done! It's going to be done!" But at the same time, fusion *itself* is represented by other groups as illustrating the real, authentic spirit of klezmer and forms part of its attraction. Members of the Rome klezmer band Klezroym say they strive to mix Sephardic melodies, Italian folk songs, Middle Eastern music, and jazz in their compositions. "I want to produce something that satisfies my sense of creativity," says Klezroym's trumpeter, Andrea Pandolfo "When I write a piece, I don't think 'klezmer'; rather, I think of what story I want to tell."

Christian Dawid, the clarinetist of the Bremen group Klezgoyim, says questioning the motivation of his own interest in klezmer music and Jewish culture led him to reflect on his relationship with all types of music. "I went through a period when I doubted why I am so interested in this music and this culture," he said. "Was it that I also want to be a very late-born victim and to get rid of my German roots, or something?" Eventually, he came to the conclusion that klezmer is just as much "his" music as any other. It might not be his ancestral musical tradition, but, he explained, "I've been occupied with a music which is not my own for all my life—[classical music] is also not 'my' music, it's just an old music, it may come from Germany and Austria, but it's also definitely not 'my' music, definitely not." With klezmer, he said, he felt the same way: "I'm not a Jew, and I also don't want to copy something or say, well, this is my music, or that I want to look Jewish, or to sound Jewish, things like that. But as a musician, I just have very, very deep feelings for this music. I just like it a lot. It's very meaningful to me to play the music that I just love very, very much."

When I first met him, in October 1995, Dawid was taking part in a weeklong klezmer music and Yiddish workshop conducted by Brave Old World, Henry Sapoznik, and other North American Jewish performers, including the Canadian Yiddishist Michael Wex. The stated goal was to demystify Jews and Jewish traditions, to provide German klezmer enthusiasts not with a sense of spiritual reconciliation vis-à-vis the music but with an idea of the context from which the music derived as well as an understanding of its unique musical form and language. In short, it was anti-Feidman. Demystifying Things Jewish, organizers hoped, would help Germans to free themselves from stereotypes and have a more "normal" relationship with the Jewish world, Jewish culture—and Jews themselves. Providing this background would give the musicians a foundation on which to build their own interpretations. The idea was to encourage them to move the music in new directions without losing sight of its roots and inherent identity.

"The unfortunate problem with German philo-Semitism is that it immediately defines the Jews as dead victims we have to feel sorry for," Wex, who taught a session on the history and contexts of Yiddish, told me. ". . . What I and [others] are trying to do is to present [Jewish] culture as a living phenomenon that has a lot of wonderful things in it but, like any living phenomenon, occasionally has to go to the bathroom, occasionally has to eat or burp or get into a fight. It's not a simple 'outpouring of the soul'—it's that sometimes, too, but it's like the old Bob Dylan line, even the president of the United States must sometimes stand naked. Even a language like Yiddish has to go to the can once in a while."

The weeklong workshop took place in the graceful, moated castle of Bad Pyrmont, a sleepy spa town in northern Germany, with mineral baths and shady parks whose trees that week were brilliant with autumn foliage. The castle, which dates to the sixteenth century, had become the site of a municipal adult education center directed by Heinz Baldermann, a middle-aged Jew born after World War II. Baldermann was the chief local organizer of the workshop and also headed Haskalah, a Jewish cultural association in Hannover whose aim was to provide living Jewish "outreach" to non-Jews to counter the stereotypical image of Jews as dead victims. For him, klezmer represented a means by which dialogue with non-Jews could take place: "Klezmer in itself is composed of dialogue," he said. "For me, it's a symbol of a Jewish tradition in which Jewish and non-Jewish themes interact."

The forty participating musicians at the Bad Pyrmont workshop were a diverse group—young men with dreadlocks, middle-aged sixties types, a punk-looking woman in her twenties with bright blue hair, an eastern German woman who had recently discovered some sort of distant Jewish connection in her background and wore a Star of David charm on a chain around her neck. Each paid 350 deutsche marks, the equivalent of U.S. $230 (DM 250, or $160, for students) for the full week, including room and board. Most came from Germany (a few came from the Netherlands). Only six of the participants were Jewish; Baldermann was the only local German Jew among the mostly Jewish staff. Baldermann told me that he had recruited participants through announcements sent to an extensive mailing list that included all Jewish communities in Germany. Eighty people responded. He had hoped to have more Jewish participants, he said, but interested Jews apparently saw the announcement too late to register: "The announcement was hanging in Jewish community centers, but the Jewish musicians were 'yontiff' [holiday] Jews: they only saw the notices when they went to the synagogue for Yom Kippur, and by then all places were filled."

Most of the participants already played in local klezmer bands, for example, the all-female group Kales (Yiddish for "young women"), Yardniks, Uftref, and Dawid's group, Klezgoyim. Each day they met for master classes and sessions on topics such as Yiddish song, eastern European Jewish dance, and Wex's Yiddish contexts. Henry Sapoznik, using vintage and contemporary recordings, taught a daily session on the history of klezmer music, from its eastern European roots through its immigrant American metamorphosis to its current eclectic styles. Evenings were devoted to performances by the workshop members and to discussion sessions whose topics ranged from Jewish history to contemporary attitudes toward Jews to attempts to analyze klezmer's current popular attraction.

More than a year later, Dawid told me that the workshop had represented a "loss of innocence" for him. The experience, he said, had had a profound effect on his musical and his personal development. The son of a Protestant minister, he had grown up knowing about some Jewish traditions from a close reading of the Old Testament. Like so many others, he had been turned on to klezmer by hearing Feidman recordings in the early 1990s and got together with friends to see what they could do. "I wrote some pieces myself, using what I understood at the time to be the right musical language," Dawid told me with a laugh. "And we had a few traditional tunes which mostly we knew from Feidman recordings. We started with very easy pieces, to find out whether we could do things with this music, things we liked. We would make our own kind of very individualistic arrangements, really doing our own thing to this music. And we weren't interested in copying something or in sounding very Jewish or looking very Jewish. We just all liked the music very much."

Still, Dawid said, it was a shock when the Bad Pyrmont instructors told them that their music didn't sound very Jewish at all—that the musical language of modes, chords, and progressions they were using was not in fact that used in the klezmer tradition. "They told us that there was much more to this music, that this musical language is much more complicated than we thought," Dawid said. This made him want to learn more. "For me it was just worth it as a musician to play better music. Just to go deeper, dive into it more."

When I spoke to him in 1997, Dawid said he considered himself simply a musician—not a "klezmer musician"—although klezmer is the music he liked best and tried to play most often. Playing music—whether in a theater orchestra, a klezmer band, or elsewhere—and teaching music were his primary sources of income. His personal as well as professional musical life revolved around klezmer, too. At the Bad Pyrmont workshop, Dawid met and fell in love with one of the other participants, a Dutch accordion player named Sanne Möricke. The two began living together and playing klezmer together as a duo called Khupe (Wedding Canopy). They use a Yiddish word as their e-mail address, and they used a Yiddish phrase on the birth announcement for their daughter, whom they gave a typical Jewish name.

A cassette that they recorded privately in January 1997 is a series of highly personal interpretations of klezmer standards. The two musicians are technically expert and express affection for each other as well as for the melodies as they play. The familiar tunes—stock tracks of many klezmer albums—sound new and fresh, part of living experience, not an archival reconstruction of a lost past, not a political act, not a sacred New Age moment, not a radical exercise in experimental jazz, and not an angst-filled apology.

Dawid's approach to the music and his apparently easy familiarity with it despite lingering qualms may represent a next stage in the klezmer phenomenon in Germany: a relationship with the music, Jewish culture, Jewish memory—and Jews—that is respectful but less haunted and emotionally laden, a relationship that also involves active collaboration with Jewish musicians. (Heiko Lehmann writes: "Klezmer music is not a museum. Even if it is hard, German performers have to try to contribute to the music.")[7] Changes in the packaging of the Klezgoyim's CDs were indicative of this change, too. The first release, which the group cut before attending the Bad Pyrmont workshop, features a sepia print photo of the band looking stereotypically somber and old-fashioned. With the second CD, recorded in late 1996, they felt relaxed and confident enough about the music, and their relationship to it, to joke. The title of the CD is *Out of the Eyebrow,* and the cover shows a montage of the group's eyes and eyebrows. The title and photo are a pun. Bremen—the band's hometown—means "eyebrows" in Yiddish. The CD notes quote Michael Wex: "Someone asked me, what is that—

a 'klezgoy'?—and I answered, that is a 'shabbes-goy' with a musical instrument."

(Dawid took this evolution further. He studied with Brave Old World clarinetist Kurt Bjorling and in 1999 was hired by Brave Old World to substitute for Bjorling during an international tour by the group. In 2000 Dawid left the Klezgoyim, and he and Möricke cofounded another group, Sukke. Sukke's singer and violinist is Claudia Koch, who helped found the pioneer East Berlin klezmer group Aufwind in 1984. Koch also has performed with established American Jewish musicians, including the Chicago Klezmer Ensemble. Heiko Lehmann, the former Aufwind bass player who also plays in Sukke, wrote of Koch and Dawid: "Here are two German musicians who were invited by Jewish klezmer music performers to contribute to their projects. They did what they could, and it was liked, by both their fellow musicians and the audiences." It still remained to be seen, he wrote in late 2000, whether "these Germans, who contributed to the music by playing with Jewish bands, will be able to contribute anything as a German band.")[8]

Afterword

"We always have the stories, from either 400 years ago or this century, that as the Jews were moved out, the locals took on their houses, and often their belongings; in a sense, they both murdered and inherited," writes the Tel Aviv University historian Raphael Vago. "But did it occur to historians that whenever Jews were removed and disappeared a gap was created, a gap that perhaps could not be filled, even if the homes, furniture and belongings were taken over by the inheritors?"[1]

The Holocaust, compounded by the Cold War, created the biggest and most wrenching Jewish gap in history—the "void," "vacuum," "black hole," "unhealable wound"—whose impact has resounded far beyond the actual killing fields of Europe and far beyond the direct damage done to Jews and to others targeted for extermination. While the recent trends I have outlined and discussed mark by no means the first time that Gentile society in Europe has manifested interest in Jews and their concerns, the contemporary embrace of the Jewish component and creation of Jewish virtualities is, consciously or not, an attempt to deal with that gap and its effects.

The memory of Jews and Jewish heritage is emotionally charged, whether because of official postwar taboos, government policy, lingering anti-Semitism, a sincere sense of loss, or guilty conscience. The remembered presence of Jews and Jewish space can become a symbol of the past, but it can also become an idealized symbol of contemporary aspirations: to multiculturalism, to identity, to "authenticity," to a pan-European ideal. "We [Jews] are the vanished race of Europe—on the national conscience, romanticized, and ascribed wisdom," the klez-mer musician Michael Alpert told me. Within political, personal, and even religious frameworks, these symbols resonate from the viewpoint of the present and in some cases are used to make sense of today's world. Through memory and loss, yearning and manipulation, the Jewish space, as Diana Pinto put it, still exists. Through contemporary approaches to studying, enjoying, participating in, resurrecting, exploiting, and sometimes sanctifying it, the "Jewish thing" is becoming universal. In "bringing it alive," or attempting to do so, the inheritors today sometimes aspire to take on the identity as well as the trappings—though sometimes what they "bring alive" is a grotesquely animated cadaver.

The manifestations of and motivations for the virtual Jewish phenomenon are many and varied. They are changing rapidly, too, as we become farther removed in time from the Holocaust, as postcommunist democratic changes shake down into normality, and as Jews themselves take advantage of the new climate to assert a positive identity—as practicing Jews, as secular Jews, as consciously Jewish living individuals adding creative input, as Jews, to society as a whole.

Jews as well as non-Jews now benefit from a wealth of information and educational material about Jews, Jewish culture, and Jewish history. It still may not be "normal" to be Jewish in Europe, but it is now no longer abnormal to recognize historic Jewish presence, to learn about Jewish history and traditions, to appreciate Jewish culture, or what is defined or perceived as such, or to participate in it. The concerts, exhibitions, books, festivals, debates, and study programs that have mushroomed in recent years fill a very real gap that existed until not too long ago. Jewish historical sites, too, are now noted as national cultural monuments, and confiscated Jewish property is being returned.

Yet the proliferation has many pitfalls. Many Jews are skeptical: philo-Semitism and anti-Semitism are seen as sides of the same coin. The non-Jewish mainstream frequently finds it easier to deal with dead Jews than with living ones; to simplify, exoticize, and view from a historical distance. Jewish culture, says the Polish sociologist Paweł Spiewak, runs the risk of being "reduced to symbols and food." In isolation, it may lose its meaning, become "just a type of folklore" that people recognize or label as "Jewish" without any deeper understanding or association.

Indeed, the virtual Jewish phenomenon frequently has little to do with Jews. It is a national phenomenon: a Polish phenomenon, an Italian phenomenon, a Czech phenomenon, a German phenomenon. Also, knowledge or sympathy for Things Jewish among a part of society is not a general cure-all for the ills and omissions of society as a whole. Surveys have shown a deep ignorance concerning the Jewish phenomenon and the persistence of prejudice and stereotype, even at the close of the 1990s in countries like Italy, Germany, and Poland that have seen a proliferation of Jewish performance, study programs, books, and the like. Educational systems have proved sorely lacking in their treatment of Jewish issues, including the Holocaust experience.

Even superficial interest, however, may serve as a means of demythologizing Jews and creating a less ignorant and, it is hoped, a more open, tolerant society. Even faddish experiences such as the "Shalom" craze in the Czech Republic, "Jewish" cafés in Poland, or the fact that klezmer songs make the charts in Germany can be the thin edge of the wedge providing easy gateways to further, deeper, and less easily assimilated knowledge. Not everyone who buys a CD or attends a concert or visits a Jewish museum or exhibition makes use of these gateways; on the contrary. But for those who do go deeper, "Jewish chic" and pop culture attraction can become an important entrée.

Moni Ovadia's impact in Italy illustrates this to some extent. At the beginning of the 1990s Ovadia was virtually alone among Italian performers in staging overtly Jewish material for the mainstream public. Regardless of its ambiguity, his style and staging touched a chord in Italy and served as a catalyst for burgeoning interest on all levels, including academic scholarship. By the latter part of the 1990s, he and his work had helped to create a receptive market for a flood of other scholarly activities, publications, and public performances and events by local and international artists, including many from Israel, which had begun to illustrate a much broader image of Jewish identity, life, and culture.

The Academy Award–winning 1997 film, *La vita è bella,* by Roberto Benigni, falls into this category. It is quite clear to me that without Ovadia Benigni would not have made the film; Benigni, who is not Jewish, was praised by Ovadia as "an honorary Jew" for his work. Debates over the movie, in Italy as elsewhere, involved the issue of whether Benigni had banalized the Holocaust by using it as a setting for his tragicomic tour de force. An extremely significant but largely overlooked point, however, was that Benigni portrayed his Jewish protagonist, Guido, as an ordinary person, an Italian—not a Woody Allen New York neurotic, a Mitteleuropean coffeehouse intellectual, a battle-scarred Israeli, or a caftaned, Yiddish-speaking, shtetl dweller. *La vita è bella* thus provided a powerful popular antidote to stereotyped public perceptions of Jews and Judaism as filtered through the media and entertainers, ironically, such as Ovadia himself.

The phenomenon I have discussed in this book is in flux and still, in some places, fairly new. Its subsequent development and ultimate effects remain to be seen. The questions I have posed—and the responses to them—are still very much open. I think, however, that we can look toward a further "universalization" of the "Jewish thing." Jews themselves may be few, but the Jewish legacy touches and will touch the mainstream, on a variety of levels. The enormous response to the European Day of Jewish Culture in September 2000 was an impressive illustration of this. And already, as we have seen, dozens of local klezmer groups have sprung up, no longer as attempts to achieve symbolic reconciliation with the past, but because the groups simply like the music. These bands are increasingly making this music "theirs," as legitimate a subject of personal rendering and interpretation as any other music in the broad spectrum of the "world beat" multicultural repertoire.

But is it good for the Jews, as the old saying goes? On the whole, I would say yes, with certain caveats. A sizable part of the European population has begun to know something of what Jews were—and are—and to recognize that Jews and Jewish culture formed a rich, integral part of their own history. Jews themselves, particularly the emerging communities in postcommunist states, have benefited in various ways from this new climate.

Yet there is a growing sense of urgency among Jews that unless they themselves take positive action, the "Jewish thing" may be hijacked, if not watered down to a homeopathic degree: Jewish cultural products displacing Jewish culture. An affirmation that Jews and Jewish culture are not simply dusty or sanctified museum relics is essential. Without a living Jewish dimension, the virtual Jewish world may become a sterile desert—or a haunted Jewish never-never land. Some Jews have begun to take positive steps to help chart future development of the phenomenon by making sure that there is actual living Jewish input, and Jewish organizations are trying to develop strategies.

Responses to these issues may be the key to the future. But these responses, too, are in flux. "There is a problem of representation," the British scholar Jonathan Webber told a February 1999 conference in Paris on Jewish culture in the twenty-first century. "There is a difference between official, established Judaism and how Jews actually live. And there is an imagined Judaism, created ex nihilo. How do we Jews represent Jewish culture in relation to ourselves, to non-Jews, in the media? Should we participate or stand by?" Not only that, he warned. "Representation is a moving target. Jewish culture is undergoing such changes that to pin it down to one representation is an illusion."

Notes

Chapter 1. Cities without Jews

1. Hugo Bettauer, *The City without Jews: A Novel of Our Time,* trans. Salomea Neumark Brainin (New York: Bloch, [1926] 1991), 78. (First published in German as *Die Stadt ohne Juden: Ein Roman von übermorgen* [Vienna: Gloriette-Verlag, 1922].)

2. Ibid., 188–89.

3. Salomea Neumark Brainin, "Introduction by the Translator," ibid., xiii. Diane R. Spielmann cites 80,000 copies sold in German by the end of 1924 and more than 250,000 printed copies in translation. See "German-Jewish Writers on the Eve of the Holocaust," in *Reflections of the Holocaust in Art and Literature,* ed. Randolf L. Braham (Boulder: Social Science Monographs; New York: Csengi Institute for Holocaust Studies of the Graduate School and University Center of the City University of New York, 1990), 62. I am grateful to Dr. Murray G. Hall of Vienna for clarifying several issues relating to Bettauer.

4. Brainin, "Introduction by the Translator," xii–xiii.

5. Miguel Angel Martínez, rapporteur, *The Jewish Contribution to European Culture,* Report of the Committee on Culture and Education (Strasbourg: Council of Europe, 1987).

6. See Diana Pinto, *A New Jewish Identity for Post-1989 Europe,* JPR Policy Paper No. 1 (London: Institute for Jewish Policy Research, June 1996), among other writings and lectures by Pinto. Also see efforts and initiatives by organizations such as the European Council of Jewish Communities and the Europe Israel Jewish Forum movement.

7. See Bernard Wasserstein, *Vanishing Diaspora: The Jews in Europe since 1945* (Cambridge, Mass.: Harvard University Press, 1996).

8. The size of Jewish communities is a matter of much discussion and conjecture. These figures are all estimates, based on the number of registered mem-

bers of the Jewish communities as well as projections of the numbers of Jews who are not formally affiliated.

9. A writer in the *Jerusalem Report* found it incongruous, too, that in 1997, amid the controversy over Swiss use of Nazi gold, one by-product of which was a backlash of grassroots anti-Semitism, the Swiss government sponsored a high-profile U.S. tour of the Swiss klezmer group Kol Simcha. See Jeremy Eichler, "But Is It Jewish?" *Jerusalem Report,* November 13, 1997.

10. Umberto Eco, *Travels in Hyperreality,* trans. William Weaver (New York: Harcourt Brace & Company, 1986), 8, 7. See the discussion of virtuality in Barbara Kirshenblatt-Gimblett, *Destination Culture: Tourism, Museums, and Heritage* (Berkeley: University of California Press, 1998).

11. In *Jewish Icons: Art and Society in Modern Europe* (Berkeley: University of California Press, 1998), Richard I. Cohen uses the term "Jewish public space" to describe areas in which Jews interacted with or portrayed themselves to the surrounding mainstream Christian world in the eighteenth and nineteenth centuries. See, for example, p. 70.

12. Pinto, *A New Jewish Identity,* 6–7.

13. Y. Michal Bodemann, "A Reemergence of German Jewry?" in *Reemerging Jewish Culture in Germany: Life and Literature since 1989,* ed. Sander L. Gilman and Karen Remmler (New York: New York University Press, 1994), 57–58. See also the book of essays edited by Bodemann, *Jews, Germans, Memory: Reconstructions of Jewish Life in Germany* (Ann Arbor: University of Michigan Press, 1996).

14. See my paper *Filling the Jewish Space in Europe,* published in 1996 by the American Jewish Committee.

15. Bodemann, "Reemergence?" 57. The exhibition coincided with the five hundredth anniversary of the expulsion of Jews from Spain and the fiftieth anniversary of the Wannsee Conference in Berlin at which Nazi leaders plotted the "Final Solution."

16. *American Jewish Yearbook,* 1994, 322. See also Aviva Kempner, "Andreas Nachama: Keeping Alive 'The Patterns of Jewish Life,'" in *Washington Jewish Week,* September 24, 1992.

17. Annette Winkelmann, ed., *Directory of Jewish Studies in Europe* (Oxford: European Association of Jewish Studies, 1998). A similar catalog for the United States and Canada was first published in 1979 by the Association of Jewish Studies, in association with the B'nai B'rith Hillel Foundations. See also Shaye J. D. Cohen and Edward L. Greenstein, eds., *The State of Jewish Studies* (New York: Jewish Theological Seminary of America, 1990). This volume includes papers presented at a 1987 conference, whose major theme was the new and increasing "normality" of Jewish studies, particularly in the United States. For a detailed examination of Jewish studies in Germany, see the special issue, "Historical Memory and the State of Jewish Studies in Germany," *Shofar: An Interdisciplinary Journal of Jewish Studies* 15, no. 4 (Summer 1997).

18. Speech by Krzysztof Śliwiński, at the time Poland's official ambassador to the Jewish Diaspora, King's College, London, November 20, 1996.

19. Many such surveys were carried out, including a series commissioned in various countries throughout the 1990s by the American Jewish Committee. Reports of various surveys are summarized in the annual "Anti-Semitism World

Report" published (as of 1999 on-line only) by the Institute for Jewish Policy Research, London.

20. I helped to coordinate this project, under the direction of American Jewish Committee research director, David Singer. The initial countries surveyed were Poland, the Czech Republic, Slovakia, Hungary, Croatia, and Ukraine.

21. Katharina Ochse, "What Could Be More Fruitful, More Healing, More Purifying? Representations of Jews in the German Media after 1989," in Gilman and Remmler, *Reemerging Jewish Culture in Germany,* 113.

22. Agata Tuszyńska, *Lost Landscapes: In Search of Isaac Bashevis Singer and the Jews of Poland,* trans. Madeline G. Levine (New York: William Morrow, 1998), 98.

23. Estimates ranged routinely from 500,000 to 5 million. Information on these surveys was obtained from Tullia Zevi, former president of the Union of Italian Jewish Communities, and Annie Sacerdoti, editor of the Milan Jewish magazine *Il Bollettino.*

24. Fritz Stern, address to the Bertelsmann Forum in Berlin, July 4, 1998. Reprinted in the *International Herald Tribune,* July 8, 1998.

25. For a detailed discussion of Germany, see Jeffrey Herf, *Divided Memory: The Nazi Past in the Two Germanys* (Cambridge, Mass.: Harvard University Press, 1997).

26. See the chilling examples detailed in Herf, *Divided Memory,* e.g., 123–24. Also see Michael C. Steinlauf, *Bondage to the Dead: Poland and the Memory of the Holocaust* (Syracuse: Syracuse University Press, 1997); Konstanty Gebert, "Jewish Identities in Poland: New, Old, and Imaginary," and András Kovács, "Changes in Jewish Identity in Modern Hungary," both in *Jewish Identities in the New Europe,* ed. Jonathan Webber (London: Littman Library of Jewish Civilization, 1994); articles in Randolph L. Braham, ed., *Anti-Semitism and the Treatment of the Holocaust in Post-Communist Europe* (New York: Columbia University Press, 1994); and books including Jonathan Kaufman, *A Hole in the Heart of the World: Being Jewish in Eastern Europe* (New York: Viking, 1996), and Charles Hoffman, *Gray Dawn: The Jews of Eastern Europe in the Post-Communist Era* (New York: HarperCollins, 1992).

27. See, e.g., the book by that name by Sabine Reichel (New York: Hill & Wang, 1989).

28. Some Vatican policies after the papal trip to the Holy Land, however, raised concern among Jews. Among other things, this included John Paul's beatification of nineteenth-century Pope Pius IX, the last pope to have confined Jews to the ghetto.

29. "Berlin 1990," by Michael Alpert, on the CD *Beyond the Pale* (Pinorrekk Records, CD 5013, 1993).

30. Ruth Beckermann, "The Glory of Austrian Resistance and the Forgotten Jews," in *Insiders and Outsiders: Jewish and Gentile Culture in Germany and Austria,* ed. Dagmar C. G. Lorenz and Gabriele Weinberger (Detroit: Wayne State University Press, 1994), 258.

31. Speech by Tullia Zevi to the 3d Congress of the Union of Italian Jewish Communities, Rome, June 21, 1998.

32. See, e.g., Jonathan Boyarin, "Europe's Indian, America's Jew: Modiano

and Vizenor," in Boyarin's *Storm from Paradise: The Politics of Jewish Memory* (Minneapolis: University of Minnesota Press, 1992). There is a growing literature on how Americans of immigrant ancestry view the American Indian. Europeans, too, have long manifested a fascination with American Indian culture. This results, in part, from the philosophical idealization of the natural world that dates back to Rousseau and earlier. A large part of the more recent fascination can be attributed to the immense popularity of the Wild West adventure books of the German author Karl May. May lived from 1842 to 1912 and never set foot in the United States. Practically unknown to American readers, his tales about the noble Apache Winnetou and his young German immigrant companion, Charley, known as "Old Shatterhand," have reached every part of Europe with their romantic and adventurous vision of the West. Translated into some twenty-eight languages, they have sold 80 million copies and spawned movies, television programs, posters, postcards, and other spin-offs. May's home is something of a pilgrimage site, and thousands of Germans, Czechs, Swedes, and others dress up like Indians, learn Indian arts and crafts, spend weekends in tepee villages or actually fly to the United States to spend their vacations on American Indian reservations. I bought Winnetou postcards and saw an Old Shatterhand movie in communist Prague in 1966. I am grateful to Carol Herselle Krinsky for providing me with information on May and the European attraction to the American West, from her work in progress on Europeans, reservation tourism, and the novels of Karl May.

33. For a discussion of white appropriation of black culture, particularly music, see Ellis Cashmore, *The Black Culture Industry* (London: Routledge, 1997). Also see Michael Rogin, *Blackface, White Noise: Jewish Immigrants in the Hollywood Melting Pot* (Berkeley: University of California Press, 1998); Daniel Belasco, "From the Streets, Jews and Hip Hop," in *CultureCurrents*, the on-line newsletter of the National Foundation for Jewish Culture, July 1999. The U.S. magazine *Common Quest* devoted much of its summer 1997 issue to the topic of black-Jewish cultural relations.

34. Flyer on the exhibition "The Motives of Memory: Commercializing the Jewish Past in Poland," by Erica Lehrer, which opened at the Terrace Gallery, Grinnell, Iowa, on June 1, 1995.

35. See particularly Rogin, *Blackface, White Noise*. In the 1970s a film clip on German television featuring a black singer who made a career in West Germany, Roberto Blanco, showed Blanco's face in a washing machine into which "Blanco 73" washing powder was poured. Blanco, of course, means "white" in Spanish. Blanco's face is shown revolving in the machine. At the end of the cycle the door of the machine opens and he is shown in chalky "whiteface." This clip was rebroadcast on German television in August 1998 during a special featuring popular singers from the 1970s.

36. I am grateful to Charles Bergengren for sending material on this to me.

37. On Holocaust memorials, see James E. Young, *The Texture of Memory: Holocaust Memorials and Their Meaning* (New Haven: Yale University Press, 1993), and *At Memory's Edge: After-Images of the Holocaust in Contemporary Art and Architecture* (New Haven: Yale University Press, 2000).

38. See, e.g., Mark R. Cohen, trans. and ed., *The Autobiography of a Seventeenth-Century Venetian Rabbi: Leon Modena's "Life of Judah"* (Princeton:

Princeton University Press, 1988). Some books on Jewish ritual and practice were published, at times by Jewish converts to Christianity, as deliberate attempts to discredit Judaism. See the discussion, for example, in Cohen, *Jewish Icons*. For an upbeat view, see Alan Edelstein, *An Unacknowledged Harmony: Philo-Semitism and the Survival of European Jewry*, Contributions in Ethnic Studies No. 4 (Westport, Conn.: Greenwood Press, 1982).

39. See Cohen, *Jewish Icons*. Also see Linda Nochlin and Tamar Garb, eds., *The Jew in the Text: Modernity and the Construction of Identity* (London: Thames and Hudson, 1995); Kirshenblatt-Gimblett, *Destination Culture;* Jacob Katz, *Out of the Ghetto: The Social Background of Jewish Emancipation, 1770–1870* (Cambridge, Mass.: Harvard University Press, 1973), among others.

40. Mark Twain [Samuel L. Clemens], "Concerning the Jews," in *How to Tell a Story and other Essays*, Author's National Edition, *The Writings of Mark Twain*, vol. 22 (New York: Harper and Brothers, 1909), 274–75; emphasis in original. For Twain's portrait of the Austrian parliament and its anti-Semitic parties, see "Stirring Times in Austria," in the same volume, pp. 227–28.

Chapter 2. A Virtual Jewish World

1. See Sheri Allen, "Petr Muk: The Faithful Star," *Prague Post,* February 17–23, 1993. Thanks also to Richard Allen Green and Silvie Wittman for information on the Shalom craze.

2. Gábor T. Szántó, "Gathering the Dispersed," in *Diaszpóra (és) Művészet/Diaspora (and) Art* (Budapest: Hungarian Jewish Museum, 1997), the catalog of an exhibition held in 1997–98. There is a wide literature on the question of Jewish art. See, for example, "What Is a Jewish Artist?" by Marc Chagall, in *The Golden Tradition: Jewish Life and Thought in Eastern Europe,* ed. Lucy S. Dawidowicz (New York: Schocken, 1967). In *Jewish Icons: Art and Society in Modern Europe* (Berkeley: University of California Press, 1998), 7, Richard I. Cohen calls Jewish art "an elusive entity that can be best encapsulated by a general definition as that 'which reflects the Jewish experience.' "

3. For example, see Stanley Waterman, *Cultural Politics and European Jewry* (London: Institute of Jewish Policy Research, 1999), a monograph prepared for an international seminar, Jewish Culture for the Twenty-first Century, held in Paris in February 1999.

4. Michael Brenner, *The Renaissance of Jewish Culture in Weimer Germany* (New Haven: Yale University Press, 1996), 5.

5. Interview with Gary Smith, then director of the Einstein Forum, an international academic center in Potsdam, Germany, March 4, 1997.

6. *Ebraica,* Nuova Era Records, 7287, 1997. Liner notes by Enrico Fubini, a Jewish scholar and Jewish community leader in Turin.

7. See Cohen, *Jewish Icons,* 174–75; see also Marta Halpert, *Jewish Life in Austria* (Vienna: Federal Press Service, [1994] 1998), 24.

8. Quoted in Konstanty Gebert, "The Rescuers of Atlantis," *Midrasz,* July–August 1998. English translation in *The Best of Midrasz 1998* (New York: American Jewish Committee/Ronald S. Lauder Foundation, 1999).

9. Interview with Konstanty Gebert, Warsaw, September 15, 1997.

10. Gebert's personal story is recounted in Małgorzata Niezabitowska and Tomasz Tomaszewski, *Remnants: The Last Jews of Poland* (New York: Friendly Press, 1986), 92 ff.

11. Alain Finkielkraut, *The Imaginary Jew* (Lincoln: University of Nebraska Press, 1994), trans. Kevin O'Neill and David Suchoff, 38 (originally published as *Le Juif imaginaire* [Paris: Editions du Seuil, 1980]). As an interesting comparison, see Alvin H. Rosenfeld's *Imagining Hitler* (Bloomington: Indiana University Press, 1986), in which he discusses how a virtual image of Hitler permeates popular culture and imagination.

12. Franz Kafka, "Letter to His Father," in *Wedding Preparations in the Country and Other Stories,* trans. Ernst Kaiser and Eithne Wilkins (London: Penguin Books, 1978). See also the discussion throughout Steven E. Aschheim, *Brothers and Strangers: The East European Jew in German and German Jewish Consciousness, 1800–1923* (Madison: University of Wisconsin Press, 1982).

13. See Brenner, *Renaissance of Jewish Culture;* Aschheim, *Brothers and Strangers;* Cohen, *Jewish Icons.* Also see Alfred Döblin, *Journey to Poland,* trans. Joachim Neugroschel (New York: Paragon House, 1991) (originally published as *Reise in Polen*); Joseph Roth, *Juden auf Wanderschaft* (Berlin: Die Schmiede, 1927) (English translation: *The Wandering Jews,* trans. Michael Hofmann [New York: Norton, 2000]). On Engel, see Jacob Weinberg, "Joel Engel, Champion of Jewish Music," in Dawidowicz, *The Golden Tradition.* Lucyna Król provides a bibliography of turn-of-the-century and pre–World War II sources on Polish Jewish ethnography in the chapter "From Birth to Wedding Day: The Culture of Polish Jews in Nineteenth- and Twentieth-Century Literature Written in Polish," in *The Jews in Poland,* vol. 1, ed. Andrzej K. Paluch (Kraków: Jagiellonian University, 1992). These include collections of Jewish folk songs, superstitions, folk culture and art, proverbs, and customs.

14. Notably, Jiří Langer, an assimilated Czech Jew who in 1913 left Prague to "find himself" among the Hasidim of Belz in eastern Galicia. Langer wrote an account of his spiritual and physical transformation, *Nine Gates.* His brother, František, wrote a book about Jiří, published in Prague in 1963, titled *Byli a bylo.* An excerpt from this, decribing Jiří's transformation and reaction to it, is included in Wilma Abeles Iggers, ed., *The Jews of Bohemia and Moravia: A Historical Reader* (Detroit: Wayne State University Press, 1992), originally published as *Die Juden in Böhmen und Mähren* (Munich: Oscar Beck, 1986.)

15. See, e.g., Cohen, *Jewish Icons.* Also, *Żydzi-Polscy: Grudzień 1989-Luty 1990,* the catalog to an exhibition on Jews as portrayed in Polish art, mainly by non-Jewish artists, held in Kraków and Warsaw in 1989–90, particularly the introductory essay by Marek Rostworowski; also *Żydzi w Polsce: Obraz i słowo* (Warsaw: Interpress, 1993), the coffee-table book based on the exhibition. See, too, Harold B. Segel, ed., *Stranger in Our Midst: Images of the Jew in Polish Literature* (Ithaca: Cornell University Press, 1996); Aschheim, *Brothers and Strangers.* Non-Jews, of course, also frequently portrayed Jews in negative ways.

16. Felicitas Heimann-Jelinek, "Heading towards the Third Millennium," in *Musei ebraici in Europa: Orientamenti e prospettive/Jewish Museums in Europe: Trends and Perspectives,* ed. Franco Bonilauri and Vincenza Maugeri (Milan: Electa, 1998), 113. See the exhaustive discussion of artists, writers, and museums throughout Cohen, *Jewish Icons.*

17. See the chapter "A New Learning," in Brenner, *Renaissance of Jewish Culture*.

18. This claim, wrote Dagmar C. G. Lorenz, a professor of German at Ohio State University, was "preposterous" and constituted "historical revisionism." See Dagmar C. G. Lorenz, "The Case of Jacob Littner: Authors, Publishers, and Jewish History in Unified Germany," in Dagmar C. G. Lorenz and Gabriele Weinberger, eds., *Insiders and Outsiders: Jewish and Gentile Culture in Germany and Austria* (Detroit: Wayne State University Press), 235-50. Rather than inaugurate its list with a work from a Jewish author, Lorenz writes, the first book published by Suhrkamp's Jüdischer Verlag was instead a reissue of a phony Holocaust memoir: a novel by a non-Jewish German, Wolfgang Koeppen, which, when it was first published in 1948, purported to be the memoirs of a real-life Jewish survivor, Jakob Littner. Lorenz's essay is a detailed examination of the publication of the Koeppen book, *Aufzeichnungen aus einem Erdloch*. "Littner's story as retold by Koeppen is a 'Jewish' story with neither a Jewish author nor a Jewish character," she writes. "The Jüdischer Verlag im Hause Suhrkamp is a 'Jewish' publishing house without Jews" (pp. 239-40). The book received extensive, largely positive reviews in the mainstream media and represented an exploitation "reminiscent of the total utilization of all raw materials that was practiced in the concentration camps: the spoils of the Holocaust are transformed into German products" (p. 247).

19. See Charles R. Eisendrath, "An Identity and Family History That Are Inextricably Linked," *International Herald Tribune*, June 16, 1999.

20. For an analysis of Polish attitudes toward the Holocaust and Jews, see Michael C. Steinlauf, *Bondage to the Dead: Poland and the Memory of the Holocaust* (Syracuse: Syracuse University Press, 1997). See Jeffrey Herf, *Divided Memory: The Nazi Past in the Two Germanys* (Cambridge, Mass.: Harvard University Press, 1997), for a graphic detailing of East German attitudes. As early as 1947 an eighty-eight-page official government report on Poland's "war losses and damages" described the Nazis' treatment of Jews in passing, only as part of the Nazis' overall policy of "total warfare against the entire Polish nation and its peoples." The specific slaughter of 3.2 million Polish Jews rated just one sentence in a detailed four-page section titled "The Extermination of Population." *Statement on War Losses and Damages of Poland in 1939-1945* (Warsaw: Presidency of the Council of Ministers, War Indemnities Office, 1947), 32. This paper, with its extensive charts and tables detailing losses, is fascinating as an example of how historic events may be viewed through different lenses.

21. East Germany's top leaders made no mention of Jewish Holocaust victims, for example, at the dedication of East German government memorials to "victims of fascism" at the sites of the Buchenwald concentration camp in 1958 and the Sachsenhausen camp in 1961. East German president Otto Grotewohl used the dedication of the Buchenwald monument, the first major East German memorial to victims of fascism, to voice support for the Arabs in the Middle East conflict. See Herf, *Divided Memory*, 175-81. At Terezín, near Prague, the fact that the Nazis had turned the entire town into a concentration camp ghetto for Jews was subordinated to the fact that the town had also been the site of a much smaller camp for anti-Nazi political prisoners. This prison, with a dramatic "Arbeit Macht Frei" gate similar to that at Auschwitz, was sit-

uated in a forbidding-looking fortress just outside the town proper and formed the centerpiece to a memorial site set up in 1947. Its large museum included no exhibit on the Jewish ghetto of Terezín. A nearby cemetery, planted with roses as a national memorial, honored "victims of fascism." It was here, at the fortress and national cemetery, that tour buses stopped and delegations were brought, not in the ghetto/town itself, or at a monument erected in the 1970s in the cemetery where 9,000 Jewish prisoners were buried, or at the small monument at the spot where the ashes of 20,000 people were thrown into the Ohře River. Many visitors, even if they knew that Terezín had been a ghetto, believed that the Jews had been held inside the fortress. *Terezín,* a coffee-table book published by the Terezín Memorial in 1988, with text in Czech and four other languages, does document the ghetto and the Jewish cemetery memorial. The photographs show crowds of people and delegations at the Small Fortress and National Cemetery, but no visitors appear in the photos of the Jewish cemetery, crematorium, and monument on the Ohře. For Holocaust memorials in general, see James E. Young, *The Texture of Memory: Holocaust Memorials and Their Meaning* (New Haven: Yale University Press, 1993), and *At Memory's Edge: After-Images of the Holocaust in Contemporary Art and Architecture* (New Haven: Yale University Press, 2000). See also discussions in Charles Hoffman, *Gray Dawn: The Jews of Eastern Europe in the Post-Communist Era* (New York: HarperCollins, 1992).

22. For a discussion specifically of the interfaith center, see the chapter "Snowbound at Auschwitz," in Ruth Ellen Gruber, *Upon the Doorposts of Thy House: Jewish Life in East-Central Europe, Yesterday and Today* (New York: Wiley, 1994).

23. *Gulliver,* November 1999, 186-248.

24. Ibid., 188.

25. See Alexander Stille, *Benevolence and Betrayal: Five Italian Jewish Families under Fascism* (New York: Simon and Schuster, 1991), 22 ff. See also Susan Zuccotti, *The Italians and the Holocaust: Persecution, Rescue, Survival* (New York: Basic Books, 1987); Mario Toscano, "The Jews in Italy from the Risorgimento to the Republic," in *Gardens and Ghettos: The Art of Jewish Life in Italy,* ed. Vivian B. Mann (Berkeley: University of California Press, 1989). See also, among others, Mario Toscano, "L'uguaglianza senza diversità: Stato, società e questione ebraica nell'Italia liberale," in *Integrazione e Identità: L'esperienza ebraica in Germania e Italia dall'Illuminismo al fascismo,* ed. Mario Toscano (Milan: FrancoAngeli, 1998); and Lynn M. Gunzberg, *Strangers at Home: Jews in the Italian Literary Imagination* (Berkeley: University of California Press, 1992).

26. *La vita è bella* (Life Is Beautiful), the most popular and honored movie in Italy in 1998 and the winner of three Academy Awards, was about an assimilated Italian Jew who suddenly faced discrimination and deportation. See also the novel by Giorgio Bassani, *Il giardino dei Finzi-Contini* (Turin: Einaudi, 1962) (English-language edition: *The Garden of the Finzi-Continis* [New York: Athenaeum, 1965]) and the film based on it; Stille, *Benevolence and Betrayal.*

27. Claudio Magris, *Lontano da dove: Joseph Roth e la tradizione ebraico-orientale* (Turin: Einaudi, [1971] 1989).

28. Letter to Gustav Kiepenheuer, June 10, 1930. Published in Joseph Roth, *Briefe 1911-1939* (Cologne: Kiepenheuer & Witsch, 1970). See the English trans-

lation of part of this letter quoted in the introduction by Michael Hofmann to Joseph Roth, *Flight without End,* trans. David le Vay (London: Dent, 1984), v.

29. Magris, *Lontano da dove.* In an afterword to a 1989 edition, Magris elaborated on how he used Roth as a pretext for writing about the lost world of eastern European Jewry and the Jewish exile as a metaphor "of a historical and existential condition that sees the individual exiled from the fullness and totality of true life" (p. 313). A German translation of the book published in 1974 emphasized this, doing away with the reference to Roth in the subtitle and appearing simply as *Weit von wo: Verlorene Welt des Ostjudentums* (Far from Where: The Lost World of Eastern European Jewry).

30. Claudio Magris, "Lei è ebreo? È solo una domanda," in Toscano, *Integrazione e identità,* 29.

31. Address to the conference Dall'Europa all'America, e ritorno: Cultura yiddish, musica klezmer e mondo moderno, Rome, November 30–December 1, 1998.

32. Magris, "Ebreo," 23–24.

33. Ibid., 31.

34. See, e.g., Agata Tuszyńska, *Lost Landscapes: In Search of Isaac Bashevis Singer and the Jews of Poland,* trans. Madeline G. Levine (New York: William Morrow, 1998). The Italian painter Lillo Bartoloni began painting fanciful, imaginary shtetl scenes based on Singer's characters after he read Singer and visited Kraków in the 1990s. There are many other examples.

35. Letter from Marcin Kacprzak, published in *Midrasz,* nos. 7–8 (November–December 1997). English translation in *The Best of Midrasz 1997* (New York: American Jewish Committee, May 1998).

36. For Poland, see Alina Cała, *The Image of the Jew in Polish Folk Culture* (Jerusalem: Magnes Press, The Hebrew University, 1995). Aleksander Hertz, *The Jews in Polish Culture* (Evanston: Northwestern University Press, 1988), 93 (originally published as *Żydzi w kulturze polskiej* [Paris: Instytut Literacki, 1961]).

37. See "A Fateful Encounter: Jews and Non-Jews in Central Europe," a paper presented by Raphael Vago at the conference Medieval Jewish Communities in Central Europe and Their Cultural Heritage, Maribor, Slovenia, October 1997. See also, among others, Diana Pinto, *A New Jewish Identity for Post-1989 Europe,* JPR Policy Paper No. 1 (London: Institute for Jewish Policy Research, June 1996), on the relationship between Jews and Europe.

38. *Yiddish Culture: Report of the Committee on Culture and Education,* rapporteur Emanuel Zingeris (Strasbourg: Council of Europe, 1996).

39. See Randolf L. Braham, ed., *Anti-Semitism and the Treatment of the Holocaust in Postcommunist Eastern Europe* (New York: Columbia University Press, 1994). See also Steinlauf, *Bondage to the Dead;* Cała, *Image of the Jew;* Hertz, *Jews in Polish Culture.*

40. See, e.g., Cała, *Image of the Jew,* 21 ("The Jews have left a vacuum of which not everyone is fully aware, but which everyone feels"); Tuszyńska, *Lost Landscapes;* Vago, "A Fateful Encounter"; Young, *Memory's Edge;* Jonathan Kaufman, *A Hole in the Heart of the World: Being Jewish in Eastern Europe* (New York: Viking, 1996), 6.

41. Daniel Libeskind, in *Daniel Libeskind—Between the Lines,* catalog of an exhibition held June 7–September 22, 1991, at the Joods Historisch Museum, Amsterdam. For details on the Berlin Museum, see Young, *Memory's Edge.*

42. For a recent elaboration of Jews (and other minorities) as the leaven of society, see Maurice Cerasi, "Ogni minoranza è un lievito nella pasta della città che l'ospita . . . ," in *Architettura judaica in Italia: Ebraismo, sito, memoria dei luoghi,* chief ed. Francesca Fatta, ed. Paola Caselli (Palermo: Flaccovio Editore, 1994).

43. Ewa Berberyusz, "The Black Hole: Conversation with Stanisław Krajewski," in *My Brother's Keeper: Recent Polish Debates on the Holocaust,* ed. Antony Polonsky (London: Routledge, 1990), 108.

44. Milan Kundera, "The Tragedy of Central Europe," *New York Review of Books,* April 26, 1998, 37–38.

45. Bernt Engelmann, *Germany without Jews* (Munich: Wilhelm Godman Verlag, 1979); English translation by D. J. Beer (New York: Bantam Books, 1984), 39. Jews, of course, also expressed this loss. For example, the Kraków-born Jewish writer Rafael Scharf wrote in 1993: "With the millions that were destroyed in unspeakable torment there perished the culture, the ethos, the thought, the achievement of a singular people. . . . How many potential Einsteins and Freuds, Maimonides' and Spinozas, Heines, Tuwims, Mandelstams, Shalom-Aleichems and Chagalls were buried in the ashes? The genetic pool of mankind has been impoverished beyond computation and the price of that is paid not by Jews alone." Introduction by Rafael Scharf to *A Tribe of Stones,* by Monika Krajewska (Warsaw: Polish Scientific Publishers, 1993), 9.

46. Ruth Beckermann, "The Austrian Resistance and the Forgotten Jews," trans. Jack Zipes, in Lorenz and Weinberger, *Insiders and Outsiders,* 257. Beckermann notes how Jews in Vienna today also idealize the Jewish experience in prewar Vienna. Among others, see catalog programs for the annual summer Mittelfest festival, held since 1991 in Cividale del Friuli, Italy; and Riccardo Calimani, ed., *Le vie del mondo, Berlino, Budapest, Praga, Vienna e Trieste: Intellettuali ebrei e cultura europea dal 1880 al 1930* (Milan: Electa, 1998), a book-length catalog of an exhibition mounted in Trieste in 1998 under the sponsorship of the Italian government and regional authorities.

47. Presentation during the German-Jewish Dialogue conference organized by the Bertelsmann Stiftung near Bonn, October 28, 1997.

48. Hugo Bettauer, *The City without Jews: A Novel of Our Time,* trans. Salomea Neumark Brainin (New York: Bloch, [1926] 1991), 142.

49. Yael Grözinger, "Oh You're Jewish? That's Okay," in *Speaking Out: Jewish Voices from United Germany,* ed. Susan Stern (Chicago: edition q, 1995), 124.

50. Daniel Passent, "Looking Each Other in the Face," in *Preserving Traces of Jewish Culture in Poland: For the Living and the Dead,* ed. Radosław Piszczek (Warsaw: Nissenbaum Foundation, Krajowa Agencja Wydawnicza, 1988).

51. Interviewed in the newspaper *Gazeta Krakowska,* June 26, 1992. Quoted in the program of the 1994 festival.

52. Aviva Kempner, "Jewish Woodstock in Cracow," *Washington Jewish Week,* July 16, 1992.

53. For a discussion of the recent Jewish awakening in Kraków's Kazimierz district, see the chapter "What's to Be Done?" in Gruber, *Upon the Doorposts of Thy House*. Also see Jack Kugelmass and Annamaria Orla-Bukowska, "'If You Build It They Will Come': Recreating an Historic Jewish District in Post-Communist Kraków," in *City & Society* annual review (1998): 315–53.

54. Interview with Janusz Makuch, Kraków, September 1997, except "Atlantis" quote from *Washington Jewish Week*.

55. His book is Jiří Kuděla and Jiří Všetečka, *The Fate of Jewish Prague* (Prague: Grafoprint, 1993).

56. Rosh, a Protestant, is widely assumed to be Jewish. She did, though, have one Jewish grandparent, her mother's father. See Jane Kramer, *The Politics of Memory: Looking for Germany in the New Germany* (New York: Random House, 1996).

57. Pinto, *A New Jewish Identity*, 6–7.

58. Rafael Seligmann, "German Jewry Squawking at the Approach of Danger," in Stern, *Speaking Out*, 174.

59. Dan Diner, "Negative Symbiose," *Babylon 1* (1986), 9, quoted in Jack Zipes, "The Negative German-Jewish Symbiosis," in Lorenz and Weinberger, *Insider and Outsider*, 144–54. Zipes argues that the German-Jewish symbiosis was always negative, even before the Holocaust.

60. Frank Stern, "German-Jewish Relations in the Postwar Period," in *Jews, Germans, Memory: Reconstructions of Jewish Life in Germany*, ed. Y. Michal Bodemann (Ann Arbor: University of Michigan Press, 1996), 93. See also, among others, Rodney Livingstone, "Germans and Jews since 1945," *Patterns of Prejudice* 29, nos. 2–3 (April–July 1995): 45–60; Bernard Wasserstein, *Vanishing Diaspora: The Jews in Europe since 1945* (Cambridge, Mass.: Harvard University Press, 1996). For a detailed analysis of differences between how West Germany and East Germany dealt with the Nazi past, see Herf, *Divided Memory*.

61. See Björn Krondorfer, *Remembrance and Reconciliation: Encounters between Young Jews and Germans* (New Haven: Yale University Press, 1995); and Stern, "German-Jewish Relations." For lengthy discussions of this phenomenon, see, among others, Ian Buruma, *The Wages of Guilt: Memories of War in Germany and Japan* (New York: Meridian, 1995); Charles S. Maier, *The Unmasterable Past: History, Holocaust, and German National Identity* (Cambridge, Mass.: Harvard University Press, 1988); Judith Miller, *One by One by One: Facing the Holocaust* (New York: Simon and Schuster, 1990); Michael Wolffsohn, *Eternal Guilt? Forty Years of German-Jewish-Israeli Relations*, trans. Douglas Bokovoy (New York: Columbia University Press, 1993) (originally published in Germany in 1988). See also Margarethe Mitscherlich, "How Do Germans Face Their Guilt?" paper presented at a symposium on April 1 and 2, 1995, at Adelphi University, reprinted in *Partisan Review*.

62. Alvin H. Rosenfeld has written that Anne Frank became a continuing, ready-at-hand formula for easy forgiveness." Rosenfeld, "Popularization and Memory: The Case of Anne Frank," in *Lessons and Legacies: The Meaning of the Holocaust in a Changing World*, ed. Peter Hayes (Evanston, Ill.: Northwestern University Press, 1991), 271. See also Cynthia Ozick, "Who Owns Anne Frank?"

New Yorker, October 6, 1997, 76–87; Ian Buruma, "Anne Frank's Afterlife," *New York Review of Books,* February 19, 1998, 4–8.

63. Krondorfer, *Remembrance and Reconciliation,* 35.

64. Susan Neiman, *Slow Fire: Jewish Notes from Berlin* (New York: Schocken, 1992), 137, 138.

65. Sales information supplied to me by Pehle. Judith Miller writes that *Holocaust* was seen by 14 million viewers. Miller, *One by One by One,* 43. See also Judith E. Doneson, "*Holocaust* Revisited: A Catalyst for Memory or Trivialization?" *Annals of the American Academy of Political and Social Sciences* 548 (November 1996): 70–77.

66. Paper delivered to a conference on second-generation memory and trauma, Vienna, September 1999.

67. See Y. Michal Bodemann, "Reconstructions of History: From Jewish Memory to Nationalized Commemoration of Kristallnacht in Germany," in Bodemann, *Jews, Germans, Memory,* 182 ff. This detailed essay chronicles this process. Bodemann notes that only one Jew—an actress reading a poem—took part in the Kristallnacht commemoration in 1988 held in the German Parliament. In 1996, Germany initiated an official Day of Commemoration for victims of National Socialism on January 27—the anniversary of the liberation of Auschwitz.

68. Robin Ostow, "Imperialist Agents, Anti-Fascist Monuments, Eastern Refugees, Property Claims: Jews as Incorporations of East German Social Trauma, 1945–94," in Bodemann, *Jews, Germans, Memory,* 227–42.

69. See Maier, *The Unmasterable Past;* Miller, *One by One by One.* See also James Knowlton and Truett Cates, trans., *Forever in the Shadow of Hitler? Original Documents of the Historikerstreit, the Controversy concerning the Singularity of the Holocaust* (Atlantic Highlands, N.J.: Humanities Press, 1993).

70. Miller, *One by One by One,* 41.

71. See the discussion in Rob Burns and Wilfried van der Will, "The Federal Republic, 1968–1990: From the Industrial Society to the Cultural Society," in *German Cultural Studies: An Introduction,* ed. Rob Burns (Oxford: Oxford University Press, 1995), 317–20. See also Doneson, "*Holocaust* Revisited"; Miller, *One by One by One,* 41–42.

72. See, e.g., Henry M. Broder, "Our Kampf," in *Jewish Voices, German Words: Growing Up Jewish in Postwar Germany & Austria,* ed. Elena Lappin, trans. Krishna Winston (North Haven, Conn.: Catbird Press, 1994), 283–96; and Kizer Walker, "The Persian Gulf War and the Germans' 'Jewish Question': Transformations on the Left," in *Reemerging Jewish Culture: Life and Literature since 1989,* ed. Sander L. Gilman and Karen Remmler (New York: New York University Press, 1994), 148–72.

73. See, among others, Kramer, *Politics of Memory;* Young, *At Memory's Edge,* esp. chaps. 6, 7.

74. See articles in Lappin, *German Voices;* Stern, *Speaking Out;* Gilman and Remmler, *Reemerging Jewish Culture;* Bodemann, *Jews, Germans, Memory.*

75. See, e.g., Richard Chaim Schneider, "Germany—Home Sweet Home?" in Stern, *Speaking Out,* 92.

76. Jerome Rothenberg, "The Wedding," in *Poland/1931* (New York: New Directions, 1960–74), 3. Writings by Jews about Poland are too numerous to

mention. Rothenberg's poem, an imagined vision of the country as it would have been in the year of his birth, which I first heard him read in London in 1975, is one of my favorites.

77. Numerous books, fiction and nonfiction, describe this. A recent English-language novel exploring repressed memory of Jews in a Polish village is Charles T. Powers, *In the Memory of the Forest* (New York: Scribner's, 1997).

78. Timothy Garton Ash, *The Uses of Adversity* (London: Penguin, 1989), 242.

79. Young, *Texture of Memory*, 116.

80. Ewa Berberyusz, "Guilt by Neglect," in Polonsky, *My Brother's Keeper?* 69–71; originally published in *Tygodnik Powszechny*, February 22, 1987. See Steinlauf, *Bondage to the Dead*, for a detailed examination of this issue.

81. Translation by A. Gillon, as reprinted in Polonsky, *My Brother's Keeper?*

82. Quote from Michael Steinlauf, paper delivered at the conference The Role of History Museums in Central and Eastern Europe, Warsaw, April 24–26, 1996. Liberal Roman Catholic intellectuals were important in this process. See Jacek Borkowicz, ed., *Under One Heaven: Poles and Jews, Więź*, Special Issue, 1998, trans. William Brand (Warsaw: Towarzyszystwo Więż, 1998), a collection of articles from a leading Catholic intellectual journal.

83. See Steinlauf, *Bondage to the Dead*, 111–13.

84. Polonsky, *My Brother's Keeper?* 1. This book presents a selection of articles that formed a public debate on the issue. Also see Steinlauf, *Bondage to the Dead*, 113 ff.; Borkowicz, *Under One Heaven*.

85. The publication of Gross's book touched off lacerating debates in the public, private, political, scholarly, and religious spheres. The debates extended beyond Poland with the publication of an English edition, *Neighbors: The Destruction of the Jewish Community in Jedwabne, Poland* (Princeton, N.J.: Princeton University Press, 2001).

86. Anna Bikont, ed., *And I Still See Their Faces: Images of Polish Jews* (Warsaw: Fundacja Shalom, 1996). Also see Jane Perlez, "Poland Turns Out for Glimpse of a Lost World," *New York Times*, May 19, 1996.

87. Hoffman, *Gray Dawn*, 247.

88. Ibid.

89. Interview in *Corriere della Sera*, Milan, March 6, 1995.

90. See the discussion throughout Harley Erdman, *Staging the Jew: The Performance of an American Ethnicity, 1860–1920* (New Brunswick: Rutgers University Press, 1997), for a description of anti-Semitic (or at least stereotypical) stage conventions in the United States. Ovadia's stage appearance is remarkably similar to a photograph in the book of the nineteenth-century actor Frank Bush in character as a comic Jew (p. 77). Bush's Jew wore "a 'tall, rusty plug hat, long black coat, shabby pants, long beard which ran to a point, and large spectacles,' [and] used pseudo-Yiddish phrases, funny gestures and lively songs to tell crazy stories of his trials and tribulations" (p. 79).

· 91. Giovanni Raboni (a poet and critic), "Riflessi di un poeta yiddish," in Claudio Cattaruzza, ed., *Dedica a Moni Ovadia* (Pordenone: Associazione Provinciale per la Prosa, 1998), 79–80. For a detailed analysis of Ovadia's work, see Lisa Sacerdoti, "Ricomporre l'infranto. La memoria ebraica tra storia e identità. Moni Ovadia e il teatro dell'esilio," thesis for the Philosophy Department,

Università degli Studi, Milan, 1996–97. Also, for an analysis of Ovadia's work as part of the Yiddish theater tradition, see Laura Quercioli Mincer, "Tradition Revisited in Moni Ovadia's Theater," paper presented at a conference on Yiddish theater, Oxford, June 1999.

92. During a discussion session with Ovadia at the Rome Jewish Community Center in 1995, a woman in the audience said she had never tasted gefilte fish but loved the concept because the words "sounded so cute."

93. This is not to say that stereotypes of Jews—frequently related to money —did not exist in Italy. But, for the most part, visible models for the physical stereotypes employed by Ovadia to denote the Jew did not exist there. See Gunzberg, *Strangers at Home;* Gadi Luzzatto Voghera, "Lo stereotipo dell' ebreo nell'Italia contemporanea," in *I nemici sono gli "altri": Convegno sull' Olocausto,* ed. Laura Fontana and Giorgio Giovagnoli (Florence: Giuntina, 1999).

94. Personal conversations. Also see descriptions of this in Sacerdoti, "Ricomporre l'infranto"; and Ovadia's autobiography, *Speriamo che tenga* (Milan: Mondadori, 1998).

95. Moni Ovadia, *Perche no? L'ebreo corrosivo* (Milan: Bompiani, 1996), 6.

96. Sacerdoti, "Ricomporre l'infranto," 171.

97. Mincer, "Tradition Revisited."

98. Moni Ovadia, liner notes to the CD *Oylem Goylem* (Fonit Cetra, CDC 60, 1996). This CD presented music from his stage shows *Dalla sabbia dal Tempo* and *Oylem Goylem.* See the critical discussion in Francesco Spagnolo, "Un' estetica del (trad.): La ricostruzione della musica klezmer tra europa e america e il caso italiano," paper based on a presentation at the conference Dall' Europa all'America, e ritorno: Cultura yiddish, musica klezmer e mondo moderno, Rome, November 30–December 1, 1998.

99. Erri di Luca, "Lo Yiddish di Moni," *il manifesto,* November 17, 1998.

100. At one performance by Ovadia that I attended, his own cell phone rang on stage during the performance! The drawing is apparently based on a public relations photograph of Ovadia that appears on his 1997 CD *Nigun* (Ricordi, 74321452162, 1997).

101. Mark Slobin, *Fiddler on the Move: Exploring the Klezmer World* (Oxford: Oxford University Press, 2000), 87.

102. Ibid., 88.

103. Abraham Brumberg, "What to Make of Poland's Jewish Rebirth?" *Forward,* January 30, 1998.

104. Gábor T. Szántó, "Floodgate or Dead End? The Presence of a Many-Faceted Culture," *Human Rights without Frontiers,* Special Issue (1997): 38.

105. The seminar was sponsored by the London-based Institute for Jewish Policy Research, with the cosponsorship of Alliance Israélite Universelle, the American Jewish Committee, and the European Council of Jewish Communities, in association with the Jewish Studies Program of the Central European University, Budapest, and the Jewish Museum, Prague. See Sonia Misak, *Highlights of the International Seminar Jewish Culture for the Twenty-first Century, Paris, February 1999* (London: Institute for Jewish Policy Research, 1999).

106. Leibl Rosenberg, "Jüdische Kultur in Deutschland: Bestandsaufnahme eines Elends," *Allgemeine Jüdische Wochenzeitung,* November 13, 1997.

Chapter 3. "There Is No Future without Memory"

1. I thank Bernhard Purin, director of the Jüdisches Museum Franken in Fürth, Germany, for bringing this to my attention. For details of the plaque, see the introduction by Eva Grabherr to *Jews in Hohenems,* the catalog of the Jewish Museum Hohenems (Hohenems: Jüdisches Museum Hohenems, 1996). Thanks especially to my brother Samuel D. Gruber, president of the International Survey of Jewish Monuments and a leading figure in Jewish heritage studies, for discussing the issues raised in this chapter with me over many years and for lending me some of the terminology.

2. In "Jewish Sites in Europe: Constructing Spatial Narratives and Collective Memory," a paper presented at the conference of the European Association of Jewish Studies in Toledo, Spain, July 1998, David Clark of the University of North London, Center for Leisure and Tourism Studies, refers to the individual versus the official role in terms of "center-margin relationships" and writes of "attempts by the center, and the agencies of the state in particular, to 'recolonize' the margins."

3. Many historic buildings that were damaged, if not totally destroyed, in the war were also rebuilt, of course, sometimes from scratch, in all countries. Most famously, the Old Town of Warsaw and historic districts in other Polish cities that were totally razed by bombing were meticulously reconstructed, using old photographs and paintings as guides.

4. See Samuel D. Gruber and Phyllis Myers, *Survey of Historic Jewish Monuments in the Czech Republic* (New York: Jewish Heritage Council, World Monuments Fund, 1995), 26–33, for lists.

5. Sabine Offe, "Sites of Remembrance? Jewish Museums in Contemporary Germany," *Jewish Social Studies* 3, no. 2 (Winter 1997): 82–83.

6. See Thea Altaras, *Synagogen in Hesse: Was geschah seit 1945?* (Königstein im Taunus: Karl Robert Langewiesche Nachfolger Hans Köster Verlagsbuchhandlung, 1988).

7. In November 1997 the Nuremberg historian Eckart Dietzfelbinger told me, "For years after the war, the Nazi history of the place was a blank spot. There was no discussion of the Nazi past." Various structures were demolished, and a new housing development was built on one part of the grounds. The grandstand was used for concerts, sports events, and even religious revivals. In the 1980s there was an abortive attempt to turn the never-completed congress hall into a shopping center. A museum tracing the evolution of Nazi terror was eventually installed at the complex.

8. Quoted in brochure material prepared by the Alte Synagoge Essen in 1999. I am grateful to Edna Brocke, director of the Alte Synagoge Essen, for having provided me with manuscript copy of these brochures. Information in this section also comes from personal communications from Edna Brocke as well as Edna Brocke and Michael Zimmermann, "Yesterday a Synagogue—The 'Old Synagogue' Today: History as Reflected in 75 Years of a Building's Con-

struction" (Essen: Alte Synagoge, 1990). Clark, "Jewish Sites in Europe," was also helpful.

9. Carol Herselle Krinsky, *Synagogues of Europe* (New York: Architectural History Foundation, 1985), 290.

10. Peter Meyer, Bernard D. Weinryb, Eugene Duschinsky, and Nicolas Sylvain, *The Jews in the Soviet Satellites* (Syracuse: American Jewish Committee/Syracuse University Press, 1953), 40-41. For a detailed description of how restitution of Jewish property was rejected in East Germany, see Jeffrey Herf, *Divided Memory: The Nazi Past in the Two Germanys* (Cambridge, Mass.: Harvard University Press, 1997).

11. Maria Piechotka and Kazimierz Piechotka, *Wooden Synagogues* (Warsaw: Arkady, 1959) (originally published as *Bóżnice Drewniane* [Warsaw, 1957]). An early survey of the postwar condition of synagogues was presented in Anna Kubiak, "Żydowska architektura zabytkowa w Polsce. Stan po wojnie," *BŻIH* 6-7 (1953): 122-68; 8 (1953): 73-96. Also see David Dawidowicz, *Synagogues in Poland and Their Destruction* (Jerusalem: Mosad Harav Kuk and Yad Vashem, 1960).

12. Phyllis Myers, "Polish Monuments Protection Law and Jewish Sites," in Samuel D. Gruber and Phyllis Myers, *Survey of Historic Jewish Monuments in Poland* (New York: Jewish Heritage Council, World Monuments Fund, 1995), 57.

13. Gruber and Myers, *Survey . . . Czech Republic*, 69.

14. The Nazis were notorious for using Jewish tombstones for paving and construction, but this happened, too, after the war. See, e.g., Tomasz Wiśniewski, "Cemeteries Outside Cemeteries," *Jewish Heritage Report* 2, nos. 1-2, (Spring–Summer 1998): 18-19.

15. To name but a few towns where synagogues stood empty, unrepaired, or in ruins well into the 1990s: Chmielnik, Przysucha, Kraków, Wodisław, Rymanów, Wrocław, and Dukla in Poland; Budapest, Mád, Tarcal, Tokaj, Kőszeg, Sopron, and Olaszliszka in Hungary; and Třebíč, Polná, Břeclav, Lučenec and Trnava, in Czechoslovakia (now the Czech Republic and Slovakia). Neglected property in general ran the gamut from churches and other religious buildings to historic structures such as castles and manor houses to simple residences, businesses, and public buildings to examples of vernacular architecture. In 1992 Polish conservationists told me that out of the 30,000 castles, palaces, stately homes, and historic residences estimated to have been in existence before World War II in Poland, only about 2,000 palaces, 350 castles, and 5,000 stately homes were believed to remain standing, most of them in poor condition. Romania's communist dictator Nicolae Ceaușescu, in particular, was infamous for bulldozing historic neighborhoods and churches to make way for grandiose urban projects. See Dinu C. Giurescu, *The Razing of Romania's Past* (New York: World Monuments Fund, 1989).

16. In 1988 there were fewer than four hundred Jews registered with Jewish communities in East Germany. But some estimates put the number of unaffiliated Jews as high as four thousand. See Marion Kaplan, "What Is 'Religion' among Jews in Contemporary Germany?" in *Reemerging Jewish Culture in Germany: Life and Literature since 1989*, ed. Sander L. Gilman and Karen Remmler

(New York: New York University Press, 1994), 94. See also Herf, *Divided Memory*.

17. Annie Sacerdoti and Luca Fiorentino, *Guida all'Italia ebraica* (Genoa: Marietti, 1986), 8.

18. Simonetta M. Bondoni and Giulio Busi, eds., *Cultura ebraica in Emilia-Romagna* (Rimini: Istituto per i Beni Culturali della Regione Emilia-Romagna, Luisè Editore, 1987).

19. A recent book on Europe's lost or destroyed architectural heritage made no mention of the destruction of Jewish historical sites: Jean Loussier and Robin Langley Sommer, eds., *Lost Europe: Images of a Vanished World* (London: Grange Books, 1997).

20. Jan Heřman, *Jewish Cemeteries in Bohemia and Moravia* (Prague: Council of Jewish Communities in the Czech Socialist Republic, n.d. [1983?]), 6. See also Jiří Fiedler, *Jewish Sights of Bohemia and Moravia* (Prague: Sefer, 1991).

21. Of course, this has also happened in North America. Former synagogues still stand in many neighborhoods such as New York's Lower East Side that were once Jewish but are now home to other groups. Synagogues and Jewish cemeteries are also found in a number of small towns that now have no formal Jewish community.

22. For a contemporary account of the squalid condition of the Jewish ghetto in Rome in the nineteenth century, see Ferdinand Gregorovius, *The Ghetto and the Jews of Rome*, trans. Moses Hadas (New York: Schocken, [1948] 1966; originally written in 1853). On the demolition of the Rome ghetto, see Salvatore Fornari, *La Roma del Ghetto* (Rome: Fratelli Palombi Editore, 1984); for Prague, see, among others, Milada Vilímková, *The Prague Ghetto*, trans. Iris Urwin (Prague: Aventinum, 1990). On Florence, see Marco Bini, "Edificazione e demolizione del Ghetto di Firenze: Prime ricostruzioni grafiche," in *Architettura judaica in Italia: Ebraismo, sito, memoria dei luoghi*, chief ed. Francesca Fatta, ed. Paola Caselli (Palermo: Flaccovio Editore, 1994).

23. Many of the designs for these grand synagogues were chosen through architecture competitions. For a fascinating account of the competition launched by the Trieste Jewish community in 1903, see Alberto Boralevi, "Il 'Tempio Israelitico' di Trieste: Storia di un Concorso," in *Comunità religiose di Trieste: Contributi di conoscenza* (Udine: Istituto per l'Enciclopedia del Friuli Venezia Giulia, 1979).

24. See, among others, Gerard Silvain, *Images et traditions juives: Un millier de cartes postales (1897–1917) pour servir à l'histoire de la Diaspora* (n.p.: Celiv, 1980). See also Eugeniusz Duda and Marek Sosenko, *Old Jewish Postcards from Marek Sosenko's Collection* (Kraków: Muzeum Historyczne Miasta Krakowa, 1997). This book notes that postcards on Jewish themes were "rather rare." Sosenko's collection of more than half a million postcards includes only about four thousand on Jewish themes.

25. David Philipson, *Old European Jewries* (Philadelphia: Jewish Publication Society of America, 1894), 76–77. Philipson also notes that a Frankfurt rabbi had been collecting and collating tombstone inscriptions. There were some art-historical studies of historic synagogues of western Europe, for example, Richard Krautheimer, *Mittelalterliche Synagogen* (Berlin: Frankfurter Verlags-Anstalt, 1927).

26. Grace Humphrey, *Poland the Unexplored* (Indianapolis: Bobbs-Merrill, 1931), 17. On Jewish travelers, see Daniel Soyer, "The Travel Agent as Broker between Old World and New: The Case of Gustave Eisner," in *YIVO Annual*, vol. 21: *Going Home*, ed. Jack Kugelmass (New York: YIVO Institute of Jewish Research, 1993), 345-68; and Roberta Newman, "Pictures of a Trip to the Old Country," in the same volume, pp. 223-29.

27. See Monika Krajewska, *A Tribe of Stones: Jewish Cemeteries in Poland* (Warsaw: Polish Scientific Publishers, 1993), 16. Krajewska cites the prints of reliefs of tombstone carvings gathered during An-Ski's expedition in 1912 and also, in particular, the work by the Polish scholars Majer Bałaban and Arian Maliniak, as well as Arthur Levy, a field rabbi during World War I who gathered information from some fifty cemeteries in Poland and Lithuania and analyzed the symbolism of the carvings. She also cites the work of Max Diamant and Rachel Wischnitzer. Among specific publications cited are Arthur Levy, *Jüdische Grabmalkunst in Osteuropa* (Berlin, 1923); Arian Maliniak, *Monumentica*, in *Stary cmentarz Żydowski w Łodzi, Dzieje i zabytki* (Łódź, 1938); Max Diamant, *Jüdische Volkskunst* (Vienna, 1939); and Majer Bałaban, *Zabytki historyczne Żydów w Polsce* (Warsaw, 1929). An early comparative work was A. Grotte, *Deutsch, bömische und polnische Synagogentypen von Anfang bis XIX Jahrhundert* (Berlin, 1915).

28. See the introduction by Jan Zachwatowicz to Piechotka and Piechotka, *Wooden Synagogues*. Also see Samuel D. Gruber, "First, We Document: ISJM Announces Prizes to Encourage Quality Surveys," in *Jewish Heritage Report* 2, nos. 1-2 (Spring-Summer 1998): 1, 5-8.

29. Marvin Lowenthal, *A World Passed By: Scenes and Memories of Jewish Civilization in Europe and North Africa* (New York: Harper & Brothers, 1933; New York: Behrman's Jewish Book House, 1938), xix-xx. Grace Humphrey, whose general travel book about Poland came out two years before Lowenthal's book, did visit synagogues, Jewish cemeteries, and Jewish quarters and devoted a chapter of her book to Jews in Poland, but her description was not calculated to persuade others to do the same: "Interesting as I found the ghettos, as much fun as it was to go poking around in twisting medieval streets and alleys, peering into courts, walking slowly when I came to open doorways[,] . . . I found that half an hour was as long as I could stay. . . . For the ghettos I saw in Warsaw, in Wilno, Lublin, Kraków, are not only ugly and dreary, they're smelly —an ancient, medieval odor plus a sour odor." Humphrey, *Poland the Unexplored*, 273.

Chapter 4. Touching the Past

1. On Hungarian synagogues and architects, see Lászlo Gerő, ed., *Magyarországi zsinagógák* (Budapest: Műszaki Könyvkiadó, 1989); János Gerle, Attila Kovács, and Imre Makovecz, *A Századforduló Magyar Építészete* (Budapest: Szépirodalmi Könyvkiadó, 1990); and Géza Komoróczy, ed., *Jewish Budapest: Monuments, Rites, History* (Budapest: Central European University Press, 1999).

2. Brian Ladd, *The Ghosts of Berlin: Confronting German History in the Urban Landscape* (Chicago: University of Chicago Press, 1997), 1.

3. Agata Tuszyńska, *Lost Landscapes: In Search of Isaac Bashevis Singer and the Jews of Poland,* trans. Madeline G. Levine (New York: William Morrow, 1998), 5.

4. Among many others, see the restored Jewish cemeteries in Oświęcim, Poland; Hranice, Czech Republic; and Fürth, Germany.

5. Cilly Kugelmann, "Jewish Museums in Germany: A German-Jewish Problem," in *Speaking Out: Jewish Voices from United Germany,* ed. Susan Stern (Chicago: edition q, 1995), 243–56.

6. See Kugelmann, "Jewish Museums in Germany"; and *Gedenkstätte/Memorial: Neuer Börneplatz, Frankfurt am Main* (Frankfurt: Amt für Wissenschaft und Kunst, 1996). Elsewhere, Kugelmann has described the Frankfurt memorial as an example of "the appropriation of Jewish memory on the part of gentile memorial strategy in the field of symbolic and aesthetic expression [that tends] to ignore those responsible for the genocide." In an article titled "The National Context of Jewish Museums in Germany" that was scheduled for publication in Italy's *La Rassegna Mensile di Israel* in 2001, she noted that "the names of nearly eleven thousand Jewish Nazi victims are engraved in tiny metal blocks, quasi-tombstones, which are built into the newly whitewashed wall surrounding the thirteenth-century Jewish cemetery. The area around the cemetery is divided in two parts. The space between the wall and a synagogue that was destroyed during 'Crystal-Night' is paved with coarse stones on which walking is hard and inconvenient. The other part of the site contains a sycamore grove with a large stone cube in its center. The cube is compiled of drift blocks of the former synagogue. The memorial is complemented by a data base computer which contains biographical information about the victims. There is no mentioning, no text or any other architectural or aesthetic hint of the Gestapo, the local police, [of] tax and custom offices or any other institutions that worked hand in hand to organize the deportation." (Quotations from unpublished manuscript.)

7. Sabine Offe, "Sites of Remembrance? Jewish Museums in Contemporary Germany," *Jewish Social Studies* 3, no. 2 (Winter 1997): 87.

8. See the chapter "Back to the Middle Again" in Marc Fisher, *After the Wall: Germany, the Germans and the Burden of History* (New York: Simon and Schuster, 1995), for a description of an Aktion Sühnezeichnen trip to Poland.

9. See the chronology in Komoróczy, *Jewish Budapest,* 446 ff. Also see, among others, Charles Hoffman, *Gray Dawn: The Jews of Eastern Europe in the Post-Communist Era* (New York: HarperCollins, 1992); Steve Lipman, "Hungarian Jewry on the Rise," *Jewish Week of New York/Jewish Telegraphic Agency,* February 17, 1989.

10. Both of these projects were fruit of 1981 legislation that created a fund for the repair of neglected historic buildings. The eighteenth-century synagogue in Mád underwent partial restoration thanks to this legislation (the structure was repaired but not the interior, and the building was left empty). Information supplied by András Román, of the Hungarian national committee of the International Council on Monuments and Sites (ICOMOS).

11. Anikó Gazda, *Zsinagógák és zsidó községek magyarországon* (Budapest: MTA Judaisztikai Kutatócsoport, 1991), 235.

12. Gerő, *Magyarországi zsinagógák*. In 1991 Gazda's notes, maps, architectural drawings, and statistical material were published (posthumously) in Gazda, *Zsinagógák,* a separate volume.

13. Gazda, *Zsinagógák,* 235–36.

14. Introduction to Monika Krajewska, *Time of Stones* (Warsaw: Interpress, 1983).

15. Eva Hoffman's *Shtetl: The Life and Death of a Small Town and the World of Polish Jews* (New York: Houghton Mifflin, 1997) presented a much more sympathetic picture. Hoffman questioned Romaniuk's self-avowed cerebral approach. She wondered "whether a sustained labor of restoration, such as his creation of the memorial cemetery, can be carried out without at least some subliminal urge to restore what has been lost and repair what has been wounded on a more symbolic level" (pp. 22–26).

16. For an appreciative Polish-Jewish view of the awards, see Konstanty Gebert, "The Rescuers of Atlantis," in *The Best of Midrasz 1998* (New York: American Jewish Committee, 1999), originally published in the Polish-Jewish monthly *Midrasz,* Warsaw, July–August 1998.

17. See the discussion by Raina Fehl, a founder of the International Survey of Jewish Monuments, of documenting Jewish monuments in East Germany, in her review of Michael Brocke, Eckehart Ruthenberg, and Kai Uwe Schulenburg, *Stein und Name: Die jüdischen Friedhöfe in Ostdeutschland (Neue Bundestländer/DDR und Berlin)* (Berlin: Veröffentlichungen aus dem Institut Kirche und Judentum, 1994). This book lists Jewish sites in the former GDR and also describes the difficulties encountered in documenting Jewish heritage there under communism. Fehl's article is in *Jewish Heritage Report* 2, nos. 1–2 (Spring–Summer 1998): 32–33.

18. Gebert, "Rescuers."

19. Charles T. Powers, *In the Memory of the Forest* (New York: Penguin, 1997), described the powerful impact of Jewish tombstones, memory, and vodka on a small fictional village in 1990 not far from Białystok.

20. See Samuel D. Gruber, "Report from Paris: State of Jewish Heritage in Europe," *Jewish Heritage Report* 2, nos. 3–4 (1999): 1, 3–4. Several reports from the Paris meeting are quoted in this issue.

21. By late 1998 surveys were under way in Ukraine and Romania and some work had been carried out in Slovakia and Hungary. (I carried out the survey of Jewish monuments in Slovenia in 1996.) Researchers in Romania said that as of December 2000 they had discovered about two hundred cemeteries that had not been on official Jewish community lists.

22. The mandate of the commission is to "1) identify and publish a list of those monuments, historic buildings and cemeteries located abroad which are associated with the foreign heritage of United States citizens from Eastern and Central Europe, particularly those monuments, historic buildings and cemeteries which are in danger of deterioration or destruction; 2) encourage the preservation and protection of such monuments, historic buildings and cemeteries by obtaining, in cooperation with the Department of State, assurances from for-

eign governments that these monuments, historic buildings and cemeteries will be preserved and protected; and 3) prepare and disseminate reports on the condition of and the progress toward preserving and protecting such monuments, historic buildings and cemeteries."

23. The full criteria appear in *Preservation Priorities: Endangered Historic Jewish Sites* (New York: World Monuments Fund, 1996).

24. The Center for Jewish Art sponsored a few research surveys in the 1980s. But, during the 1990s, it sent research teams to document synagogues or other Jewish sites, such as cemeteries and shtetl architecture, in Azerbaijan, Belarus, Bulgaria, the Czech Republic, Daghestan, Georgia, Germany, Greece, Hungary, Italy, Lithuania, Moldova, Poland, Romania, Russia, Turkey, Ukraine, England, Uzbekistan, Bosnia-Hercegovina, and Croatia. The Dorfmans carried out extensive photographic and other documentation work on synagogues in east central Europe in the 1980s and 1990s. Their book, *Synagogues without Jews,* was published in 2000 (Philadelphia: Jewish Publication Society of America).

Chapter 5. What to Do?

1. See, e.g., the collection of papers from a seminar on tourism and historic preservation in Krzysztof Broński, Krzysztof Görlich, Stefan Kłosowski, Jacek Purchla, and Zbigniew Zuziak, eds., *Managing Tourism in Historic Cities* (Kraków: International Cultural Center, 1992).

2. Andrew Herscher, "Remembering and Rebuilding in Bosnia," *Transitions: Changes in Post-Communist Societies* 5, no. 3 (March 1998): 77.

3. Robert Graefrath, "Die Ruine der Neuen Synagoge Berlin—konservieren oder rekonstruieren," *Bildende Kunst* 12 (1989): 16–20, quoted in Hermann Simon, *The New Synagogue, Berlin: Past-Present-Future* (Berlin: Edition Hentrich, 1992), 22–23.

4. See Sabine Offe, "Sites of Remembrance? Jewish Museums in Contemporary Germany," *Jewish Social Studies* 3, no. 2 (Winter 1997): 86. Hermann Simon, in *The New Synagogue, Berlin,* 26, refers to the discovery of the lamp as "close to a miracle."

5. See Eli Valley, *The Great Jewish Cities of Central and Eastern Europe* (Northvale, N.J.: Jason Aronson, 1999), 460.

6. For a breakdown for Třebíč, see material provided by the Fond Třebíč, the public-private fund overseeing the Třebíč development, including its 1994 Annual Report.

7. In December 2000 the Jewish Heritage Program of the World Monuments Fund awarded a grant of $70,000 to fund the final phase of restoration of the Boskovice synagogue, including fresco conservation.

8. Numerous monuments and cemetery restoration projects were carried out through the 1990s. For a vividly detailed description of the Hasidic pilgrimage experience in southern Poland and the restoration of the cemetery in Pilzo, see Adam Bartosz, "A Pilgrimage from Bobowa to Bobowa," in *Polin,* vol. 11, ed. Antony Polonsky (London: Littman Library of Jewish Civilization).

9. See his testimony before the U.S. House of Representatives International Relations Committee on August 6, 1998.

10. See, e.g., the letter by Rabbi Hertz Frankel, from Brooklyn, printed in the *Forward,* December 12, 1995.

11. Anikó Gazda, *Zsinagógák és zsidó községek magyarországon* (Budapest: MTA Judaisztikai Kutatócsoport, 1991), 238.

12. Ruth Ellen Gruber and Samuel D. Gruber, *Survey of Jewish Monuments in Slovenia* (Washington, D.C.: U.S. Commission for the Preservation of America's Heritage Abroad, 1996).

Chapter 6. Seeing Is Believing

1. Philip Gourevitch, "God, Genocide and the Fashions of Popular History," New York Times Service, *International Herald Tribune,* February 14, 1995.

2. "Should one take snapshots of the gas chambers and crematoria? Is this a trivialization?" Judith E. Doneson wrote in *"Holocaust* Revisited: A Catalyst for Memory or Trivialization?" *Annals of the American Academy of Political and Social Sciences* 548 (November 1996): 72. The German artist Joachim Seinfeld, whose work frequently deals with the Holocaust and its effects, has taken numerous photographs of tourists posing for photographs beneath the "Arbeit Macht Frei" gate at Auschwitz.

3. At the time Luzzatto was cultural representative of the Union of Italian Jewish Communities. In 1998 he became president of the Union. Amos Luzzatto, presentation published in Frano Bonilauri and Vincenza Maugeri, eds., *Musei ebraici in Europa: Orientamenti e prospettive/Jewish Museums in Europe: Trends and Perspectives* (Milan: Electa, 1998).

4. On the American Jewish artist Shimon Attie's response to the Schindler tour phenomenon, see James E. Young, *At Memory's Edge: After-Images of the Holocaust in Contemporary Art and Architecture* (New Haven: Yale University Press, 2000), 85–89.

5. Franciszek Palowski, *Retracing "Schindler's List"* (Kraków: Jordan Art, 1994), 12.

6. Michael C. Steinlauf, paper presented at a conference in Warsaw on the role of history museums in contemporary central and eastern Europe, April 24–26, 1996.

7. See, e.g., Stanisław Markowski, *Krakowski Kazimierz: Dzielnica Żydowska 1870–1988* (Kraków: Arka, 1992). On the relationship among tourists, modern tourism, and photography, see the works of John Urry, e.g., "Tourism and the Photographic Eye," in *Touring Cultures: Transformations of Travel and Theory,* ed. Chris Rojek and John Urry (London: Routledge, 1997), 176–95.

Chapter 7. The Tourist Track

1. Gabe Levenson, "Falling Walls, Rising Curtain," *Jewish Week,* February 9, 1990.

2. I list a selection of these books in the bibliography.

3. Eli Valley, "Letter from Prague," *Forward,* March 17, 1995. See also the

chapter "The Jurassic Park of Judaism" in Eli Valley, *The Great Jewish Cities of Central and Eastern Europe* (Northvale, N.J.: Jason Aronson, 1999), 53 ff.

4. There is, however, what *Moment* magazine described as a "Hasidic theme park" in Israel, set up by Chabad-Lubavitch in Kfar Chabad, south of Tel Aviv, to celebrate the three hundredth anniversary of the birth of the Baal Shem Tov, the founder of Hasidism: "In Chabad's reimagining of an 18th-century Eastern European shtetl young visitors can make olive oil with the shtetl oil maker, draw water from the village well, pet sheep and goats, ride in a horse-drawn cart, and hear stories and music from the Baal Shem Tov's time." "Shtetl Chic," *Moment*, December 1998, 37.

5. Donald Horne, *The Great Museum: The Re-presentation of History* (London: Pluto Press, 1984), 19–20. A large and varied literature on tourism theory, sociology, and anthropology has grown up since the 1980s, as leisure studies has become an academic discipline.

6. See, among others, the essays in Barbara Kirshenblatt-Gimblett, *Destination Tourism: Tourism, Museums, and Heritage* (Berkeley: University of California Press, 1998); and Ivan Karp and Steven D. Lavine, eds., *Exhibiting Cultures: The Poetics and Politics of Museum Display* (Washington, D.C.: Smithsonian Institution Press, 1991).

7. Stanley Waterman, *Cultural Politics and European Jewry* (London: Institute for Jewish Policy Research, 1999), 17.

8. Bernard Postal and Samuel H. Abramson, *The Landmarks of a People: A Guide to Jewish Sites in Europe* (New York: Hill and Wang, 1962), touched nearly three dozen countries and targeted the Jews who were among those who participated in the postwar boom in American tourism to Europe, which, the authors noted in the preface, brought an estimated 750,000 Americans to Europe annually by the early 1960s: "Whether as businessmen or as pleasure-seekers, as students or as pilgrims come to honor parents and other kinfolk buried abroad, as World War II veterans who want to see the postwar Continent, or as former refugees from the Nazi terror visiting their old homes, American Jews are pouring into Europe by the tens of thousands annually" (p. vi). My own family was part of this wave. We made three family trips to Europe, in 1959, 1962, and 1966. The only Jewish sites I remember visiting were the Old Jewish Cemetery and the Jewish Museum in Prague in 1966 and the synagogue in Florence in 1962, where we saw a wedding taking place. Near Prague, we also visited the memorial at Lidice, commemorating a town wiped out by the Nazis in retaliation for a resistance attack. On a summer-long hitchhiking tour of Europe in 1970, I may have visited the Jewish sites of Prague, though I don't remember doing so. What I most remember is being determined not to spend the night, or spend any money, in Germany. See also travel articles by writers such as Gabe Levenson and Alan Tigay in the Jewish media and the guides written and published by Oscar Israelowicz. The Jewish Travel Guides published annually by the London *Jewish Chronicle* provide information mainly on synagogues and infrastructure.

9. Miriam Weiner's "Roots and Branches" column, *Jewish Advocate of South Broward*, October 5–18, 1990.

10. Slogan from *A la découverte du judaïsme alsacien* (Strasbourg/Colmar: Tourisme Alsace, 1998). It is interesting, again, to note parallels with treatment

of Native American heritage in the United States. A billboard I saw in January 1999 along Interstate 95 in Connecticut advertised the Mashantucket Pequot Museum with the slogan, "Discover a Nation in Your Own Backyard."

11. Collections from the Cluny and other museums were merged to form the core of the exhibitions at the Museum of Jewish Art and History that opened in Paris in December 1998.

12. See *Monuments Historiques,* no. 191 (February 1994), a special issue dedicated to the Jewish heritage of France. It includes a detailed summary of state legislation regarding the protection of Jewish monuments in France.

13. Ben G. Frank, *France for the Jewish Traveler* (no publication information available). Frank thanks the French Government Tourist Office "for their help and cooperation in making possible" the booklet, whose cover bears the logo of the French tourist office and lists French government tourist offices in five U.S. cities.

14. Information from Catherine Lehmann, of the Agence de Développement Touristique du Bas-Rhin in Strasbourg.

15. Albert Stalzer, *Jewish Vienna & Austria: Heritage and Mission* (Vienna: Vienna Tourist Board/Austrian National Tourist Office, 1993–94); *Shalom: Jewish Relics in Hungary* (Budapest: Hungarian Travel Magazine/National Tourist Board of Hungary). The Hungary booklet was commissioned by the National Tourist Board, with "the support of the Hungarian Chapter of WIZO"—the Women's Zionist Organization. Its cover bears the logo of the Hungarian National Tourist Board.

16. Information in this section is from the presentation by Catherine Lehmann, Claude Bloch, of the B'nai B'rith in Strasbourg, and Gilbert Weil, president of the Association of Friends of the Jewish Museum of Bouxwiller, at the International Conference on Jewish Heritage in Europe, Paris, January 28, 1999, as well as subsequent information provided by Lehmann and Bloch.

17. Aron Hirt-Manheimer, "Poland: Realm of Restless Spirits," *Reform Judaism* (Fall 1994): 20–27.

18. For a detailed discussion of Prague, see Ruth Ellen Gruber, *Upon the Doorposts of Thy House: Jewish Life in East-Central Europe, Yesterday and Today* (New York: Wiley, 1994); and *Filling the Jewish Space in Europe* (New York: American Jewish Committee, 1996).

19. According to official statistics, more than 90 million foreign visitors went to the Czech Republic in the first eleven months of 1995. Preliminary statistics released in August 1998 showed that 48.2 million foreigners crossed the border in the first half of 1998.

20. Eli Valley, in his exhaustive resource book and tourist guide to Prague and other Jewish cities of central Europe, is a scolder. See Valley, *Great Jewish Cities,* 63. He himself worked as a tour guide for a Jewish travel agency during his time in Prague.

21. For details on Wittmann, see Jonathan Kaufman, *A Hole in the Heart of the World: Being Jewish in Eastern Europe* (New York: Viking, 1996).

22. Jack Kugelmass, "The Rites of the Tribe," in *Going Home: YIVO Annual 21,* ed. Jack Kugelmass (New York: YIVO Institute for Jewish Research/Evanston, Ill.: Northwestern University Press, 1993), 410–11.

23. See the chapter "What Does It Do for Me?" in Tom Segev, *The Seventh Million: The Israelis and the Holocaust* (New York: Hill and Wang, 1993). Also the chapter "Snowbound in Auschwitz," in Gruber, *Doorposts*.

24. "There is no more Jewish life in Poland," a handbook for participants said. "Some remaining synagogues, most of which are used for other purposes, and cemeteries. Being there, with our consciousness and our identity, returning to these towns and these villages, these cities and markets, we . . . will fill these places with a Jewish vitality and a renewed Jewish hope. We will be surrounded everywhere by the local Polish population, and we will have ambivalent feelings toward them. We will hate them for having participated in atrocities, but we will also pity them for their woeful living conditions today. Let us not be carried away by negative emotions. We won the war, we can march there, before the entire world, with our national white and blue flag, and not with the 'yellow star.'" (The handbook did go on to mention that some Righteous Gentiles who saved Jews were Polish.)

25. In the late 1990s and particularly from 2000, changes were introduced for some groups participating in the March of the Living. Some eight hundred Gentiles, most of them Polish (including President Aleksander Kwasniewski), took part in 2000, and there were attempts to instruct visiting participants about present Polish conditions and current efforts to revive Jewish communal life. As part of a preparatory program sponsored by the American Jewish Committee, several members of the Polish Jewish community traveled to the United States ahead of the March to hold encounters with some of the participants. The program was expanded in 2001.

26. Many personal accounts have been published over the years in *Avotaynu*, the international journal of Jewish genealogy. High-profile accounts include Theo Richmond, *Konin: A Quest* (London: Jonathan Cape, 1996); Arnold Zable, *Jewels and Ashes* (New York: Harcourt Brace & Company, 1994); Stephen J. Dubner, *Turbulent Souls: A Catholic Son's Return to His Jewish Family* (New York: Morrow, 1998).

27. Hillel Halkin, "The Road to Naybikhov," *Commentary*, November 1998. Halkin tries to remain immune to the same reactions he dismisses, but his account is similar to many. For an original take, see Jonathan Safran Foer, "The Very Rigid Search," *New Yorker*, June 18–25, 2001.

Chapter 8. Structuring Memory

1. I am grateful to Sabine Offe, of Bremen University, and to several other people for sharing with me their experience and their insights on the issues discussed in this chapter, in particular, Eva Grabherr, of Vienna; Bernhard Purin, director of the Jüdisches Museum Franken of Fürth and Schnaittach; and Franco Bonilauri, director of the Jewish Museum in Bologna.

2. On museums as destinations, see the chapter "Destination Museum" in Barbara Kirshenblatt-Gimblett, *Destination Culture: Tourism, Museums, and Heritage* (Berkeley: University of California Press, 1998).

3. Museums "stand for the idea that some things are culturally more valuable than others; hierarchies do exist." Herbert Muschamp, "Culture's Power

Houses: The Museum Becomes an Engine of Urban Redesign," *New York Times,* special section on museums, April 21, 1999. See Kirshenblatt-Gimblett, *Destination Culture,* 138–39, on the multiple roles of museums.

4. See Carol Duncan, "Art Museums and the Ritual of Citizenship," in *Exhibiting Cultures: The Poetics and Politics of Museum Display,* ed. Ivan Karp and Steven D. Lavine (Washington, D.C.: Smithsonian Institution Press, 1991), 88–103, for a discussion of the ritual aspect and political use of museums in general in the fostering of a positive image of the society that founds the museum. Duncan elaborated this further in *Civilizing Rituals: Inside Public Art Museums* (London: Routledge, 1995).

5. See Sabine Offe, "Sites of Remembrance? Jewish Museums in Contemporary Germany," *Jewish Social Studies* 3, no. 2 (Winter 1997): 79.

6. A vast literature on exhibitions, museums, and museum theory has been published since the late 1980s in particular, some examples of which are noted in the bibliography and footnotes.

7. For example, Julius H. Schoeps, the first director of the Jewish Museum in Vienna, raised many of these questions in an article in the main catalog of the museum that set out the museum's aims and responsibilities: "What is a Jewish museum? What are its tasks? . . . [I]s it permitted at all to talk about a 'Jewish' history? Is it not more appropriate to talk about a history of German-Jewish or Austrian-Jewish relations?" See Julius H. Schoeps, "Memories—Enlightenment and Commemoration," in *Jewish Museum Vienna,* ed. Felicitas Heimann-Jelinek and Hannes Sulzenbacher (Vienna: Jewish Museum of the City of Vienna, 1996). See also, e.g., Felicitas Heimann-Jelinek, "Heading towards the Third Millennium," in *Musei ebraici in Europa: Orientamenti e prospettive/ Jewish Museums in Europe: Trends and Perspectives,* ed. Franco Bonilauri and Vincenza Maugeri (Milan: Electa, 1998); Offe, "Sites of Remembrance?"; Cilly Kugelmann, "Jewish Museums in Germany: A German-Jewish Problem," in *Speaking Out: Jewish Voices from United Germany,* ed. Susan Stern (Chicago: edition q, 1995); David Clark, *Developing Jewish Museums in Europe* (London: Institute for Jewish Policy Research, 1999); *Musée d'art e d'histoire du Judaïsme: Rappel de l'historique du project, entretien avec Laurence Sigal* (press kit material for the Musée d'art e d'histoire du Judaïsme, which opened in Paris in 1998); James E. Young, *At Memory's Edge: After-Images of the Holocaust in Contemporary Art and Architecture* (New Haven: Yale University Press, 2000); and the numerous articles about the Berlin Jewish Museum.

8. Offe, "Sites of Remembrance?" 79. See also her book *Ausstellungen, Einstellungen, Enstellungen: Jüdisches Museen in Deutschland und Österreich* (Berlin: Philo, 2000).

9. Clark, *Developing Jewish Museums,* 3, 6. In 1999 Clark was working on a Ph.D. on Jewish museums.

10. Alan Levy, "Goyish Voices Raised High in Yiddish Song," *International Herald Tribune,* April 26, 1991, 15.

11. Marvin Lowenthal, *A World Passed By: Scenes and Memories of Jewish Civilization in Europe and North Africa* (New York: Harper & Brothers, 1933; New York: Behrman's Jewish Book House, 1938), 337. See Richard I. Cohen, *Jewish Icons: Art and Society in Modern Europe* (Berkeley: University of California Press, 1998), esp. 187 ff., about nineteenth-century exhibitions of Judaica and

the "institutionalization of Jewish art" in early Jewish museums; Kirshenblatt-Gimblett, *Destination Culture,* 81 ff.; Heimann-Jelinek, "Heading towards the Third Millennium."

12. Yeshayahu Weinberg, "Story-Telling Exhibitions and Their Impact on Modern History Museums," paper presented at the conference The Role of History Museums in Contemporary Central and Eastern Europe, Warsaw, April 24–26, 1996.

13. *Jüdisches Museum Westfalen* (Dorsten: Nordrhein-Westfalen-Stiftung, 1992).

14. Offe, "Sites of Remembrance?" 78.

15. See, among others, Kirshenblatt-Gimblett, *Destination Culture,* 81 ff.; Cohen, *Jewish Icons,* esp. 155 ff.

16. On Toledo, see Carmen Betegon, "Il museo Sefardi di Toledo, Rimodellazione e prospettive," in Bonilauri and Maugeri, *Musei ebraici in Europa/Jewish Museums in Europe,* 32–35.

17. Eva Grabherr, ed., *Jews in Hohenems,* catalog of the Jewish Museum Hohenems (Hohenems: Jüdisches Museum Hohenems, 1996), 10. See discussion of Shimon Attie's projection installations in Berlin and elsewhere in Young, *At Memory's Edge,* 62 ff.

18. See A. Z. Idelsohn, *Jewish Music in Its Historical Development* (New York: Henry Holt, 1929), 256–57.

19. Grabherr, *Jews in Hohenems,* 81.

20. Ibid., 10.

21. I am grateful to Richard Mitten for his discussions with me on this issue, and for allowing me to read an unpublished version of his article, "Jews and Other Victims: The 'Jewish Question' and Discourses of Victimhood in Postwar Austria."

22. Marta Halpert, *Jewish Life in Austria* (Vienna: Federal Press Service, [1994] 1998), 10.

23. Alan Levy, "Goyish Voices."

24. Grabherr, *Jews in Hohenems,* 10.

25. See the remarks by Otto Lohr, of the office in charge of nonstate museums in Bavaria, which include nearly a dozen Jewish museums, in a presentation to the Paris international conference on European Jewish heritage in January 1999. Published in *Jewish Heritage Report* 2, nos. 3–4 (1999): 24–26.

26. Ibid.

27. See Bernhard Purin, *The Franconian Jewish Museum in Schnaittach,* information paper, Jüdisches Museum Franken, Fürth. The major part of the *Heimat* museum's Jewish collection was taken over by the Jewish Cultural Reconstruction Organization in 1951; items from the collection are now in the Israel Museum in Jerusalem, the Jewish Museum in New York, and the Skirball Museum in Los Angeles.

28. Purin, *Franconian Jewish Museum.*

29. On the use of objects and artifacts and the question of authenticity in exhibitions, see Spencer R. Crew and James E. Sims, "Locating Authenticity: Fragments of a Dialogue," in Karp and Lavine, *Exhibiting Cultures,* 159–75.

30. See Sandro Servi, *Il Museo Ebraico di Roma* (Rome: Comunità Israelitica di Roma, 1984).

31. The museum was under reconstruction and expansion in 2000–2001, and it was not clear whether it would be possible to maintain this policy of personal touch with the new arrangement, which was to place the museum collections in a historical context.

32. The project, including a description of it as a "virtual museum" is elaborated in detail in Franco Bonilauri, "Il museo ebraico di Bologna. Il progetto culturale," in Bonilauri and Maugeri, *Musei ebraici in Europa/Jewish Museums in Europe,* 48–55.

33. See, among others, Leo Pavlát, "Perspectives of the Jewish Museum in Prague," in Bonilauri and Maugeri, *Musei ebraici in Europa/Jewish Museums in Europe;* Eli Valley, *The Great Jewish Cities of Central and Eastern Europe* (Northvale, N.J.: Jason Aronson, 1999); David Altshuler, ed., *The Precious Legacy: Judaic Treasures from the Czechoslovak State Collections* (New York: Summit Books, 1983).

34. Carved reliefs on the Arch of Titus in Rome famously (or infamously) show the menorah brought back in 70 C.E. as plunder from the destroyed Temple in Jerusalem.

35. Jiří Weill, *Mendelssohn Is on the Roof,* trans. Marie Winn (London: Flamingo, 1991), 67; originally published in 1960 as *Na Strese Je Mendelssohn.*

36. Leo Pavlát, unpublished remarks prepared in October 1994. See also Hana Volavková, *The Jewish Museum of Prague: A Guide through the Collections* (Prague: Council of Jewish Religious Communities of Bohemia, Moravia, and Silesia, 1948); Valley, *Great Jewish Cities;* Altshuler, *Precious Legacy.*

37. See Charles Hoffman, *Gray Dawn: The Jews of Eastern Europe in the Post-Communist Era* (New York: HarperCollins, 1992), 15. See also Valley, *Great Jewish Cities.*

38. See Valley, *Great Jewish Cities,* 53–55 ff. See also the chapter on the Prague museum in Itamar Levin, *The Last Chapter of the Holocaust?* 2d rev. and updated ed. (n.p.: Jewish Agency for Israel, 1998), 174–77. The director of the Prague Jewish Museum, Leo Pavlát, issued a lengthy rebuttal of the information in Levin's report, which included a copy of Levin's chapter on the Prague museum.

39. See Richard Allen Greene, "Leo Pavlát: Context for a Community," *Prague Post,* April 9–15, 1997.

40. At this writing, the new Jewish Museum in Berlin was not yet complete.

41. See Bernhard Purin, "Palais Eskeles in Vienna's Dorotheergasse: The Eventful History of a Building," *Jüdisches Museum Wien Newsletter,* June 1994.

42. Umberto Eco, *Travels in Hyperreality,* trans. William Weaver (New York: Harcourt Brace & Company, 1986), 4.

43. Felicitas Heimann-Jelinek, "On the Historical Exhibition at the Jewish Museum of the City of Vienna," in Heimann-Jelinek and Sulzenbacher, *Jewish Museum Vienna,* 62. See also her article "On the Re-Organization of the Jewish Museum of the City of Vienna," *Jüdisches Museum Wien Newsletter,* nos. 8–9 (March 1996): 2.

44. Felicitas Heimann-Jelinek, "Memoria, Intelligentia, Providentia," in Heimann-Jelinek and Sulzenbacher, *Jewish Museum Vienna,* 129.

45. On the concept of the viewable storage area, see Gabriele Kohlbauer-

Fritz, "A Viewable Storage Area," in Heimann-Jelinek and Sulzenbacher, *Jewish Museum Vienna,* 119–25.

46. Recounted to me by Rebecca Anderson of New York.

Chapter 9. Making (and Remaking) Jewish Music

1. I am deeply indebted to many musician friends for discussing issues explored in these pages, for inviting me to their concerts and rehearsals, and for sending me their CDs. The list is long, but Alan Bern, Michael Alpert, Bob Cohen, Francesco Spagnolo, Judith Frigyesi, Rudi Assuntino, Heiko Lehmann, and Moni Ovadia have been of particular help.

2. The most comprehensive klezmer music site on the web is Ari Davidow's Klezmer Shack: www.klezmershack.com. It includes listings and addresses for bands in many countries.

3. Andrea Cangioli, "Hai mai sentito il Klezmer?" *Glamour* (Italy), October 1997, 144–45.

4. Gebrider Moischele, *Shtil, di nacht is ojsgeschternt* (Extraplatte, EX 238–2, 1995).

5. Interview with Luca Di Volo by Miria Fracassi in *Avvenimenti,* June 11, 1997, 77.

6. The title of a recent Italian book illustrates this. See Gabriele Coen and Isotta Toso, *Klezmer! La musica popolare ebraica dallo shtetl a John Zorn* (*Klezmer! Jewish Folk Music from the Shtetl to John Zorn*) (Rome: Castelvecchi, 2000).

7. For background on klezmer music, see, among others: Michael Alpert, "As If It Were Yesterday," in *Klezmer Music: A Marriage of Heaven & Earth,* CD and book, produced by Michael Shapiro (Roslyn, N.Y.: ellipsis arts, 1996); Henry Sapoznik, *Klezmer! Jewish Music from Old World to Our World* (New York: Schirmer, 1999), and *The Compleat Klezmer* (Cedarhurst, N.Y.: Tara Publications, 1987), 5–6; and A. Z. Idelsohn, *Jewish Music in Its Historical Development* (New York: Henry Holt, 1929), 455 ff. See also Mark Slobin, *Tenement Songs: The Popular Music of the Jewish Immigrants* (Urbana: University of Illinois Press, 1982); *Old Jewish Folk Music: The Collections and Writings of Moshe Beregovski* (Philadelphia: University of Pennsylvania Press, 1982); and *Fiddler on the Move* (New York: Oxford University Press, 2000). Also see Seth Rogovoy, *The Essential Klezmer: A Music Lover's Guide to Jewish Roots and Soul Music, from the Old World to the Downtown Avant-Garde* (Chapel Hill, N.C.: Algonquin, 2000); Coen and Toso, *Klezmer!*

8. See Mark Slobin, "The Neo-Klezmer Movement and Euro-American Musical Revivalism," *Journal of American Folklore* 97, no. 383 (January–March 1984): 98–104. See also Barbara Kirshenblatt-Gimblett, "Sounds of Sensibility," *Judaism* 47, no. 1 (Winter 1998): 49–78.

9. Sapoznik, *The Compleat Klezmer,* 14. See also Sapoznik, *Klezmer!* 180–81.

10. Mark Slobin, "Rethinking 'Revival' of American Ethnic Music," *New York Folklore* 9, nos. 3–4 (Winter 1983).

11. Slobin, "Neo-Klezmer," 102.

12. See the film about Kozłowski, *The Last Klezmer,* made by American photographer, filmmaker, and klezmer fiddler, Yale Strom.

13. This holds increasingly true for younger groups in America, too. See Slobin, *Fiddler.*

14. La'om, *". . . spielt!" Klezmer-musik von Chicago bis Odessa* (Raumer Records, RR 10696, 1997).

15. See Kirshenblatt-Gimblett, "Sounds of Sensibility."

16. Alan Levy, "Goyish Voices Raised High in Yiddish Song," *International Herald Tribune,* April 26, 1991.

17. *Music in Izaak Synagogue Cracow* (Extraplatte, EX 281–096–2, 1996).

18. Peter Sichrovsky, *Born Guilty: Children of Nazi Families,* trans. Jean Steinberg (New York: Basic Books, 1988), 8–10; originally published as *Schuldig geboren: Kinder aus Nazifamilien* (Cologne: Verlag Kiepenheuer & Witsch, 1987). Sichrovsky does not cite the family name but clearly refers to Strobl. (Sichrovsky's own story eventually reflected the complex aftermath of the Kurt Waldheim affair. In 1996 he caused a furor by running in European Parliament elections as a candidate on the list of Jörg Haider's Freedom Party, the chief right-wing force to emerge out of the post-Waldheim ideological entrenchments.)

19. Catalog of the Seventh Jewish Culture Festival, June 29–July 6, 1997, 45.

20. Dire Gelt, *Klezmer Music, Yiddish Songs* (dona ruy project, Harmony Music, ESS 6, 1996).

21. At my urging, the Klezroym made a brief mention of the holiday when they played their set.

22. The lecture for the first festival, in 1996, was given by Moni Ovadia. In 1997 I gave the lecture—on the revival of klezmer music in Europe. In 1998 it was given by Ovadia and Francesco Spagnolo, the director of the new Center for the Study of Jewish Music in Milan. In 1999 the American Willy Schwarz gave a combined concert and talk.

Chapter 10. Klezmer in Germany

1. For an exhaustive treatment of the strained relationship between German Jews and *Ostjuden,* see Steven E. Aschheim, *Brothers and Strangers: The East European Jew in German and German Jewish Consciousness, 1800 –1923* (Madison: University of Wisconsin Press, 1982). See also the novel by Sholem Asch, *The War Goes On,* trans. Willa Muir and Edwin Muir (New York: Putnam, 1936).

2. A. Z. Idelsohn, *Jewish Music in Its Historical Development* (New York: Henry Holt, 1929), 458–59. See also Henry Sapoznik, *Klezmer! Jewish Music from Old World to Our World* (New York: Schirmer, 1999), 1–5; *Encyclopaedia Judaica* (Jerusalem: Keter, 1972), 7:983.

3. In the late 1990s Germany saw a kitsch revival of exaggerated *schlager* in all its sequined-jacket glory.

4. In Rob Burns, ed., *German Cultural Studies: An Introduction* (Oxford: Oxford University Press, 1995), 312–13, Burns and Wilfried van der Will note that "record sales of American rock and pop artists far outstripped those of their

German counterparts" and that American hit bands and rock cult artists alike would be guaranteed sellout tours.

5. Zupfgeigenhansel, *Jiddische Lieder* (Dortmund: pläne, 1979).

6. Notes to the CD *Europäisches Jiddisch-Festival, Leverkusen 1993* (Edition Künstlertreff, EK 171062, 1994).

7. Information from the German klezmer collector Bertram Nickolay and Aufwind member Andreas Rohde and former member Heiko Lehmann. See also the lecture "Klezmer in Germany/Germans and Klezmer: Reparation or Contribution" given by Lehmann in Berlin, October 19, 2000. Text can be found at http://sukke.de/lecture.html. Other early German performers singing Yiddish songs were ESPE, Hein & Oss, and Peter Rohland. Also see Sapoznik, *Klezmer!* 275; Blake Eskin, "Keeping Time," *Forward,* November 21, 1997. In the chapter "Stasi" in *The Politics of Memory: Looking for Germany in the New Germany* (New York: Random House, 1996), Jane Kramer writes about the alternative literature scene in the 1980s in East Berlin and the way it was infiltrated with Stasi secret police informers.

8. Jalda Rebling, "Yiddish Culture—A Soul Survivor of East Germany," in *Speaking Out: Jewish Voices from United Germany,* ed. Susan Stern (Chicago: edition q, 1995). See also Sapoznik, *Klezmer!* 276; Lehmann, "Klezmer in Germany."

9. Another American neoklezmer pioneer, Andy Statman, played in Germany that same year, at a Berlin jazz festival, and Giora Feidman also performed in Germany in 1984. See Sapoznik, *Klezmer!* 223 ff.

10. For a description of the jazz scene in Germany, mainly Berlin, in the 1920s, see the introduction to Michael H. Kater, *Different Drummers: Jazz in the Culture of Nazi Germany* (Oxford: Oxford University Press, 1992), esp. 16–27. This affords a fascinating comparison with the reception of klezmer music today and the efforts by local German musicians to master the new foreign musical idiom. Kater also describes the "hunger" of local audiences for foreign music crazes including tango and gypsy music, often played by foreign musicians: p. 27.

11. One is reminded of George Gershwin and Ira Gershwin's 1918 song, "The Real American Folksong (Is a Rag)."

12. See Michael Wolffsohn, *Eternal Guilt? Forty Years of German-Jewish-Israeli Relations,* trans. Douglas Bokovoy (New York: Columbia University Press, 1993), 200–202. For a discussion of German productions of *Ghetto* in the 1990s, see Alan Bern, "Who Is Weiskopf? Representing Jewish Identity in 'Ghetto' on East and West German Stages," paper presented at the symposium Identität und Gedächtnis in der jüdischen Literatur nach 1945, Institut für Allgemeine und Vergleichende Literaturwissenschaft, Joh. Gutenberg-Universität, Mainz, October 15–17, 2000.

13. On Feidman's connection with Hasidic and kabbalistic tradition, see Francesco Spagnolo, "'Io non suono musica klezmer: io sono klezmer!': Riflessioni a margine di una conversazione con Giora Feidman," program notes for a concert by Feidman in Siena, Italy, August 5, 1998.

14. This discussion describes a concert I attended in Venice in November 1995, but it is virtually identical to other Feidman concerts.

15. Information from Heiko Lehmann, e-mail communication, February 4, 1998.

16. Personal communication. Also, see Lehmann, "Klezmer in Germany," for his insider description of this process.

17. It also conjures up colorful images of the prewar underworld as portrayed in novels such as *Berlin Alexanderplatz,* by Alfred Döblin. See, among others, Brian Ladd, *The Ghosts of Berlin: Confronting German History in the Urban Landscape* (Chicago: University of Chicago Press, 1997), 110–15.

18. See Alan Bern, "Van Klezmer tot Nieuwe Joodse Muziek," *Mens en Melodie,* July–August 1998. In this article Bern describes Brave Old World's approach to klezmer and its evolution as a band. An English-language text of the article, "From Klezmer to New Jewish Music," is available at www. klezmershack.com/articles/bern.new.html.

19. See Y. Michal Bodemann, "Reconstructions of History: From Jewish Memory to Nationalized Commemoration of Kristallnacht in Germany," in *Jews, Germans, Memory: Reconstructions of Jewish Life in Germany,* ed. Y. Michal Bodemann (Ann Arbor: University of Michigan Press, 1996).

20. la'om, *". . . spielt!" Klezmer-musik von Chicago bis Odessa.* (Raumer Records, RR 10696, 1996).

Chapter 11. Whose Music?

1. See also the collaborations between the highlander band Trebunia-Tutki Family and the reggae group Twinkle Brother, including the CD *Comeback Twinkle 2 Trebunia Family* (Ryszard Music/Kamahuk, CD 0007, 1994). Brave Old World has collaborated with a Ukrainian-Canadian group, Paris to Kyiv, in performances called "Night Songs from a Neighboring Village," which illustrate the mutual influences between Yiddish and Ukrainian folk music. In Italy there are frequent concerts and festivals of klezmer and Roma (Gypsy) music.

2. The cultural anthropologist and folklorist Barbara Kirshenblatt-Gimblett has written widely on this. See, e.g., her article "Objects of Ethnography" in *Exhibiting Cultures: The Poetics and Politics of Museum Display,* ed. Ivan Karp and Steven D. Lavine (Washington, D.C.: Smithsonian Institution Press, 1991). See also Ellis Cashmore, *The Black Culture Industry* (London: Routledge, 1997). Michael H. Kater, *Different Drummers: Jazz in the Culture of Nazi Germany* (Oxford: Oxford University Press, 1992), 17–28, has a fascinating discussion of German, particularly Berlin, musicians in the 1920s trying to play jazz and the music scene's (and society's) reaction to black American jazz musicians, "the true originators of [the] idiom," who, Kater writes, were relegated "to the periphery of the jazz scene" there. Kater continues, "The public and private attitude toward blacks, including Afro-Americans, was an ambivalent one. . . . The German star cult around black personalities such as Josephine Baker really was an inverted form of racial prejudice. . . . Baker was popular *because* she was an outsider who afforded audiences the titillating illusion of sin while never endangering the moral standard" (p. 18).

3. Review of the CD *Awek di junge jorn,* by Aufwind (Misrach Music, MSR 0144–2, 1996). Posted on Ari's Klezmer Shack web site January 1, 1998. See also

Heiko Lehmann, "Klezmer in Germany/Germans and Klezmer: Reparation or Contribution," a lecture given in Berlin, October 19, 2000. Text can be found at http://www.sukke.de/lecture.html.

4. Margaret Talbot, "Bonn Diarist: Recycled," *New Republic,* May 29, 1995.
5. Ensemble Klesmer, *Live in Prag* (Extraplatte, EX-317–2, 1997).
6. Budowitz, *Mother Tongue* (Koch International, CD 3–1261–2, 1997).
7. Lehmann, "Klezmer in Germany."
8. Ibid.

Afterword

1. "A Fateful Encounter: Jews and non-Jews in Central Europe," paper presented at the conference, Medieval Jewish Communities in Central Europe and Their Cultural Heritage, in Maribor, Slovenia, October 1997.

Posters for klezmer music concerts by the Klezmatics and Giora Feidman join posters for other events on a billboard in Budapest, 1999. (Photo by Ruth Ellen Gruber.)

Selected Bibliography

Books, Articles, and Periodicals

Altaras, Thea. *Synagogen in Hessen: Was geschah seit 1945?* Königstein im Taunus: Karl Robert Langewiesche Nachfolger Hans Köster Verlagsbuchhandlung, 1988.

Altshuler, David, ed. *The Precious Legacy: Judaic Treasures from the Czechoslovak State Collections.* New York: Summit Books, 1983.

Ambrosewicz-Jacobs, Jolanta, and Annamaria Orla-Bukowska. "After the Fall: Attitudes towards Jews in Post-1989 Poland." *Nationalities Papers* 26, no. 1 (1998): 265–82.

The American Jewish Yearbook. Vols. 90–100. New York: The American Jewish Committee, 1990–2000.

And I Still See Their Faces: Images of Polish Jews. Warsaw: Fundacja Shalom, 1996.

Annals of the American Academy of Political and Social Sciences. Special issue, "The Holocaust: Remembering for the Future," vol. 548 (November 1996).

Aschheim, Steven E. *Brothers and Strangers: The East European Jew in German and German Jewish Consciousness, 1800–1923.* Madison: University of Wisconsin Press, 1982.

Bartosz, Adam. "A Pilgrimage from Bobowa to Bobowa." In *Polin,* vol. 11, ed. Antony Polonsky, 66–76. London: Littman Library of Jewish Civilization, 1998.

Baumhorn Lipót, építész: 1860–1932. Exhibition catalog. Budapest: Architart Kiadó, 1999.

Berchiellaro, Davide, and Elena Vaghi. "Vedi alla Voce Talmud . . . e anche Cabalà, Klezmer, Kosher." *Panorama* 35, no. 40 (October 8, 1998): 268–74.

Bern, Alan. "Who Is Weiskopf? Representing Jewish Identity in 'Ghetto' on

East and West German Stages." Paper presented at the symposium Identität und Gedächtnis in der jüdischen Literatur nach 1945, Institut für Allgemeine und Vergleichende Literaturwissenschaft, Joh. Gutenberg-Universität, Mainz, October 15–17, 2000.

Bettauer, Hugo. *The City without Jews: A Novel of Our Time*. Trans. Salomea Neumark Brainin. New York: Bloch, [1926] 1991.

Blasius, Dirk, and Dan Diner, eds. *Zerbrochene Geschichte: Leben und Selbsverständnis der Juden in Deutschland*. Frankfurt: Fischer, 1991.

Bodemann, Y. Michal, ed. *Jews, Germans, Memory: Reconstructions of Jewish Life in Germany*. Ann Arbor: University of Michigan Press, 1996.

Bondoni, Simonetta M., and Giulio Busi, eds. *Cultura ebraica in Emilia-Romagna*. Rimini: Istituto per i Beni Culturali della Regione Emilia-Romagna, Luisè Editore, 1987.

Bonilauri, Franco, and Vincenza Maugeri, eds. *Musei ebraici in Europa: Orientamenti e prospettive/Jewish Museums in Europe: Trends and Perspectives*. Milan: Electa, 1998.

———. *La tutela dei beni culturali ebraici in Italia*. Bologna: Istituto per Beni Culturali della Regione Emilia-Romagna, 1996.

Borkowicz, Jacek, ed. *Więź Special Issue (1998)*. Warsaw: Towarzyszystwo Więż, 1998.

Braham, Randolf L., ed. *Anti-Semitism and the Treatment of the Holocaust in Postcommunist Eastern Europe*. New York: Columbia University Press, 1994.

———. *Reflections of the Holocaust in Art and Literature*. Boulder: Social Science Monographs; New York: Csengi Institute for Holocaust Studies of the Graduate School and University Center of the City University of New York, 1990.

Brenner, Michael. *The Renaissance of Jewish Culture in Weimar Germany*. New Haven: Yale University Press, 1996.

Broński, Krzysztof, Krzysztof Görlich, Stefan Kłosowski, Jacek Purchla, and Zbigniew Zuziak, eds. *Managing Tourism in Historic Cities*. Kraków: International Culture Center, 1992.

Burns, Rob, ed. *German Cultural Studies: An Introduction*. Oxford: Oxford University Press, 1995.

Buruma, Ian. *The Wages of Guilt: Memories of War in Germany and Japan*. New York: Meridian, 1994.

Cashmore, Ellis. *The Black Culture Industry*. London: Routledge, 1997.

Cattaruzza, Claudio, ed. *Dedica a Moni Ovadia*. Pordenone: Associazione Provinciale per la Prosa, 1998.

Clark, David. *Developing Jewish Museums in Europe*. London: Institute for Jewish Policy Research, 1999.

———. "Jewish Sites in Europe: Constructing Spatial Narratives and Collective Memory." Paper presented at the conference of the European Association of Jewish Studies, Toledo, July 1998.

Coen, Gabriele, and Isotta Toso. *Klezmer! La musica popolare ebraica dallo shtetl a John Zorn*. Rome: Castelvecchi, 2000.

Cohen, Mark R., trans. and ed. *The Autobiography of a Seventeenth-Century*

Venetian Rabbi: Leon Modena's "Life of Judah." Princeton: Princeton University Press, 1988.

Cohen, Mitchell. "Imaginary Jews and Jewish Imagination." In *Literary Strategies: Jewish Texts and Contents*, ed. Ezra Mendelsohn, 251–58. Studies in Contemporary Jewry 12. Oxford: Oxford University Press, 1996.

Cohen, Richard I. *Jewish Icons: Art and Society in Modern Europe.* Berkeley: University of California Press, 1998.

Comunità religiose di Trieste: Contributi di conoscenza, a cura dei Civici Musei di Storia e Arte Trieste. Udine: Istituto per l'Enciclopedia del Friuli Venezia Giulia, 1979.

Dawidowicz, Lucy S., ed. *The Golden Tradition: Jewish Life and Thought in Eastern Europe.* New York: Schocken, 1967.

Diaszpóra (és) Művészet/Diaspora (and) Art. Exhibition catalog. Budapest: Hungarian Jewish Museum, 1997.

Döblin, Alfred. *Journey to Poland.* Trans. Joachim Neugroschel. New York: Paragon House, 1991.

Dugulin, Adriano, ed. *Shalom Trieste: Gli itinerari dell' ebraismo.* Trieste: Comune di Trieste, 1998.

Eco, Umberto. *Travels in Hyperreality.* Trans. William Weaver. New York: Harcourt Brace & Company, 1986.

Edelstein, Alan. *An Unacknowledged Harmony: Philo-Semitism and the Survival of European Jewry.* Contributions in Ethnic Studies No. 4. Westport, Conn.: Greenwood Press, 1982.

Eichler, Jeremy. "But Is It Jewish?" *Jerusalem Report,* November 13, 1997.

Erdman, Harley. *Staging the Jew: The Performance of an American Ethnicity, 1860–1920.* New Brunswick: Rutgers University Press, 1997.

. . . és beszéld el fiadnak . . . Catalog, photographic exhibition by Tamás Fenér. Budapest: Néprajzi Múzeum, 1983.

Fatta, Francesca, chief ed., and Paola Caselli, ed. *Architettura judaica in Italia: Ebraismo, sito, memoria dei luoghi.* Palermo: Flaccovio Editore, 1994.

Finkielkraut, Alain. *The Imaginary Jew.* Trans. Kevin O'Neill and David Suchoff. Lincoln: University of Nebraska Press, 1994.

Fisher, Marc. *After the Wall: Germany, the Germans and the Burdens of History.* New York: Simon and Schuster, 1995.

Fontana, Laura, and Giorgio Giovagnoli, eds. *I nemici sono gli "altri": Convegno sull'Olocausto.* Florence: Giuntina, 1999.

Forgács, Éva. *Lászlo Fehér.* Budapest: Új Művészet Könyvek, 1993.

Friedlander, Saul. *Memory, History and the Extermination of the Jews of Europe.* Bloomington: Indiana University Press, 1993.

Gazda, Anikó. *Zsinagógák és zsidó községek magyarországon: Térképek, rajzok, adatok.* Budapest: MTA Judaisztikai Kutatócsoport, 1991.

Gebirtig, Mordechai. *Le mie canzoni.* Trans. Laura Quercioli Mincer and ed. Rudi Assuntino. Florence: Giuntina, 1997.

Gennari, Anna. "Il boom della cultura ebraica." *Grazia,* February 17, 1999.

Gerle, János, Attila Kovács, and Imre Makovecz. *A századforduló magyar építészete.* Budapest: Szépirodalmi Könyvkiadó, 1990.

Gerő, Lászlo, ed. *Magyarországi zsinagógák.* Budapest: Műszaki Könyvkiadó, 1989.

Gilman, Sander L. *Jews in Today's German Culture*. Bloomington: Indiana University Press, 1995.

Gilman, Sander L., and Karen Remmler, eds. *Reemerging Jewish Culture in Germany: Life and Literature since 1989*. New York: New York University Press, 1994.

Giurescu, Dinu C. *The Razing of Romania's Past*. New York: World Monuments Fund, 1989.

Grabherr, Eva, ed. *Jews in Hohenems*. Catalog of the Jewish Museum Hohenems. Hohenems: Jüdisches Museum Hohenems, 1996.

Gruber, Ruth Ellen. *Filling the Jewish Space in Europe*. New York: American Jewish Committee, 1996.

———. *Upon the Doorposts of Thy House: Jewish Life in East-Central Europe, Yesterday and Today*. New York: Wiley, 1994.

Gruber, Samuel D. *Synagogues*. New York: MetroBooks, 1999.

———. "The Synagogues of Eastern Europe." *Metropolis,* June 1993, 27–31.

Gruber, Samuel D., and Phyllis Myers. *Survey of Historic Jewish Monuments in Poland*. New York: Jewish Heritage Council, World Monuments Fund, 1995.

———. *Survey of Historic Jewish Monuments in the Czech Republic*. New York: Jewish Heritage Council, World Monuments Fund, 1995.

Gunzberg, Lynn M. *Strangers at Home: Jews in the Italian Literary Imagination*. Berkeley: University of California Press, 1992.

Halpert, Marta. *Jewish Life in Austria*. Vienna: Federal Press Service, [1994] 1998.

Hayes, Peter, ed. *Lessons and Legacies: The Meaning of the Holocaust in a Changing World*. Evanston, Ill.: Northwestern University Press, 1991.

Heimann-Jelinek, Felicitas, and Hannes Sulzenbacher, eds. *Jewish Museum Vienna*. Vienna: Jewish Museum of the City of Vienna, 1996.

Heller, Janet. "Out of Cracow's Shadows." *Historic Preservation News,* February–March, 1994.

Herf, Jeffrey. *Divided Memory: The Nazi Past in the Two Germanys*. Cambridge, Mass.: Harvard University Press, 1997.

Heřman, Jan. *Jewish Cemeteries in Bohemia and Moravia*. Prague: Council of Jewish Communities in the Czech Socialist Republic, n.d. (1983?).

Hoffman, Charles. *Gray Dawn: The Jews of Eastern Europe in the Post-Communist Era*. New York: HarperCollins, 1992.

Hoffman, Eva. *Shtetl: The Life and Death of a Small Town and the World of Polish Jews*. New York: Houghton Mifflin, 1997.

Honigmann, Peter. *La centralisation des informations concernant les projets de documentation d'inscriptions funéraires juives sur le territoire de la République Fédérale Allemande*. Paper presented at the International Conference on European Jewish Heritage, Paris, January 26–28, 1999.

Horne, Donald. *The Great Museum: The Re-presentation of History*. London: Pluto Press, 1984.

Idelsohn, A. Z. *Jewish Music in Its Historical Development*. New York: Henry Holt, 1929.

Jewish Heritage in Europe: Taking Stock and Developing an Approach. Case studies prepared for the General Assembly of the European Council of Jewish Communities, Thessaloniki, 1997.

Jewish Heritage Report. Periodical of the International Survey of Jewish Monuments.

Jewish Restitution and Compensation Claims in Eastern Europe and the Former USSR. London: Institute of Jewish Affairs, 1992 (with updated material published 1994).

John Paul II. *On Jews and Judaism, 1979–86.* Washington, D.C.: United States Catholic Conference, 1987.

Karp, Ivan, and Steven D. Lavine, eds. *Exhibiting Cultures: The Poetics and Politics of Museum Display.* Washington, D.C.: Smithsonian Institution Press, 1991.

Kater, Michael H. *Different Drummers: Jazz in the Culture of Nazi Germany.* Oxford: Oxford University Press, 1992.

Kaufman, Jonathan. *A Hole in the Heart of the World: Being Jewish in Eastern Europe.* New York: Viking, 1996.

Kaufman, Michael T. *Mad Dreams, Saving Graces—Poland: A Nation in Conspiracy.* New York: Random House, 1989.

Kaufmann, Uri R., ed. *Jewish Life in Germany Today.* Bonn: Inter Nationes, 1994.

Kazimierz. Special (English-language) issue 2000. Kraków. Summer 2000.

Kazimierz Action Plan. Kraków, 1994.

Kirshenblatt-Gimblett, Barbara. *Destination Culture: Tourism, Museums, and Heritage.* Berkeley: University of California Press, 1998.

———. "Sounds of Sensibility." *Judaism* 47, no. 1 (Winter 1998): 49–78.

Knowlton, James, and Truett Cates, trans. *Forever in the Shadow of Hitler? Original Documents of the Historikerstreit, the Controversy Concerning the Singularity of the Holocaust.* Atlantic Highlands, N.J.: Humanities Press, 1993. Originally published as *Historikerstreit: Die Dokumentation der Kontroverse um die Einzigartigkeit der nationalsozialistischen Judenvernichtung.* Munich: R. Piper, 1991.

Kol haKEHILA, the Newsletter of the Greek Jewish Monuments. Vol. 1, no. 1 (Summer 1998).

Koshar, Rudy. *Germany's Transient Past: Preservation and National Memory in the Twentieth Century.* Chapel Hill: University of North Carolina Press, 1998.

Kramer, Jane. *The Politics of Memory: Looking for Germany in the New Germany.* New York: Random House, 1996.

Krondorfer, Björn. *Remembrance and Reconciliation: Encounters between Young Jews and Germans.* New Haven: Yale University Press, 1995.

Kugelmass, Jack, ed. *Going Home: YIVO Annual 21.* New York: YIVO Institute for Jewish Research; Evanston, Ill.: Northwestern University Press, 1993.

Kugelmass, Jack, and Annamaria Orla-Bukowska. "'If You Build It They Will Come': Recreating an Historic Jewish District in Post-Communist Kraków." *City & Society,* annual review (1998): 315–53.

Kundera, Milan. "The Tragedy of Central Europe." *New York Review of Books,* April 26, 1984, 33–38.

Lappin, Elena, ed. *Jewish Voices, German Words: Growing up Jewish in Postwar Germany and Austria*. Trans. Krishna Winston. New Haven: Catbird Press, 1994.

Lehmann, Heiko. "Klezmer in Germany/Germans and Klezmer: Reparation or Contribution." Lecture given in Berlin, October 19, 2000. Text available at http://www.sukke.de/lecture.html.

Lorenz, Dagmar C. G., and Gabriele Weinberger. *Insiders and Outsiders: Jewish and Gentile Culture in Germany and Austria*. Detroit: Wayne State University Press, 1994.

Loussier, Jean, and Robin Langley Sommer, eds. *Lost Europe: Images of a Vanished World*. London: Grange Books, 1997.

Lowenthal, Marvin. *The Jews of Germany: A Story of Sixteen Centuries*. Philadelphia: Jewish Publication Society of America, 1938.

———. *A World Passed By: Scenes and Memories of Jewish Civilization in Europe and North Africa*. New York: Harper & Brothers, 1933; New York: Behrman's Jewish Book House, 1938.

Luzzatto, Amos. "Il lavoro della 'Rassegna Mensile di Israel.'" *La Rassegna Mensile di Israel* 63, no. 1 (January–April 1997): 3–15.

Magris, Claudio. *Lontano da dove: Joseph Roth e la tradizione ebraico-orientale*. Turin: Einaudi, [1971] 1989.

Maier, Charles S. *The Unmasterable Past: History, Holocaust, and German National Identity*. Cambridge, Mass.: Harvard University Press, 1988.

Mann, Vivian B., ed. *Gardens and Ghettos: The Art of Jewish Life in Italy*. Berkeley: University of California Press, 1989.

Martínez, Miguel Angel, rapporteur. *The Jewish Contribution to European Culture*. Report of the Committee on Culture and Education. Strasbourg: Council of Europe, 1987.

Meyer, Peter, Bernard D. Weinryb, Eugene Duschinsky, and Nicolas Sylvain. *The Jews in the Soviet Satellites*. Syracuse: American Jewish Committee/Syracuse University Press, 1953.

Miller, Judith. *One by One by One: Facing the Holocaust*. New York: Simon and Schuster, 1990.

Mincer, Laura Quercioli. "Tradition Revisited in Moni Ovadia's Theatre." Paper presented at the conference on Yiddish theater, Oxford, June 1999.

Misak, Sonia. *Highlights of the International Seminar Jewish Culture for the Twenty-first Century, Paris, February 1999*. London: Institute for Jewish Policy Research, 1999.

Monuments Historiques. Special issue, "Le patrimoine juif français," no. 191 (February 1994).

Mortara Di Veroli, Elena, and Laura Quercioli Mincer, eds. *Il mondo Yiddish: Saggi. La Rassegna Mensile di Israel* 62, nos. 1–2. Rome: Unione delle Comunità Ebraiche Italiane, 1996.

Mortkowitz, Siegfried. "One Man's Fight against a 'Disneyland' Prague." *Prague Post*, October 8–14, 1997.

Neiman, Susan. *Slow Fire: Jewish Notes from Berlin*. New York: Schocken, 1992.

Nissenbaum Foundation. *Preserving Traces of Jewish Culture in Poland: For the Living and the Dead*. Warsaw: Krajowa Agencja Wydawnicza, 1988.

Nochlin, Linda, and Tamar Garb, eds. *The Jew in the Text: Modernity and the Construction of Identity.* London: Thames and Hudson, 1995.

Offe, Sabine. "Sites of Remembrance? Jewish Museums in Contemporary Germany." *Jewish Social Studies* 3, no. 2 (Winter 1997): 72–89.

Ovadia, Moni. *L'ebreo che ride: L'umorismo ebraico in otto lezioni e duecento storielle.* Turin: Einaudi, 1998.

———. *Perchè no? L'ebreo corrosivo.* Milan: asSaggi Bompiani, 1996.

———. *Speriamo che tenga: Viaggio di un saltimbanco sospeso tra cielo e terra.* Milan: Mondadori, 1998.

Paluch, Andrzej K., ed. *The Jews in Poland* Vol. 1. Kraków: Jagiellonian University, 1992.

Pavlát, Leo. *The Treatment of Jewish Themes in Czech Schools.* The Central and Eastern European Curriculum Review Project. New York: American Jewish Committee, 1998. [See also the other reports in the series, on Poland (1998), Slovakia (1999), Hungary (2000), etc.]

Philipson, David. *Old European Jewries.* Philadelphia: Jewish Publication Society of America, 1894.

Piechotka, Maria, and Kazimierz Piechotka. *Bramy Nieba: Bóżnice drewiane.* Warsaw: Wydawnictwo Krupski I S-Ka Sp., 1996.

———. *Wooden Synagogues.* Warsaw: Arkady, 1959. Originally published as *Bóżnice Drewniane.* Warsaw, 1957.

Pinto, Diana. *Beyond Anti-Semitism: The New Jewish Presence in Europe.* New York: American Jewish Committee, 1994.

———. *A New Jewish Identity for Post-1989 Europe.* JPR Policy Paper No. 1. London: Institute for Jewish Policy Research, June 1996.

Powers, Charles T. *In the Memory of the Forest.* New York: Penguin, 1997.

Preservation Priorities: Endangered Historic Jewish Sites. New York: World Monuments Fund, 1996.

Reinharz, Jehuda, and Walter Schatzberg, eds. *The Jewish Response to German Culture: From the Enlightenment to the Second World War.* Hanover, N.H.: University Press of New England, 1985.

Rogin, Michael. *Blackface, White Noise: Jewish Immigrants in the Hollywood Melting Pot.* Berkeley: University of California Press, 1998.

Rogovoy, Seth. *The Essential Klezmer: A Music Lover's Guide to Jewish Roots and Soul Music, from the Old World to the Jazz Age to the Downtown Avant-Garde.* Chapel Hill, N.C.: Algonquin, 2000.

Rojek, Chris, and John Urry, eds. *Touring Cultures: Transformations of Travel and Theory.* London: Routledge, 1997.

Rosenfeld, Alvin H. "The Popularization of Memory: The Case of Anne Frank." In *Lessons and Legacies: The Meaning of the Holocaust in a Changing World,* ed. Peter Hayes, 243–78. Evanston, Ill.: Northwestern University Press, 1991.

Sacerdoti, Lisa. Ricomporre l'infranto. "La memoria ebraica tra storia e identità. Moni Ovadia e il teatro dell'esilio." Thesis, Università degli Studi, Milan, 1996–97.

Sandler, Boris. "The Risk of 'Museomania.'" *Forward,* September 18, 1998.

Sapoznik, Henry. *The Compleat Klezmer.* Cedarhurst, N.Y.: Tara Publications, 1987.

————. *Klezmer! Jewish Music from Old World to Our World.* New York: Schirmer, 1999.

Segel, Harold B., ed. *Stranger in Our Midst: Images of the Jew in Polish Literature.* Ithaca: Cornell University Press, 1996.

Serotta, Edward. *Jews, Germany, Memory: A Contemporary Portrait.* Berlin: Nicolai, 1996.

Shapiro, Michal, producer, and Candace Ward, ed. *Klezmer Music: A Marriage of Heaven & Earth.* Roslyn, N.Y.: ellipsis arts, 1996 (book and CD).

Sichrovsky, Peter. *Born Guilty: Children of Nazi Families.* Trans. Jean Steinberg. New York: Basic Books, 1988.

Simon, Hermann. *The New Synagogue, Berlin: Past-Present-Future.* Berlin: Edition Hentrich, 1992.

Slobin, Mark. *Fiddler on the Move: Exploring the Klezmer World.* New York: Oxford University Press, 2000.

————. "The Neo-Klezmer Movement and Euro-American Musical Revivalism." *Journal of America Folklore* 97, no. 383 (January–March 1984): 98–104.

————. "Rethinking 'Revival' of American Ethnic Music." *New York Folklore* 9, nos. 3–4 (Winter 1983).

————. *Tenement Songs: The Popular Music of the Jewish Immigrants.* Urbana: University of Illinois Press, 1982.

Smolar, Aleksander. "The Jews as a Polish Problem." *Daedalus* 116, no. 2 (Spring 1987): 31–74.

Spagnolo, Francesco. *Un' estetica del (trad.): La ricostruzione della musica klezmer tra Europa e America e il caso italiano.* Manuscript based on paper presented at conference Dall'Europa all'America, e ritorno: Cultura yiddish, musica klezmer e mondo moderno, Rome, December 1998.

La Speranza: Attraverso l'ebraismo goriziano. Istituto per gli Studi Ebraici della Mitteleuropa. Monfalcone: Edizioni della Laguna, 1991.

Stavans, Ilan. "Where History and Fetishism Become One: The European Rage for Building Jewish Museums Raises Questions about What Is Being Preserved." *Forward,* May 21, 1999.

Stegeman, Wolf, and Johanna Eichmann. *Jüdisches Museum Westfalen.* Dorsten: Nordrhein-Westfalen-Stiftung, 1992.

Steinlauf, Michael C. *Bondage to the Dead: Poland and the Memory of the Holocaust.* Syracuse: Syracuse University Press, 1997.

Stern, Susan, ed. *Speaking Out: Jewish Voices from United Germany.* Chicago: edition q, 1995.

Stille, Alexander. *Benevolence and Betrayal: Five Italian Jewish Families under Fascism.* New York: Simon and Schuster, 1991.

Strehlen, Martina, Michael Brocke, and Doris Fischer, eds. *"Ein edler Stein sei sein Baldachin . . .": Jüdische Friedhöfe in Rheinland-Pfalz.* N.p.: Landesamt für Denkmalpflege Rheinland-Pfalz, 1996.

Szántó, Gábor T. "Floodgate or Dead End? The Presence of a Many-Faceted Culture." *Human Rights without Frontiers,* special issue (1997): 37–40.

Terezín. Ústí nad Labem: Památnik Terezín, 1988.

Toscano, Mario, ed. *Integrazione e identità: L'esperienza ebraica in Germania e Italia dall'Illuminismo al fascismo.* Milan: FrancoAngeli, 1998.

Tuszyńska, Agata. *Lost Landscapes: In Search of Isaac Bashevis Singer and the Jews of Poland.* Trans. Madeline G. Levine. New York: William Morrow, 1998.

Vago, Raphael. "A Fateful Encounter: Jews and Non-Jews in Central Europe." Paper presented at conference Medieval Jewish Communities in Central Europe and Their Cultural Heritage, Maribor, Slovenia, October 1997.

Volavková, Hana. *The Jewish Museum of Prague: A Guide through the Collections.* Prague: Council of Jewish Religious Communities of Bohemia, Moravia, and Silesia, 1948.

Wasserstein, Bernard. *Vanishing Diaspora: The Jews in Europe since 1945.* Cambridge, Mass.: Harvard University Press, 1996.

Waterman, Stanley. *Cultural Politics and European Jewry.* London: Institute for Jewish Policy Research, 1999.

Weiner, Miriam. *Jewish Roots in Poland: Pages from the Past and Archival Inventories.* New York: YIVO/Routes to Roots Foundation, 1998.

Winkelmann, Annette. *Directory of Jewish Studies in Europe.* Oxford: European Association for Jewish Studies, 1998.

Wirth, Péter. *Itt Van Elrejtve.* Budapest: Európa Könyvkiadó, 1985.

Wolffsohn, Michael. *Eternal Guilt? Forty Years of German-Jewish-Israeli Relations.* Trans. Douglas Bokovoy. New York: Columbia University Press, 1993.

The World Directory of Jewish Museums. Jerusalem: Center for Jewish Art, The Hebrew University, 1994.

Yiddish Culture: Report of the Committee on Culture and Education and Related Documents. Rapporteur Emanuelis Zingeris. Doc. 7489. Strasbourg: Council of Europe, Parliamentary Assembly, 1996.

Young, James E. *At Memory's Edge: After-Images of the Holocaust in Contemporary Art and Architecture.* New Haven: Yale University Press, 2000.

———. *The Texture of Memory: Holocaust Memorials and Their Meaning.* New Haven: Yale University Press, 1993.

Zpravodaj/Newsletter. Quarterly. Prague: Jewish Museum Prague.

Zuccotti, Susan. *The Italians and the Holocaust: Persecution, Rescue, Survival.* New York: Basic Books, 1987.

Post–World War II Jewish Travel Guidebooks and Pamphlets (A Representative Selection)

A la découverte du judaïsme alsacien. Tourisme Alsace, Agence de Développement Touristique du Bas-Rhin/Association B'nai B'rith/Association Départementale du Tourisme du Haut-Rhin, 1998.

Bárkány, Eugen, and L'udovít Dojč. *Židovské Náboženské Obce na Slovensku.* Bratislava: Vesna, 1991.

Bartosz, Adam. *Tarnowskie Judaica.* Warsaw: Wydawnictwo PTTK Kraj, 1992.

Bergman, Eleonora, and Jan Jagielski. *Zachowane Synagogi i domy modlitwy w Polsce: Katalog.* Warsaw: Jewish Historical Institute, 1996.

Burchard, Przemysław. *Pamiątki i Zabytki Kultury Żydowskiej w Polsce.* Warsaw: Zakładach Graficznych "Reprint" Piotr Piotrowski, 1990.

Duda, Eugeniusz. *Krakowskie judaica*. Warsaw: Wydawnictwo PTTK Kraj, 1991.

Fiedler, Jiří. *Jewish Sights of Bohemia and Moravia*. Prague: Sefer, 1991.

Frank, Ben G. *A Travel Guide to Jewish Europe*. Gretna: Pelican, [1992] 1996.

Girona e les Juifs. Ajuntament de Girona (Spain), Patronat Municipal "Call de Girona."

Gruber, Ruth Ellen. *Jewish Heritage Travel: A Guide to East-Central Europe*. New York: Wiley, [1992] 1994; Northvale, N.J.: Jason Aronson, 1999.

Hirsch, Peter, and Billie Ann Lopez. *Reiseführer durch das jüdische Deutschland*. Munich: Verlag Roman Kovar, 1993.

Jagielski, Jan, and Robert Pasieczny. *A Guide to Jewish Warsaw*. Warsaw: Our Roots, 1990. [See the Our Roots guidebooks to Jewish Kraków, Lublin, and Łódź.]

Jewish Heritage in Central Europe. Vienna: Jewish Welcome Service, 1991.

Jüdisches Europa: Amsterdam, Brüssel, Budapest, Madrid, Prag, Warschau, Wien. Vienna: Austrian National Travel Agency Corp./Jewish Welcome Service.

Klenovský, Jaroslav. *Židovské Památky Mikulova*. Mikulov: 1994. [See the series of similar local Jewish guidebooks to various other Moravian towns, by the same author.]

Komoróczy, Géza, ed. *Jewish Budapest: Monuments, Rites, History*. Budapest: Central European University Press, 1999. Originally published as *A zsidó Budapest*. Budapest: MTA Judaisztikai Kutatocsoport, 1995.

Kovac, Vlasta, ed. *Jewish Heritage in Zagreb and Croatia*. Zagreb: Jewish Community of Zagreb and Tourist Association of the City of Zagreb, 1993.

Orbán, Ferenc. *Magyarország zsidó emlékej, nevezetességej*. Budapest: Panoráma, 1991.

Palowski, Franciszek. *Retracing "Schindler's List."* Kraków: Jordan Art, 1994.

Pivirotto, Riccardo, and Monica Sideri. *L'ebreo errante: Guida ai luoghi ebraici tra arte e storia nella Maremma collinare*. Orbetello: Edizioni Best Service, 1997.

Postal, Bernard, and Samuel H. Abramson. *The Landmarks of a People: A Guide to Jewish Sites in Europe*. New York: Hill and Wang, 1962. Republished as *The Traveler's Guide to Jewish Landmarks of Europe*. New York: Fleet Press Corporation, 1971.

Reuter, Fritz. *Jewish Worms: Rashi House and Judengasse*. Worms: Jüdisches Museum Raschi-Haus, 1992.

The Road to Jewish Heritage in the South of France. Comité Départemental du Tourisme de N.p.: Vaucluse, 1993.

Sacerdoti, Annie, and Luca Fiorentino. *Guida all'Italia ebraica*. Genoa: Marietti, 1986.

Sacerdoti, Annie, and Annamarcella Tedeschi Falco, eds. *Emilia-Romagna: Itinerari ebraici; I luoghi, la storia, l'arte*. Venice: Marsilio, 1992. [See the other volumes in this continuing series, each devoted to an Italian region, including Tuscany, Lazio, Veneto, and Piedmont.]

Seidel, Peter. *Germany for the Jewish Traveler*. N.p.: German National Tourist Office, 1989(?).

Šosberger, Pavle. *Sinagoge u Vojvodini: pomenica minulog vremena.* Novi Sad: Prometej, 1998.

Stalzer, Albert. *Jewish Vienna & Austria: Heritage and Mission.* Trans. Susi Schneider. Vienna: Vienna Tourist Board/Jewish Welcome Service, 1993–94.

Stavrolakis, Nicholas P., and Timothy J. DeVinney. *Jewish Sites and Synagogues of Greece.* Athens: Talos Press, 1992.

"Yiddish & Europa/Tendenze/Humour/Itinerari." *Gulliver* (Milan) 7, no. 11 (November 1999): 186–248.

Valley, Eli. *The Great Jewish Cities of Central and Eastern Europe.* Northvale, N.J.: Jason Aronson, 1999.

Wiśniewski, Tomasz. *Jewish Białystok and Surroundings in Eastern Europe: A Guide for Yesterday and Today.* Ipswitch, Mass.: Ipswitch Press, 1998.

———. *Synagogues and Jewish Communities in the Białystok Region: Jewish Life in Eastern Europe before 1939.* Białystok: David, 1992.

Selected Discography

A selection of CDs and tapes by some of the groups mentioned in the text or working in the region.

10 Saiten 1 Bogen. *Schpil ess noch amol!* Austro Mechana, MC 297 131, 1992.

Ahava Raba. *Ahava Raba.* Nebelhorn, 018, 1993.

Aufwind. *Awek di Junge Jorn.* Misrach Music, MSR 0144-2, 1996.

Barbapedana. *Sherele: Balkan, Gypsy and Klezmer Music.* BFP, 003, 1997.

Brave Old World. *Beyond the Pale.* Pinorrekk Records, CD 5013, 1993.

———. *Blood Oranges.* Pinorrekk Records, PRCD 3405027, 1997.

———. *Klezmer Music.* Flying Fish Records, FF 70560, 1990.

Budapester Klezmer Band. *The Train 7.40.* Klezmer Music, BKB 97/1, 1997.

———. *Yiddish Folklore from Central Europe.* Quint Records, HMA 1903070, 1992.

Budowitz. *Klezmermusik des 19. Jahrhunderts/Mother Tongue: Music of the 19th-Century Klezmorim.* Koch International, 3-1261-2, 1997.

'Ch Hob a Nign: Jiddisches Lied & Klezmer. 4 Internationales Festival Fürth. Swiss Pan, 510404, 1994.

Colalaila. *The Train to Massada.* Boulevard Records/Hammer Music, 7838411, 1996.

Dire Gelt. *Klezmer Music, Yiddish Songs.* Dona Ruy Project, Harmony Records, ESS 6, 1996.

Ensemble Klesmer. *Live in Prag.* Extraplatte, EX 317-2, 1997.

Europäisches Jiddisch-Festival Leverkusen 1993. Edition Künstlertreff, EK 17 1062, 1994.

Giora Feidman. *Gershwin and the Klezmer.* ROM Productions, ROM 104, 1991.

———. *Klassic Klezmer.* ROM Productions, 106 CD, 1993.

———. *The Magic of Klezmer.* ROM Productions, ROM 101, 1986.

———. *The Singing Clarinet of Giora Feidman.* ROM Productions, ROM 102, 1987.

————. *The Soul Chai*. pläne, 88786, 1995.

Enrico Fink. *Lokshen*. Materiali Sonori, CD 90117, 2000.

Gebrider Moischele. *Schtil, di nacht is ojsgeschternt: Jiddische Lieder*. Austro-Star, EX 238-2, 1995.

Geduldig und Thimann. *A Haymish Groove*. Extraplatte, EX 316155, 1992.

————. *A Schtetl Is Amerike*. WEA Musik-GesmbH, 240 939-2, 1986.

Gojim. *Tscholent*. Extraplatte, EX 207-2, 1994.

Harry's Freilach. *Klezmer Tov!* Nightengale Records, Meistersinger Musik, NGH-CD-457, 1997.

Jüdische Lebenswelten—Patterns of Jewish Life. Highlights from the concerts "Traditional and Popular Jewish Music," Berlin, 1992. Wergo Schallplatten, SM 1604-2, 1993.

Klezgoyim. *Out of the Eyebrow*. Globe Records, CD 015019701, 1996.

The Klezmatics. *Jews with Horns*. Xeno/Green Linnet, Xeno 4032, 1995.

————. *Possessed*. Xeno/Green Linnet, Xeno 4050, 1997.

————. *Rhythm + Jews*. Flying Fish, FF 70591, 1992.

Klezmer Music: A Marriage of Heaven & Earth. ellipsis arts (P.O. Box 305, Roslyn, N.Y. 11576), CD 4090, 1996.

Klezmischpoche Berlin. *Oifn Jorid*. Profile, 0004, 1995.

Klezroym. *KlezRoym*. Anagrumba, GDL 1093, 1998.

Kol Simcha. *Klezmer Soul*. World Class, 11303-2, 1997.

Kroke. *Klezmer Acoustic Music*. Gauss, 1993.

————. *Trio (Klezmer Acoustic Music)*. ART-CD, AMC 00, 1995.

la'om. *Riffkele: Klezmermusik—Live*. Megaphon, LC 03050, 1998.

————. *". . . Spielt!" Klezmer-Musik von Chicago bis Odessa*. Raumer Records, RR 10696, 1996.

Riccardo Moretti. *Ebraica*. Nuova Era Records, 7287, 1997.

Die Naye Kapelye. *Die Naye Kapelye*. Riente Musik, RIEN CD 17, 1998.

————. *Old Time East European Klezmer Music from Not So Long Ago*. Privately published, Die Naye Kapelye, 1996.

André Ochodlo. *André Ochodlo Sings Mordechaj Gebirtig*. Sound-Pol, CD 050, 1996.

Moni Ovadia. *Oylem Goylem*. Change Performing Art/Fonit Cetra, CDC 60, 1991.

Moni Ovadia and Carlo Boccadoro. *Nigun*. BMI Music, BMG Ricordi SpA, 74321452162, 1997.

Itzhak Perlman + Various Artists. *In the Fiddler's House*. Angel Records, 7243 5 55555 26, 1995.

————. *Live in the Fiddler's House*. Angel Records, 7243 5 56209 27, 1996.

Rhapsodija Trio. *Spartacus*. Nota, CD 2.44, 1997.

Joel Rubin Jewish Music Ensemble. *Beregovski's Khasene: Beregovski's Wedding—Forgotten Instrumental Treasures from the Ukraine*. Schott Wergo Music Media, SM 1614-2, 1997.

The Joel Rubin Klezmer Band. *Brave Old World*. Stebo, S 509.

Herwig Strobl. *Music in the Izaak Synagogue*. Extraplatte, EX 281-096-2, 1996.

Index

Text/Display: Galliard
Compositor: G&S Typesetters, Inc.
Printer/Binder: Sheridan Books, Inc.